International Human Resource Management

FOURTH EDITION

Managing people in a multinational context

Peter J. Dowling, University of Canberra, Australia

Denice E. Welch, Mt Eliza Business School and
University of Queensland, Australia

THOMSON

Australia · Canada · Mexico · Singapore · Spain · United Kingdom · United States

International Human Resource Management, 4th edition

Copyright © 2004 Thomson Learning

The Thomson logo is a registered trademark used herein under license.

For more information, contact Thomson Learning, High Holborn House; 50–51 Bedford Row, London WC1R 4LR or visit us on the World Wide Web at:
http://www.thomsonlearning.co.uk

British Library Cataloguing-in-Publication Data
A catalog record for this book is available from the British Library

ISBN 1-84480-013-X

Typeset by Gray Publishing, Tunbridge Wells
Text design by Design Deluxe, Bath
Printed in Italy by Canale

International Human Resource Management

Contents

III Global HR issues 183

CHAPTER 8 HRM in the host country context 185

CHAPTER 9 Industrial relations 209

CHAPTER 10 Performance management 231

Preface

According to 2003 figures from the United Nations Conference on Trade and Development, there are currently a total of 65 000 transnational corporations, with 850 000 affiliates. These organizations now employ a total number of 54 million people worldwide, compared with 24 million in 1990 – the year the first edition of this textbook was published. The spread of international business, of course, is not confined to transnational corporations. However, these figures do serve to demonstrate how global the world of international business has become. The role of human resource management in sustaining international business in this complex, ever-changing world is the central theme of our book.

This, the fourth edition of our textbook, represents a significant change in terms of scope, presentation and publication. The first two editions were part of the International Dimensions of Business Series, which was discontinued while we were preparing the third edition, as reflected in its title – *International Human Resource Management: Managing People in a Multinational Context*. The discontinuation of the International Dimensions Series has meant that its constraints no longer apply. This has allowed us to provide what our colleagues who have adopted previous editions have consistently requested: teaching cases and exercises, a website instructor's guide, teaching aids and other supplementary material.

Reflecting the growth in international human resource issues, we have 11 chapters in this edition. We have divided these into four parts. Part I contains three chapters dealing with the multinational context and the consequences of international growth on human resource management (HRM). Those of our colleagues familiar with previous editions will notice that Chapter 3, new in this edition, presents staffing approaches in the context of the reasons for and types of international assignments, and the key roles played by expatriates and non-expatriates (that is, international business travelers). Part II deals with areas deemed critical in managing and supporting international assignments. Its four chapters cover activities relating to expatriate management. Part III concerns global HRM issues. It contains a new chapter dealing with subsidiary management and HRM issues, a chapter on industrial relations, and we have repositioned the chapter on performance management to this part, to reflect both corporate and individual performance issues. The final chapter identifies future trends and international HRM (IHRM) challenges, including research issues and theoretical developments. Part IV contains new, unpublished, cases and exercises, selected on the basis of how they reinforce topics or themes covered in the various chapters. By grouping these into a self-contained section, instructors can decide which case or exercise they feel best suits their pedagogical needs and styles. A list of useful websites can be found in the Appendix.

The new structure enables us to give more emphasis to broader HR issues than expatriate management, although international assignments continue to be given weight owing to their importance in international business operations, and the continuing focus of research into expatriate management activities. Indeed, the shape and contents of the fourth edition provide a clear indication of how the field of IHRM has evolved from its early focus on the selection and training of expatriate managers. However, those of our colleagues who have adopted previous editions will recognize that we endeavor to maintain a familiar approach while injecting freshness into the contents of each revised chapter.

The second major change has been the decision by our colleague, Randall Schuler, to withdraw from authorship of the book owing to work commitments. We respect his decision and take this opportunity to acknowledge publicly his contributions to earlier editions, particularly during the book's initial inception as part of the International Dimensions Series.

The change in format has been accompanied by a change in production location – across the Atlantic to the United Kingdom in terms of place of publication. Perhaps appropriate for authors writing in the area of staff relocation, since the publication of the third edition, the Dowling family relocated from the island state of Tasmania to mainland Australia, and the Welch family repatriated themselves from Norway back home to Australia.

The contribution of this book to the globalization of the business curriculum

This book can be used in various ways:

- As the main text for a course on IHRM. We also recommend the current edition of *Readings and Cases in International Human Resource Management* by Mark Mendenhall and Gary Oddou, ITP South-Western, as a supplementary text.
- As one of several texts in a comparative management or international management course.
- As a supplement to a traditional introductory HRM course to bring an international dimension into the course, and assist in meeting AACSB and EQIS requirements.

For all instructors teaching in the areas of IHRM, we recommend the *International Encyclopedia of Business and Management* (edited by M. Warner, Thomson Learning, London, 2002) as an excellent library reference.

Acknowledgements

As with the previous editions, we have received encouraging and helpful assistance from numerous colleagues in various educational institutions around the world. Their comments, along with those from students and book reviewers, have provided us with suggestions and general feedback that has aided us in adding, deleting and refining sections and chapters of the book for each edition. Particular thanks go to the following colleagues for their assistance with chapters and the provision of teaching cases:

- Ingmar Björkman, Swedish School of Economics and Business Administration, Finland and INSEAD France
- Helen De Cieri, Monash University
- Allen Engle Sr, Eastern Kentucky University
- Marilyn Fenwick, Monash University
- Lisa Hewerdine, University of New South Wales
- Ali Niazi, University of Canberra
- Günter Stahl, INSEAD – Singapore
- Catherine Welch, University of New South Wales
- Lawrence Welch, Mt Eliza Business School and University of Queensland.

We also express our appreciation to the following colleagues for their timely feedback and comments: Chris Brewster, John Boudreau, Pawan Budhwar, Marion Festing, Pervez Ghauri, Runar Framnes, Klaus Macharzina, Rebecca Marschan-Piekkari, Michael Poole, Hugh Scullion, Adam Steen, Marja Tahvanianen, Wolfgang Weber and Verner Worm.

We also acknowledge the support of Lynn Materne, University of Canberra, and Les Johnson, Lynette Francis, Mark Suares and Carole Christopherson, Mt Eliza Business School.

The assistance from staff at Thomson Learning UK has been appreciated. We thank in particular Jennifer Pegg for ensuring a smooth transition of the book from the USA to the UK, Amie Barker, Development Editor, and Fiona Freel and her production team.

Finally, we thank Fiona Dowling for her patience and support through all four editions, and Lawrence Welch, for his significant academic contribution and encouragement.

Peter J. Dowling
Canberra
Denice E. Welch
Melbourne

About the authors

Peter J. Dowling (PhD, The Flinders University of South Australia) is Pro Vice-Chancellor of the Division of Business, Law & Information Sciences and Professor of International Management & Strategy at the University of Canberra, Australia. His previous appointments include the University of Tasmania, Monash University, the University of Melbourne and California State University at Chico. He has also held visiting appointments in the USA at Cornell University and Michigan State University, and in Germany at the University of Paderborn and the University of Bayreuth. His current research interests are concerned with International Human Resource Management and Strategic Management. He has co-authored three books: *Human Resource Management in Australia*; *People in Organizations: an Introduction to Organizational Behaviour in Australia*; and *Strategic Management: Competitiveness and Globalization – Pacific Rim Edition*. He has written or co-authored over 60 journal articles and book chapters, and serves on the editorial boards of *Asia Pacific Journal of Human Resources*, *International Journal of Human Resource Management*, *Journal of International Business Studies*, *Journal of World Business*, *Management International Review* and *Thunderbird International Business Review*. He is a former national Vice-President of the Australian Human Resources Institute, past Editor of *Asia Pacific Journal of Human Resources* and a Life Fellow of the Australian Human Resources Institute. He is also a Senior Research Affiliate of the Center for Advanced Human Resource Studies at Cornell University and a member of the Australian Defence College Advisory Board.

Denice E. Welch (PhD, Monash University) is Professor of International Management at the Mt Eliza Business School and University of Queensland, Australia. Previous teaching appointments include the Norwegian School of Management, Oslo, and Monash University, Australia. She has held visiting positions at the Helsinki School of Economics and Business Administration, Finland and the Copenhagen Business School, Denmark. She maintains her link with the Norwegian School of Management and is an adjunct professor of the University of Canberra, Australia. Her current research interests include the effect of language standardization in multinationals, the link between international human resource management strategies and international business operations, the role of non-expatriates in knowledge generation and competence, the viability of non-standard and virtual assignments and the use of qualitative methods in international business research. She has published extensively in international journals such as *Management International Review*, *Journal of Management Studies*, *Journal of International Marketing*, *International Business Review* and *International Journal of Human Resource Management*. Her work has also been published as chapters in a variety of books, including reprinted journal articles. She has contributed to in-house training programs and workshops for multinational managers and HR directors, and has organized and co-chaired various academic workshops in France, Finland and Norway.

Book layout

The fourth edition contains four parts. Part I has three chapters dealing with the multinational context and the consequences of international growth on human resource management (HRM). Part II deals with areas deemed critical in managing and supporting international assignments. Its four chapters cover the main areas of expatriate management: selection, training and development, compensation and re-entry. Part III concerns global issues pertaining to multinational IHRM: subsidiary management, industrial relations and performance management. It concludes with a chapter identifying trends and future challenges for IHRM. Part IV contains new teaching cases and exercises. The accompanying diagram illustrates how the various parts are connected and build into a solid treatment of *International Human Resource Management: Managing People in a Multinational Context.*

Preface

PART I. The multinational context
- The enduring context of IHRM
- The organizational context
- IHRM: sustaining international business operations

PART II. Managing and supporting international assignments
- Recruitment and selection
- Training and development
- Compensation
- Re-entry and career issues

PART III. Global HR issues
- HRM in the host country context
- Industrial relations
- Performance management
- IHRM trends and future challanges

PART IV. Cases and exercises

Visit the *International Human Resource Management* 4th edition
accompanying website at www.thomsonlearning.co.uk/businessandmanagement/
dowlingandwelch to find valuable further material for students and lecturers
including:

For Students

- Overviews of each chapter
- Human Resource Management definitions from *The IEBM Pocket Encyclopedia of Business and Management*
- Related weblinks to direct you to further resources

For Lecturers

- Instructors Manual – including:
  - Teaching notes to cases and exercises
  - Suggested answers to discussion questions and exercises for each chapter
- Downloadable PowerPoint$^{(TM)}$ slides featuring diagrams and models from the book

The multinational context

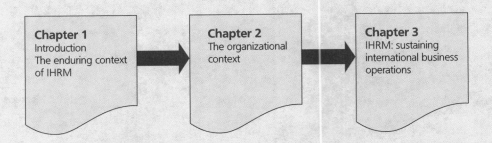

Chapter 1
Introduction
The enduring context
of IHRM

Chapter 2
The organizational
context

Chapter 3
IHRM: sustaining
international business
operations

Part I contains three chapters that deal with the multinational context within which international human resource management (IHRM) functions and activities take place. Chapter 1 introduces the scope of the book and outlines the differences between domestic and international HRM and the variables that moderate these differences. We then look at the enduring context of IHRM – demonstrating how trends and challenges in the global work environment force changes on the operations of internationalizing firms that have consequences for the management of people in the multinational context.

Chapter 2 examines in detail the organizational and managerial responses to international growth. We trace the international firm along the path to multinational status and examine structural responses, control and coordination mechanisms and the mode of operation used in various international markets. The implications for IHRM are highlighted.

Chapter 3 provides the final contextual section. We examine the approaches to staffing international operations, the reasons for, and types of, international assignments and the roles played by expatriates. The impact on international growth on the corporate HR function is also discussed.

These three inter-related chapters provide a useful foundation for examining the specific IHRM functions and activities to sustain international business operations.

Introduction
The enduring context of IHRM

Chapter objectives

In this introductory chapter, we establish the scope of the textbook. We:

- define key terms in international human resource management (IHRM)
- outline the differences between domestic and international human resource management and the variables that moderate these differences
- discuss trends and challenges in the global work environment and the enduring context in which IHRM functions and activities are conducted – including the way in which forces for change affect the operations of the internationalizing firm and have consequences for the management of people in the multinational context.

Scope of the book

The field of IHRM has been characterized by three broad approaches.[1] The first[2] emphasizes cross-cultural management: examining human behaviour within organizations from an international perspective. A second approach developed from the comparative industrial relations and HRM literature[3] and seeks to describe, compare and analyze HRM systems in various countries. A third approach seeks to focus on aspects of HRM in multinational firms.[4] These approaches are depicted in Figure 1-1. In this book, we take the third approach. Our objective is to explore the implications that the process of internationalization has for the activities and policies of HRM. In particular, we are interested in how HRM is practiced in multinationals – hence the subtitle of this book, 'Managing People in a Multinational Context'.

As Figure 1-1 demonstrates, there is an inevitable overlap between the three approaches when one is attempting to provide an accurate view of the global realities

| Figure 1-1 | Inter-relationships between approaches to the field |

of operating in the international business environment. Obviously, cross-cultural management issues are important when dealing with the cultural aspects of foreign operations. Some of these aspects will be taken up in Chapter 8, where we deal with HRM in the host country context – indicated by (a) in Figure 1-1. Chapter 9 deals with industrial relations issues and draws on literature from the comparative IR field – (b) in Figure 1-1.

While the focus of much of this book is on the established multinational enterprise (MNE) – a firm which owns or controls business activities in more than one foreign country – we recognize that small, internationalizing firms which are yet to reach multinational firm status and family-owned firms also face international HRM issues.[5]

Defining international HRM

Before we can offer a definition of IHRM, we should first define the general field of HRM. Typically, HRM refers to those activities undertaken by an organization to utilize its human resources effectively. These activities would include at least the following:

1 human resource planning
2 staffing (recruitment, selection, placement)
3 performance management
4 training and development
5 compensation (remuneration) and benefits
6 industrial relations.

The question is, of course, which activities change when HRM goes international. A model (shown in Figure 1-2) developed by Morgan[6] is helpful. He presents IHRM on three dimensions:

1 The broad human resource activities of procurement, allocation and utilization (these three broad activities can be easily expanded into the six HR activities listed above).
2 The national or country categories involved in IHRM activities:

- the host country where a subsidiary may be located
- the home country where the firm is headquartered and
- 'other' countries that may be the source of labour, finance and other inputs.

A model of IHRM **Figure 1-2**

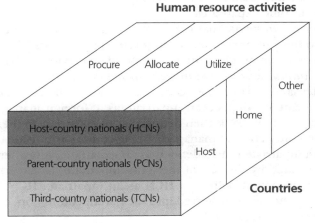

Source: Adapted from P.V. Morgan, International Human Resource Management: Fact or Fiction. *Personnel Administrator,* Vol. 31, No. 9 (1986) p. 44.

3 The three categories of employees of an international firm:

- host-country nationals (HCNs)
- parent-country nationals (PCNs) and
- third-country nationals (TCNs).

Thus, for example, the US multinational IBM employs Australian citizens in its Australian operations (HCNs), often sends US citizens (PCNs) to Asia-Pacific countries on assignment and may send some of its Singaporean employees on an assignment to its Japanese operations (as TCNs). The nationality of the employee is a major factor in determining the person's 'category'.

Morgan defines IHRM as the interplay among these three dimensions – human resource activities, types of employees and countries of operation. We can see that in broad terms IHRM involves the same activities as domestic HRM, e.g. procurement refers to HR planning and staffing. However, domestic HRM is involved with employees *within only one national boundary*. Increasingly, domestic HRM is taking on some of the flavor of IHRM as it deals more and more with a multicultural workforce. Thus, some of the current focus of domestic HRM on issues of managing workforce diversity may prove to be beneficial to the practice of IHRM. However, it must be remembered that the way in which diversity is managed within a single national context may not necessarily transfer to a multinational context without some modification.

What is an expatriate?

One obvious difference between domestic and international HRM is that staff are moved across national boundaries into various roles within the international firm's foreign operations – these employees have traditionally been called 'expatriates'. An expatriate is an employee who is working and temporarily residing in a foreign country. Some firms prefer to call such employees 'international assignees'.

Although it is clear in the literature that PCNs are always expatriates, it is often overlooked that TCNs are expatriates, as are HCNs who are transferred into parent-country operations outside their home country.[7] Figure 1-3 illustrates how all three categories may become expatriates.

Lately, the term '*inpatriate*' has come into vogue to signify the transfer of subsidiary staff into the parent country (headquarters) operations.[8] Its use has added a level of confusion surrounding the definition of an expatriate. For example, the *International Human Resource Management Reference Guide*, published by the Institute for International Human Resources (a division of the US Society for Human Resource Management), defined an inpatriate as a 'foreign manager in the US'. A 'foreign manager in the US' is then defined as 'an expatriate in the US where the US is the host-country and the manager's home-country is outside of the US'.[9] In other words, an inpatriate is also defined as an expatriate. A further indication of the confusion created by the use of the term 'inpatriate' is that some writers in international management define an HCN as an inpatriate. HCNs only become 'inpatriates' when they are transferred into the parent country operations as expatriates, as illustrated in Figure 1-3.

Given the substantial amount of jargon in international HRM, it is questionable as to whether the term 'inpatriate' adds enough value to justify its use. However, companies now use the term. For example, the Finnish multinational Nokia uses 'expatriate' to signify staff who are transferred out of, and 'inpatriate' to signify staff transferred into, a particular country. These terms are regarded as a constant reminder to all managers that there are movements of staff that need to be managed and not all are PCNs. Nokia does not confine the use of the term 'inpatriate' to an employee who is transferred into its parent country operations in Finland, but uses it as a generic term.[10] To complicate matters further, the term 'transpatriate' has recently been coined. It is used by some writers to refer to employees who are moved between subsidiaries. Again, these employees are expatriates.

| **Figure 1-3** | International assignments create expatriates |

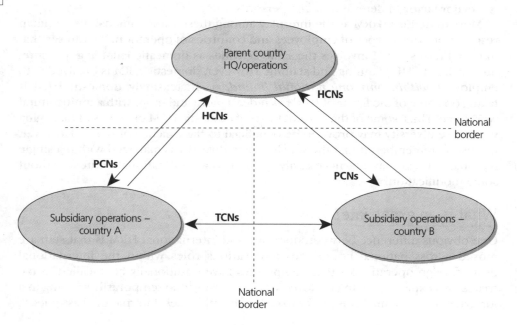

For clarity, we will use the term **expatriate** throughout this text to refer to employees who are transferred out of their home base into some other area of the firm's international operations, unless we are directly quoting from another source.

Differences between domestic and international HRM

In our view, the complexities of operating in different countries and employing different national categories of workers is a key variable that differentiates domestic and international HRM, rather than any major differences between the HRM activities performed. Dowling[11] argues that the complexity of international HR can be attributed to six factors:

- more HR activities
- the need for a broader perspective
- more involvement in employees' personal lives
- changes in emphasis as the workforce mix of expatriates and locals varies
- risk exposure
- broader external influences.

Each of these factors is now discussed in detail to illustrate its characteristics.

More HR activities

To operate in an international environment, a human resources department must engage in a number of activities that would not be necessary in a domestic environment: international taxation; international relocation and orientation; administrative services for expatriates; host-government relations; and language translation services.

Expatriates are subject to international taxation and often have both domestic (i.e. home-country) and host-country tax liabilities. Therefore, tax equalization policies must be designed to ensure that there is no tax incentive or disincentive associated with any particular international assignment.[12,13] The administration of tax equalization policies is complicated by the wide variations in tax laws across host countries and by the possible time lag between the completion of an expatriate assignment and the settlement of domestic and international tax liabilities. In recognition of these difficulties, many multinational firms retain the services of a major accounting firm for international taxation advice.

International relocation and orientation involve arranging for pre-departure training; providing immigration and travel details; providing housing, shopping, medical care, recreation and schooling information; and finalizing compensation details such as delivery of salary overseas, determination of various overseas allowances and taxation treatment. [The issue of expatriates returning to their home-country (repatriation) is covered in detail in Chapter 7.] Many of these factors may be a source of anxiety for the expatriate and require considerable time and attention to resolve potential problems successfully – certainly much more time than would be involved in a domestic transfer/relocation such as New York to Dallas, Sydney to Melbourne, London to Cardiff, Frankfurt to Munich or Beijing to Shanghai.

A multinational firm also needs to provide administrative services for expatriates in the host countries in which it operates. Providing these can often be a time-consuming and complex activity because policies and procedures are not always clear-cut and may conflict with local conditions. For example, ethical questions can arise when a practice that is legal and accepted in the host country may be at best unethical and at worst illegal in the home country. For example, a situation may arise in which a host country requires an AIDS test for a work permit for an employee whose parent firm is headquartered in the USA, where employment-related AIDS testing remains a controversial issue. How does the corporate HR manager deal with the potential expatriate employee who refuses to meet this requirement for an AIDS test and the overseas affiliate which needs the services of a specialist expatriate from headquarters? These issues add to the complexity of providing administrative services to expatriates.

Host-government relations represent an important activity for an HR department, particularly in developing countries where work permits and other important certificates are often more easily obtained when a personal relationship exists between the relevant government officials and multinational managers. Maintaining such relationships helps resolve potential problems that can be caused by ambiguous eligibility and/or compliance criteria for documentation such as work permits. US-based multinationals, however, must be careful in how they deal with relevant government officials, as payment or payment-in-kind such as dinners and gifts may violate the US Foreign Corrupt Practices Act.

Provision of language translation services for internal and external correspondence is an additional international activity for the HR department. Morgan[6] notes that if the HR department is the major user of language translation services, the role of this translation group is often expanded to provide translation services to all foreign operation departments within the multinational.

The need for a broader perspective

HR managers working in a domestic environment generally administer programs for a single national group of employees who are covered by a uniform compensation policy and taxed by one national government. Because HR managers working in an international environment face the problem of designing and administering programs for more than one national group of employees (e.g. PCN, HCN and TCN employees who may work together in Zurich at the European regional headquarters of a US-based multinational), they need to take a broader view of issues. For example, a broader, more international perspective on expatriate benefits would endorse the view that all expatriate employees, regardless of nationality, should receive a foreign service or expatriate premium when working in a foreign location. Yet some multinationals which routinely pay such premiums to their PCN employees on overseas assignment (even if the assignments are to desirable locations) are reluctant to pay premiums to foreign nationals assigned to the home country of the firm. Such a policy confirms the common perception of many HCN and TCN employees that PCN employees are given preferential treatment.[14] Complex equity issues arise when employees of various nationalities work together and the resolution of these issues remains one of the major challenges in the IHRM field. (Equity issues with regard to compensation are discussed in Chapter 6).

More involvement in employees' personal lives

A greater degree of involvement in employees' personal lives is necessary for the selection, training and effective management of both PCN and TCN employees.

The HR department or professional needs to ensure that the expatriate employee understands housing arrangements, health care and all aspects of the compensation package provided for the assignment (cost-of-living allowances, premiums, taxes and so on). Many multinationals have an 'International HR Services' section that coordinates administration of the above programs and provides services for PCNs and TCNs such as handling their banking, investments and home rental while on assignment and coordinating home visits and final repatriation.

In the domestic setting, the HR department's involvement with an employee's family is limited. The firm may, for example, provide employee insurance programs, or, if a domestic transfer is involved, the HR department may provide some assistance in relocating the employee and family. In the international setting, however, the HR department must be much more involved in order to provide the level of support required and will need to know more about the employee's personal life. For example, some governments require the presentation of a marriage certificate before granting a visa to an accompanying spouse. Thus, marital status could become an aspect of the selection process, regardless of the best intentions of the firm to avoid using a potentially discriminatory selection criterion. In such a situation, the HR department should advise all candidates being considered for the position of the host country's visa requirements with regard to marital status and allow candidates to decide whether they wish to remain in the selection process. Apart from providing suitable housing and schooling in the assignment location, the HR department may also need to assist children left behind at boarding schools in the home country.[15] In more remote or less hospitable assignment locations, the HR department may be required to develop and even run, recreational programs. For a domestic assignment, most of these matters either would not arise or would be primarily the responsibility of the employee rather than the HR department.

Changes in emphasis as the workforce mix of PCNs and HCNs varies

As foreign operations mature, the emphases put on various human resource activities change. For example, as the need for PCNs and TCNs declines and more trained locals become available, resources previously allocated to areas such as expatriate taxation, relocation and orientation are transferred to activities such as local staff selection, training and management development. The latter activity may require the establishment of a program to bring high-potential local staff to corporate headquarters for developmental assignments. The need to change emphasis in HR operations as a foreign subsidiary matures is clearly a factor that would broaden the responsibilities of local HR activities such as human resource planning, staffing, training and development and compensation.

Risk exposure

Frequently, the human and financial consequences of failure in the international arena are more severe than in domestic business. For example, while we discuss the topic in more detail in Chapter 4, expatriate failure (the premature return of an expatriate from an international assignment) and underperformance while on international assignment are potentially high-cost problems for international companies. Direct costs (salary, training costs and travel and relocation expenses) per failure to the parent firm may be as high as three times the domestic salary plus relocation expenses, depending on currency exchange rates and location of assignments. Indirect costs such as loss of foreign market share and damage to key host-country relationships may be considerable.

Another aspect of risk exposure that is relevant to international HRM is terrorism, particularly in the current political climate since the tragic events in New York on 11 September 2001. Most major multinationals must now consider political risk and terrorism when planning international meetings and assignments and it is estimated that they spend 1–2 per cent of their revenues on protection against terrorism. Terrorism has also clearly had an effect on the way in which employees assess potential international assignment locations.[16] The HR department may also need to devise emergency evacuation procedures for highly volatile assignment locations.

Our IHRM in Action Case 1-1 presents an example of how a firm operating internationally can become unwittingly caught up in larger political events. The situation was extremely stressful for the captain and crew of *The Tampa*, and also for company staff at headquarters in Oslo and in the Australian subsidiary. Having clear policy and procedure guidelines in place for emergencies encountered at sea assisted personnel to handle the crisis.

IHRM in Action Case 1-1

International staff all at sea

Captain Arne Rinnan and his ship *The Tampa*

Sunday 26 August 2001

The Norwegian-registered container ship, *The Tampa*, is sailing from Fremantle, Australia, towards Singapore on its homeward bound journey. Its cargo includes steel pipes, non-perishable dairy products and timber – in total worth about US$30 million. En route, it answers a distress signal advising that a boat, the *MK Palapa*, is drifting nearby. Under the 'rules of the sea', Captain Rinnan, as the nearest vessel, is obliged to go to its assistance. He and his crew, with advice from the Australian Government, take on board 460 refugees, mostly from Afghanistan and, again following the 'rules of the sea', *The Tampa* sets sail to the nearest harbor, which is the Indonesian port of Merak.

However, when the refugees find that they are being taken back to Indonesia, from which they had sailed some days previously, they become distressed and angry and demand to be taken to Christmas Island off the Australian coast. Captain Rinnan contacts the Australian Maritime Safety Authority who advise that, as the ship's captain, it is his decision. Captain Rinnan orders the ship to turn around and head for Christmas Island: the safety of his crew, the passengers and his ship are paramount.

When the Australian government is informed that *The Tampa* is about to seek permission to dock at Christmas Island, the Prime Minister, John Howard, announces that the refugees will not be allowed to set foot on Australian soil and refuses to allow the ship to dock. *The Tampa* waits outside Australian territorial waters. Captain Rinnan is informed that if he attempts to dock and land his rescued passengers, he will face a possible jail sentence of 20 years and his company will receive massive fines.

Wednesday 29 August, 2001

The Indonesian government informs the Australian government that it will not accept the refugees.

The Norwegian government tries to intervene and is informed by the Australian government that the fate of the refugees is between the Indonesian government (the nearest port to where the refugees were taken on board) and the Norwegian government (the ship is registered in Norway). The Norwegian Foreign Minister, Torbjorn Jagland, informs his Australian counterpart there is a medical crisis on board. Faced with suicide threats by some of the refugees if medical help did not arrive, Captain Rinnan issues a Mayday signal. He advises he is sailing into Australian waters as matters are becoming difficult for all on board. Australian troops board *The Tampa* to prevent it from docking on Christmas Island.

Monday 3 September, 2001

Australian troops move the refugees to an Australian vessel. *The Tampa* sails for Singapore.

The Tampa is owned by the Norwegian shipping company, Wallenius Wilhelmsen. The company has regional offices in the Americas, Asia, Europe and Oceania, employing 2900 people globally. Its Oceania Region covers Australia, New Zealand, Noumea and French Polynesia. In the 1980s, the company had been involved in rescuing post-Vietnam boat people and had policies in place as a consequence. *The Tampa* incident, though, involved the largest number of rescued persons.

The shipping line's owner, Wilh Wilhelmsen and his top management team at headquarters in Oslo immediately set up a Contingency Room from where they directed the situation, attending meetings with Norwegian government ministers and consulting maritime lawyers and were in constant communication with Captain Rinnen. At the local level, the Australian subsidiary's head office in Sydney was actively involved. Sydney staff handled local and international media, liaised with customers, particularly those who had cargo on board and managed relationships with key stakeholders. There was daily communication between Sydney and Oslo.

However, Rinnan was captain of *The Tampa* and responsible for the ship and its crew. He was also responsible for the lives of the refugees while they were on his ship.

Source: Various Australian and Norwegian newspaper reports, company information and D. Marr and M. Wilkinson, *Dark Victory*, Sydney: Allen and Unwin, 2003. We thank Runar Rabben and Scott Wilkinson for their assistance in preparing this case.

Broader external influences

The major external factors that influence IHRM are the type of government, the state of the economy and the generally accepted practices of doing business in each of the various host countries in which the multinational operates. A host government can, for example, dictate hiring procedures, as has been the case in Malaysia. The government during the 1970s introduced a requirement that foreign firms comply with an extensive set of affirmative action rules designed to provide additional employment opportunities for the indigenous Malays who constitute the majority of the population but tend to be under-represented in business and professional employment groups relative to Chinese Malays and Indian Malays. Various statistics showing employment levels of indigenous Malays throughout the firm were required to be forwarded to the relevant government department.

In developed countries, labor is more expensive and better organized than in less-developed countries and governments require compliance with guidelines on issues such as labor relations, taxation and health and safety. These factors shape the activities of the subsidiary HR manager to a considerable extent. In less-developed countries, labor tends to be cheaper and less organized and government regulation is less pervasive, so these factors take less time. The subsidiary HR manager must spend more time, however, learning and interpreting the local ways of doing business and the general code of conduct regarding activities such as gift giving. It is also likely that the subsidiary HR manager will become more involved in administering benefits either provided or financed by the multinational such as housing, education and other facilities not readily available in the local economy.

Variables that moderate differences between domestic and international HRM

Earlier, we argued that the complexity involved in operating in different countries and employing different national categories of employees is a key variable that differentiates domestic and international HRM, rather than any major differences between the HRM activities performed. Many firms underestimate the complexities involved in international operations and there has been consistent evidence to suggest that business failures in the international arena are often linked to poor management of human resources. In addition to complexity, there are four other variables that moderate (that is, either diminish or accentuate) differences between domestic and international HRM. As Figure 1-4 illustrates, these four moderators are:

● the cultural environment
● the industry (or industries) with which the multinational is primarily involved

Figure 1-4

Variables that moderate differences between domestic and international HRM

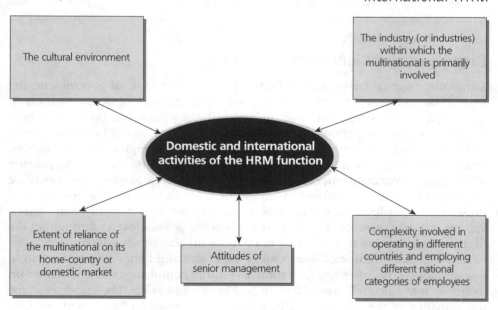

Source: P.J. Dowling, Completing the Puzzle: Issues in the Development of the Field of International Human Resource Management. *Management International Review*, Special Issue No. 3 (1999) p. 31. Reproduced with permission.

- the extent of reliance of the multinational on its home-country domestic market and
- the attitudes of senior management.

The cultural environment

There are many definitions of *culture*, but the term is usually used to describe a shaping process. That is, members of a group or society share a distinct way of life with common values, attitudes and behaviors that are transmitted over time in a gradual, yet dynamic, process. As Phatak[17] explains:

> A person is not born with a given culture: rather, she or he acquires it through the socialization process that begins at birth: an American is not born with a liking for hot dogs, or a German with a natural preference for beer: these behavioral attributes are culturally transmitted.

An important characteristic of culture is that it is so subtle a process that one is not always conscious of its effect on values, attitudes and behaviors. One usually has to be confronted with a different culture in order to appreciate this effect fully. Anyone traveling abroad, either as a tourist or on business, experiences situations that demonstrate cultural differences in language, food, dress, hygiene and attitude to time. Whereas the traveler can perceive these differences as novel, even enjoyable, for people required to live and work in a new country, such differences can prove difficult. They experience **culture shock** – a phenomenon experienced by people who move across cultures. The new environment requires many adjustments in a relatively short period of time, challenging people's frames of reference to such an extent that their sense of self, especially in terms of nationality, comes into question. People, in effect, experience a shock reaction to new cultural experiences that cause psychological disorientation because they misunderstand or do not recognize important cues. Culture shock can lead to negative feelings about the host country and its people and a longing to return home.[18]

Because international business involves the interaction and movement of people across national boundaries, an appreciation of cultural differences and when these differences are important is essential. Research into these aspects has assisted in furthering our understanding of the cultural environment as an important variable that moderates differences between domestic and international HRM. However, while cross-cultural and comparative research attempts to explore and explain similarities and differences, there are problems associated with such research. A major problem is that there is little agreement on either an exact definition of culture or on the operationalization of this concept. For many researchers, culture has become an omnibus variable, representing a range of social, historic, economic and political factors that are invoked *post hoc* to explain similarity or dissimilarity in the results of a study. As Bhagat and McQuaid[19] have noted,

> *Culture* has often served simply as a synonym for *nation* without any further conceptual grounding. In effect, national differences found in the characteristics of organizations or their members have been interpreted as cultural differences.

To reduce these difficulties, culture needs to be defined *a priori* rather than *post hoc*, and it should not be assumed that national differences necessarily represent cultural differences.

Another issue in cross-cultural research concerns the *emic–etic* distinction.[20] **Emic** refers to culture-specific aspects of concepts or behaviour and **etic** refers to culture-common aspects. These terms have been borrowed from linguistics: a phon*emic* system documents meaningful sounds specific to a given language and a phon*etic* system organizes all sounds that have meaning in any language.[21] Both the emic and etic approaches are legitimate research orientations. A major problem may arise, however, if a researcher imposes an etic approach (that is, assumes universality across cultures) when there is little or no evidence for doing so. A well-known example of an imposed etic approach is the convergence hypothesis that dominated much of US and European management research in the 1950s and 1960s. This approach was based on two key assumptions.[22] The first assumption was that there were principles of sound management that held regardless of national environments. Thus, the existence of local or national practices that deviated from these principles simply indicated a need to change these local practices. The second assumption was that the universality of sound management practices would lead to societies becoming more and more alike in the future. Given that the USA was the leading industrial economy at that time, the point of convergence was the US model.

To use Kuhn's[23] terminology, the convergence hypothesis became an established paradigm that many researchers found difficult to give up, despite a growing body of evidence supporting a divergence hypothesis. In an important paper reviewing the convergence–divergence debate, Child[24] made the point that there is evidence for both convergence and divergence. The majority of the convergence studies, however, focus on macrolevel variables (for example, structure and technology used by firms across cultures), and the majority of the divergence studies focus on microlevel variables (for example, the behavior of people within firms). His conclusion was that although firms in different countries are becoming more alike (an etic or convergence approach), the behavior of individuals within these firms is maintaining its cultural specificity (an emic or divergence approach). As noted above, both emic and etic approaches are legitimate research orientations, but methodological difficulties may arise if the distinction between these two approaches is ignored or if unwarranted universality assumptions are made.[25] The debate on assumptions of universality is not limited to the literature in international management. This issue has become a topic of debate in the field of international relations and strategic studies where research from international management is cited.[26]

The importance of cultural awareness

Despite the methodological concerns about cross-cultural research, it is now generally recognized that culturally insensitive attitudes and behaviors stemming from ignorance or from misguided beliefs ('my way is best', or 'what works at home will work here') not only are inappropriate but often cause international business failure. Therefore, an awareness of cultural differences is essential for the HR manager at corporate headquarters as well as in the host location.[27] Activities such as hiring, promoting, rewarding and dismissal will be determined by the practices of the host country and often are based on a value system peculiar to that country's culture. A firm may decide to head up a new overseas operation with an expatriate general manager but appoint as the HR department manager a local, a person who is familiar with the host country's HR practices. This practice can cause problems, though, for the expatriate general manager, as happened to an

Australian who was in charge of a new mining venture in Indonesia. The local manager responsible for recruitment could not understand why the Australian was upset to find that he had hired most of his extended family rather than staff with the required technical competence. The Indonesian was simply ensuring that his duty to his family was fulfilled – since he was in a position to employ most of them, he was obligated to do so. The Australian, however, interpreted the Indonesian's actions as nepotism, a negative practice according to his own value system.[28]

Wyatt[29] recounts a good example of the fallacy of assuming 'what works at home will work here' when dealing with work situations in another culture. HR department staff of a large firm in Papua New Guinea were concerned over a number of accidents involving operators of very large, expensive, earth-moving vehicles. The expatriate managers investigating the accidents found that local drivers involved in the accidents were chewing betel nut, a common habit for most of the coastal peoples of Papua New Guinea and other Pacific islands. Associating the betel nut with depressants such as alcohol, the expatriate managers banned the chewing of betel nut during work hours. In another move to reduce the number of accidents, free coffee was provided at loading points and drivers were required to alight from their vehicles at these locations. What the managers did not realize was that betel nut, like their culturally acceptable coffee, is, in fact, a stimulant, although some of the drivers were chewing it to cover up the fact that they drank beer before commencing work. As Wyatt points out, many indigenous workers used betel nut as a pick-me-up in much the same way as the expatriates used coffee.

Coping with cultural differences, and recognizing how and when these differences are relevant, are a constant challenge for international firms. Helping to prepare staff and their families for working and living in a new cultural environment has become a key activity for HR departments in those multinationals that appreciate (or have been forced, through experience, to appreciate) the impact that the cultural environment can have on staff performance and well-being. We shall address key issues relating to cultural differences and staff preparation and adjustment in Part II.

Industry type

Porter[30] suggests that the industry (or industries if the firm is a conglomerate) in which a multinational firm is involved is of considerable importance because patterns of international competition vary widely from one industry to another. At one end of the continuum of international competition is the *multidomestic industry*, one in which competition in each country is essentially independent of competition in other countries. Traditional examples include retailing, distribution and insurance. At the other end of the continuum is the *global industry*, one in which a firm's competitive position in one country is significantly influenced by its position in other countries. Examples include commercial aircraft, semiconductors and copiers. The key distinction between a multidomestic industry and a global industry is described by Porter as follows:

> The global industry is not merely a collection of domestic industries but a series of linked domestic industries in which the rivals compete against each other on a truly worldwide basis ... In a multidomestic industry, then, international strategy collapses to a series of domestic strategies. The issues that are uniquely international revolve around how to do business abroad, how to select good countries in which to compete (or assess country risk),

and mechanisms to achieve the one-time transfer of know-how. These are questions that are relatively well developed in the literature. In a global industry, however, managing international activities like a portfolio will undermine the possibility of achieving competitive advantage. In a global industry, a firm must in some way integrate its activities on a worldwide basis to capture the linkages among countries.

The role of the HRM function in multidomestic and global industries can be analysed using Porter's value-chain model.[31] In Porter's model, HRM is seen as one of four support activities for the five primary activities of the firm. Since human resources are involved in each of the primary and support activities, the HRM function is seen as cutting across the entire value chain of a firm. If the firm is in a multidomestic industry, the role of the HR department will most likely be more domestic in structure and orientation. At times there may be considerable demand for international services from the HRM function (for example, when a new plant or office is established in a foreign location and the need for expatriate employees arises), but these activities would not be pivotal – indeed, many of these services may be provided via consultants and/or temporary employees. The main role for the HRM function would be to support the primary activities of the firm in each domestic market to achieve a competitive advantage through either cost/efficiency or product/service differentiation.[32] If the multinational is in a global industry, however, the 'imperative for coordination' described by Porter would require a HRM function structured to deliver the international support required by the primary activities of the multinational.

Reliance of the multinational on its home-country domestic market

A pervasive but often ignored factor which influences the behavior of multinationals and resultant HR practices is the extent of reliance of the multinational on its home-country domestic market. When, for example, we look through lists of very large firms (such as those that appear in *Fortune* and other business magazines), it is frequently assumed that a global market perspective would be dominant in the firm's culture and thinking. However, size is not the only key variable when looking at a multinational – the extent of reliance of the multinational on its home-country domestic market is also very important. In fact, for many firms, a small home market is one of the major motives for 'going international'.

The United Nations Conference on Trade and Development (UNCTAD) in its annual survey of foreign direct investment calculates what it refers to as an 'index of transnationality', which is an average of ratios of foreign assets to total assets; foreign sales to total sales; and foreign employment to total employment.[33] The 'top ten' multinationals are as follows:

1   Rio Tinto (UK/Australia)
2   Thomson Corporation (Canada)
3   ABB (Switzerland)
4   Nestlé (Switzerland)
5   British American Tobacco (UK)
6   Electrolux (Sweden)
7   Interbrew (Belgium)
8   Anglo American (UK)

9 AstraZeneca (UK)

10 Philips Electronics (The Netherlands).

There is not a US firm in the first 15 multinationals listed and Coca-Cola and McDonald's are ranked 27th and 39th, respectively. The reason for this is as obvious as it is important – *the size of the domestic market* for US firms. A very large domestic market influences all aspects of how a multinational organizes its activities. For example, it will be more likely to use an international division as the way it organizes its international activities (see Chapter 2) and, even if it uses a global product structure, the importance of the domestic market will be pervasive. A large domestic market will also influence the attitudes of senior managers towards their international activities, and will generate a large number of managers with an experience base of predominantly or even exclusively domestic market experience. Thus, multinationals from small advanced economies such as Switzerland (population 7 million), Belgium (just over 10 million), Sweden (almost 9 million) and The Netherlands (16 million) are in a very different position to US multinationals based in the largest single national market in the world with over 290 million people. The demands of a large domestic market present a challenge to the globalization efforts of many US firms. As Cavusgil[34] noted in an important book on internationalizing business education, the task of internationalizing business education in the USA is a large one. So, too, is the task facing many US firms in terms of developing global managers.

The enduring context of IHRM

To a certain extent, our discussion of the factors that differentiate domestic and international HRM, and the variables that moderate these differences, demonstrates a degree of consistency in the global context within which international business operates. Internationalizing firms rely on having the right people to manage and operate in what has become an increasingly complex environment. However, the need for good IHRM practices that are appropriate to the context in which they occur has been a constant critical success factor in international business ventures. For example, the following quotation is taken from a detailed case study of a large US multinational, where the authors, Desatnick and Bennett[35] concluded:

> The primary causes of failure in multinational ventures stem from a lack of understanding of the essential differences in managing human resources, at all levels, in foreign environments. Certain management philosophies and techniques have proved successful in the domestic environment: their application in a foreign environment too often leads to frustration, failure and underachievement. These 'human' considerations are as important as the financial and marketing criteria upon which so many decisions to undertake multinational ventures depend.

The study was reported in 1978, but many international managers today would concur with the sentiments expressed in this quotation. They would also identify with the experiences and challenges confronting a 14th-century Italian merchant (see IHRM in Action Case 1-2). Datini faced an environment fraught with peril (pirates, land-robbers, pestilence), political events (wars, election of a new Pope, government regulations) and economic changes (fluctuating prices, import restrictions) that generated barriers to be overcome in order to grow internationally as well as at home in Tuscany. As will be gathered from the case, Datini had to deal with communication and control issues and to devise ways of staffing his foreign operations.

Managers in the 21st century face similar challenges. The recent outbreak of severe acute respiratory syndrome (SARS) reminds us of medieval plagues. Wars continue to place lives at risk, and have positive and negative effects on the flow of international trade and business. The key difference between Datini's world and

IHRM in Action Case 1-2

Managing international business in the 14th century

Francesco di Marco Datini (da Prato) was a 14th-century merchant based in Prato in Tuscany. His business was international: his trading houses were based in Florence, Pisa, Genoa, Avignon (at that time one of the most important trading cities in Europe), and Spain and Majorca, all controlled from what we would call today his headquarters, situated in the small town of Prato.

The 14th-century merchant was said to be a risk-taker who attempted to diminish risks by spreading them over the widest possible area in terms of both geography and products. According to trading manuals at the time, to be successful abroad, a merchant needed to be acquainted with foreign languages and foreign ways of operating. Datini spent his early working years in Avignon (in modern day France) before returning to Prato.

Among his various businesses was the production of cloth. Wool from Spain and England was imported for spinning, weaving, dyeing and finishing. The finished cloth was sent to overseas markets or sold in markets in other Italian states. Surplus wool was sold in Italy. To support his activities, Datini established an office in Pisa to handle his importing activities, and another in Genoa to handle the import of special ingredients for fixing dyes. An overseas branch in Barcelona, initially for the purchase of wool, later became a sales office for finished cloth. Datini used other Tuscany merchants as his agents in England.

His Spanish operations began with the use of agents; then several years later, these were replaced with his own branch offices. One of his trusted partners was sent to Barcelona. This person then set up other offices – in Valencia and on the island of Majorca. Carefully selected managers (*fattori* in medieval Italian), some of whom were relatives or connected to his partners or friends, were sent by Datini to run these branches. His partner became what we would now call Spanish Regional Manager. The *fattore* in charge of the branch in Barcelona, after a couple of years in his role, complained about his salary and requested to be made a partner. After some discussion, Datini relented. Those sent to Majorca and other parts of the Balearic Islands viewed their years abroad with an eye to their repatriation back to Prato, when younger men would replace them. Datini, though, found that the young Tuscans sent to the Spanish operations liked their new life so well they did not want to come home.

Datini wrote lengthy weekly letters to the managers of his branches. These people were expected to report weekly in return. Some of Datini's letters that have survived the passing of time reveal that he was capable of instructing his *fattori* on personal matters as well as business matters. All correspondence was carefully filed.

The Venetian Republic maintained a regular postal service between Venice and Bruges (Flanders) that took only seven days. Letters to England, though, depended on favorable winds and tides at the Channel Ports. Those to Spain and Majorca had to survive possible encounters with pirates. Confidential correspondence was sent by trusted couriers, often with outriders as protection. Sometimes, Datini would send a partner, or a correspondent, or one of his *fattori* to travel between his various branches – so it was not unusual for a 14th-century merchant to ride about the world on his company's business. This was not without risk given the perils of such travel: shipwreck, piracy, land-robbers, dishonest agents, closed ports and pestilence.

Source: Iris Origo, *The Merchant of Prato: Daily Life in a Medieval Italian City*, London: Penguin Books, 1992.

that which we face today is perhaps the greater complexity of global business with increasing interdependencies between countries through regional integration (such as the European Union and the Asia Pacific Economic Cooperation) and trade agreements (such as the North American Free Trade Agreement); and increasing numbers of very large multinational firms linked in intra- and inter-organizational networks and alliances. It is a dynamic environment still fraught with peril. A report in the British newspaper *The Financial Times* relates the first two days of the then incoming Chief Executive Officer (CEO) of the US multinational General Electric. Mr Immelt is quoted as saying, 'I was Chairman for two days; I had an airplane with my engines that hit a building [one of the World Trade Center towers] I insured, covered by a network I owned.'[36]

The internationalizing firm, regardless of size and geographic reach, faces continuing forces for change that affect its characteristics and operations, which in turn places demands on its management. As depicted in Figure 1-5, environmental changes provoke managerial responses that then alter the global work environment. We shall briefly look at the interaction of these elements in terms of IHRM.

Forces for change

Of course, one could argue that the greatest force is change itself, and that a feature of our current environment is one of rapid change. However, rather than engage here in a philosophical debate, we shall confine our discussion to key trends that are generally accepted to be forces for change in the current global workplace.

Global competition.   It is generally recognized that levels of competition are increasing with the spread and diversity of international business and as firms from developing nations and transitional economies become more involved with global activities (such as the emergence of Chinese multinationals). As more and more firms from numerous countries become internationalized, concerns have been expressed about the desirability of the globalization of trade and business activity. The recent debate and demonstrations against 'globalization' are perhaps indicative of this.

There has been, though, a consistent concern for some decades about the operations of very large multinational firms (particularly those labelled as transnational corporations). Some regard the multinational as a force for convergence through the transfer of standardized work practices across their global operations. Stakeholder pressure [particularly from lobby and environmental groups, themselves often

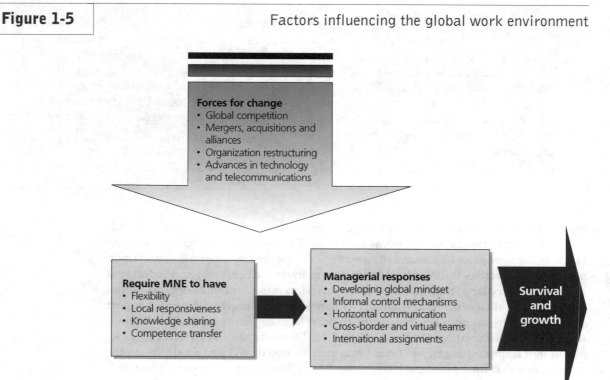

Figure 1-5   Factors influencing the global work environment

international organizations – sometimes referred to as non-government organizations (NGOs)] is seen as a countervailing force. Thus, not only does increased global competition have an impact on a firm's competitive position, but also dealing with issues related to business ethics and social responsibility has now become a priority for multinationals, involving HR managers, as we will discuss later.

Growth in mergers, acquisitions and alliances.   A contributing element, and also response, to global competition has been an increase in the number of mergers and acquisitions (M&As) and the continued trend to the formation of strategic alliances. The merger between Daimler-Benz and Chrysler (German and US automobile manufacturers) to form DaimlerChrysler and between BHP and Billiton (Australian and South African mining companies) are examples of the creation of large multinationals through a cross-border M&A. Over a four-year period, the Finnish Merita Bank merged first with Nordbanken from Sweden, then with Unidanmark from Denmark, and later with Bank of Norway, to form Nordea Bank. In Chapter 2, we look at these trends and draw out the implications for IHRM.

Organization restructuring.   It has long been recognized that firms constantly realign their operations and activities to support changes in strategic direction, as a consequence of growth and changes in the firm's environment.[37] The past decade has seen large-scale retrenchments as firms outsource activities, sell underperforming units, engage in plant rationalization, integrate acquired operations and merge businesses. Although one could argue that organizational change is a fact of work life, it would seem that the rate of structural changes has increased exponentially with global competition. Again, in Chapter 2, we explore the HR implications of structural change as the internationalizing firm adapts to strategic imperatives.

Advances in technology and telecommunication. Perhaps the most striking example here has been the rapid adoption of the Internet, although its anticipated contribution to developing new ways of conducting international business has not yet lived up to expectations.[38] However, arrangements such as virtual teams have facilitated project work across time zones and national borders, constant communication via digital mobile telephones and e-mail has assisted managerial handling of crises and situations and computerized processes and procedures have enhanced production and improved working conditions. Naturally, these changes have had implications for the way in which people are managed.

Impacts on multinational management

A consequence of the above forces for change has been the need for flexibility in terms of management approaches and action, as indicated in Figure 1-5. Large firms have tended to become bureaucratic over time as control and coordination concerns arise. Often, the need for central control has meant slow response to local issues and concerns at the subsidiary level. The mantra of the 1990s was 'think global, act local' – a slogan to remind managers in global organizations that subsidiaries required some freedom to act according to their local environment, with a simultaneous requirement for an overall view of the firm's global position. The challenge, of course, was how to enable local responsiveness without affecting overall corporate cohesion, and firms are still grappling with ways in which to achieve this objective. In Chapter 2, we discuss issues relating to autonomy and control mechanisms, drawing out the IHRM implications.

Two other major requirements that have been identified as important to multinational management's responses to the above forces for change have been knowledge sharing and transfer of competence.

Knowledge sharing. Although some may regard this aspect as self-evident given the so-called Information Age and the rise of the Knowledge Organization, providing the avenues for knowledge sharing remains an important consideration for firms growing internationally. Indeed, the push for reduced layers of hierarchy within organizations was to facilitate horizontal communication across world-wide operations, and also flexibility and responsiveness.[39] Structural changes have been made in order to dismantle functional and unit boundaries to counter what has been termed 'the silo mentality', where employees protect their territory and are unwilling to share resources and knowledge. How effective these structural changes are depends in part on how the personnel concerned respond to structural changes and workplace arrangements. For example, a recent study[40] on the adoption of intranet technology in a large global bank found that, rather than assisting integration of activities and people through project-based work arrangements, the intranet actually helped to reinforce existing functional and national borders – through the creation instead of what the authors of the study termed 'electronic fences'.

The managerial challenge is how to leverage knowledge and information that is imbedded in the various parts of the multinational so that the necessary know-how can be transferred where needed. Knowledge – which has been defined as 'what we know' – is generally divided into two types: explicit (articulated) and tacit (non-verbal, intuitive). It is transferred through the process of codification, diffusion and absorption.[41] Teaching a person to drive a motorcar is often used as an example of how we transfer knowledge. As Zack[42] comments, 'the most valuable knowledge is the tacit knowledge existing within people's heads, augmented or shared via interpersonal interaction and social relationships'. Writers in the area of knowledge management concur that, because of its 'sticky' nature, the transfer of tacit knowledge is difficult. Organizations need to provide an encouraging environment – using rewards systems and communication networks that promote knowledge sharing.

As we will discuss in Chapter 3, expatriates play a key role in tacit knowledge transfer as they move across borders and operations, demonstrating and implementing organizational routines, systems and work practices. Staff movements facilitate the establishment of personal working relationships and interaction that assist in knowledge transfer and informal information flow. Kamoche argues that 'the scope for organizational learning exists if the knowledge acquired by individuals in international assignments can be diffused across the organization'.[43] The constraint is that tacit knowledge is person-bound and depends on the person's preparedness and ability to share relevant knowledge with others. Information is data and is less sticky; however, individuals can act as gatekeepers, deciding when and with whom they share information. Further, uncodified information that flows through informal information networks is difficult for multinational managers to harness and utilize, yet can be an effective way of transferring critical knowledge and information, complementing and sometimes surpassing formal information systems. The role of personal networks in international business has long been recognized as a key component for success.

Transfer of competence.   Human competence refers to the knowledge, skills and abilities required in competent work performance and is fundamental to organizational viability.[44] Firms through hiring practices and training programs develop required levels of competence. Competence is also regarded as a source of competitive advantage, if the firm is able to coordinate and deploy these in a way that is difficult for competitors to imitate. Hamel and Prahalad[45] define a core competence as 'the sum of learning across individual skill sets and individual organizational units'. In other words, it is the collective stock of human competence that provides an organization with certain capabilities and processes. The management challenge, of course, is to identify what is a core competence, where it resides and how it can be protected, nurtured and exploited for competitive advantage, and is more difficult for the dispersed multinational, with diverse global units and employees from different national backgrounds. There need to be effective mechanisms in place that encourage openness to new ideas and new ways of working, to counter the 'not-invented-here' attitudes that form barriers to the transfer of new skills. Aspects related to the development and transfer of competence will be addressed further in Chapter 8, where we examine HR practices in the host-country (subsidiary) context.

The managerial requisites of flexibility, responsiveness, knowledge sharing and competence transfer have engendered various managerial responses, as indicated in Figure 1-5. It has been suggested that one way of assisting the firm's ability to leverage its resources, knowledge and competencies is through the development of a 'global mindset' or perspective throughout the firm – to encourage employees in various locations and functions to view activities as part of the corporate whole.[46] Regional and global meetings and training programs held in rotating locations, staff exchanges and cross-border teams are ways in which multinationals can provide opportunities for employees to 'see the bigger picture'. In the next chapter, we will discuss how informal control mechanisms (personal networks and corporate culture) have been advocated as a way of devolving responsibility to enhance local responsiveness and flexibility. Horizontal communication, fostered as we mentioned above through the use of less hierarchical structures, flowing through informal conduits such as personal networks, has also been suggested as a way of enhancing a global perspective and encouraging knowledge sharing. The formation of cross-border, even virtual, teams is another way of encouraging network building, knowledge sharing and competence development and transfer. International assignments have been a time-honored way of achieving a broader perspective at the individual level and as a mechanism for transferring information, knowledge and skills for the benefit of the organization, while maintaining cohesion and control.

Although the forces for change in the global environment are more complex owing to interdependencies of operations, markets, trading blocs and the like, and managerial responses reflect technological advances and attitudinal changes to workplace arrangements, there have remained consistent requirements across the centuries of international business and trade. The role of people in driving international expansion is one such constant factor. Just as our 14th-century merchant worried about whom to place in control of his Spanish branches, and then how to monitor their performance, so do those of the 21st century. For small- and medium-sized and family-owned, firms, internationalization often stretches resources and the availability of reliable staff becomes a major constraint on further expansion. How people are recruited, deployed and managed in the multinational context therefore remains a critical component of success.

Summary

This chapter has established the scope of this book. We have:

- Defined international HRM and the term 'expatriate'.
- Discussed the differences between domestic and international HRM – looking at six factors: more HR activities, the need for a broader perspective, more involvement in employees' personal lives, changes in emphasis as the workforce mix of expatriates and locals varies, risk exposure and more external influences.
- Examined what we have called the enduring context of IHRM.
  The focus is on the current global work environment, looking at the forces for change that have prompted managerial responses that have implications for the way in which people are being managed in multinationals at the turn of the 21st century. However, we have made a brief comparison with the situation that confronted a 14th-century merchant as a way of drawing out some of the constants in international business.

This treatment has enabled us to provide an overview of the field of IHRM and establish how the general environment affects IHRM. The next chapter examines the organizational context where we explore how IHRM activities are determined by, and influence, various internal changes as the firm internationalizes.

Discussion questions and exercises

1 What are the similarities and differences between domestic and international HRM?

2 Define international HRM.

3 What aspects of international HRM are illustrated by the case of Captain Rinnan and his ship *The Tampa*?

4 Can you identify other forces for change than those noted in Figure 1-5? If so, what managerial responses have you observed?

5 You are the Human Resource Director, Global Services, of a large multinational in the oil industry. You are concerned for the safety of 15 expatriate staff currently working in the oilfields in a Middle Eastern country. Given the political volatility of the area, devise a set of policies and procedures that will enable you to evacuate all 15 persons should the need arise.

6 Form small groups. You are managers from various subsidiaries of a global firm. Your organization has embraced the concept of cross-border teamwork and you are all expected to contribute, where possible, resources, expertise and other assistance. Assume that you have a project that will suit a cross-border teamwork approach. How will you form such a team? What issues will have to be addressed? For example, is it feasible to work as a virtual team, and how you will share resources, particularly staff.

Further reading

K. Desouza and R. Evaristo, 2003. Global Knowledge Management Strategies, *European Management Journal*, Vol. 21, No. 1, pp. 62–67.

L. Gratton and S. Ghoshal, 2003. Managing Personal Human Capital: New Ethos for the 'Volunteer' Employee, *European Management Journal*, Vol. 21, No. 1, pp. 1–10.

R.S. Blagat, B.L. Kedia, P.D. Harveston and H.C. Triandis, 2002. Cultural Variations in the Cross-border Transfer of Organizational Knowledge: an Integrative Framework, *Academy of Management Review*, Vol. 27, No. 2, pp. 204–221.

M. Harvey, M.M. Noviceviv and T. Kiessling, 2001. Hypercompetition and the Future of Global Management in the Twenty-first Century. *Thunderbird International Business Review*, Vol. 43, No. 5, pp. 599–616.

Y. Doz, J. Santos and P. Williamson, 2001. *From Global to Metanational*, Cambridge, MA: Harvard Business School Press.

S. McGaughey and H. De Cieri, 1999. Reassessment of Convergence and Divergence Dynamics: Implications for International HRM, *International Journal of Human Resource Management*, Vol. 10, No. 2, pp. 235–250.

I. Nonaka and H. Takeuchi, 1995. *The Knowledge Creating Company*, Oxford: Oxford University Press.

P.J. Dowling, 1988. International and Domestic Personnel/Human Resource Management: Similarities and Differences, in *Readings in Personnel and Human Resource Management* (3rd edn), ed. R.S. Schuler, S.A. Youngblood and V.L. Huber, St. Paul, MN: West Publishing.

Notes and references

1 H. De Cieri and P.J. Dowling, Strategic Human Resource Management in Multinational Enterprises: Theoretical and Empirical Developments, in P. Wright *et al.* (eds), *Research and Theory in SHRM: an Agenda for the 21st Century*, Greenwich, CT: JAI Press, 1999.

2 For examples of this approach, see N. Adler, *International Dimensions of Organizational Behaviour*, 3rd edn, Cincinnatti, OH: South-Western, 1997, and A. Phatak, *International Management: Concept and Cases*, Cincinnati, OH: South-Western, 1997. See also the Special Issue on Asia-Pacific HRM, *International Journal of Human Resource Management*, Vol. 11, No. 2 (2000).

3   See, for example, C. Brewster and A. Hegewisch, *Policy and Practice in European Human Resource Management – The Price Waterhouse Cranfield Survey*, London: Routledge, 1994.

4   See P. Dowling and R. Schuler, *International Dimensions of Human Resource Management,* 1st edn, Boston, MA: PWS-Kent, 1990; P. Dowling, R. Schuler and D. Welch, *International Dimensions of Human Resource Management,* 2nd edn, Belmont, CA: Wadsworth, 1994; P.J. Dowling, D.E. Welch and R.S. Schuler, *International Human Resource Management: Managing People in a Multinational Context*, 3rd edn, Cincinnati OH: South-Western, 1998.

5   T.M. Welbourne and H. De Cieri, How New Venture Initial Public Offerings Benefit from International Operations, *International Journal of Human Resource Management*, Vol. 12, No. 4 (2001) pp. 652–668.

6   P. Morgan, International Human Resource Management: Fact or Fiction, *Personnel Administrator*, Vol. 31, No. 9 (1986) pp. 43–47.

7   See H. De Cieri, S.L. McGaughey and P.J. Dowling, Relocation in *International Encyclopaedia of Business and Management*, ed. M. Warner, Vol. 5, London: Routledge, 1996, pp. 4300–4310, for further discussion of this point.

8   For an example of the way in which the term is being used, see M.G. Harvey, M.M. Novicevic and C. Speier, Strategic Global Human Resource Management: the Role of Inpatriate Managers, *Human Resource Management Review*, Vol. 10, No. 2 (2000) pp. 153–175.

9   Curiously, the Reference Guide also states that the word inpatriate 'can also be used for US expatriates returning to an assignment in the US'. This is a contradiction of the first part of the definition of an inpatriate being a 'Foreign manager in the US' and is illogical. US expatriates returning to the US are PCNs and cannot also be classed as 'foreign managers in the US' – perhaps they are 'repatriates', but they are not inpatriates. As defined, this term is only of use in the USA.

10 From a discussion on this issue among members of the Finnish International HRM Club meeting, 7 February 2003.

11 P.J. Dowling, International and Domestic Personnel/Human Resource Management: Similarities and Differences, in *Readings in Personnel and Human Resource Management* 3rd edn. R.S. Schuler, S.A. Youngblood and V.L. Huber, St. Paul, MN: West Publishing, 1988.

12 D.L. Pinney, Structuring an Expatriate Tax Reimbursement Program, *Personnel Administrator*, Vol. 27, No. 7 (1982) pp. 19–25.

13 M. Gajek and M.M. Sabo, The Bottom Line: What HR Managers Need to Know About the New Expatriate Regulations, *Personnel Administrator*, Vol. 31, No. 2 (1986) pp. 87–92.

14 R.D. Robinson, *International Business Management: a Guide to Decision Making,* 2nd edn, Hinsdale, IL: Dryden, 1978.

15 Although less common in the USA, the use of private boarding schools is common in countries (particularly European countries) which have a colonial tradition, where both colonial administrators and business people would often undertake long assignments overseas and expect to leave their children at a boarding school in their home country. This is especially true of the UK, which also has a strong cultural tradition of the middle and upper classes sending their children to private boarding schools (curiously described by the British as 'public' schools, even though they are all private institutions which charge fees) even if the parents were working in Britain.

16 See Terrorism, Chapter 4 in T.M. Gladwin and I. Walter, *Multinationals Under Fire: Lessons in the Management of Conflict*, New York: Wiley, 1980; M. Harvey, A Survey of Corporate Programs for Managing Terrorist Threats, *Journal of International Business Studies*, Vol. 24, No. 3 (1993) pp. 465–478; C. Solomon, Global Business Under Siege, *Global Workforce*, January (1997) pp. 20.

17 A.V. Phatak, *International Dimensions of Management*, 4th edn, Cincinnati, OH: South-Western, 1995, p. 48.

18 J.E. Harris and R.T. Moran, *Managing Cultural Differences*, Houston: Gulf, 1979.

19 R.S. Bhagat and S.J. McQuaid, Role of Subjective Culture in Organizations: a Review and Directions for Future Research, *Journal of Applied Psychology*, Vol. 67 (1982) pp. 653–685.

20 See J.W. Berry, Introduction to Methodology, in *Handbook of Cross-cultural Psychology,* Vol. 2: *Methodology,* ed. H.C. Triandis and J.W. Berry, Boston: Allyn and Bacon, 1980; H. De Cieri and P.J. Dowling, Cross-cultural Issues in Organizational Behaviour, in *Trends in Organizational Behaviour,* Vol. 2, ed. C.L. Cooper and D.M. Rousseau, Chichester: Wiley, 1995, pp. 127–145; M.B. Teagarden and M.A. Von Glinow, Human Resource Management in Cross-cultural Contexts: Emic Practices versus Etic Philosophies, *Management International Review,* 37 (1 – Special Issue) (1997) pp. 7–20.

21 See H. Triandis and R. Brislin, Cross-cultural Psychology, *American Psychologist*, Vol. 39 (1984) pp. 1006–1016.

22   See G. Hofstede, The Cultural Relativity of Organizational Practices and Theories, *Journal of International Business Studies*, Vol. 14, No. 2 (1983) pp. 75–89.

23   T.S. Kuhn, *The Structure of Scientific Revolution*, 2nd edn, Chicago, IL: University of Chicago Press, 1962.

24   J.D. Child, Culture, Contingency and Capitalism in the Cross-national Study of Organizations, in *Research in Organizational Behaviour*, Vol. 3, ed. L.L. Cummings and B.M. Staw, Greenwich, CT: JAI Press, 1981.

25   See D.A. Ricks, *Blunders in International Business*, Cambridge, MA: Blackwell, 1993, for a comprehensive collection of mistakes made by multinational firms which paid insufficient attention to their cultural environment in their international business operations. For further literature on this topic see the following: P.S. Kirkbride and S.F.Y. Tang, From Kyoto to Kowloon: Cultural Barriers to the Transference of Quality Circles from Japan to Hong Kong, *Asia Pacific Journal of Human Resources*, 32, No. 2 (1994) pp. 100–111; M. Tayeb, Organizations and National Culture: Methodology Considered, *Organisation Studies*, 15, No. 3 (1994) pp. 429–446; P. Sparrow, R.S. Schuler and S.E. Jackson, Convergence or Divergence: Human Resource Practices and Policies for Competitive Advantage Worldwide, *International Journal of Human Resource Management*, Vol. 5, No. 2 (1994) pp. 267–299; M. Morishima, Embedding HRM in a Social Context, *British Journal of Industrial Relations*, Vol. 33, No. 4 (1995) pp. 617–643; J.E. Delery and D.H. Doty, Modes of Theorizing in Strategic Human Resource Management: Tests of Universalistic, Contingency, and Configurational Performance Predictions, *Academy of Management Journal*, Vol. 39 (1996) pp. 802–835.

26   S.P. Huntington, The West: Unique, Not Universal, *Foreign Affairs,* November/December (1996) pp. 28–46.

27   R.L. Tung, Managing Cross-national and Intra-national Diversity, *Human Resource Management*, Vol. 32, No. 4 (1993) pp. 461–477.

28   P.J Dowling, D.E. Welch and H. De Cieri, International Joint Ventures: a New Challenge for Human Resource Management, in *Proceedings of the Fifteenth Conference of the European International Business Association,* ed. R. Luostarinen, Helsinki, December 1989.

29   T. Wyatt, Understanding Unfamiliar Personnel Problems in Cross-cultural Work Encounters, *Asia Pacific HRM,* Vol. 27, No. 4 (1989) p. 5.

30   M.E. Porter, Changing Patterns of International Competition, *California Management Review,* Vol. 28, No. 2 (1986) pp. 9–40.

31   M.E. Porter, *Competitive Advantage: Creating and Sustaining Superior Performance*, New York: Free Press, 1985.

32   See R.S. Schuler and I.C. MacMillan, Gaining Competitive Advantage Through Human Resource Management Practices, *Human Resource Management*, Vol. 23, No. 3 (1984) pp. 241–255, for a discussion of these strategies.

33   This section is based on the World Investment Report, 2002, United Nations Conference on Trade and Development, Division on Investment, Technology and Enterprise Development, Transnational Corporations, Vol. 11, No. 3, December 2002.

34   S. Tamer Cavusgil, *Internationalising Business Education: Meeting the Challenge*, East Lansing, MI: Michigan State University Press, 1993.

35   R.L. Desatnick and M.L. Bennett, *Human Resource Management in the Multinational Company*, New York: Nichols, 1978.

36   A. Hill, Two Days that Shook GE into a New Age, *Financial Times*, 11 May 2002.

37   As a reminder that restructuring is not new, some authors like to refer to a statement supposedly made by a Roman soldier – attributed, probably inaccurately to Petronius: 'We tend to meet any new situation by reorganizing and a wonderful method it can be for creating the illusion of progress while creating confusion, inefficiency and demoralization'; see C. Pollitt, Institutional Amnesia: a Paradox of the 'Information Age', *Prometheus*, Vol. 18, No. 1 (2000) pp. 5–16.

38   For a review of the Internet and international management, see B. Petersen (ed.) International Management and the Internet – Post-hype, *Management International Review*, Special Issue No. 1 (2003).

39   R. Marschan, D. Welch and L. Welch, Control in Less-hierarchical Multinationals: the Role of Networks and Informal Communication, *International Business Review*, Vol. 5, No. 2 (1996) pp. 137–150.

40   S. Newell, H. Scarbrough and J. Swan, From Global Knowledge Management to Internal Electronic Fences: Contradictory Outcomes of Intranet Development, *British Journal of Management*, Vol. 12 (2001) pp. 97–111.

41   J. Howells and J. Roberts, From Innovation Systems to Knowledge Systems *Prometheus*, Vol. 18, No. 1 (2000) pp. 17–31.

42 M.H. Zack, Developing a Knowledge Strategy, *California Management Review*, Vol. 41, No. 3, (1999) pp. 125–145.

43 K. Kamoche, Knowledge Creation and Learning in International HRM, *International Journal of Human Resource Management*, Vol. 8, No. 3 (1997) pp. 213–225.

44 J. Sandberg, Understanding Human Competence at Work: an Interpretative Approach, *Academy of Management Journal*, Vol. 43, No. 1 (2000) pp. 9–25.

45 G. Hamel and C.K. Prahalad, *Competing for the Future*, Cambridge, MA: Harvard Business School Press, 1994, pp. 202–203.

46 J.B. Boudreau, P.M. Ramstad and P.J. Dowling, Global Talentship: Toward a Decision Science Connecting Talent to Global Strategic Success, in *Advances in Global Leadership*, Vol. 3, ed. W.H. Mobley and P.W. Dorfman, Oxford: Elsevier Science, 2003, pp. 63–99.

The organizational context

Chapter objectives

In this chapter, we examine how international growth places demands on management, and the factors that impact on how managers of internationalizing firms respond to these challenges. We start with the premise that the human resource (HR) function does not operate in a vacuum, and that HR activities are determined by, and influence, organisational factors. We cover the following areas:

- structural responses to international growth
- control and coordination mechanisms
- mode of operation used in various international markets
- effect of responses on human resource management approaches and activities.

It builds upon material covered in Chapter 1 to provide a meaningful global and organizational context for drawing out the international dimension of human resource management – the central theme of this book.

Introduction

Before we look at the way in which the shift from a domestic to global orientation affects the HR function and the human resource management consequences involved, we need to develop an appreciation of the way in which various internationalizing firms have responded to the challenges of international growth. In Chapter 1, we looked at the general global environment in which firms compete. Here we focus on internal responses as firms attempt to deal with global environment challenges. Figure 2-1 illustrates the major elements encountered as a result of international growth that place demands on management.

The various elements in Figure 2-1 are not mutually exclusive. For example, geographical dispersion affects firm size, creating pressure upon control mechanisms

Figure 2-1	Management demands of international growth

IHRM in Action Case 2-1

GE's acquisition in Hungary

In January 1990, the US multinational General Electric (GE) invested in Tungsram, the Hungarian lighting company as part of its European market expansion strategy. By 1994, its equity had risen to 99.6%. The Hungarian operation had 13 existing factories employing 17600 workers. GE initially appointed a Hungarian-born US expatriate as its top manager, although he was later replaced when Tungsram was brought under the direct control of GE Lighting Europe in 1993. Staff transfers played an important role in training and developing the Hungarian staff. Key executives were brought over from the USA for varying lengths of time (3–6 months) to assist in knowledge and skills transfer. Management training also involved sending Tungsram staff to the USA, giving selected Hungarians exposure to GE's working environment, and American life in general. In order to improve Tungsram's competitiveness, GE reduced staff levels by almost half, closing five plants, despite the unionized environment, and invested heavily in training (e.g. quality programs) to improve production workers' output. During this period, its European market share increased from 5% in 1989 to 15% in 1994.

In 1999, the Hungarian operation was renamed GE Hungary, Tungsram Lighting. Currently, its eight manufacturing plants form the base of GE Lighting operations that supply Europe, the Middle East and Africa; 95% of its output is exported to Europe, USA and Asia. It employs approximately 11000 people. Hungary is also 'home' to GE Lighting's regional headquarters – the region covering Europe, the Middle East and Africa. In October 2000, a female, Golnar Motahari Pour, was appointed as President of GE Lighting Europe, Middle East and Africa. It also has a center of excellence for research and development.

Source: *International Management*, December, 1992, pp. 42–45; N. Denton, Tungsram Fails to Shine for GE, *Financial Times*, March 17, 1993, p. 18; *Business Central Europe* Tungsram Turns a Corner, March 1994, p. 25; GE press release obtained from GE website, accessed 28 April 2003.

that, in turn, will influence structural change. Growth (size of the firm) will affect the flow and volume of information, which may reinforce a control response (such as what functions, systems and processes to centralize and what to decentralize). As we will examine later in this chapter, the mode of operation involved (such as exporting, fully own subsidiary, international joint venture or combinations thereof) will affect the rate of geographical dispersion. Geographical dispersion will involve more encounters with national cultures and languages, thus affecting the flow and volume of information. The demands of the host country can influence mode of operation (such as a demand for local joint venture partners) and/or country selection (such as barriers to market entry), which will affect geographical dispersion.

An in-depth examination of all these elements is beyond the scope of this book. Rather, the purpose of this chapter is to explore some of the managerial responses to these influences that concern HRM. Our focus remains on the connection between organizational factors, management decisions and HR consequences. To a certain extent, how the internationalizing firm copes with the HR demands of its various foreign operations determines its ability to execute its chosen expansion strategies. Indeed, Finnish research suggests that personnel policies should lead rather than follow international operation decisions,[1] yet one could argue that most companies take the opposite approach – that is, follow market-driven strategies.

General Electric (GE) is a large multinational with experience and resources to draw upon. The IHRM in Action Case 2-1 concerns GE's experience with an acquisition. After reading the case, do you think that GE top managers fully anticipated the HR investment that the Tungsram acquisition would entail prior to its decision to purchase the Hungarian firm? As one can see, a decade later, GE is still making staffing decisions as a result of its attempt to integrate fully its European operations into its 'global family'.

GE's experience with its Lighting Division in Europe also illustrates the dynamic nature of international business. We will now follow the path that a domestic firm takes as it evolves into a global entity, and illustrate how IHRM is affected by the way in which the internationalization process itself is managed.

The path to global status

Most firms pass through several stages of organizational development as the nature and size of their international activities grow. As they go through these evolutionary stages, their organizational structures[2] change, typically due to:

- the strain imposed by growth and geographical spread
- the need for improved coordination and control across business units and
- the constraints imposed by host-government regulations on ownership and equity.

Multinationals are not born overnight; the evolution from a domestic to a truly global organization may involve a long and somewhat tortuous process with many and diverse steps, as illustrated in Figure 2-2. Although research into internationalization has revealed a common process, it must be stressed that this process is not exactly the same for all firms. As Figure 2-2 shows, some firms may use licensing, subcontracting or other operation modes, instead of establishing their own foreign production or service facilities.

Figure 2-2   Stages of internationalization

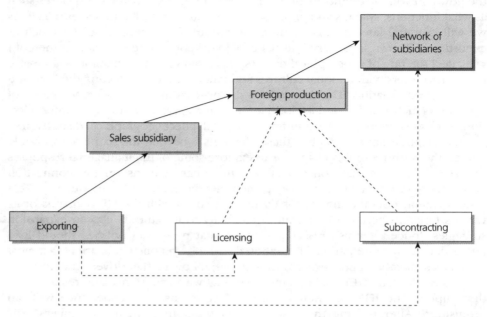

Some firms go through the various steps rapidly whereas others evolve slowly over many years, although recent studies have identified a speeding up of the process. For example, some firms are able to accelerate the process through acquisitions, thus leapfrogging over intermediate steps (that is, move directly into foreign production through the purchase of a foreign firm, rather than initial exporting, followed by sales subsidiary, as per Figure 2-2). Nor do all firms follow the same sequence of stages as they internationalize – some firms can be driven by external factors such as host-government action (for example, forced into a joint venture), or an offer to buy a company. Others are formed expressly with the international market in mind – often referred to as **born globals**.[3] In other words, the number of steps, or stages, along the path to multinational status varies from firm to firm, as does the time frame involved.[4] However, the concept of an evolutionary process is useful in illustrating the organizational adjustments required of a firm moving along the path to multinational status. As mentioned earlier, linked to this evolutionary process are structural responses, control mechanisms and HRM policies, which we now examine.

Export

This typically is the initial stage for manufacturing firms entering international operations. As such, it rarely involves much organizational response until the level of export sales reaches a critical point. Of course, simple exporting may be difficult for service companies (such as legal firms) so that they may be forced to make an early step into foreign direct investment operations (via a branch office or joint venture[5]).

Exporting often tends to be handled by an intermediary (for example, a foreign agent or distributor, as local market knowledge is deemed critical). As export sales increase, however, an export manager may be appointed to control foreign sales

Export department

Figure 2-3

and actively seek new markets. This person is commonly from the domestic operations. Further growth in exporting may lead to the establishment of an export department at the same level as the domestic sales department, as the firm becomes more committed to, or more dependent upon, its foreign export sales, as Figure 2-3 shows.

At this stage, exporting is controlled from the domestic-based home office, through a designated export manager. The role of the HR department is unclear, as indicated by the dotted arrow between these two functional areas in Figure 2-3. Welch and Welch[6] argue that there is a paucity of empirical evidence about HR responses at this early internationalization stage, even though there are HR activities involved (such as the selection of export staff), and perhaps training of the foreign agency staff. They suggest that, as these activities are handled by the marketing department, or exporting staff, the HR department has little, if any, involvement with the development of policies and procedures surrounding the HR aspects of the firm's early international activities.

Sales subsidiary

As the firm develops expertise in foreign markets, agents and distributors are often replaced by direct sales with the establishment of sales subsidiaries or branch offices in the foreign market countries. This stage may be prompted by problems with foreign agents, more confidence in the international sales activity, the desire to have greater control and/or the decision to give greater support to the exporting activity, usually due to its increasing importance to the overall success of the organization. The export manager may be given the same authority as other functional managers, as illustrated in Figure 2-4.

Exporting is still controlled at corporate headquarters, but the firm must make a decision regarding the coordination of the sales subsidiary, including staffing. If it wishes to maintain direct control, reflecting an ethnocentric attitude, it opts to staff the sales subsidiary from its headquarters through the use of parent country nationals (PCNs). If it regards country-specific factors – such as knowledge of the

Figure 2-4 Sales subsidiary

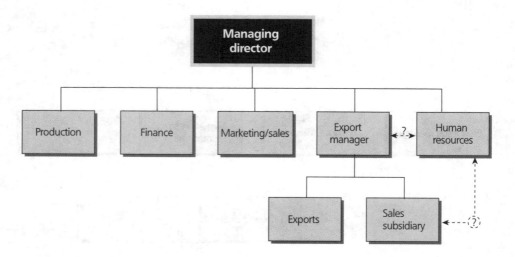

foreign market, language, sensitivity to host-country needs – as important, it may staff the subsidiary with host country nationals (HCNs). However, it would appear that many firms use PCNs in key sales subsidiary positions.

The decision to use PCNs leads into expatriation management issues and activities. It may be that, at this point, the HR department becomes actively involved in the personnel aspects of the firm's international operations, although there is little empirical evidence as to when, and how, HR-designated staff become involved (as indicated by the question marks in Figure 2-4).

International division

For some firms, it is a short step from the establishment of a sales subsidiary to a foreign production or service facility. This step may be considered small if the firm is already assembling the product abroad to take advantage of cheap labor or to save shipping costs or tariffs, for example. Alternatively, the firm may have a well-established export and marketing program that enables it to take advantage of host-government incentives or counter host-government controls on foreign imports by establishing a foreign production facility. For some firms, however, the transition to foreign direct investment is a large step.[7] However, having made the decision to produce overseas, the firm may establish its own foreign production facilities, enter into a joint venture with a local firm or buy a local firm. Regardless of the method of establishment, foreign production/service operations tend to trigger the creation of a separate international division in which all international activities are grouped, as Figure 2-5 demonstrates.

With the spread of international activities, typically the firm establishes what has been referred to as 'miniature replicas', as the foreign subsidiaries are structured to mirror that of the domestic organization. The subsidiary managers report to the head of the international division, and there may be some informal reporting to the various functional heads directly. For example, as shown in Figure 2-5, there may be contact between the HR managers in the two subsidiaries and the HR manager at corporate headquarters regarding staffing issues.

International division   Figure 2-5

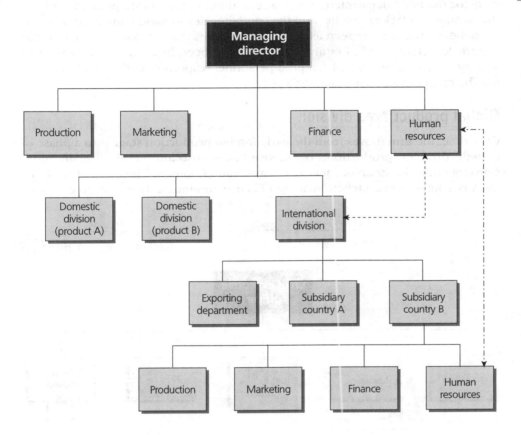

Many firms at this stage of internationalization are concerned about maintaining control of the newly established subsidiary, and will place PCNs in all key positions in the subsidiary. However, some firms decide that local employment conditions require local handling and place an HCN in charge of the subsidiary HR function, thus making an exception to the overall ethnocentric approach. Others may place HCNs in several key positions, including HRM, to comply with host-government directives.

The role of corporate HR staff is primarily concerned with expatriate management, although there will be some monitoring of the subsidiary HR function – formally through the head of the International Division. Pucik[8] suggests that, initially, corporate HR activities are confined to supervising the selection of staff for the new international division. Expatriate managers perform a major role: 'identifying employees who can direct the daily operations of the foreign subsidiaries, supervising transfer of managerial and technical know-how, communicating corporate policies, and keeping corporate HQ informed'. As the firm expands its foreign production or service facilities into other countries, increasing the size of its foreign workforce, accompanied by a growth in the number of expatriates, more formal HR policies become necessary. Welch and Welch[9] argue that the capacity of corporate HR staff to design appropriate policies may depend on how institutionalized existing approaches to expatriate management concerns have become, especially policies for compensation and pre-departure training; and that the more isolated the corporate HR function has been from the preceding international activities, the more difficult the task is likely to be. These authors add that 'an additional difficulty for the HRM department, when attempting to play a more proactive role, is that it may well lack credibility and the competencies to handle international personnel demands may be seen as residing outside its current domain'. That is, the export department (or its equivalent) may have been in charge of international staffing issues and instigated required personnel responses, and now considers it has the competence to manage expatriates.

Global product/area division

Over time, the firm moves from the early foreign production stage into a phase of growth through production, or service, standardization and diversification. Consequently, the strain of sheer size may create problems. The international division becomes overstretched, making effective communication and efficiency of

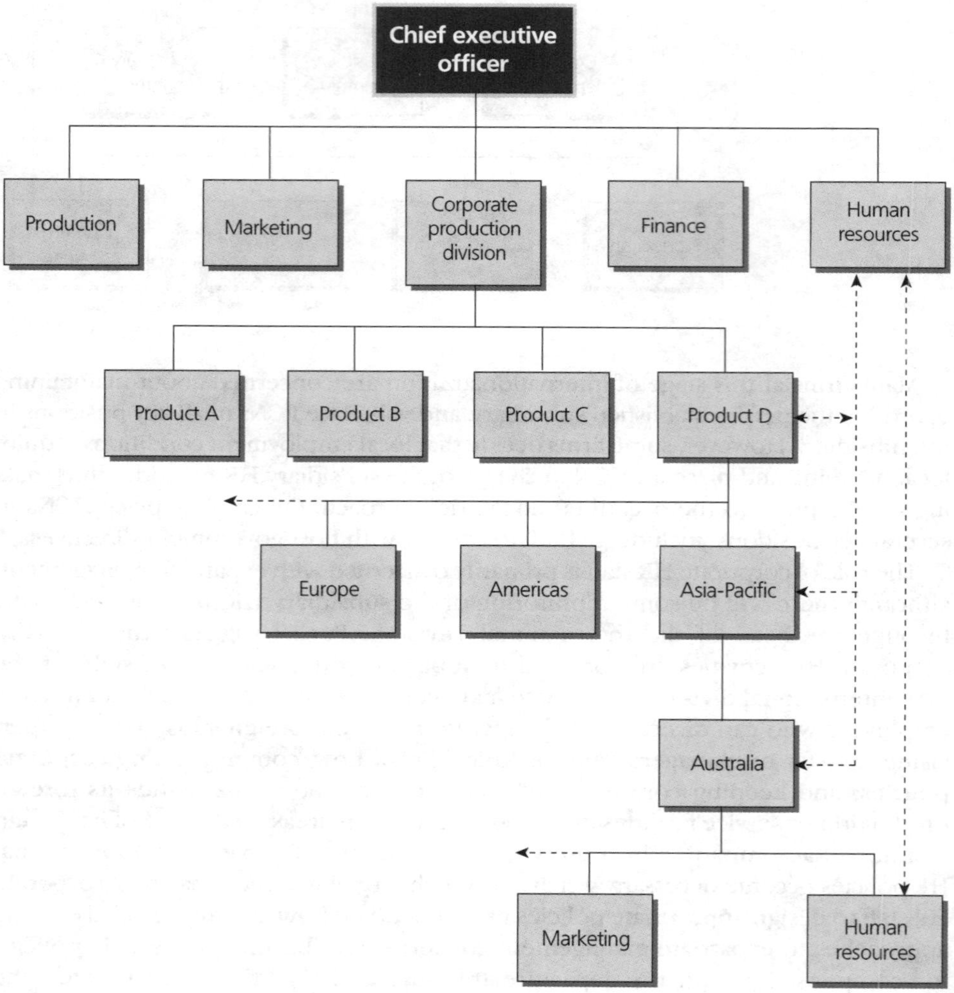

Figure 2-6a   Global product division

operation difficult. In some cases, corporate top managers may become concerned that the international division has enjoyed too much autonomy, acting so independently from the domestic operations that it operates as a separate unit – a situation that cannot be tolerated as the firm's international activities become strategically more important.

Typically, tensions will emerge between the parent company (headquarters) and its subsidiaries, stemming from the need for national responsiveness at the subsidiary unit and global integration imperatives at the parent headquarters. The demand for national responsiveness at the subsidiary unit develops because of factors such as differences in market structures, distribution channels, customer needs, local culture and pressure from the host government. The need for more centralized global integration by the headquarters comes from having multinational customers, global competitors and the increasingly rapid flow of information and technology, and from the quest for large volume for economies of scale.

Global area division

Figure 2-6b

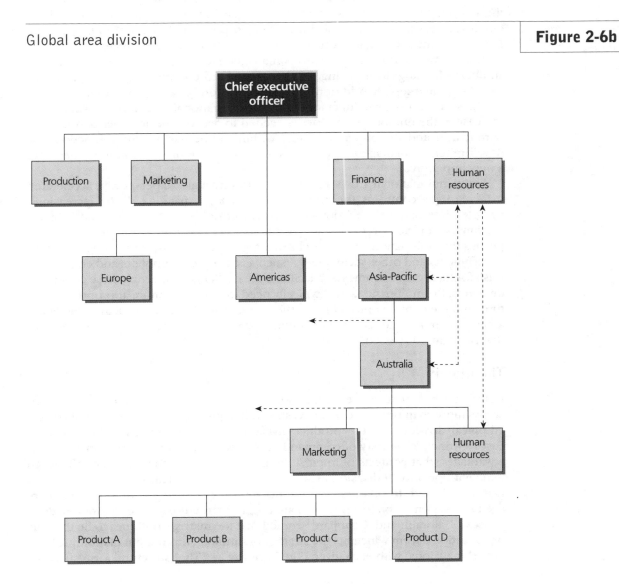

As a result of these various forces for change, the multinational confronts two major issues of structure:

- the extent to which key decisions are to be made at the parent country headquarters or at the subsidiary units (centralization versus decentralization) and
- the type or form of control exerted by the parent over the subsidiary unit.

The structural response, at this stage of internationalization, can be either a product/service-based global structure (if the growth strategy is through product or service diversification) or an area-based structure (if the growth strategy is through geographical expansion); see Figures 2-6a and 2-6b.

As part of the process of accommodating subsidiary concerns through decentralization, the MNE strives to adapt its HRM activities to each host country's specific requirements. This naturally impacts on the corporate HRM function (the dotted arrows denote functions other than HRM and marketing). As indicated by the dashed arrows, there is an increasing devolution of responsibility for local employee decisions to each subsidiary, with corporate HR staff performing a monitoring role, intervening in local affairs only in extreme circumstances.

This HRM monitoring role reflects management's desire for central control of strategic planning; formulating, implementing and coordinating strategies for its worldwide markets. In addition, the growth in foreign exposure combined with changes in the organizational structure of international operations results in an increase in the number of employees needed to oversee the activities between the parent firm and its foreign affiliates. Within the human resource function, the development of managers able to operate in international environments becomes a new imperative.[8]

As the multinational grows and the trend toward a global perspective accelerates, it increasingly confronts the 'think global, act local' paradox.[10] The increasingly complex international environment – characterized by global competitors, global customers, universal products, rapid technological change and world-scale factories – pushes the multinational towards global integration whereas, at the same time, host governments and other stakeholders (such as customers, suppliers and employees) push for local responsiveness. To facilitate the challenge of meeting these conflicting demands, the multinational will typically need to consider a more appropriate structure, and the choice appears to be either the matrix, the mixed structure, the heterarchy, the transnational or the multinational network. These options are now described and discussed.

The matrix

In the matrix structure, the multinational is attempting to integrate its operations across more than one dimension. As shown in Figure 2-7, the international or geographical division and the product division share joint authority, thus violating Fayol's principle of unity of command. Advocates of this structural form see, as its advantages, that conflicts of interest are brought out into the open, and that each issue with priority in decision-making has an executive champion to ensure that it is not neglected. In other words, the matrix is considered to bring into the management system a philosophy of matching the structure to the decision-making process. Galbraith and Kazanjian[11] argued that the matrix 'continues to be the only organizational form which fits the strategy of simultaneous pursuit of multiple business dimensions, with each given equal priority ... [The] structural form succeeds because it fits the situation'. In practice, firms that have adopted the matrix structure have met with mixed success. One reason is that it is an expensive form that requires careful implementation and commitment on the part of top management to be successful. (See also Refs 12 and 13 for a discussion on the matrix structure.)

In Figure 2-7, area managers are responsible for the performance of all three products within the various countries that comprise their regions, and product managers are responsible for sales of their specific product ranges across the areas. For example, Product A Manager would be concerned with sales of product

The matrix **Figure 2-7**

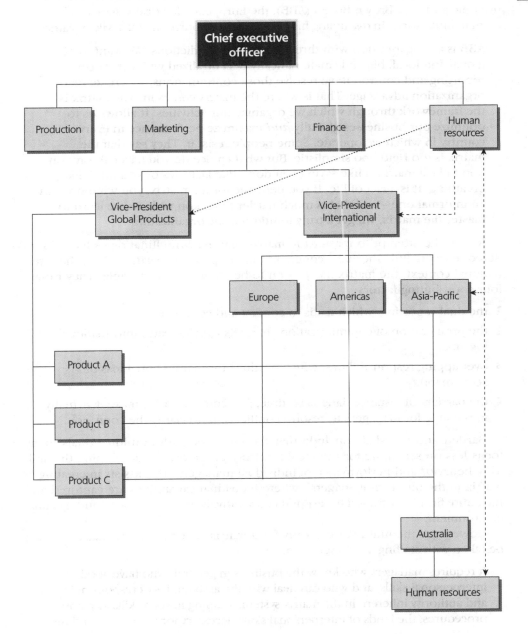

A in Europe, the Americas and the Asia-Pacific area. Product managers report to the Vice-President Global Products for matters pertaining to products and to the Vice-President International for geographical matters. There is a similar dual reporting line for functional staff. This is illustrated in Figure 2-7 through the HR departments to the corporate level (dotted arrows), and to country managers and subsidiary HR managers (dashed arrows). The HR manager in the Australia subsidiary would report to the country manager (Australia) and also to the Asia-Pacific Area Manager (and thus indirectly to the Vice-President, International). Country HR managers may also be involved in staffing issues involving product division staff (reporting indirectly to Vice-President Global Products). There may be additional reporting requirements to corporate HR at headquarters.

One supporter of the matrix organization has been Barnevik, former chief executive officer of Asea Brown Boveri (ABB), the European electrical systems and equipment manufacturer. In discussing his organization's approach, Barnevik explained:[14]

> ABB is an organization with three internal contradictions. We want to be global and local, big and small, radically decentralized with centralized reporting and control. If we resolve those contradictions, we create real organization advantage. That is where the matrix comes in. The matrix is the framework through which we organize our activities. It allows us to optimize our businesses globally *and* maximize performance in every country in which we operate. Some people resist it. They say that the matrix is too rigid, too simplistic. But what choice do you have? To say you don't like a matrix is like saying you don't like factories or you don't like breathing. It is a fact of life. If you deny the formal matrix, you wind up with an informal one – and that is much harder to reckon with. As we learn to master the matrix, we get a truly multidomestic organization.

It is in the attempt to master the matrix that many multinationals have floundered. Bartlett and Ghoshal[15] comment that, in practice, particularly in the international context, the matrix has proven to be all but unmanageable. They isolate four contributing factors:

1 the dual reporting, which leads to conflict and confusion
2 the proliferation of communication channels which creates informational logjams
3 overlapping responsibilities, which produce turf battles and a loss of accountability
4 the barriers of distance, language, time, and culture, which make it virtually impossible for managers to resolve conflicts and to clarify the confusion.

Bartlett and Ghoshal conclude that the most successful multinationals today focus less on searching for the ideal structure and more on developing the abilities, behavior and performance of individual managers. This assists in creating 'a matrix in the minds of managers', where individual capabilities are captured and the entire firm is motivated to respond cooperatively to a complicated and dynamic environment.

However, if the multinational opts for a matrix structure, particular care must be taken with staffing. As Ronen[16] notes:

> It requires managers who know the business in general, who have good interpersonal skills, and who can deal with the ambiguities of responsibility and authority inherent in the matrix system. Training in such skills as planning procedures, the kinds of interpersonal skills necessary for the matrix, and the

kind of analysis and orderly presentation of ideas essential to planning within a group is most important for supporting the matrix approach. Moreover, management development and human resource planning are even more necessary in the volatile environment of the matrix than in the traditional organizations.

Mixed structure

In an attempt to manage the growth of diverse operations, or because attempts to implement a matrix structure have been unsuccessful, some firms have opted for what can only be described as a mixed form. In a survey conducted by Dowling,[17] more than one-third (35 per cent) of respondents indicated that they had mixed forms, and around 18 per cent had product or matrix structures. Galbraith and Kazanjian[11] also identify mixed structures that seem to have emerged in response to global pressures and trade-offs:

> For example, organizations that pursued area structures kept these geographical profit centers, but added worldwide product managers. Colgate-Palmolive has always had strong country managers. But, as they doubled the funding for product research, and as Colgate Dental Creme became a universal product, product managers were added at the corporate office to direct the R & D funding and coordinate marketing programs worldwide.
>
> Similarly, the product-divisionalized firms have been reintroducing the international division. At Motorola, the product groups had worldwide responsibility for their product lines. As they compete with the Japanese in Japan, an international group has been introduced to help coordinate across product lines.

Although all structural forms that result from the evolutionary development of international business are complex and difficult to manage effectively, given a firm's developing capabilities and experience at each new stage, mixed structures appear even more complex and harder to explain and implement, and also control. Thus, as our discussion of the matrix structure emphasized, it is important that all employees understand the mixed framework and that attention is also given to supporting mechanisms, such as corporate identity, interpersonal relationships, management attitudes and HR systems, particularly promotion and reward policies.

Beyond the matrix

Early studies of headquarter–subsidiary relationships tended to stress resources, people and information flows from headquarters to subsidiary, examining these relationships mainly in the context of control and coordination. However, in the large, mature, multinational, these flows are multidirectional: from headquarters to subsidiary, from subsidiary to subsidiary and between subsidiaries. The result can be a complex network of inter-related activities and relationships and the multinational management literature identifies three descriptions of organizational structures – the heterarchy, the transnational and the network firm. Whilst they have been given different terms, each form recognizes that, at this stage of internationalization, the concept of a superior structure that neatly fits the corporate strategy becomes inappropriate. The proponents of these forms are in agreement that multinationals at this stage become less hierarchical. As Marschan[18] explains, reconsidering the long-standing principle that 'the parent knows best' requires a radical change in the way the entire multinational is managed, turning it from an organizational pyramid into an integrated network. We shall take a brief look at each of these forms.

The heterarchy.   This structural form proposed by Hedlund[19] recognizes that a multinational may have a number of different kinds of centers apart from that traditionally referred to as 'headquarters'. Hedlund argued that competitive advantage does not necessarily reside in any one country (the parent country, for example). Rather, it may be found in many, so that each subsidiary center may be simultaneously a center and a global coordinator of discrete activities, thus performing a strategic role not just for itself, but for the MNE as a whole (the subsidiary labeled 'center' in Figure 2-8). For example, some multinationals may centralize research and development in a particular subsidiary. In a heterarchical MNE, control is less reliant on the top-to-bottom mechanisms of previous hierarchical modes and more on normative mechanisms, such as the corporate culture and a widely shared awareness of central goals and strategies.

From an HRM perspective, the heterarchy is interesting in that its success appears to rest solely on the ability of the multinational to formulate, implement and reinforce the required human resource elements. Hedlund recognizes that the heterarchy demands skillful and experienced personnel in addition to sophisticated reward and punishment systems in order to develop the normative control mechanisms necessary for effective performance. The use of staff as an informal control mechanism is important, which we shall explore later in this chapter.

In a later article, Hedlund[20] proposed a structural model he termed the *N-form*. This model builds upon his heterarchy concept and integrates work from knowledge organization scholars. Hedlund argued that a new structural form is required to allow for knowledge management. His N-form takes away divisions, allows for

| **Figure 2-8** | The networked organization |

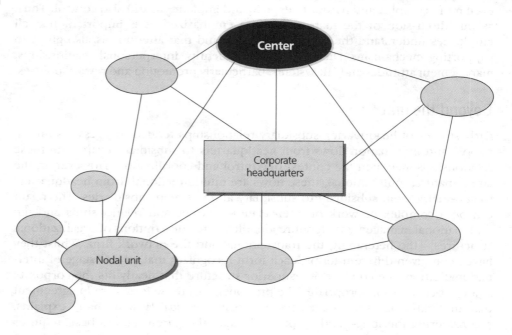

temporary constellations and the use of project teams and places stress on lateral communication and dialogue between units and individuals. The top management role was presented as that of a catalyst, architect and protector of knowledge rather than a monitor and resource allocator. The use of mechanisms such as cross-functional teams and empowerment of lower level employees was advocated to further support the N-form.

The transnational.   The term transnational has been coined to describe an organizational form that is characterized by an interdependence of resources and responsibilities across all business units regardless of national boundaries. The term has also become a descriptor of a particular type of multinational that tries to cope with the large flows of components, products, resources, people and information among its subsidiaries, while simultaneously recognizing distributed specialized resources and capabilities. As such, the transnational demands a complex process of coordination and cooperation involving strong cross-unit integrating devices, a strong corporate identity and a well-developed worldwide management perspective. In their study, Bartlett and Ghoshal[21] noted:

> Among the companies we studied, there were several that were in the process of developing such organizational capabilities. They had surpassed the classic capabilities of the *multinational* company that operates as decentralized federations of units able to sense and respond to diverse international needs and opportunities; and they had evolved beyond the abilities of the global company with its facility for managing operations on a tightly controlled worldwide basis through its centralized hub structure. They had developed what we termed *transnational* capabilities – the ability to manage across national boundaries, retaining local flexibility while achieving global integration. More than anything else this involved the ability to link local operations to each other and to the center in a flexible way, and in so doing, to leverage those local and central capabilities.

In fact, the matrix, the heterarchy and the transnational share a common theme regarding the human resource factor. Therefore, developing transnational managers or global leaders who can think and act across national and subsidiary boundaries emerges as an important task for top management introducing these complex organizational forms. Staff transfers play a critical role in integration and coordination.

The multinational as a network.   Some scholars are advocating viewing certain large and mature internationalized firms as a network, in situations where:

● Subsidiaries have developed into significant centers for investments, activities and influence, and can no longer be regarded as at the periphery.[22] For example, GE has established a 'center of excellence' in Hungary for research and development in its lighting division. Interaction between headquarters and each subsidiary is likely to be dyadic, taking place between various actors at many different organizational levels and covering different exchanges, the outcome of which will be important for effective global performance.

● Such MNEs are loosely coupled political systems rather than tightly bonded, homogeneous, hierarchically controlled systems.[23] This runs counter to the traditional structure where linkages are described formally via the organization's structure and standardized procedures, and informally through interpersonal contact and socialization.[24]

Figure 2-8 attempts to depict such an intricate criss-crossing of relationships. One subsidiary may act as a nodal unit linked to a cluster of satellite organizations. Thus, one center can assume responsibility for other units in its country or region. In line with this view, Ghoshal and Bartlett[25] have expanded their concept of the transnational to define the MNE as an inter-organizational system. This is comprised of a network of exchange relationships among different organizational units, including headquarters and national subsidiaries, in addition to external organizations, such as host governments, customers, suppliers and competitors, with which the different units of the multinational must interact. These authors argue that a new way of structuring is not the issue – it is more the emerging management philosophy, with its focus on management processes: 'The actual configuration of the processes themselves, and the structural shell within which they are imbedded, can be very different depending on the businesses and the heritage of each company'.[26] Ghoshal and Bartlett cite GE, ABB and Toyota as prime examples of companies involved in developing such processes, with Intel and Corning, Philips and Alcatel, and Matsushita and Toshiba regarded as companies embarking upon a network-type configuration.

The management of a multi-centered networked organization is complex. Apart from the intra-organizational network (comprising headquarters and the numerous subsidiaries), each subsidiary also has a range of external relationships (involving local suppliers, customers, competitors, host governments and alliance partners). The management of both the intra-organizational and inter-organizational spheres, and of the total integrated network, is crucial to global corporate performance. It involves what has been termed a less-hierarchical structure, featuring five dimensions:

- delegation of decision-making authority to appropriate units and levels
- geographical dispersal of key functions across units in different countries
- delayering of organizational levels
- de-bureaucratization of formal procedures and
- differentiation of work, responsibility and authority across the networked subsidiaries.[27]

The place of the HR function in structural forms

As we point out in our treatment of the various forms, there has been little direct investigation into how the HR function develops in response to structural changes as a consequence of international growth. An exception is a study of the changing role of the corporate HR function in 30 UK firms.[28] The authors, Scullion and Starkey, found three distinct groups which they describe as follows:

- Centralized HR companies, characterized by large, well-resourced HR departments responsible for a wide range of functions. The key role for corporate HR was to establish and maintain control over worldwide top-level management positions, such as divisional and subsidiary managers, so that strategic staffing was under central control. Companies in this group operated within product-based or matrix structures.

- Decentralized HR companies, characterized by devolving the HR responsibilities to a small group who confined their role to senior management at corporate HQ. This was consistent with the decentralized approach to other functions. Companies within this group operated within product- or regional-based structures, with only one reporting using a matrix.

- Transition companies, characterized by medium-sized corporate HR departments staffed by a relatively small group at corporate HQ. They operated in a decentralized, product-based structure, although again one company reported using a matrix structure.

Scullion and Starkey note that the varied roles of corporate HR within these three groups impacted upon the way in which activities such as training and performance appraisal were handled, and the ability of corporate HR to plan for staff movements throughout the worldwide operations. We shall take up these issues in Chapter 3.

Different countries take different paths

The above discussion takes a generalist view of the growth of the internationalizing firm through the various stages to multinational status, and the corresponding organizational structures. However, it is important to note a cultural element.

As can be seen from Figure 2-9, European firms have tended to take a different structural path than their US counterparts. Franko's study of 70 European multinationals revealed that European firms moved directly from a functional 'mother–daughter' structure to a global structure with worldwide product or area divisions, or to a matrix organization without the transitional stage of an international division.[29] Human resource management practices, changing to serve the needs of the new structure, adjusted accordingly. Swedish firms have traditionally adopted the mother–daughter structure, but Hedlund suggests that this is changing. The Swedish multinationals in his study tended to adopt a mixture of elements of the mother–daughter structure and elements of the product division at this stage of

US, European and Japanese structural changes   **Figure 2-9**

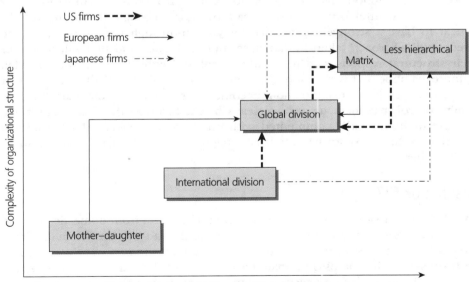

Source: R. Marschan, *New Structural Forms and Inter-unit Communication in Multinationals*, (Helsinki: Helsinki School of Economics, 1996). Reproduced with permission.

their internationalization process.[30] Although there are few empirical data to sub-stantiate this, it would appear that there is a preference for matrix-type structures within European firms, particularly Nordic multinationals. One could suggest that this structural form has better suited the more collaborative, group-oriented work organization found within these firms. Needless to say, as can be seen from the above figure, some European multinationals have also tried and abandoned the matrix, as the backward arrows in Figure 2-9 portray.

US firms that have experimented with the matrix form appear to have met with limited success. For example, as part of a reorganization process termed 'Ford 2000', the Ford Motor Company abandoned its regional structure in 1993. It adopted a form of global matrix organization characterized by a multidisciplinary product team approach with networked plants across regions. In the process, the European regional headquarters was moved to the USA in an attempt to develop global decision-making. In November 2001, Ford announced a restructuring and plant rationalization that effectively has taken the company back to a regional structure.[31]

Japanese multinationals are evolving along similar lines to their US counter-parts. Export divisions have become international divisions but, according to Ronen,[32] the rate of change is slower. The characteristics of Japanese organiza-tional culture (such as the control and reporting mechanisms and decision-making systems), the role of trading companies and the systems of management appear to contribute to the slower evolution of the international division. In some cases, despite their high degree of internationalization, Japanese firms may not adapt their structure as they become more dispersed. As mentioned previously, Ghoshal and Bartlett were able to include Japanese firms in their description of the net-work multinational. A 1996 study[33] of 54 companies, taken from the *Fortune* 1991 list of the world's 500 largest industrial corporations, revealed that the degree of internationalization differed between firms from the USA, Europe and Japan. The study also reports that the US multinationals in the sample gave more autonomy to their international operations than did their Japanese counterparts.

We should mention that internationalizing firms from other Asian nations may also vary in structural form and growth patterns. Korean conglomerates (*chaebols*) appear to have a stronger preference for growth-through-acquisitions than the 'greenfield' approach taken by Japanese multinationals, and this will influence their structural responses in terms of control and coordination. The so-called Chinese bamboo network/family firms may face significant challenges as their international activities expand and it becomes more difficult to maintain the tight family control that characterizes overseas-Chinese firms. As the Chairman of one Chinese multinational[34] commented with regard to the effects of international growth, 'You have no choice but to trust foreigners and to delegate. You run out of family rather rapidly.'

Fashion or fit?

The above discussion has traced the evolution of the firm from domestic-oriented into a global-oriented firm. A note of caution should be added. Growth in the firm's international business activity does require structural responses, but the evolution-ary process will differ across multinationals. Apart from the country of origin aspect, other variables – size of organization, pattern of internationalization, management policies and so on – also play a part. Further, as the case of the Ford Motor Company mentioned above, and as Figure 2-9 illustrates, firms undergo stages of restructur-ing as they attempt to grapple with environment changes that require strategic responses. Figure 2-9 also is a useful reminder that the networked firm is *not* the ultimate end state, although one can often get the impression from some writers that all internationalizing firms aspire one day to be referred to as 'transnational/ networked'. Researchers have identified the pattern described here, but the danger is to treat the stages as normative rather than descriptive.

Control mechanisms

As indicated in Figure 2-1, international operations place additional stresses on control mechanisms. There is also additional stress on the firm's ability to coordinate resources and activities. As the chairman and chief executive officer of the French hotel and travel company, Accor, explained in a newspaper interview:[35]

> Accor has to be a global company, in view of the revolution in the service sector which is taking place ... National [hotel chains] cannot optimize their operations. They cannot invest enough money ... Globalization brings considerable challenges which are often under-estimated. The principal difficulty is getting our local management to adhere to the values of the group ... Every morning when I wake I think about the challenges of coordinating our operations in many different countries.

Figure 2-10 illustrates the range of formal control mechanisms, including organizational structure, along with reporting systems, budgets and performance targets. In Chapter 10, we will explore the role that HRM plays in supporting formal control systems, particularly bureaucratic control. However, international firms also rely on information control mechanisms. In fact, there is a strong argument that organizations are tending to place more weighting on the informal mechanisms to facilitate control and coordination, as will have been gathered from the discussion of the heterarchy, the N-form and the transnational/networked organizations.

Control mechanisms   **Figure 2-10**

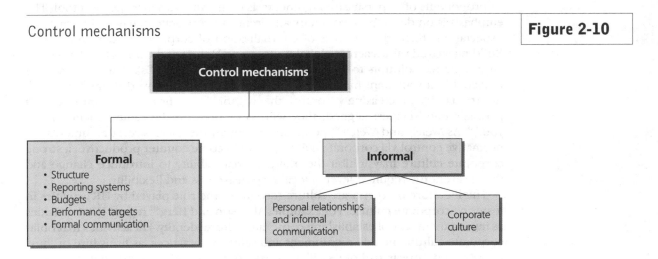

Source: Adapted from R. Marchan, D. Welch and L. Welch, Control in Less-hierarchical Multinationals: the Role of Personal Networks and Informal Communication, *International Business Review*, Vol. 5, No. 2, (1996) p. 139.

Control through personal relationships

A consistent theme in the descriptions of transnational and networked organiza-tion forms is the need to foster vital knowledge generation and diffusion through lateral communication via a network of working relationships. Given that network relationships are built and maintained through personal contact, organizations need processes and forums where staff from various units can develop types of personal relationships that can be used for organizational purposes. For example, working in cross-functional and/or cross-border teams can assist in developing personal contacts. Training and development programs, held in regional centers or at headquarters, become an important forum for the development of personal networks that foster informal communication channels. However, research by Marschan *et al.* suggests that the ability to participate in such forums depends on fluency in the common corporate language.[36] For most large international firms, a common reporting language is necessary for formal and information communication, reporting systems and information flow. Whether deliberately or by default, the language tends to be English. Such language standardization is both a facilitator and a barrier. It does facilitate formal reporting and communication, but only to the extent that people have a required level of fluency in the corporate language. This aspect will be more fully explored in Chapter 8, where we deal with HRM issues from the subsidiary perspective.

Control through corporate culture

Some advocates of more complex structural forms regard the use of cultural control as an effective informal control mechanism. Corporate culture is variously defined, but essentially it refers to a process of socializing people so that they come to share a common set of values and beliefs that then shape their behavior and perspectives. It is often expressed as 'our way of doing things'. Cultural control may be a contentious issue for some – evidence of multinational imperialism where corporate culture is superimposed upon national cultures in subsidiary operations. However, its proponents offer persuasive arguments as to its value as a management tool. The emphasis is on developing voluntary adherence to corporate behavioral norms and expectations through a process of internalization of corporate values and beliefs. Building shared values across global units, argue Nohria and Ghoshal,[37] 'represents an alternative solution to the governance problem in MNCs'. This sentiment is reflected in a statement made by a senior executive in the Swedish multinational, Electrolux: 'We increasingly control the organization through the mindset... If people's mindsets are aligned, they will come up with the same conclusions as you.'[38] As Welch and Welch[39] point out, although there are strong arguments for normative control via corporate culture, it can become counter-productive: a strong corporate culture may inhibit the multinational's ability to introduce change and thus prevent the required level of local responsiveness and flexibility.

The literature on corporate culture recognizes the role played by HR activities in fostering corporate culture. For example, Alvesson and Berg[40] regard HRM activities as important means of establishing corporate culture identity. HR activities that build corporate culture include recruitment and selection practices, as firms hire or 'buy' people who appear to hold similar values. Training and development programs, reward systems and promotion are also activities that reinforce company value systems. Placement of staff is another method. The case of GE in Hungary (IHRM in Action Case 2-1) is a good example of how staff transfers were an important part of

GE's attempts to integrate its new acquisition. Hungarian staff transferred into GE's US operations post-acquisition were exposed to the 'GE way' of operating.

Mode of operation

One of the elements depicted in Figure 2-1 is mode of operation. We will now take a brief look at forms of operation mode utilized by internationalizing firms and the managerial and HR issues involved.

The discussion on the range of structural adjustments and control mechanisms has been based on the literature relating to the growth of the multinational enterprise. The organizational forms illustrated are primarily concerned with integrating wholly owned subsidiaries. However, as Welch and Welch argue,[41] internationalizing firms may also adopt contractual (such as licensing, franchising, management contracts and projects) and cooperative (such as joint ventures) modes in order to enter and develop foreign markets. Naturally, these modes are not mutually exclusive: a firm may have licensing arrangements with a foreign joint venture, or have a general strategy of growth through international franchising, but combine this with a wholly owned subsidiary or a joint venture in some markets. These authors present a framework to illustrate how IHRM activities, such as staff placement, simultaneously link and influence the mode of operation utilized to support an internationalization strategy. This framework is reproduced in Figure 2-11. Welch and Welch explain:[42]

> The many forms of operation modes may demand different skills and place
> varying stresses on the resources of the company, particularly on its personnel.
> For example, licensing might involve only limited commitments of staff,
> whereas the availability of key people becomes particularly critical for the

Linking operation mode and HRM | **Figure 2-11**

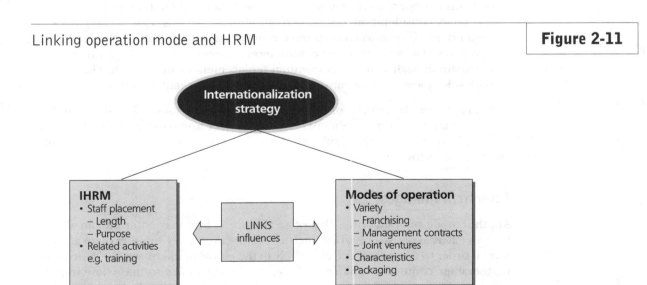

Source: D. Welch and L. Welch, Linking Operation Mode Diversity and IHRM, *International Journal of Human Resource Management*, Vol. 5, No. 4 (1994) p. 915. Reproduced with permission of the Editor.

success of a management contract in which the company is required to transfer a number of experienced managerial and technical staff to run a foreign facility.

Although decrying the paucity of empirical evidence regarding the IHRM demands of the contractual modes of operation, the authors suggest that HRM concerns affect, and may even govern, the choice of market entry mode. They use the entry of the US hamburger chain McDonald's into Russia to illustrate the interconnection between mode of entry, an international joint venture, and IHRM. Expatriates were involved in assisting with the selection and training of local staff: each crew member received the standard McDonald's training (60 hours of training per crew member). Russians selected for managerial positions were sent to McDonald's Institute of Hamburgerology in Toronto, Canada, and to the Hamburger University in Oakbrook, IL, USA. When the first restaurant opened, they had a staff of 630.[43]

Another way of operating in foreign markets is through the use of **management contracts**. They involve a management role in the foreign company for a specified period of time and fee, and therefore require the posting of staff for extended periods of time. Walt Disney is an example of a firm that utilizes this mode of operation. The establishment of Euro-Disney (France) combined 49 per cent equity with a management fee of 3 per cent of gross revenue.[44] Management contracts are also used in the hotel and airline industries.

By its very nature, this form of contractual mode means that skilled, usually talented staff will be needed. Knowledge transfer is an important component, involving the training of HCN staff. However, there is little treatment of the HR demands of a successful management contract in the IHRM literature. In one of the few international business texts that covers this contractual mode of operation, the authors comment:[45]

> The overall success of the contract operation, including the training aspect, depends on the quality of staff transferred or appointed to the contract venture, and therefore overall international human resource management by the company. Because management contracts are normally not a mainstream operational method, when used they will often receive secondary consideration in staffing requirements. For this reason, companies tend not to be keen to commit large numbers of quality staff to contract operations. Likewise the client organization prefers not to have large numbers of expatriate staff as it makes eventual replacement more difficult. Thus, for both sides there is an incentive to keep down foreign staff numbers.

There is a similar paucity of information associated with the IHRM demands of international project management – for the project firm itself, and also the range of contributing firms (that is, subcontractors, joint-venture partners, etc.) that may be involved in the international project.

Interfirm linkages

Another mode of operation is that of an alliance. A firm may enter into an alliance with an external party (or parties) such as a competitor, a key supplier or an affiliated firm in order to compete more effectively in the global marketplace.[46,47] Since these partnerships come in all shapes and sizes,[48] the term *alliance* has come to mean different things to different people: strategic alliance, cooperative venture, collaborative agreement or corporate linkage, of which one form may be a joint venture.[45] For the purpose of this discussion, we will use a broad definition: 'A corporate alliance is a formal and mutually agreed commercial collaboration between companies. The partners pool, exchange, or integrate specified business resources for mutual gain. Yet the partners remain separate businesses.'[49] The key point is that an alliance is a form of business relationship that:

- Involves some measure of interfirm integration that goes beyond the traditional buyer-seller relationship.
- Stops short of a full merger or acquisition, though some alliances can develop into mergers or takeovers at a later date.[49]
- The particular type of venture that emerges is a function of the strategic importance of the venture to the parent company and the extent to which the parent seeks control over the resources allocated to the venture.

There has been a marked growth in alliance formation over the last two decades. Alliances are found in such diverse industries as telecommunications, aerospace, automobiles, electronics, and transportation equipment. Shared activities can include research and development, production and marketing. An alliance can involve arrangements such as licensing agreements, marketing or distribution partnerships and consortia.

Regardless of the motive for entering into such an arrangement, the resultant partnership adds another dimension to a firm's structure. In order to meet the objectives of the collaborative partnership within the context of broader corporate strategy, the firm needs to integrate or link the partnership venture to its own existing activities and functions and to devise a method of monitoring its performance. The way the partnership is interlinked naturally depends on the form that the collaboration takes.

As we have seen with other modes of operation, the various forms of interfirm linkages affect HRM in different ways, depending upon the type of alliance involved. For example, in an international joint venture, a new entity that brings together managers from two or more firms, the managers must become accustomed to working with a foreign partner (or partners). 'Staffing the joint venture with managers who are flexible in terms of different management styles and philosophies is probably the single most important task facing the human resource function at this critical time.'[50] Indeed, Lorange links success to a match between the form of cooperative venture and human resource components, maintaining that: 'the human resource function is particularly critical to successful implementation of such cooperative ventures'.[51] In their analysis of strategic alliances, Cascio and Serapio[52] classify these collaborative forms of business relationships according to the extent of interaction required among people from the collaborating companies; they point out, for example, that a joint venture involves more interaction than does a marketing or distribution partnership. HR factors play a crucial role in these types of inter-firm linkages, as Schuler points out in his review of HR issues and activities in international joint ventures.[53] Assigning managers to the joint venture, evaluating their performance, handling aspects pertaining to career path and compensation benefits are some of the HR issues and activities that affect the successful conduct of international joint ventures.

Mergers and acquisitions

The past decade has seen a plethora of mergers and acquisitions (M&As) as a form of market entry and expansion. According to UNCTAD (United Nations Conference on Trade and Development), acquisition is the preferred mode of entry by firms from developed countries when entering other developed countries.

There are considerable challenges involved in successful M&As. It is never a simple process to integrate two existing firms into one entity. As the President of Dow Performance Chemicals explained:[54]

> Most M&As fail because the integration of the acquired into the new company does not go well … You have to have the human side of it done very well: who is leaving, who is staying, have you sifted and sorted it so those who are staying buy into your company's value proposition.

The recent merger of the computer firms Hewlett-Packard and Compaq highlights the complexity of the integration process. We will return to explore some of these aspects in Chapter 8.

Summary

The purpose of this chapter has been to identify the HR implications of the various options and responses that international growth places on the firm. This chapter focused on:

- The organizational context in which IHRM activities take place. Different structural arrangements have been identified as the firm moves along the path to multinational status – from export department through to more complex varieties such as the matrix, heterarchy, transnational and networked.

- Control and coordination aspects. Formal and informal mechanisms were outlined, with emphasis on control through personal networks and relationships, and control through corporate culture, drawing out HRM implications.

- The various modes – such as wholly owned, franchising, management contracts and international joint ventures – used by multinationals for foreign market entry and expansion. Again, we attempted to demonstrate the IHRM implications of these various modes, although noting that most of the literature focuses on wholly owned subsidiaries and international joint ventures.

- How international growth affects the firm's approach to HRM. Firms vary from one another as they go through the stages of international development, and react in different ways to the circumstances they encounter in the various foreign markets. There is a wide variety of matches between IHRM approaches, organizational structure and stage of internationalization. For example, almost half the US firms surveyed by Dowling[55] reported that the operations of the HR function were unrelated to the nature of the firm's international operations. A study of nine subsidiaries of multinationals operating in Ireland by Monks[56] found that the majority adopted a local approach to the HR function, with headquarters involvement often limited to monitoring the financial implications of HR decisions.

- Stages of development, organizational forms and mode of operation should not be taken as normative. Research does suggest a pattern and a process of internationalization but firms do vary in how they adapt to international operations – we use nationality of the parent firm to demonstrate this.

Through the approach taken in this chapter, we have been able to demonstrate that there is an interconnection between international HRM approaches and activities and the organizational context and that HR managers have a crucial role to play. In order to perform this role better, it would seem important that HR managers understand the various international structural options – along with the control and coordination demands imposed by international growth – and the HR implications that accompany the range of operation modes outlined in this chapter.

Discussion questions and exercises

1 What are the stages a firm typically goes through as it grows internationally and how does each stage affect the HR function?

2 What are the specific HRM challenges in a networked firm?

3 The opening of McDonald's in Moscow demonstrates the HR demands associated with new market entry. What did the company do to handle these? What role did staff transfers play?

4 Why are many multinationals adopting English as their common corporate language?

5 International growth places particular stress on the resources of small firms. Form small groups. Imagine you are the management team of a small project company operating in the highly competitive international construction industry. You have just been advised that your company's tender for part of an airport runway extension and facilities in a South-East Asian country has been successful. Although you are very pleased to have won such a prestigious contract, you are now faced with a dilemma. The project will require sending at least six key specialist staff, for varying periods of time, into the foreign location. Your employees are working on other projects and only three will be available for the new venture, assuming that the current projects run to schedule. Should you accept the new project? If so, how will you handle the staffing situation?

6 'Companies can hire or buy in values by the way they recruit and select staff.' In pairs, or in small groups, discuss this statement in the context of the following:

● The recruitment and selection processes in your country.

● How would these 'fit' with the concept of hiring and buying in corporate values?

● Do you think a multinational would be able to hire values, or buy values, when staffing its subsidiary operations in your country?

Further reading

B. McKern (ed.), 2003. *Managing the Global Network Corporation*, London: Routledge.

R.S. Schuler, S.E. Jackson and Y. Luo, 2003. *Managing Human Resources in Cross-border Alliances*, New York: Routledge.

J.G. Morgan, W. Kelly, D. Sharpe and R. Whitley, 2003. Global Managers and Japanese Multinationals: Internationalisation and Management in Japanese Financial Institutions, *International Journal of Human Resource Management*, Vol. 14, No. 3, pp. 389–407.

M.J. Robson, N. Paparoidamis and D. Ginoglu, 2003. Top Management Staffing in International Strategic Alliances: A Conceptual Explanation of Decision Perspective and Objective Formation, *International Business Review*, Vol. 12, No. 2, pp. 173–191.

G. Fryxell, R. Dooley and M. Vryza, 2002. After the Ink Dries: the Interaction of Trust and Control in US-based International Joint Ventures, *Journal of Management Studies*, Vol. 3, No. 6, pp. 885–886.

T.W. Malnight, 2001. Emerging Structural Patterns within Multinational Corporations: Towards Process-based Structures, *Academy of Management Journal*, Vol. 44, No. 6, pp. 1187–1210.

P.J. Buckley and P. Ghauri (eds), 1999. *The Internationalisation of the Firm: a Reader*, 2nd edn, London: ITP.

J. Wolf, 1997. From 'Starworks' to Networks and Heterarchies? *Management International Review*, Vol. 37, No. 1 (Special Issue), pp. 145–169.

Notes and references

1   M. Svard and R. Luostarinen, Personnel Needs in the Internationalising Firm, FIBO Publication No. 19, Helsinki: Helsinki School of Economics, 1982.

2   The organization's structure defines the tasks of individuals and business units within the firm and the processes that result from the intertwined tasks: identifying how the organization is divided up (differentiated) and how it is united (integrated).

3   B.M. Oviatt and P.P. McDougall, Towards a Theory of International New Ventures, *Journal of International Business Studies*, Vol. 25, No. 1 (1994) pp. 45–64.

4   J. Johanson and J.E. Vahlne, The Mechanism of Internationalisation, *International Marketing Review*, Vol. 7, No. 4 (1990) pp. 11–24; L.S. Welch and R. Luostarinen, Internationalisation; Evolution of a Concept, *Journal of General Management*, Vol. 14, No. 2 (1988) pp. 34–55.

5   A study of US service firms involved in international operations showed that the wholly owned subsidiary/branch office was the most common method, although engineering and architecture firms used direct exports; and consumer services used licensing/franchising: K. Erramilli, The Experience Factor in Foreign Market Entry Behaviour of Service Firms, *Journal of International Business Studies*, Vol. 22, No. 3 (1991) pp. 479–501. Similar results were found in a study of Australian service firms: LEK Partnership, *Intelligent Exports and the Silent Revolution in Services*, Canberra: Australian Government Publishing Service, 1994.

6   D.E Welch and L.S. Welch, Pre-expatriation: the Role of HR Factors in the Early Stages of Internationalization, *International Journal of Human Resource Management*, Vol. 8, No. 4 (1997) pp. 402–413.

7   In fact, there are some companies that have internationalized extensively through modes other than foreign direct investment – for example via licensing: A. Taylor, Pilkington Emerges with Advantages, *Financial Times*, 27 May (1994) p. 6.

8   See V. Pucik, Strategic Human Resource Management in a Multinational Firm, in *Strategic Management of Multinational Corporations: the Essentials*, ed. H.V. Wortzel and L.H. Wortzel, New York: Wiley, 1985, p. 425.

9   Ref. 6, p. 409.

10   C.A. Bartlett and S. Ghoshal, Organizing for Worldwide Effectiveness: The Transnational Solution in *Global Marketing Management: Cases and Readings*, 3rd edn, ed. R.D. Buzzell, J.A. Quelch, and C.A. Bartlett, Reading, MA: Addison-Wesley, 1992.

11   J.R. Galbraith and R.K. Kazanjian, Organizing to Implement Strategies of Diversity and Globalization: the Role of Matrix Designs, *Human Resource Management*, Vol. 25, No. 1 (1986) p. 50.

12   T.T. Naylor, The International Strategy Mix, *Columbia Journal of World Business*, Vol. 20, No. 2 (1985).

13   R.A. Pitts and J.D. Daniels, Aftermath of the Matrix Mania, *Columbia Journal of World Business*, Vol. 19, No. 2 (1984).

14   W. Taylor, The Logic of Global Business: an Interview with ABB's Percy Barnevik, *Harvard Business Review*, March–April (1991) pp. 95–96.

15   C.A. Bartlett and S. Ghoshal, Matrix Management: Not a Structure, a Frame of Mind, *Harvard Business Review*, July–August (1990) pp. 138–145.

16   S. Ronen, *Comparative and Multinational Management*, New York: Wiley, 1986, p. 330.

17   P.J. Dowling, International HRM, in *Human Resource Management: Evolving Roles and Responsibilities*, Vol. 1, ed. L. Dyer, ASPA/BNA Handbook of Human Resource Management Series, Washington, DC: BRA, 1988.

18 R. Marschan, *New Structural Forms and Inter-unit Communication in Multinationals*, Helsinki: Helsinki School of Economics, 1996, p. 15.

19 G. Hedlund, The Hypermodern MNC – A Heterarchy? *Human Resource Management*, Vol. 25, No. 1 (1986) pp. 9–35.

20 G. Hedlund, A Model of Knowledge Management and the N-form Corporation, *Strategic Management Journal*, Vol. 15 (1994) pp. 73–90.

21 Ref. 10, p. 66.

22 J. Birkinshaw and N. Hood, *Multinational Corporate Evolution and Subsidiary Development*, London: Macmillan Press, 1998.

23 M. Forsgren, Managing the International Multi-centre Firm: Case Studies from Sweden, *European Management Journal*, Vol. 8, No. 2 (1990) pp. 261–267. Much of this work has been based on the concepts of social exchange theory and interaction between actors in a network.

24 J.I. Martinez and J.C. Jarillo, The Evolution of Research on Coordination Mechanisms in Multinational Corporations, *Journal of International Business Studies*, Fall (1989) pp. 489–514.

25 S. Ghoshal and C.A. Bartlett, The Multinational Corporation as an Interorganisational Network, *Academy of Management Review*, Vol. 8, No. 2 (1990) pp. 603–625.

26 S. Ghoshal and C, Bartlett, Building the Entrepreneurial Corporation: New Organizational Processes, New Managerial Tasks, *European Management Journal*, Vol. 13, No. 2 (1995) p. 145.

27 R. Marschan, Dimensions of Less-hierarchical Structures in Multinationals, in *The Nature of the International Firm*, ed. I. Björkman and M. Forsgren, Copenhagen: Copenhagen Business School Press, 1997.

28 H. Scullion and K. Starkey, In Search of the Changing Role of the Corporate Human Resource Function in the International Firm, *International Journal of Human Resource Management*, Vol. 11, No. 6, (2000) pp. 1061–1081.

29 L. Leksell, *Headquarter–Subsidiary Relationships in Multinational Corporations*, Stockholm, 1981.

30 G. Hedlund, Organization In-between: the Evolution of the Mother–Daughter Structure of Managing Foreign Subsidiaries in Swedish MNCs, *Journal of International Business Studies*, Fall (1984) pp. 109–123.

31 *Financial Times* series on The Global Company, 15 October (1997), p. 14; *The Economist*, October (2000) p. 82; *The Economist*, 13 November (2001).

32 S. Ronen, *Comparative and Multinational Management*, New York: J Wiley, 1986.

33 R.B. Peterson, J. Sargent, N.K. Napier and W.S. Shim, Corporate Expatriate HRM Policies, Internationalisation and Performance, *Management International Review*, Vol. 36, No. 3 (1996) pp. 215–230.

34 Victor Fung, Chairman of Li Fung, one of Hong Kong's oldest and largest trading groups, A Multinational Trading Group with Chinese Characteristics, *Financial Times*, 7 November (1997) p. 12.

35 Interview by Andrew Jack, *Financial Times*, 13 October (1997) p. 14.

36 R. Marschan, D. Welch and L. Welch, Language: the Forgotten Factor in Multinational Management, *European Management Journal*, Vol. 15, No. 5 (1997) pp. 591–598; R. Marschan-Piekkari, D. Welch and L .Welch, In the Shadow: the Impact of Language on Structure, Power and Communication in the Multinational, *International Business Review*, Vol. 8, No. 4 (1999) pp. 421–440.

37 N. Nohria and S. Ghoshal, Differentiated Fit and Shared Values: Alternatives for Managing Headquarters-Subsidiary Relations, *Strategic Management Journal*, Vol. 15 (1994) pp. 491–502.

38 T. Lester, Close the Personnel Department? *International Management*, April (1994) pp. 40–41.

39 D. Welch and L. Welch, Being Flexible and Accommodating Diversity: the Challenge for Multinational Management, *European Management Journal*, Vol. 15, No. 6 (1997) pp. 677–685.

40 M. Alvesson and P.O. Berg, *Corporate Culture and Organizational Symbolism*, Walter de Gruyter: Berlin, 1992.

41 D. Welch and L. Welch, Linking Operation Mode Diversity and IHRM, *The International Journal of Human Resource Management*, Vol. 5, No. 4 (1994) pp. 911–926.

42 Ref. 41, p. 915.

43 O. Vikhanski and S. Puffer, Management Education and Employee Training at Moscow McDonald's, *European Management Journal*, Vol. 11, No. 1 (1993) pp. 102–107.

44 *The Economist*, 26 September (1992).

45 R. Luostarinen and L.S. Welch, *International Business Operations*, Helsinki: Export Consulting, 1990, p. 100.

46 R.N. Osborn and C.C. Baughn, Forms of Interorganisational Governance for Multinational Alliances, *Academy of Management Journal*, Vol. 33, No. 3 (1990) pp. 503–519.

47 J.C. Jarillo and H.H. Stevenson, Co-operative Strategies – the Payoffs and the Pitfalls, *Long-Range Planning*, Vol. 24, No. 1 (1991) pp. 64–70.

48 D. Scott-Kemmis, T. Darling, R. Johnston, F. Collyer and C. Cliff, *Strategic Alliances in the Internationalisation of Australian Industry*, Canberra: Australian Government Publishing Service, 1990.

49 Business International, *Making Alliances Work: Lessons from Companies' Successes and Mistakes*, London: Business International, 1990, p. 27.

50 D. Lei and J.W. Slocum, Jr, Global Strategic Alliances: Payoffs and Pitfalls, *Organizational Dynamics*, Winter (1991) p. 57.

51 P. Lorange, Human Resource Management in Multinational Cooperative Ventures, *Human Resource Management*, Vol. 25, No. 1 (1986) pp. 133.

52 W.F. Cascio and M.G. Serapio, Human Resources Systems in an International Alliance: the Undoing of a Done Deal? *Organizational Dynamics*, Winter (1991) pp. 63–74; R.S. Schuler and E. Van Slujis, Davidson Marley BV: Establishing and Operating an International Joint Venture, *European Management Journal*, Vol. 10, December, (1992) pp. 428–436.

53 R. Schuler, Human Resource Issues and Activities in International Joint Ventures, *International Journal of Human Resource Management*, Vol. 12, No. 1 (2001) pp. 1–52.

54 A. Ferguson and D. James, Secrets and Traps of Overseas Expansion, *Business Review Weekly*, 5–11 June (2003) pp. 40–46.

55 P.J. Dowling, Hot Issues Overseas, *Personnel Administrator*, Vol. 34, No. 1 (1989) pp. 66–72.

56 K. Monks, Global or Local? HRM in the Multinational Company: the Irish Experience, *International Journal of Human Resource Management*, Vol. 7, No. 3 (1996) pp. 721–735.

IHRM: sustaining international business operations

Chapter objectives

The previous two chapters concentrated on the global environment and organizational contexts. We now focus on the 'managing people' aspect. The aim is to establish the role of HRM in sustaining international business operations and growth. We cover the following:

- issues relating to the various approaches to staffing foreign operations
- the reasons for using international assignments: position filling, management development and organizational development
- the various types of international assignments: short-term, extended and longer-term; and non-standard arrangements: commuter, rotator, contractual and virtual
- the role of expatriates and non-expatriates (international business travelers) in supporting international business activities
- the role of the corporate HR function.

Introduction

The purpose of this chapter is to expand on the role of IHRM in sustaining international business operations. We examine the various approaches taken to staffing international operations and the allocation of human resources to the firm's various international operations to insure effective strategic outcomes. The pivotal role of international assignments is outlined. We conclude with a discussion on the role of the HR function within this context, particularly examining the issue of centralization and decentralization of the HR function and its activities.

Approaches to staffing

There are staffing issues that internationalizing firms confront that are either not present in a domestic environment or are complicated by the international context in which these activities take place. Take, for example, this scenario. A US multinational wishes to appoint a new finance director for its Irish subsidiary. It may decide to fill the position by selecting from finance staff available in its parent operations (that is, a PCN), or to recruit locally (an HCN) or seek a suitable candidate from one of its other foreign subsidiaries (a TCN). How it responds is partly determined by factors such as:

- its general staffing policy on key positions in headquarters and subsidiaries (that is, ethnocentrism, polycentrism, geocentrism and regiocentrism)
- the constraints placed by the host government on hiring policies
- staff availability.

The IHRM literature uses four terms to describe MNE approaches to managing and staffing their subsidiaries. These terms are taken from the seminal work of Perlmutter,[1] who claimed that it was possible to identify among international executives three primary attitudes – **ethnocentric**, **polycentric** and **geocentric** – towards building a multinational enterprise, based on top management assumptions upon which key product, functional and geographical decisions were made. To demonstrate these three attitudes, Perlmutter used aspects of organizational design, such as decision-making, evaluation and control, information flows and complexity of organization. He also included 'perpetuation', which he defined as 'recruiting, staffing, development'. A fourth attitude – **regiocentric** – was added later.[2] We shall consider the connection between these four categories and staffing practices and examine the advantages and disadvantages of each approach.

Ethnocentric

Few foreign subsidiaries have any autonomy and strategic decisions are made at headquarters. Key positions in domestic and foreign operations are held by headquarters' personnel. Subsidiaries are managed by staff from the home country (PCNs).

There are often sound business reasons for pursuing an ethnocentric staffing policy:

- A perceived lack of qualified host-country nationals (HCNs).
- The need to maintain good communication, coordination and control links with corporate headquarters. For firms at the early stages of internationalization, an ethnocentric approach can reduce the perceived high risk. When a multinational acquires a firm in another country, it may wish initially to replace local managers with PCNs to ensure that the new subsidiary complies with overall corporate objectives and policies, or because local staff may not have the required level of competence. Thus, an ethnocentric approach to a particular foreign market situation could be perfectly valid for a very experienced multinational. Having your own person, in whom you can place a degree of trust to 'do the right thing', can moderate the perceived high risk involved in foreign activities. This has been referred to by Bonache *et al*. as 'assignments as control'.[3]

An ethnocentric policy, however, has a number of disadvantages:[4]

- It limits the promotion opportunities of HCNs, which may lead to reduced productivity and increased turnover among that group.

- The adaptation of expatriate managers to host countries often takes a long time, during which PCNs often make mistakes and poor decisions, as the case in IHRM in Action Case 3-1 illustrates.

- When PCN and HCN compensation packages are compared, the often-considerable income gap in favour of PCNs is viewed by HCNs as unjustified.

- For many expatriates a key overseas position means new status, authority and an increase in standard of living. These changes may affect expatriates' sensitivity to the needs and expectations of their host-country subordinates.

Expatriates are also very expensive to maintain in overseas locations. A US study[5] found that 50 per cent of responding firms estimated that the average cost of expatriates was three to four times that of normal salary, and 18 per cent indicated more than four times the salary.

Polycentric

The MNE treats each subsidiary as a distinct national entity with some decision-making autonomy. Subsidiaries are usually managed by local nationals (HCNs), who are seldom promoted to positions at headquarters, and PCNs are rarely transferred to foreign subsidiary operations. The main advantages of a polycentric policy, some of which address shortcomings of the ethnocentric policy identified above, are:

- Employing HCNs eliminates language barriers, avoids the adjustment problems of expatriate managers and their families and removes the need for expensive cultural awareness training programs.

IHRM in Action Case 3-1

What works at home does not necessarily work abroad

A four-day strike and pay rises of 10–15 per cent were part of the cost paid by a South Korean textile firm for an incident involving one of the expatriate managers in its Vietnamese factory. A Vietnamese worker was confronted by his South Korean boss. Speaking in Korean, the manager yelled at him for being in the wrong place in the factory. As he did not understand her, the Vietnamese did not respond. The South Korean manager kicked and slapped him – as 'in South Korea it is common for employers to scold or even beat employees if they make a big mistake'. Here, though, such behaviour resulted in 10 of the Vietnamese's co-workers retaliating in kind. The manager was rushed to hospital and the workers went on strike. The South Korean manager was subsequently deported.

Source: Based on an article by A. Schwartz, 'Love Thy Neighbour?' *Far Eastern Economic Review*, August 10 (1995) p. 63.

- Employment of HCNs allows a multinational company to take a lower profile in sensitive political situations.

- Employment of HCNs is less expensive, even if a premium is paid to attract high-quality applicants.

- Gives continuity to the management of foreign subsidiaries. This approach avoids the turnover of key managers that, by its very nature, results from an ethnocentric approach.

A polycentric policy, however, has its own disadvantages:

- Bridging the gap between HCN subsidiary managers and PCN managers at corporate headquarters. Language barriers, conflicting national loyalties and a range of cultural differences (for example, personal value differences and differences in attitudes to business) may isolate the corporate headquarters staff from the various foreign subsidiaries. The result may be that a multinational firm could become a 'federation' of independent national units with nominal links to corporate headquarters.

- Career paths of HCN and PCN managers. Host-country managers have limited opportunities to gain experience outside their own country and cannot progress beyond the senior positions in their own subsidiary. Parent-country managers also have limited opportunities to gain overseas experience. As headquarters positions are held only by PCNs, the senior corporate management group will have limited exposure to international operations and, over time, this will constrain strategic decision-making and resource allocation.

Of course, in some cases the host government may dictate that key managerial positions are filled by its nationals. Alternatively, the multinational may wish to be perceived as a local company as part of a strategy of local responsiveness. Having HCNs in key, visible positions assists this.

Geocentric

Here, the MNE is taking a global approach to its operations, recognizing that each part (subsidiaries and headquarters) makes a unique contribution with its unique competence. It is accompanied by a worldwide integrated business and nationality is ignored in favor of ability. For example, the Chief Executive Officer of the Swedish multinational Electrolux claims that, within this global company, there is not a tradition to hire managing directors from Sweden, or locally, but to find the person best suited for the job.[6] That is, the 'color of one's passport' does not matter when it comes to rewards, promotion and development. PCNs, HCNs and TCNs can be found in key positions anywhere, including those at senior management level at headquarters and on the board of directors.

There are three main advantages to this approach:

- It enables a multinational firm to develop an international executive team which assists in developing a global perspective and an internal pool of labor for deployment throughout the global organization.

- It overcomes the 'federation' drawback of the polycentric approach.

- It supports cooperation and resource sharing across units.

As with the other staffing approaches, there are disadvantages associated with a geocentric policy:

- Host governments want a high number of their citizens employed and may utilize immigration controls in order to force HCN employment if enough people and adequate skills are unavailable.

- Many Western countries require companies to provide extensive documentation if they wish to hire a foreign national instead of a local national. Providing this documentation can be time consuming, expensive and, at times, futile. Of course, the same drawback applies to an ethnocentric policy. A related issue, that will be discussed later, is the difficulty of obtaining a work permit for the accompanying spouse or partner.

- A geocentric policy can be expensive to implement because of increased training and relocation costs. A related factor is the need to have a compensation structure with standardized international base pay, which may be higher than national levels in many countries.

- Large numbers of PCNs, TCNs, and HCNs need to be sent abroad in order to build and maintain the international team required to support a geocentric staffing policy. To implement a geocentric staffing policy successfully, therefore, requires a longer lead time and more centralized control of the staffing process. This necessarily reduces the independence of subsidiary management in these issues, and this loss of autonomy may be resisted by the subsidiary.

As can be seen in Figure 3-1, Welch[7] identifies IHRM barriers that may impede a multinational from building the staffing resources required to sustain the geocentric

Geocentric staffing requirements

Figure 3-1

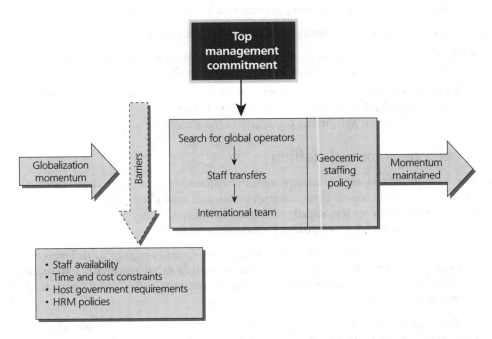

Source: D. Welch, HRM Implications of Globalisation, *Journal of General Management*, Vol. 19, No. 4 (1994) p. 57. Reproduced with permission.

policy that is implicit in globalization literature. The barriers – staff availability, time and cost constraints, host-government requirements and ineffective HRM policies – reflect the issues surrounding the geocentric approach listed in the literature reviewed above. Welch argues that top management commitment to a geocentric staffing policy is necessary to overcome these barriers. While there may be a genuine predisposition among top managers at headquarters regarding the staffing of its global operations, leveraging critical resources in order to build the necessary international team of managers may prove to be a major challenge.

Regiocentric

This approach reflects the geographic strategy and structure of the multinational. Like the geocentric approach, it utilizes a wider pool of managers but in a limited way. Staff may move outside their countries but only within the particular geographic region. Regional managers may not be promoted to headquarters positions but enjoy a degree of regional autonomy in decision making.[8] For example, a US-based firm could create three regions: Europe, the Americas and Asia-Pacific. European staff would be transferred throughout the European region (say a Briton to Germany, a French national to Belgium and a German to Spain). Staff transfers to the Asian-Pacific region from Europe would be rare, as would transfers from the regions to headquarters in the USA.

The advantages of using a regiocentric approach are:

- It allows interaction between executives transferred to regional headquarters from subsidiaries in the region and PCNs posted to the regional headquarters.
- It reflects some sensitivity to local conditions, since local subsidiaries are staffed almost totally by HCNs.
- It can be a way for a multinational to move gradually from a purely ethnocentric or polycentric approach to a geocentric approach.[9]

There are some disadvantages in a regiocentric policy:

- It can produce federalism at a regional rather than a country basis and constrain the organization from taking a global stance.
- While this approach does improve career prospects at the national level, it only moves the barrier to the regional level. Staff may advance to regional headquarters but seldom to positions at the parent headquarters.

A philosophy toward staffing

In summary, based on top management attitudes, a multinational can pursue one of several approaches to international staffing. It may even proceed on an *ad hoc* basis, rather than systematically selecting one of the four approaches discussed above. A danger with this approach, according to Robinson[10] is that:

The firm will opt for a policy of using parent-country-nationals in foreign management positions by default, that is, simply as an automatic extension of domestic policy, rather than deliberately seeking optimum utilization of management skills.

This option is really a policy by default; there is no conscious decision or evaluation of appropriate policy. The 'policy' is a result of corporate inertia, inexperience or both. The major disadvantage here (apart from the obvious one of inefficient use of resources) is that the firm's responses are reactive rather than proactive, and a consistent human resources strategy that fits its overall business strategy is difficult to achieve.

Table 3-1 summarizes the advantages and disadvantages of using the three categories of staff – PCNs, HCNs and TCNs.

While the various attitudes have been a useful way of demonstrating the various approaches to staffing foreign operations, it should be stressed that:

- The above categories refer to managerial attitudes that reflect the socio-cultural environment in which the internationalizing firm is imbedded, and are based on Perlmutter's study of US firms.

The advantages and disadvantages of using PCNs, TCNs and HCNs	Table 3-1

Parent country nationals

Advantages
- Organizational control and coordination are maintained and facilitated
- Promising managers are given international experience
- PCNs may be the best people for the job because of special skills and experience
- There is assurance that subsidiary will comply with company objectives, policies, etc.

Disadvantages
- The promotional opportunities of HCNs are limited
- Adaptation to host country may take a long time
- PCNs may impose an inappropriate HQ style
- Compensation for PCNs and HCNs may differ

Third-country nationals

Advantages
- Salary and benefit requirements may be lower than for PCNS
- TCNs may be better informed than PCNs about the host-country environment

Disadvantages
- Transfers must consider possible national animosities (e.g. India and Pakistan)
- The host government may resent hiring of TCNs
- TCNs may not want to return to their own countries after assignment

Host-country nationals

Advantages
- Language and other barriers are eliminated
- Hiring costs are reduced and no work permit is required
- Continuity of management improves, since HCNs stay longer in positions
- Government policy may dictate hiring of HCNs
- Morale among HCNs may improve as they see career potential

Disadvantages
- Control and coordination of HQ may be impeded
- HCNs have limited career opportunity outside the subsidiary
- Hiring HCNs limits opportunities for PCNs to gain foreign experience
- Hiring HCNs could encourage a federation of national rather than global units

- These attitudes may reflect a general top management attitude, but the nature of international business often forces adaptation upon implementation. That is, a firm may adopt an ethnocentric approach to all its foreign operations, but a particular host government may require the appointment of its own people in the key subsidiary positions, so, for that market, a polycentric approach is mandatory. In such instances, a uniform approach is not achievable. A Korn/Ferry International survey of 35 businesses active in Russia found that Western companies tended to maintain an ethnocentric approach to staffing despite attempts to 'Russify' the local operations.[11]

- The strategic importance of the foreign market, the maturity of the operation and the degree of cultural distance between the parent and host country influence the way in which the firm approaches a particular staffing decision.[12,13] In some cases an MNE may use a combination of approaches. For example, it may operate its European interests in a regiocentric manner and its Southeast Asian interests in an ethnocentric way until there is greater confidence in operating in that region of the world.

| **Figure 3-2** | Determinants of IHRM approaches and activities |

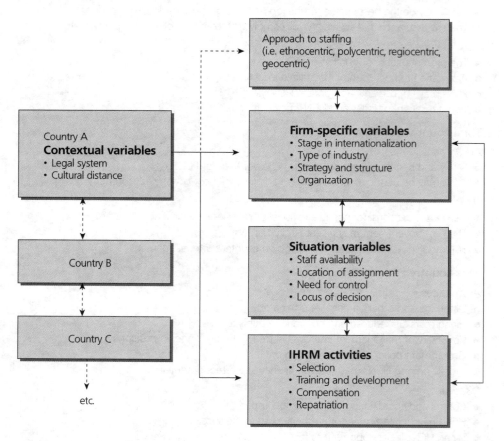

Source: Adapted from D. Welch, Determinants of International Human Resource Management Approaches and Activities: a Suggested Framework, *Journal of Management Studies*, Vol. 31, No. 2 (1994) p. 150.

- The approach to policy on executive nationality tends to reflect organizational needs. For instance, if the multinational places a high priority on organizational control, then an ethnocentric policy will be adopted. However, there are difficulties in maintaining a uniform approach to international staffing. Therefore, strategies in different countries may require different staffing approaches.

Because of these operating realities, it is sometimes difficult to equate precisely managerial attitudes towards international operations with the structural forms that were presented in Chapter 2. The environmental contingencies facing the particular internationalizing firm influence its strategic position, managerial mindset, organizational structure and staffing approaches. Figure 3-2 illustrates the linkages as:

- Firm-specific variables (such as stage in internationalization, organizational structure, and organizational culture).
- Situation variables (such as staff availability, need for control) with IHRM approaches and activities.
- Contextual variables (such as cultural distance and host country legal requirements).
- IHRM activities that may determine a firm's approach to the staffing of overseas operations, that is, whether a multinational adopts an ethnocentric, polycentric, geocentric or regiocentric approach to staff subsidiary operations.

The above model may be helpful in drawing together the various organizational factors and HR issues. Staffing approaches do influence and are influenced by organizational factors and also country factors. For example, a firm that is maturing into a networked organization (firm-specific variable) will require IHRM approaches and activities that will assist its ability to develop a flexible global organization that is centrally integrated and coordinated yet locally responsive – a geocentric approach. However, a key assumption underlying the geocentric staffing philosophy is that the multinational has sufficient numbers of high-calibre staff (PCNs, TCNs and HCNs) constantly available for transfer anywhere, whenever global management needs dictate.[7] As was discussed earlier, it is not easy to find or nurture the required numbers of high-quality staff (firm-specific and situation variables), or to assign them to certain operations owing to host-country requirements (country-specific variables). For example, a study by Richards[14] of staffing practices and subsidiary performance of US multinationals in the UK and Thailand found a link between perceptions of subsidiary performance, subsidiary location and staffing. Subsidiaries in Thailand appeared to perform better with an HCN in charge than a PCN. The IHRM activities – selection, training and development, compensation and repatriation – covered in Part II – play an important role in the development of the effective policies required to sustain a preferred approach to staffing.

Transferring staff for international business activities

The above discussion demonstrates the options for staffing key positions in foreign operations. We will now look at the HR consequences of these approaches and the broader implications in terms of:

- the reasons for using international assignments
- types of international assignments
- the role of expatriates and non-expatriates.

Reasons for international assignments

Given the difficulties surrounding international assignments, it is reasonable to question why multinationals persist in using expatriates. Certainly, there are ebbs and flows associated with the number of staff moved internationally. Frequently, predictions are made that expatriates will become like dinosaurs as firms implement localization strategies, replacing expatriates with HCNs as a way of containing employment costs. However, firms expect staff movements to increase. For example, in a 2002 survey of 273 companies from 17 countries by PricewaterhouseCoopers,[15] participants expected that their use of expatriates would continue to grow in response to pressures for internationally mobile staff. This trend was despite the global environment volatility and may be regarded as evidence of a continuing commitment to international business operations. Why? As a practitioner involved in expatriate management explains:[16]

> As I talk to people, they say they wish they could shrink the expatriate population because of the expense in terms of benefits, services and support. And as long as I've been in this business, people say they are going to scale down on expats but it never happens. Until we have people all over the world with the skills they need, employers are going to have to continue to send expatriates.

The international management and IHRM literature has consistently identified three key reasons for transferring staff through the use of various forms of international assignments:

- **Position filling**. The organization has a need and depending on the type of position and the level involved will either employ someone locally or transfer a suitable candidate. Another 2002 global survey, by the consulting firm GMAC Global Relocation Services,[17] asked respondents to indicate their primary objectives for international assignments. The most common reason was to fill a skills gap, followed by the launch of a new endeavor, and technology transfer. Likewise, Wong's study[18] of two Japanese department stores in Hong Kong found that short-term job filling was the main reason for using expatriate staff rather than for long-term development and socialization of individuals.

- **Management development**. Staff can be moved into other parts of the organization for training and development purposes, and to assist in the development of common corporate values. For this reason, we see headquarters staff transferred to subsidiary operations, or subsidiary staff transferring into the parent operations or to other subsidiary operations. Assignments may be for varying lengths of time and may involve project work in addition to a trainee position. The perceived link between international experience and career development can be a motivation for staff to agree to such transfers.

- **Organisation development**. Here strategic objectives of the operation come into play: the need for control; the transfer of knowledge, competence, procedures and practices into various locations; and to exploit global market opportunities, as outlined in Chapter 1. Indeed, the 2002 PricewaterhouseCoopers report[15] found that greater staff mobility assisted in supporting a global corporate culture and assisted the cross-fertilization of ideas and practices. One participant from an insurance firm is quoted as saying, 'To create a truly global organization, we will have to imbed a culture of cross-border mobility into the organization's genetic code, which will take 10 years.' International assignments allow staff to gain a broader perspective as they become familiar with more than one operation.

Types of international assignments

Employees are transferred internationally for varying lengths of time depending on the purpose of the transfer and the nature of the task to be performed. Companies tend to classify types according to the length or duration of the assignment:

- **Short term**: up to 3 months. These are usually for troubleshooting or project supervision or are a stopgap measure until a more permanent arrangement can be found.

- **Extended**: up to 1 year. These may involve similar activities to those for short-term assignments.

- **Long-term**: varies from 1 to 5 years, involving a clearly defined role in the receiving operation (such as managing director of a subsidiary). The long-term assignment has also been referred to as a **traditional expatriate assignment**.

Within these three broad categories, it is possible to find what are termed non-standard assignments:

- **Commuter assignments** – Special arrangements where the person concerned commutes from the home country on a weekly or bi-weekly basis to the place of work in another country. For example, the person lives in London but works in Moscow.

- **Rotational assignments** – Employees commute from the home country to a place of work in another country for a short, set period followed by a break in the home country – used on oil rigs, for example.

- **Contractual assignments** – Used in situations where employees with specific skills vital to an international project are assigned for a limited duration of 6–12 months. Research and development (R&D) is one area that is using multinational project teams and lends itself to short-term contractual assignments in conjunction with longer term assignments and virtual teams.[19]

- **Virtual assignments** – Where the employee does not relocate to a host location but manages, from home-base, international responsibilities for a part of the organization in another country. A PricewaterhouseCoopers[20] survey in 2000 of 82 multinational companies across 13 countries found that 28 per cent of the surveyed firms anticipated increasing use of virtual assignments, compared with 17 per cent in a similar survey 2 years previous. A total of 65 per cent of respondents who use virtual assignments reported having seen an increase in the number of virtual assignments used by their company and the same proportion indicated an expected increase in the next 2 years. The main reasons given by responding firms for experimenting with the virtual assignment were similar to those for other non-standard forms of international assignments: the shortage of mobile staff prepared to accept longer term postings and for cost containment reasons.

Some of these arrangements assist in overcoming the high cost of international assignments. However, non-standard assignments are not always effective substitutes for the traditional expatriate assignment. As the 2000 PricewaterhouseCoopers report's authors point out:[21]

> There are real concerns about the viability of commuter arrangements over an extended period of time due to the build up of stress resulting from intensive travel commitments and the impact on personal relationships.

Most of the research into assignment issues has been around the long-term assignment type, mainly because it forms the bulk of international assignments. In contrast, short-term and extended assignments have received limited research attention.[22] It is similar in terms of the non-standard assignments. For example, Welch et al.[23] comment, 'while non-standard assignments have long been used in conjunction with, or instead of, traditional expatriate assignments, this has yet to translate into a comparable body of academic inquiry'. Their study into the use of virtual assignments in Australian and Danish firms suggested that although there are certain advantages of operating virtually (such as not having to relocate a family unit), there are disadvantages that may affect successful work outcomes. As Figure 3-3 illustrates, these are:

- Role conflict, dual allegiance and identification issues – between the person in the home location and the virtual work group in the foreign location. For example, to whom does the virtual assignee 'belong' – the home location where the person physically resides for most of the time, or the foreign unit? How much time should be devoted to the 'virtual' work responsibilities versus the 'real' work?
- Interpersonal relations and work relationships – given that much of the work is done through electronic media, the potential for cultural misunderstandings increases, and the geographical distance means normal group interaction is not possible. Communication is mainly through conference calls, videoconferencing and e-mails, and depends on good skills in using these media. Frequent visits between the two locations are required to support the working of this arrangement as not everything can be settled virtually. Face-to-face meetings are still required.

Figure 3-3   Factors influencing virtual assignments

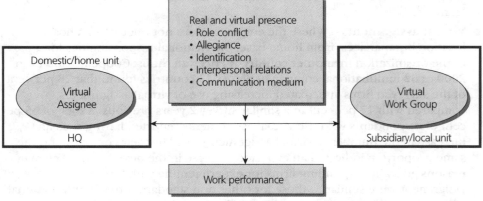

Source: D.E. Welch, V. Worm and M. Fenwick, Are Virtual Assignments Feasible?, *Management International Review*, Special Issue 1 (2003) p. 103. Reproduced with permission.

Virtual assignments tend to be used for regional positions, such as European Marketing Manager, where the person is mainly coordinating a number of countries' marketing activities but is based at a regional center. The 2000 PricewaterhouseCoopers study found that virtual assignments were more common in Europe with no companies indicating the use of such arrangements in the Asia-Pacific region. Geographical distance in terms of flight hours and time zones were the main difficulties encountered in operating virtually between operations in Europe and Asia-Pacific.

The roles of an expatriate

The reasons for using expatriates are not mutually exclusive. They do, however, underpin expectations about the roles staff play as a consequence of being transferred from one location to another country. These roles are delineated in Figure 3-4. We shall now take a look at these roles.

The expatriate as an agent of direct control

The use of staff transfers can be regarded as a bureaucratic control mechanism,[24] where the primary role is that of ensuring compliance through direct supervision. Harzing[25] found that German companies tend towards this form of control (*personnel zentral*). She labels expatriates who are such agents as 'bears', arguing that the analogy reflects the level of dominance of this type of expatriate control. To a certain extent, using expatriates for control reflects an ethnocentric predisposition, but this can be important in ensuring subsidiary compliance, enabling strategic objectives for local operations to be achieved.

The expatriate as an agent of socialization

This role is related to the use of corporate culture as an informal control mechanism we examined in Chapter 2. There is an implicit expectation that expatriates assist in the transfer of shared values and beliefs. Harzing likens expatriates who transfer corporate values to 'bumble-bees'. However, as Fenwick *et al.*[26] point out, there has been little empirical investigation as to how effective expatriates have been as agents of socialization. In fact, attempts to instil corporate values and norms ritualized in the form of certain expected behaviors often have negative results at the subsidiary level. Staff in the German operations of the US global retailer Wal-Mart hid in the toilets to escape the Wal-Mart morning cheer.[27]

The roles of an expatriate   **Figure 3-4**

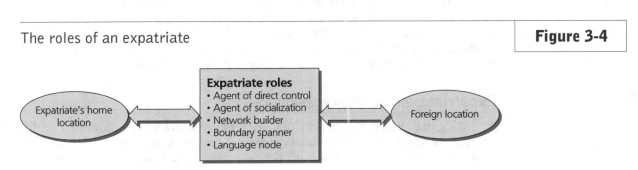

International assignments do assist in knowledge sharing and competence transfer, and encourage adoption of common work practices, aspects of which may comprise elements of corporate culture. Staff in the various organizational units may be exposed to different viewpoints and perspectives that will shape their behavior and may reinforce their feeling of belonging. In their study, Goodall and Roberts[28] relate a reaction by a Chinese employee in the Chinese operation of a European oil company. Her time in the parent's operation in Europe enabled her to appreciate how the company valued its name and reputation, and she was able to understand better the company's code of conduct and attitude towards occupational health and safety.

Expatriates as network builders

As discussed in Chapter 2, international assignments are viewed as a way of fostering interpersonal linkages that can be used for informal control and communication purposes. Naturally, as employees move between various organizational units, their network of personal relationships changes, leading to Harzing's analogy of expatriates as 'spiders' to describe this role. How these employees are utilized is person dependent. People tend to nurture and protect their networks, to be very selective about the way they use their connections and to evaluate the potential damage to key individuals in their networks if the connection was to be used inappropriately. In their study of project teams and networks, Schweiger et al.[29] provide the following example of how international assignments assisted network development:

> I depended heavily on the contacts I had developed over the years. The time spent in international assignments was invaluable. I knew important people in several key operations. I knew how they operated and what was important to them. They also knew that I was credible and would help them when the opportunity arose.

Further, as Marschan et al.[30] explain, 'People may be introduced to each other but not form the type of relationship on which productive networks are built.' Take the case of Laura, an American expatriate, who has worked in India for several years and built up a strong network comprising subsidiary staff, key host-government officials, clients, suppliers and the like. She is now being transferred to the Canadian operations and Angelo, from the Italian subsidiary, is taking her place. Laura may take Angelo around and introduce him to key individuals in this personal network, but it will not guarantee that Angelo will be readily accepted into that network of critical contacts. However, Laura may be able to activate her Indian contacts to assist in her new tasks, or be prepared to assist her various Indian contacts where necessary or appropriate in the Canadian operations.

Although short-term assignments may not allow the expatriate to develop as wide a range of contacts in one location as a traditional assignment allows, over time they can increase the number and variety of networks, giving the opportunity for the transfer of ideas and competence.[31] Duration of the assignment, therefore, will have an impact on the person's ability to develop networks.

Expatriates as boundary spanners

Boundary spanning refers to activities, such as gathering information, that bridge internal and external organizational contexts. Expatriates are considered boundary spanners because they can collect host-country information, act as representatives of their firms in the host country and can influence agents. For example, attending a social function at a foreign embassy can provide the expatriate with an opportunity to network, gather market intelligence and promote the firm's profile at a high level. Networking activity emerged as a way in which expatriates from various nationalities operating in Hong Kong were able to engage in boundary-spanning activities.[32]

Expatriates as language nodes

In Chapter 2, we discussed how many multinational firms operate through language standardization – or a common corporate language, usually English. Marschan-Piekkari et al.[33] found that Finnish expatriates working for the elevator company Kone sometimes became what they termed language nodes. They give as an example a Finn (whom they refer to as Mr X) who learned to speak Spanish while working as an expatriate in the firm's South American operations. Upon repatriation back to the Finnish headquarters, Mr X finds that he becomes 'the man in Finland who speaks Spanish'. Kone employees from the firm's Spanish-speaking operations, including Mexico, would call Mr X, preferring to conduct queries and gain information from him in Spanish, and check information sent to them in English. Mr X in effect plays a role as a language node and his linkages extend beyond the areas where he was posted as an expatriate. The language node role is not confined to PCNs. Other Kone expatriates who spoke the corporate language, English, also acted as language nodes.

Transfer of competence and knowledge

Overall, international assignments are seen as an effective way of accomplishing multiple objectives. In fact, one could argue that there are elements of competence and knowledge transfer in all the roles we have identified. However, evidence as to the effectiveness of expatriates in conducting their numerous roles is sparse. Factors that may affect effectiveness include:

- The creation of an environment of openness and support for cross-fertilization of ideas and implementation of 'best practice'.

- In Figure 3-4, the double-headed arrows indicate the need for knowledge and information to travel dyadically, that is, between the expatriate and the host location, and back to the expatriate's home location, if the multinational is to benefit from international assignments as a mechanism for competence and knowledge transfer.

- Despite the recognition of the importance of personal networks in knowledge and information transfer, staffing decisions are often made without regard to their effect on network relationships.[34]

- There is a link between the duration of the assignment and the effective transfer of knowledge and competences. Some knowledge and competence may be transferred quickly whereas other skills and knowledge (particularly where a high level of tacitness is present) may take longer.

- Naturally, much of what is transferred depends on the expatriate concerned in terms of ability to teach others and motivation to act as an agent of knowledge and competence transfer. For example, Goodall and Roberts[35] quote the experience of a Colombian HCN working for a European oil company:

> It is important that there is really a transfer of technology between expat [expatriate] and Colombian. And during the last two years nothing is

learned. The expat goes and then they bring another expat … There should be more of a formal commitment to training, a follow-up. They [expatriates] should be evaluated on coaching with Columbians.

A final point: Bolino and Feldman[36] make an interesting observation that when expatriates are assigned for position filling owing to a lack of appropriate local staff, such expatriates are often forced to take over some of the responsibilities of their colleagues owing to differences in knowledge and competence levels. Consequently, they argue that expatriates often spend significant time on less challenging tasks to help out co-workers and train them. In such cases, although the expatriates may assist in skills transfer, over time their own level of competence may decrease as they are not developing their own expertise. Hence, when expatriates return to their home operation, they may find that their knowledge is obsolescing.

The role of non-expatriates

The above discussion has centered on the international assignment. What has tended to be overlooked is that a considerable amount of international business involves what can be called non-expatriates: people who travel internationally yet are not considered expatriates, as they do not relocate to another country. That is, non-expatriates are international business travelers – persons for whom a large proportion of their role involves constant international visits to foreign markets, subsidiary units, international projects and the like. Where this group is referred to, they are popularly termed 'road warriors', 'globetrotters' or 'frequent fliers'.

International travel is an essential component of the work of non-expatriates such as international sales staff whose job is almost totally comprised of international travel and managers whose job entails numerous, periodic visits to international operations.[37] International sales representatives attend trade fairs, visit foreign agents and distributors, demonstrate new products to potential clients and negotiate sales contracts. Various staff will visit foreign locations to deal with host-country government officials, alliance partners, subcontracting firms and foreign suppliers.

In spite of e-mails and videoconferencing, international business travel is increasing.[38] People still prefer to conduct certain business activities, hold meetings and interact face-to-face. As Mintzberg et al.[39] note:

> Why do so many effective international managers get into airplanes rather
> than pick up telephones when they need to communicate seriously? As
> we move from written communication (letters, e-mail) to strictly oral
> (telephones) to face-to-face forms, communication appears to become
> richer and more nuanced.

However, international business travel can make heavy demands on staff. For example, the Norwegian firm Moelven, a global player in the timber industry, when developing its operations in the Russian market in the early 1990s, initially through importing, had to become highly involved in building personal relationships with key individuals in Russia:[40]

> One manager from the purchasing department responsible for imports
> commented: 'Personal contacts were so important that during the first three
> years [of] dealing with the Russians, I had between 50 and 100 trips to Russia,
> talking to suppliers and maintaining the personal networks.'

Apart from the resource implications, there are issues relating to the management of international business travelers that do not seem to be addressed in the IHRM literature. This may be because this category of staff are not expatriates on traditional or non-standard assignments. The international component of their work is performed within the context of their 'normal' duties. Regardless, there are several important issues that should be considered. There is a high level of stress involved for those whose job responsibilities contain a large proportion of international business travel. In one of the few articles on this issue, DeFrank *et al.*[41] identify the following factors as stressors:

- **Home and family issues** – Examples are missing important anniversaries and school events. The more frequent the travel, the greater is the potential for family and marital relationships to be strained.

- **Work arrangements** – The 'domestic' side of the job still has to be attended to even though the person is traveling internationally. Modern communications allow work to accompany them, so the business traveler is expected to deal with home-base issues while remote from the office via modem (see IHRM in Action Case 3-2). When the traveler returns to the home office, they may face crises, backlogs of paperwork and so forth.

- **Travel logistics** – Airline connections, hotel accommodation and meeting schedules.

- **Health concerns** – Poor diet, lack of physical exercise, lack of sleep, coping with jetlag and exposure to disease and other illnesses (such as SARS and deep vein thrombosis).

- **Host culture issues** – As international business is conducted in other cultural settings, the person is still expected to be able to operate in unfamiliar environments and handle cultural differences effectively. However, the limited

---

IHRM in Action Case 3-2

Connecting mobile workers

Sinclair Knight Merz, a global professional services consulting firm, based in Australia, has a worldwide workforce of 3000. The firm is involved in more than 1000 projects at any one time. Currently 700 staff are classified as 'mobile' – working in Australia, New Zealand, Asia and the UK. These project staff need access to a company intranet data and document base. To facilitate access and control costs, the company has installed a global remote access solution – referred to as WiSE – that assists staff gain access, including home access, to a wide range of documents such as drawings, proposals, contracts and specifications. About 15 sites across Australia, Asia and the UK are currently connected via the VPN (virtual private network) gateways. Staff working on international projects, for example, will no longer have difficulty in finding an access number for the country they are working in, or have to deal with difficulties associated with downloading large document files in remote locations. The company believes that staff productivity has already improved dramatically.

Source: Based on an article by Kelly Mills, Home link for global staff on mobile VPN, *The Australian IT Section*, 17 June (2003) p. 4, and the company's website.

empirical and anecdotal evidence suggests that non-expatriates do not receive the same level of cross-cultural training as expatriates, if any.

The above list contains the negatives associated with international business travel. However, there are positives. People involved in this side of international business will relate the excitement and thrills of conducting business deals in foreign locations, the life style (top hotels, business class travel, duty-free shopping) and its general exotic nature as the reasons why they enjoy international business travel, despite its very real negatives.

Non-expatriate business travelers also perform many of the roles of expatriates – in terms of being agents for socialization, network builders, boundary spanners and language nodes. From the limited evidence available, however, it would seem that the management of staff using these forms of arrangements falls to the functional or line managers involved rather than the HR department as such. The 2002 PricewaterhouseCoopers survey, for example, found that many respondents did not offer short-term project workers traditional expatriate compensation packages.

The role of the corporate HR function

Having considered the approaches to staffing and examined international assignments and the role of expatriates and non-expatriates, we now turn our attention to the role played by the corporate HR function in managing people in a multinational context.

Much of the IHRM literature is focused on whom to place in control of foreign operations and activities. However, like other functional areas, HR professionals in multinationals face strategic choices. First, can we manage our people like a global product? The concept of a global internal labor market does imply some belief that it is possible to deploy human resources in much the same way as other resources. However, comparative HRM and cross-cultural management literature suggests that standardizing work practices and HRM activities is not the same as product standardization. We will focus our attention on this strategic choice in Chapter 8, where we deal with HRM in the host-country context.

Second, what HR matters require central control and what can be delegated to subsidiary HR managers? The answer partly depends on organizational and administrative imperatives and the economic and political imperatives of the host location. For example, the desire for control and coordination may stress a geocentric approach to staffing that requires standardized policies to encourage equal treatment to all staff on international assignments (that is, an administrative imperative). Legal constraints, cost considerations and host-government directives may require compromises in terms of staffing (economic and political imperatives).

Scullion and Starkey[42] remark that there has been little empirical research into the corporate HR function's role and how it may change over time. As discussed in Chapter 2, as the firm internationalizes it is required to make structural and processual changes and we indicated ways in which the HR department may need to respond. We outlined Scullion and Starkey's finding from a study of 30 British-owned international companies where they identified centralized, decentralized and transition HR companies. The roles of the various HR departments in these three organizational categories reflect the structural differences. These are summarized in Table 3-2. As would be expected, there is a direct link between the structure of the company and the roles of the HR function. However, there was a common approach to the management of key executive staff across the three organizational types, suggesting the need for coordination and integration of international activities that, in turn, requires greater central control over key managerial staff.

A related aspect in terms of centralization and decentralization is the nature of the activities performed by the HR function. Table 3-2 indicates a primary concern of corporate HR departments to be able to deploy staff throughout the worldwide operations of the multinational and this is a major driver of centralization, whether supported by formal mechanisms or not. The 2002 PricewaterhouseCoopers survey mentioned earlier reported that 58 per cent of responding firms centralized international assignment transfers, 18 per cent devolved such responsibilities to regional headquarters and 14 per cent to business units. Some firms, however, were prepared to outsource the administrative activities associated with international transfers (12 per cent of North American firms compared with 7 per cent of European firms). Multinationals may also centralize training and development programs. For example, Motorola, a US multinational, has its own 'university'; Lufthansa, the German airline, and Ikea, the Swedish furniture retailer, have their own 'business schools'. Hiring of HCNs tends to be devolved to the local level given the need for adherence to local hiring practices.

Another driver is the level of sophistication within the firm regarding its international business operations generally. The more mature the firm, the more likely it has centralized those HR activities which it considers strategic. The position of the corporate HR function is also dependent on its profile within the top executive team. For many firms, despite the impact that international growth has on a firm's

	Various roles of corporate HR	**Table 3-2**

Centralized HR companies	Decentralized HR companies	Transition HR companies
• Large, well-resourced HR departments	• Small HR departments	• Medium-sized HR departments
• Key role management of all high-grade management positions worldwide	• Key role managing elite corporate managers	• Key role management and career development of senior managers and expatriates
• Key activities: planning international assignments and performance management globally, identifying high-potential staff	• Key activities: influencing operating units to support international assignments, supporting decentralized HR	• Key activities: persuading divisional managers to release key staff using informal and subtle methods, strategic staffing.

Source: Based on H. Scullion and K. Starkey, In Search of the Changing Role of the Corporate Human Resource Function in the International Firm, *International Journal of Human Resource Management*, Vol. 11, No. 6 (2000) pp. 1061–1081.

HR activities, the precise nature and extent of that impact on corporate performance are not well understood by many senior managers. Possible explanations are:

- HR managers only become involved in strategic decisions when there is a critical mass of expatriates to be managed.
- Senior management is more likely to recognize HR issues when international assignments become of significant strategic value, and therefore are more likely to leverage the required resources.
- There is often a considerable time lag before HR constraints on international expansion come to the attention of senior corporate management.
- As discussed in Chapter 1, a global perspective, through a broader view of issues, allows the development of more effective corporate policies. The need for a global perspective applies to staff in the corporate HR department, at the regional HR level and divisional and business units HR managers. HR managers could undertake international assignments themselves to gain appreciation of both global corporate and local unit concerns. The use of international assignments can be supplemented with frequent meetings of corporate and subsidiary HR managers. Smaller firms with limited resources may find it impossible to finance international assignments, but they may be able to identify other ways to orientate HR staff globally, such as an annual visit to key overseas subsidiaries.

In line with the above issues, Novicevic and Harvey[43] argue that corporate HR staff need to redefine their traditional role as bureaucratic administrators and become 'influencers' over areas of subsidiary practices, such as encouraging career ladders to assist in global staffing decisions and designing performance appraisal and compensation systems and policies that support lateral integration and informal communication. These types of activities, it is suggested, will enhance what these authors call homogenization of best practices while endeavouring to maintain specific capabilities and responsiveness at the local subsidiary level, thus ensuring the relevance of the corporate HR function. However, if the trend to devolve HR management activities to line managers continues, then the role of corporate HR may be reduced to the management of key international assignments, confirming in many people's minds that IHRM equals managing expatriates.

Summary

This chapter has expanded on the role of IHRM in sustaining international business operations. We have:

- Looked at the various approaches to staffing international operations – ethnocentric, polycentric, geocentric and regiocentric – examining their advantages and disadvantages and factors that may determine the choice of these options.
- Considered the reasons for using international assignments: position filling, management development and organization development.
- Discussed the various types of international assignments: short, extended and long-term (traditional); and non-standard forms such as commuter, rotational, contractual and virtual assignments.

- Examined the various roles of the expatriate: as an agent for direct control, as an agent for socialization, as network builders, as boundary spanners and as language nodes. These various roles of the expatriate help to explain why expatriates are utilized and illustrates why international assignments continue to be an important aspect of international business from the organization's perspective.

- Recognized that non-expatriates are also critical to international business operations. International business travelers present their own challenges, such as the effect of frequent absences on family and home life, the possible negative health effects and other stress factors. The management of such individuals, however, does not appear to fall within the domain of the HR department.

- Looked at the role of the corporate HR function as the firm grows internationally, building on sections from Chapters 1 and 2.

Discussion questions and exercises

1 Outline the main characteristics of the four approaches to international staffing.

2 What are the reasons for using international assignments?

3 How effective are expatriates in transferring knowledge and competences?

4 What are the positives and negatives associated with being an international business traveler?

5 As a newly appointed Project Manager of a research team, you consider that you will be able to manage the project virtually from your office in London, even though the other six members are located in Munich. This will solve your personal dilemma as your family do not want to be relocated. The project has a 6-month deadline. What factors should you need to consider in order to make this virtual assignment effective?

Further reading

O. Tregraskis, 2003. Learning Networks, Power and Legitimacy in Multinational Subsidiaries, *International Journal of Human Resource Management*, Vol. 14, No. 3, pp. 431–447.

I.M. Manev, 2003. The Managerial Network in a Multinational Enterprise and the Resource Profiles of Subsidiaries, *Journal of International Management*, Vol. 9, pp. 133–151.

D.E. Welch, V. Worm and M. Fenwick, 2003. Are Virtual Assignments Feasible? *Management International Review*, Special Issue 1, pp. 95–114.

A.W. Harzing, 2001. Of Bears, Bumble-Bees, and Spiders: the Role of Expatriates in Controlling Foreign Subsidiaries, *Journal of World Business*, Vol. 36, No. 4, pp. 366–379.

M. Janssens, 2001. Developing a Culturally Synergistic Approach to International Human Resource Management, *Journal of World Business*, Vol. 36, No. 4, pp. 429–450.

M. Novicevic and M. Harvey, 2001. The Changing Role of the Corporate HR Function in Global Organizations of the Twenty-first Century, *International Journal of Human Resource Management*, Vol. 12, No. 8, pp. 1251–1268.

H. Scullion and K. Starkey, 2000. In Search of the Changing Role of the Corporate Human Resource Function in the International Firm, *International Journal of Human Resource Management*, Vol. 11, No. 6, pp. 1061–1081.

R.S. DeFrank, R. Konopaske and J.M. Ivancevich, 2000. Executive Travel Stress: Perils of the Road Warrior, *Academy of Management Executive*, Vol. 14, No. 2, pp. 58–71.

Notes and references

1   H.V. Perlmutter, The Tortuous Evolution of the Multinational Corporation, *Columbia Journal of World Business*, Vol. 4, No. 1 (1969) pp. 9–18.

2   D.A. Heenan and H.V. Perlmutter, *Multinational Organization Development*, Reading, MA: Addison-Wesley, 1979.

3   J. Bonache, C. Brewster and V. Suutari, Expatriation: a Developing Research Agenda, *Thunderbird International Business Review*, Vol. 43, No. 1 (2001) pp. 3–20.

4   Y. Zeira, Management Development in Ethnocentric Multinational Corporations, *California Management Review*, Vol. 18, No. 4 (1976) pp. 34–42.

5   The Conference Board, *Managing Expatriates' Return*, Report No. 1148-96RR, 1997.

6   Electrolux, In-house magazine *Appliance*, E-26 (1995).

7   D. Welch, HRM Implications of Globalisation, *Journal of General Management*, Vol. 19, No. 4 (1994) pp. 52–68.

8   D.A. Heenan and H.V. Perlmutter, *Multinational Organization Development*, Reading, MA: Addison-Wesley, 1979.

9   A.J. Morrison, D.A. Ricks and K. Roth, Globalisation Versus Regionalisation: Which Way for the Multinational? *Organizational Dynamics*, Winter (1991) pp. 17–29.

10 R.D. Robinson, *International Business Management: a Guide to Decision Making*, 2nd edn, Hinsdale, IL: Dryden, 1978, p. 297.

11 J. Thornhill, Opportunities Blossom in the Wild East, *Financial Times*, 2 August (1996), Recruitment Section, p. I.

12 N. Boyacigiller, The Role of Expatriates in the Management of Interdependence, Complexity and Risk in Multinational Corporations, *Journal of International Business Studies*, Vol. 21, No. 3 (1990) pp. 357–381.

13 D.E. Welch, Determinants of International Human Resource Management Approaches and Activities: a Suggested Framework, *Journal of Management Studies*, Vol. 31, No. 2 (1994) pp. 139–164.

14 M. Richards, U.S. Multinational Staffing Practices and Implications for Subsidiary Performance in the U.K. and Thailand, *Thunderbird International Business Review*, Vol. 34, No. 2 (2001) pp. 225–242.

15 PricewaterhouseCoopers, *International Assignments: Global Policy and Practice Key Trends 2002*, PricewaterhouseCoopers, 2002.

16 K. Blassingame, 'C' Change Recommended for Expat. Management, *Employee Benefit News*, Vol. 15, No. 10 (2001) p. 12.

17 GMAC Global Relocation Services in Conjunction with US National Foreign Trade Council Inc. and SHRM Global Forum, *Global Relocation Trends: 2002 Survey Report*.

18 M.M.L. Wong, Internationalising Japanese Expatriate Managers, *Management Learning*, Vol. 32, No. 2 (2001) pp. 237–251.

19 A. Mendez, The Coordination of Globalised R&D Activities Through Project Teams Organization: an Exploratory Empirical Study, *Journal of World Business*, Vol. 38, No. 2 (2003) pp. 96–109.

20 PricewaterhouseCoopers, *Managing a Virtual World: International Non-standard Assignments, Policy and Practice*. PricewaterhouseCoopers Europe, 2000.

21 Ref. 20 p. 11.

22 D.E. Welch and L.S. Welch, Linking Operation Mode Diversity and IHRM, *International Journal of Human Resource Management*, Vol. 5, No. 4 (1994) pp. 911–926; M. Tahvanainen, Short-term International Assignments: Popular Yet Largely Unknown Way of Working Abroad, Working Paper W-352, Helsinki School of Economics.

23 D.E. Welch, V. Worm and M. Fenwick, Are Virtual Assignments Feasible? *Management International Review*, Special Issue 1 (2003) pp. 98.

24 For a literature review and discussion on the use of staff transfers as a control mechanism, see D. Welch, M. Fenwick and H. De Cieri, Staff Transfers as a Control Strategy: an Exploratory Study of Two Australian Organizations, *International Journal of Human Resource Management*, Vol. 5, No. 2 (1994) pp. 473–489.

25 A.-W. Harzing, Of Bears, Bumble Bees, and Spiders: the Role of Expatriates in Controlling Foreign Subsidiaries, *Journal of World Business*, Vol. 36, No. 4 (2001) pp. 366–379.

26 M.S. Fenwick, H.L. De Cieri and D.E. Welch, Cultural and Bureaucratic Control in MNEs: the Role of Expatriate Performance Management, *Management International Review*, Vol. 39, (1999) pp. 107–124.

27 Wal Around the World, *The Economist*, 8 December (2001), p. 60.

28 K. Goodall and J. Roberts, Only Connect: Teamwork in the Multinational, *Journal of World Business*, Vol. 38, No. 2 (2003) pp. 150–164.

29 D.M. Schweiger, T. Atamer and R. Calori, Transnational Project Teams and Networks: Making the Multinational More Effective, *Journal of World Business*, Vol. 38 (2003) pp. 127–140.

30 R. Marschan, D. Welch and L. Welch, Control in Less-hierarchical Multinationals: the Role of Personal Networks and Information Communication, *International Business Review*, Vol. 5, No. 2 (1996) pp. 1367–150.

31 J. Birkinshaw and N. Hood, Unleash Innovation in Foreign Subsidiaries, *Harvard Business Review*, March (2001) pp. 131–137.

32 K.Y. Au and J. Fukuda, Boundary Spanning Behaviours of Expatriates, *Journal of World Business*, Vol. 37 (2002) pp. 285–296.

33 R. Marschan-Piekkari, D. Welch and L. Welch, Adopting a Common Corporate Language: IHRM Implications, *International Journal of Human Resource Management*, Vol. 10, No. 3 (1999) pp. 377–390.

34 D.E. Welch and L.S. Welch, Using Personnel to Develop Networks: an Approach to Subsidiary Management, *International Business Review*, Vol. 2, No. 2 (1993).

35 Ref. 28, p. 159.

36 M.C. Bolino and D.C. Feldman, Increasing the Skill Utilization of Expatriates, *Human Resource Management*, Vol. 39, No. 4 (2000) pp. 367–379.

37 D. Welch, L. Welch and V. Worm, Just Passing Through: the International Business Traveller and Knowledge Transfer, Paper presented at the European International Business Academy Meeting, Copenhagen, 11–13 December 2003.

38 American Express, International Travellers Optimistic about Travel for 2003, press release, 9 October 2002; website accessed 19 May 2003.

39 H. Mintzberg, D. Dougherty, J. Jorgensen and F. Westley, Some Surprising Things About Collaboration – Knowing How People Connect Makes it Work Better, *Organizational Dynamics*, Vol. 25, No. 1 (1996) p. 62.

40 L.S. Welch, G.R.G. Benito, P.R. Silseth and T. Karlsen, Exploring Inward–Outward Linkages in Firms' Internationalisation: a Knowledge and Network Perspective, in *Network Knowledge in International Business*, ed. S. Lundan, Cheltenham: Edward Elgar, 2002, pp. 216–231.

41 R.S. DeFrank, R. Konopaske and J.M. Ivancevich, Executive Travel Stress: Perils of the Road Warrior, *Academy of Management Executive*, Vol. 14, No. 2 (2000) pp. 58–71.

42 H. Scullion and K. Starkey, In Search of the Changing Role of the Corporate Human Resource Function in the International Firm, *International Journal of Human Resource Management*, Vol. 11, No. 6 (2000) pp. 1061–1081.

43 M. Novicevic and M. Harvey, The Changing Role of the Corporate HR Function in Global Organizations of the Twenty-first Century, *International Journal of Human Resource Management*, Vol. 12, No. 8 (2001) pp. 1251–1268.

Managing and supporting international assignments

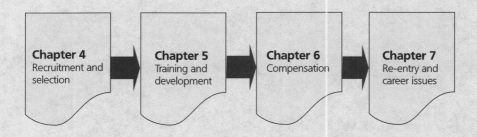

Chapter 4
Recruitment and selection

Chapter 5
Training and development

Chapter 6
Compensation

Chapter 7
Re-entry and career issues

Building on the three chapters in Part I, we further develop the central theme of the book: people are critical in sustaining international business operations. As international assignments are an important vehicle for multinationals to achieve competitive advantage and sustained international growth, Part II is concerned with the IHRM activities that manage and support international assignments.

Chapter 4 is concerned with recruiting and selecting personnel to support staffing of international business activities. The chapter starts with an examination of 'the global manager' and then covers various issues relating to expatriate failure, predictors of success, the factors that moderate performance on assignment, selection criteria and dual career couples and concludes with the question: are female expatriates different?

Chapter 5 explores the role of training and development. Pre-departure training and cultural awareness programs are the focus of this chapter, reflecting both its importance and dominance in the relevant literature. However, we also consider how the international assignment is, in itself, training. The developmental aspect of international assignments and its relation to individual career paths and the formation of international management teams, are also addressed.

Chapter 6 covers the various approaches and issues to compensation – or remuneration – of expatriates. The discussion of global pay systems highlights aspects at the local level – including international taxation and currency fluctuations – that affect individual compensation packages. The need simultaneously to build and maintain a unified, strategic pattern of compensation policies and practices is also discussed.

Chapter 7 concludes Part II. It concerns the re-entry process and repatriation of the individual back into the home operation. We deal with the process itself and explore the factors that affect readjustment into work and social settings. From the multinational's perspective, we consider the return on investment from international assignments and knowledge transfer. The discussion on re-entry illustrates how the various sections in Part II interact and influence the multinational's ability to attract and retain key personnel for international assignments.

Recruiting and selecting staff for international assignments.

Chapter objectives

In Part I, we demonstrated how people play a central role in sustaining international operations. As international assignments are an important vehicle for staffing, it is critical that they are managed effectively, and the expatriates are supported so that performance outcomes are achieved. The focus of this chapter, then, is on recruitment and selection activities in an international context. We will address the following issues:

- the myth of the global manager
- the debate surrounding expatriate failure
- factors moderating intent to stay or leave the international assignment
- selection criteria for international assignments
- dual-career couples
- are female expatriates different?

Introduction

Hiring and then deploying people to positions where they can perform effectively is a goal of most organizations, whether domestic or international. **Recruitment** is defined as searching for and obtaining potential job candidates in sufficient numbers and quality so that the organization can select the most appropriate people to fill its job needs. **Selection** is the process of gathering information for the purposes of evaluating and deciding who should be employed in particular jobs.[1] The major differences between domestic and international staffing are the firm's predisposition towards who should hold key positions in headquarters and subsidiaries (ethnocentric, polycentric, regiocentric and geocentric), the constraints imposed by host governments and the firm's ability to attract the right candidates. Further, as most expatriates are recruited internally rather than externally, persuading managers to release their best employees for international assignments is emerging as a key role for corporate HR.

In this chapter, we will explore the key issues surrounding international recruitment and selection, with a focus on selection criteria. Implicit in much of the discussion and research about selecting staff for international assignments is that there are common attributes shared by persons who have succeeded in operating in other cultural work environments – that is, the so-called global manager. Our discussion on this topic centers around four myths: that there is a universal approach to management; that all people can acquire appropriate behaviors; that there are common characteristics shared by global managers; and that there are no impediments to global staff mobility. We then consider various factors – such as expatriate failure, selection criteria, dual-career couples and gender – that impact on the multinational's ability to recruit and select high-caliber staff for deployment internationally.

For convenience, we will use the term 'multinational' throughout this chapter, but it is important to remember that the issues pertain variously to all internationalizing companies, regardless of size, industry, stage in internationalization, nationality of origin and geographical diversity. We continue to use the term expatriate to include all three categories: PCNs (parent-country nationals), TCNs (third-country nationals) and HCNs (host-country nationals) transferred into headquarters' operations, although much of the literature on expatriate selection deals only with PCNs.

Issues in staff selection

The myth of the global manager

Multinationals depend on being able to develop a pool of international operators from which they can draw as required, as we discussed in Chapter 3. Such individuals have been variously labeled 'international managers' or 'global managers'. The concept of a global manager appears to be based on the following myths or assumptions.

Myth 1: There is a universal approach to management.
This myth persists despite evidence from cross-cultural studies to the contrary, supported by reports of how many multinationals have blundered when trying to introduce home-based work practices into their foreign operations. The persistence of a belief in universal management may be evidence of a lingering ethnocentric attitude. However, as we discussed in Chapter 1 in relation to the convergence–divergence debate, work practices have, to a certain extent, converged through the transfer of ideas and 'best practice', supported by the global spread of education programs that reflect a common approach to management. Linked to this is the belief in the power of organizational culture as a moderator of cultural differences in the work setting. We will return to this aspect in Chapter 8, where we discuss standardization of work practices in the host context.

Myth 2: People can acquire multicultural adaptability and behaviors.
Some people can adopt culturally appropriate behaviors but that does not apply all the time in all cultural settings. It depends, as we will examine later, on the individual's reaction to a particular cultural environment,[2] as it is not always easy to put into

practice what one knows is the right way to behave. Some individuals have good effectiveness and coping skills.[3] Effectiveness skills are defined as the ability to translate successfully the managerial or technical skills into the foreign environment, whereas coping skills enable the person to become reasonably comfortable, or at least survive, in a foreign environment. Those who are able to function adequately in other cultural settings may be regarded as having good effectiveness and coping skills. As we examine later in this chapter, cultural adjustment has been linked to expatriate performance and influences how international assignments are perceived.

Myth 3: There are common characteristics shared by successful international managers. The body of literature on expatriate selection tends to reflect this approach, as we will explore in the next section. It is possible to identify predictors of success, in that a person who has certain characteristics, traits and experience is more likely to perform effectively in foreign environments than a person who does not share this profile. However, this has to be countered by other factors involved – not just in the selection process, but also in the way the person responds to the foreign location. It is also unclear how the identified predictors of success should be measured.

Myth 4: There are no impediments to mobility. We have mentioned that particularly large multinationals are endeavoring to develop and exploit an internal labour market from which expatriates – international managers – can be drawn. As Forster[4] points out, firms may have become more global in their operations but their people have not. The barriers to furthering a geocentric staffing policy – staff availability, time and cost constraints and host government requirements – reveal how the multinational's ability to deploy what may be the best person into a particular position can be curtailed. That some multinationals are experimenting with alternatives such as the virtual assignment is indicative of this constraint.

Compounding the above myths is the way in which the term 'global manager' is sometimes used to describe a person who has a global 'mindset', although often international experience is a prerequisite for building the global perspective required. Baruch[5] argues that there is no consistent way to characterize a global manager. He suggests that the basic qualities commonly listed – intelligence, motivation, adaptability and entrepreneurship – are the same requirements for any successful manager today.

Profile of an expatriate

Table 4-1 shows the current profile of an expatriate, drawn from results of a 2002 survey of 181 multinationals worldwide. Responding firms were operating in more than 130 countries, although the majority (77 per cent) were headquartered in the USA.

Given the important roles commonly assigned to expatriates, it is logical to assume that MNEs take great care in their selection process. What is evident from the now considerable literature on the topic is that the selection of expatriates is complex. Indeed, predicting future performance potential when hiring or promoting staff is challenging at the best of times, but operating in foreign environments certainly adds another level of uncertainty. For this reason, before we take a critical look at criteria for expatriate selection, we should consider the current debate surrounding expatriate non-performance.

Expatriate failure

There are three questions related to failure: its definition, the magnitude of the phenomenon and the costs associated with failure. We shall treat these separately before examining the reasons attributed to expatriate failure and the link to selection criteria.

What do we mean by expatriate failure?   The term expatriate failure has been defined as the premature return of an expatriate (that is, a return home before the period of assignment is completed). In such a case, an expatriate failure represents a selection error, often compounded by ineffective expatriate management policies. Lately, there has been some discussion in the literature about the usefulness of defining expatriate failure so narrowly. An expatriate may be ineffective and poorly adjusted yet, if not recalled, the person will not be considered a failure. Because of an inability either to handle the new responsibilities effectively or to adjust to the country of assignment, performance levels may be diminished. These results will not be immediately apparent but can have long-term negative consequences in terms of subsidiary performance. However, as the expatriate remains for the duration of the assignment, to all intents and purposes, the assignment will have been considered a success.

Thus, the premature return rate is not a perfect measure of success or failure, and may underestimate the problem. For example, in his study of 36 British-based firms, Forster[6] used the broadest definition of failure (that is, including underperformance and retention upon completion of the assignment). Forster found that a high proportion of staff do struggle to cope with their overseas assignments, concluding:

> If we accept that a broader definition of EFRs [expatriate failure rates] is warranted, then it can be argued that the actual figure of those who are 'failing' on IAs [international assignments] could be somewhere between 8 and 28 per cent of UK expatriates and their partners.

Table 4-1	Current expatriate profile

Category	PCN (42%)	HCN (16%) TCN (42%)
Gender	Male (82%)	Female (18%)
Age (years)	30–49 (60%)	20–29 (17%)
Marital status	Married (65%)	Single (26%)
		Partner (9%)
Accompanied by	Spouse (86%)	Children (59%)
Duration	1–3 years (52%)	Short-term (9%)
Location	Within Europe (35%)	Within Asia-Pacific (24%)
Primary reason	Fill a position	
Prior international experience	30%	

Source: Based on data from *Global Relocation Trends: 2002 Survey Report*, GMAC Global Relocation Services, National Foreign Trade Council and SHRM Global Forum, GMAC-GRS, 2003.

Support for broadening the definition of expatriate failure comes from a 1997/98 Price Waterhouse[7] study of international assignment policy and practice among European multinationals (including US subsidiaries). Unlike previous surveys of this kind, the study added 'underperformance' to its definition of assignment failure and found:

> The rates for employees currently underperforming on assignment as a result of difficulties in adapting to their cultural surroundings are even higher. 29% of companies report a rate in excess of one in twenty, with 7% reporting a rate over one in ten.

What is the magnitude of the phenomenon we call expatriate failure?   Harzing[8] questioned the reported failure rates in the US literature, claiming that there is 'almost no empirical foundation for the existence of high failure rates when measured as premature re-entry'. She further argued that there has not been any reliable large-scale empirical work on this subject for more than 15 years. As Harzing rightly points out, Tung's 1981 article[9] could be said to have started the discussion about the inability of US nationals to handle an international assignment. Tung's results[9-11] suggested that expatriate failure was of more concern to US firms: 24 per cent of the US firms in her sample ($n = 80$) had recall rates below 10 per cent, compared with 59 per cent of the West European ($n = 29$) and 76 per cent of the Japanese firms ($n = 35$) reporting recall rates of less than 5 per cent. Later studies[12-14] appear to confirm Tung's European results in terms of expatriate failure. However, many studies that explore expatriate failure and expatriate adjustment persist in quoting high US rates of failure, variously reporting it as falling between 30 and 50 per cent and even higher.

When we delve further into this issue to establish how large the problem actually is, one finds a suggestion of a declining rate. Recent evidence can be gained from two global surveys, conducted in 2002. The first was a survey of 300 multinationals (46 per cent North American, 28 per cent European and 9 per cent UK) from a wide range of industries by US-based consulting firm ORC Worldwide.[15] They report that almost 56 per cent of respondents **did not know** the return rate of their expatriates. Those who keep records indicated, on average, that less than 10 per cent of their international assignments ended in early recall. The second survey by GMAC Global Relocation Services (GMAC-GRS) mentioned earlier asked responding firms to indicate their attrition rate – that is, expatriate turnover, including early recall from an international assignment, and upon completion of the assignment. Again, we find that some firms (39 per cent) could not answer, as they **did not have the figures**. Those that did have the information indicated failure rates of around 17 per cent (which appears to be an average for all the firms in the survey). It would have been useful to find out why a majority of the responding firms in these two surveys did not keep records on assignment failures. Is it because it is not an issue?

Respondents in the ORC Worldwide survey were also asked to define a failed assignment. Some 72 per cent defined it as 'early return of the expatriate'. The other definitions were 'unmet business objectives' (71 per cent); 'problems at assignment location' (49 per cent); and 'unmet career development objectives' (32 per cent). It would appear that multinationals are recognizing that there are many aspects to a failed assignment, although it is not clear from the report if responding firms were separating out underperformance from early recall. Unmet business objectives, problems at assignment location and unmet career development may be reasons for early recall rather than a definition.

From the above discussion, though, we can draw several conclusions:

1 Broadening the definition of expatriate failure beyond that of premature return is warranted. Following up broad surveys with interviews with responding firms may assist in this.

2 Regardless of the definition or precise amount of 'failure', its very exposure as a problem has broadened the issue to demonstrate the complexity of international assignments. In fact, one could argue that the so-called persistent myth of high US expatriate failure rates has been a positive element in terms of the attention that has subsequently been directed towards expatriation practices. It has certainly provoked considerable research attention into the causes of expatriate failure.

3 The evidence about expatriate failure rates is somewhat inconclusive. Recent studies suggest that high failure rates reported in the 1980s have not persisted for all nationalities. Although recent reports do not break results down into nationality groups, US firms form the largest group in these surveys. The European studies reported above were conducted at various intervals since Tung's original study and do not include the same countries. Further, non-US researchers have been reporting from regional or single country perspectives (see, for example, Björkman and Gertsen,[16] who found expatriate failure rates of less than 5 per cent for Nordic firms; Dowling and Welch[17] reported similar results for Australian firms).

IHRM in Action Case 4-1

Happy to be going home

A US family, from the mid-west, was posted to Melbourne, Australia. The expatriate's role was to assist the Australian subsidiary improve its quality control and supplier relationships. Chuck was placed in charge of the purchasing department. After 12 months, he had successfully established good links with the company's key component suppliers and was in the process of arranging joint company quality training programs with these suppliers to ensure the newly-instigated *just-in-time* inventory procedure was on a sound footing. Chuck was enjoying his new role. Meanwhile, his 10-year-old daughter was finding it difficult to make friends in the expensive private school the company had arranged for her to attend. His wife was also finding life in Australia somewhat hard to cope with. 'On the surface, it seems so much like home, but Australians are not at all the same as us Americans, and some people make disparaging remarks about us. They use terms such as 'Yanks'. I miss not being able to find familiar things, such as brownie mix, in the supermarket.' Both wife and daughter were very happy when circumstances provided an acceptable reason for an early end to Chuck's assignment. His elderly mother suffered a bad fall, and there were no other family members to take care of her. The family was repatriated after 14 months into a 3-year assignment. The expatriate was replaced by another PCN.

Source: Based on an interview with the person concerned. Names have been changed to protect identities.

4 The above studies tend not to differentiate between types of expatriate assignments, the level of 'international' maturity[18] or firm size – factors that may influence failure in its broadest sense.

5 It may be that companies operating internationally have since become more aware of the problems associated with expatriate failure and have learned how to avoid them. That is, multinationals have become more sophisticated in their approach to IHRM activities. Benchmarking against other firms may have assisted in the development of an awareness of international assignment issues.

6 One has to be careful in making assumptions, given that a large number of firms do not keep the necessary records, so we are only getting a partial picture.

What are the costs of failure?   These can be both **direct** and **indirect**. Direct costs include airfares and associated relocation expenses and salary and training. The precise amount varies according to the level of the position concerned, country of destination, exchange rates and whether the 'failed' manager is replaced by another expatriate. The 'invisible' or indirect costs are harder to quantify in money terms but can prove to be more expensive for the company. Many expatriate positions involve contact with host government officials and key clients. Failure at this level may result in loss of market share, difficulties with host-government officials and demands that expatriates be replaced with HCNs (thus affecting the multinational's general staffing approach). The possible effect on local staff is also an indirect cost factor, since morale and productivity could suffer.[19]

Failure also, of course, has an effect on the expatriate concerned, who may lose self-esteem, self-confidence and prestige among peers.[20] Future performance may be marked by decreased motivation, lack of promotional opportunities or even increased productivity to compensate for the failure. Finally, the expatriate's family relationships may be threatened. These are additional costs to organizations that are often overlooked. The IHRM In Action Case 4-1 illustrates some of the factors involved in expatriate failure.

Factors moderating performance

Naturally, the debate about the degree to which expatriate failure occurs has been accompanied by investigation and speculation about why failure occurs. Expatriates tend to have a higher profile, so reducing the rate of incidence is of some strategic importance as multinationals continue to rely on expatriates and therefore wish to encourage mobility. Consequently, there has been considerable research that has attempted to identify factors that may moderate performance and affect the decision to stay or leave the international assignment. The primary intention has been to link reasons for early recall to predictors of success and thereby generate selection criteria that may assist multinationals in their staffing decisions. Although the focus has predominately been on cross-cultural adjustment, other factors have been identified, as shown in Figure 4-1. We will base our examination of the issue around this figure.

Inability to adjust to the foreign culture

This factor has been a consistent reason given for expatriate failure, and has been the subject of considerable interest in the past 10 years at least. Again, we must acknowledge the contribution of Tung's study[10] in providing the impetus for this interest. She found national differences in the responses between the US and Japanese firms. Asked to rank reasons for failure in descending order of importance, US firms ranked 'inability of the spouse to adjust' as the most important, whereas this was ranked fifth for the Japanese firms. For the European firms, 'inability of the spouse to adjust' was the only consistent response provided.

Tung[10] noted that the relatively lower ranking of 'inability of spouse to adjust' by Japanese respondents is not surprising, given the role and status to which Japanese society relegates the spouse. However, other social factors may contribute to this finding. Because of the competitive nature of the Japanese education system, the spouse commonly opts to remain in Japan with the children, particularly where male offspring are concerned. The Japanese word for these unaccompanied male expatriates is *tanshin funin* or bachelors-in-exile.[21] Thus, in many cases, the spouse is not a factor in expatriate failure. However, one should not assume that adjustment is not a problem for the Japanese. A tragic case that received front-page news treatment in Melbourne, Australia, involved a Japanese spouse.[22] Police treated the incident as an apparent suicide: the unhappy, home-sick woman drove her car, containing herself and her 4-year-old son, off a pier into the water, drowning both. An extreme, terrible event, it serves to remind us that the global movement of staff may produce severe adjustment problems for some families.

Unlike the debate around the magnitude of the problem, research over the past 20 years has shown a consistent ranking of 'inability of the spouse/partner/family' as a primary cause of early recall. While the data collected do not lend themselves to comparative tables, the ORC Worldwide 2002 and GMAC-GRS 2002 global surveys mentioned above reported that difficulties associated with the international assignment were:

- spouse/partner dissatisfaction
- inability to adapt
- difficulties with family adjustment in the new location
- difficulties associated with different management styles

Figure 4-1	International assignments: factors moderating performance

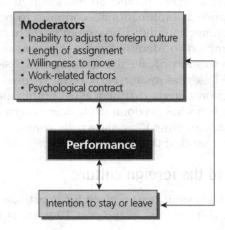

- culture and language difficulties
- issues associated with the accompanying partner's career development.

Another survey conducted in 2000 on global relocation trends,[23] although not indicating levels of expatriate failure, reported that when failure occurred, it was prompted by issues related to partner satisfaction, family concerns and inability to adapt. The persistence of these reasons for failure over the two decades since Tung's findings were published, despite company programs to try to alleviate the problem, indicates how difficult an international assignment can be for some. It certainly explains why so much attention has been given to expatriate adjustment and confirms the importance of the selection process.

Although there is limited evidence (at least readily accessible and in English) regarding expatriate experiences from other Asian countries, accounts indicate that expatriates from these countries may face similar adjustment problems. For example, Selmer *et al.*[24] report that spouses and children of Chinese expatriates in Hong Kong were normally not permitted to accompany the expatriates. While adjustment was not the focus of this study, the authors found that most of the respondents would have liked to have had their family with them and conclude that the precarious situation of the families was not conducive to the pursuit of an international career.

The process of adjustment

The dilemma is that adjustment to a foreign culture is multifaceted and individuals vary in terms of their reaction and coping behaviors. The concept of an adjustment cycle or curve, depicted in Figure 4-2, is helpful in demonstrating the typical phases that may be encountered during cultural adjustment. The curve (sometimes referred to as the U-Curve) is based on psychological reactions to the assignment and comprises certain phases.[25]

Phase 1 commences with reactions prior to the assignment – the expatriate may experience a range of positive and negative emotions such as excitement, anxiety,

---

The phases of cultural adjustment   **Figure 4-2**

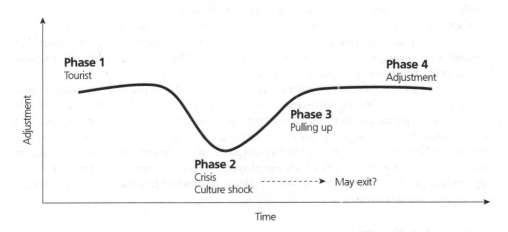

Source: Adapted from H. De Cieri, P.J. Dowling and K.F. Taylor, 'The Psychological Impact of Expatriate Relocation on Partners', *International Journal of Human Resource Management*, Vol. 2, No. 3 (1991) p. 380.

fear of the unknown or a sense of adventure. There can be an upswing of mood upon arrival in the assignment country that produces what has been referred to as the 'honeymoon' or 'tourist' phase. Then, as the novelty wears off, realities of everyday life in the foreign location begin to intrude, homesickness sets in and a downswing may commence – a feeling that 'the party is over'[26,27] – which can create negative appraisals of the situation and the location leading to a period of crisis – **Phase 2**. This can be a critical time and how the individual copes with the psychological adjustment at this phase has an important outcome in terms of success or failure. There is a suggestion that 'failure as an early recall' may be triggered at this point (indicated by the dotted arrow in Figure 4-2). Once past this crisis point, as the expatriate comes to terms with the demands of the new environment, there is a pulling up – **Phase 3** – as the person begins to adjust to the new environment. This levels off over time to what has been described as healthy recovery – **Phase 4**.

However, when considering the above U-Curve, one should remember the following points:

- The U-Curve is **not** normative. Some people do not experience this U-Curve. Individuals will differ in their reactions to the foreign location.

- The time period involved varies and there is no conclusive statistical support for the various phases. Black and Mendenhall[25] point out that the U-Curve describes these phases but does not explain how and why people move through the various phases.

- There may be other critical points during the assignment – beyond Phase 4 – that may produce downturns, negative reactions and upswings (that is, a cyclical wave rather than a U-Curve).

- As we will discuss in Chapter 7, the return home after completion of the assignment may require some psychological adjustment.

Despite these limitations, however, expatriates often relate experiencing these phases and awareness of the psychological adjustment process can assist the expatriate in adopting positive coping behaviors. It should also be noted that family members experience the phases differently, and do not necessarily move through the various phases at the same time as each other. How accompanying family members handle cultural adjustment is important, as there can be a spill-over effect – an unhappy spouse may affect the expatriate's ability to adjust and thus impact on performance. For example, in their study of American managers in Japan, Korea, Taiwan and Hong Kong, Black and Stephens[28] found a high correlation between spouse and expatriate adjustment.

Companies can assist in the cultural adjustment of the expatriate and employee. Recognizing that cultural adjustment is a major problem when bringing HCNs (including Americans) into its home operations, the Norwegian multinational Norsk Hydro has developed a family mentoring program. Supervised by Corporate Expatriate Services staff, Norsk Hydro employees volunteer to 'adopt' a visiting family. The volunteers are generally employees who have been working abroad as expatriates and therefore have an understanding of what it is like to move a family unit into another country.

Length of assignment

There is some evidence that length of assignment does contribute to adjustment and performance. For example, the average assignment for Japanese firms is

4–5 years, compared with 2–3 years for American firms. This longer assignment allows the expatriate more time to adjust to the foreign situation.[10] Also, Japanese firms do not expect the expatriate to perform up to full capacity until the third year; the first year of the foreign assignment is seen mainly as a period of adjustment to the foreign environment.

Willingness to move

The argument here is that a person who is a reluctant expatriate or accompanied by reluctant family members is more prone to interpret negatively events and situations encountered in the new environment. In their survey of 405 US managers and their spouses/partners, Brett and Stroh[29] found a significant causal relationship between the manager and the spouse's willingness to move. They conclude that managers who are most ready for international relocations are those whose spouses are also supportive of that move – a not surprising finding. Other studies support the importance of a positive outlook. For example, Hamill[13] reported that the reasons for lower British expatriate failure rates were that British managers were more internationally mobile than US managers and that perhaps British companies had developed more effective expatriate policies. Welch[30] notes that the respondents in her study perceived an expatriate posting as a desirable appointment – an opportunity to travel and live overseas – leading to a positive outlook on the foreign assignment. Willingness to relocate as a predictor of success should, however, include family members. It is also associated with the desirability of the location of the international assignment. Some countries are deemed more desirable than others.

Work environment-related factors

Gregersen and Black[31] studied 220 American expatriates in four Pacific Rim countries. They found a positive correlation between what they term 'intent to stay in the overseas assignment' and the PCN's commitment to the local company, adjustment to interaction with HCNs and adjustment to general living conditions. Adjustment to the work role itself however, was negatively associated with 'intent to stay'. Support for these factors as moderators has come from a study by Shaffer *et al.*[32] of expatriates working in 10 US multinationals. However, Bolino and Feldman[33] extended this to include skills utilization and commitment to the organization. Their study of 268 expatriates from six Fortune 500 companies found that effective skill utilization was significantly related to job satisfaction, organization commitment and intent to finish the international assignment.

Job autonomy is also a powerful factor influencing expatriate turnover.[34] Another moderator is the perceived level of organizational support – both from home and from the host unit.[35] Further, once the expatriate has mastered, or nearly completed, the assigned work, other factors may surface and assume relative importance. For instance, if the work becomes less demanding and no longer so time consuming, the expatriate may have time to pay more attention to negative cross-cultural experiences that the family is encountering. These negative experiences can become distorted when combined with lack of challenge at work and thus sow seeds for early recall, or underperformance.

The employment relationship[36]

Another moderating factor can be the employment relationship between the expatriate and the multinational. Figure 4-3 depicts the two elements that comprise the employment relationship between employer and employee. The nature of this relationship may be viewed as a continuum. At one end is the relational contract, characterized by broad, open-ended and long-term obligations based not only on exchanges around monetizable elements (pay for service, etc.), but also on socio-emotional elements (such as loyalty and support). At the other end is the transactional contract, comprising specific short-term monetized obligations.[37]

The *condition* or state of the psychological contract, shown as the horizontal axis in Figure 4-3, is regarded as a regulator of the employment relationship over time.[37,38] The psychological contract refers to an employee's belief regarding reciprocal obligations between the person and the employing organization. Intactness may be regarded as the positive side of the psychological contract. The employee considers that there has been fair treatment, reciprocal trust and both parties have 'delivered on the deal', thus creating a perception of balance between what the employee has contributed and the inducements proffered by the employer. Violation is the emotional and affective state brought about by a belief that the organization has not fulfilled its obligations.[39,40] Unspoken expectations about behaviors and attitudes that may predate the current work situation, along with feelings about trust and loyalty, are aspects of the psychological contract. Shifts along the relational–transactional continuum may occur owing to the changes in the condition of the psychological contract. As Figure 4-3 attempts to demonstrate, perceived changes in treatment, or unmet expectations, can produce movement between intactness and violation. This, in turn, will move a person along the transactional–relational continuum, affecting the nature of the employment relationship.

Guest's concept[39] of the content of the psychological contract, with its components of fairness, trust and delivery of the deal, is useful in explaining the

| Figure 4-3 | The dynamics of the employment relationship |

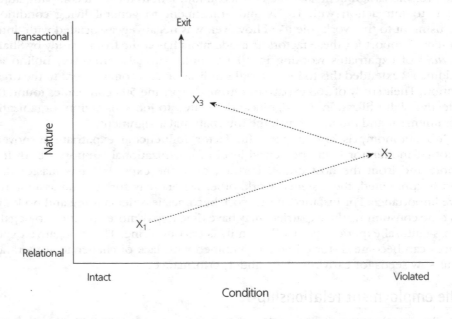

Source: D. Welch, Globalisation of Staff Movements: Beyond Cultural Adjustment, *Management International Review*, Vol. 43, No. 2 (2002) p. 156. Reproduced with permission.

dynamic shifts that occur along both continua in Figure 4-3. For example, Birgita, a long-serving employee, may have an intact relational contract (position X_1 in Figure 4-3) with a multinational until it restructures and widespread downsizing results in dismissal of members of her cohort of senior managers. A cognitive evaluation of the content of the psychological contract may produce a feeling of betrayal of trust and unfairness – loyalty to the company over many years has been overlooked. This leads to a perception of psychological contract violation and prompts a reassessment that results in movement along the relational–transactional continuum (position X_2 in Figure 4-3). The movement along both these axes will be determined by the intensity of feelings of violation and betrayal.

Suppose Birgita subsequently agrees to undertake an international assignment. As a result of the cognitive reassessment, negotiations concerning terms and conditions center more strongly on the transactional component, with emphasis on monetary compensation and a redundancy package should a suitable position not be available upon repatriation. When the assignment is completed, Birgita decides that the multinational has 'delivered on the deal' during the assignment, and that she has performed to the terms of the contract. This more positive assessment of the condition and nature of the relationship will prompt a movement back along the axes, although it may not result in a positive reassessment of the **nature** of the relationship, despite a change in the **condition** of the psychological contract causing a shift towards intactness (position X_3 in Figure 4-3). Shifts along both axes could be wave-like or a zigzag, although we depict them here as linear.

It would seem that the condition of the psychological contract acts as a regulator of the employment relationship over time. Movements between relational–transactional and intactness–violation are likely to affect the **quality** of the employment relationship that, in turn, influences the decision to stay or to exit the organization – which, of course, is of interest in terms of explaining reasons for expatriate failure and underperformance.

The two-by-two matrix in Figure 4-4 depicts an individual's likelihood of exiting based on an assessment of the combination of the nature, condition and quality of two factors: nature of the employment relationship and the condition of the psychological contract. The probability of exit is highest if the individual perceives that the psychological contract has been violated and considers the nature of the employment relationship as transactional rather than relational (Quadrant 4). Conversely, an individual in Quadrant 2 (relational–intact) is more likely to stay. Quadrant 3 indicates that, although the employment relationship is more relational than transactional, a perception of violation may provoke the individual to leave. The likelihood of exit is lower than in Quadrant 4, but may be higher than in Quadrant 1, where the condition of the psychological contract is intact, but the employment relationship is more transactional.

The question marks in Quadrants 1 and 3 in Figure 4-4 suggest consideration of exit. Whether the individual does exit appears to be related to another construct: **organizational commitment**. Allen and Meyer[41] regard the commitment construct as comprising three dimensions:

- The affective component – the employee's emotional attachment to, identification with and involvement in, the organization.

- The continuance component – the employee's commitment based on assessed costs associated with exiting the organization.

- The normative component – which refers to the employee's feelings of obligation to remain.

Figure 4-4   Likelihood of exit

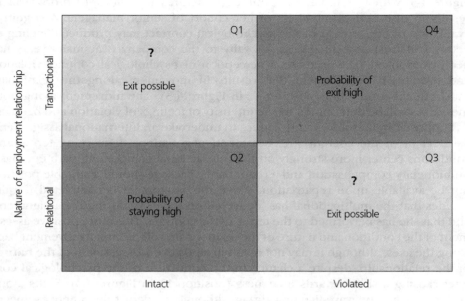

Source: D. Welch, Globalisation of Staff Movements: Beyond Cultural Adjustment, *Management International Review*, Vol. 43, No. 2 (2002) p. 158. Reproduced with permission.

The link between organizational commitment and the psychological contract would appear to be trust. As Morrison[42] explains: 'Reliability in individuals and organizations makes them credible. Credibility generates loyalty. Predictability, reliability, credibility, loyalty and trust all reinforce each other.'

Our hypothetical employee, Birgita, in the above example may have moved back towards the relational end of the continuum in Figure 4-3 (X_3) but the initial violation, involving a sense of betrayal of trust, is likely to have lowered her affective and normative components of commitment. Her tenure with the organization – continuance commitment – will be based on conditional trust: a sense of delivery of the negotiated deal this time, but the previous violation has raised doubts about future deals and trustworthiness and exiting the organisation is a considered possibility. In terms of the matrix in Figure 4-4, we can position Birgita in Quadrant 1: transactional–intact. Continuance commitment, therefore, may be the moderating variable, explaining why exit is less likely to occur in Quadrants 1 and 3 than in Quadrant 4. Of course, continuance commitment may depend also on potential opportunities to exit the organization.

What is the connection between the employment relationship, international assignment experience and expatriate failure?

● The nature, location and duration of the international assignment has the capacity to generate intense, individual reactions to perceived violations of the psychological contract.

● Given the nature of an international assignment, expatriates will have broad, elaborate, employment relationships, with greater emphasis on its relational nature.

- Expectations and promises underpin the psychological contract. When accepting an international assignment, an expatriate forms expectations regarding factors such as career-related outcomes, level of organizational support during the international assignment particularly to the accompanying family members and the position and length of the international assignment. These expectations may have been explicitly formed based on discussions with organizational representatives such as HR personnel or implicitly through perceptions based on company rhetoric.

- Regardless of the basis on which they are derived, whether real or perceived, expectations influence the content of the psychological contract in that the expatriate trusts that the organization will act fairly and in good faith when 'delivering on the deal'. They are important factors given the interruption to the lives of accompanying family members in addition to the expatriate's current career path, as we will discuss in Chapter 7. The sending organization also has expectations in a number of areas, for example commitment, performance, and satisfactory completion of the international assignment.

- Expectations provide the backdrop for the international assignment, making it a volatile situation especially as agents of the organization (such as the HR manager) are often unaware of what other agents have promised. Line managers, for example, may have encouraged the expatriate to accept the assignment on career path grounds, although such a message is not part of the formal 'deal' in the explicit international assignment contract.

- Promises will reinforce expectations, particularly those of level of organizational support to the expatriate and the accompanying family members. As we discuss later in this chapter, with the increase in dual-career couples, it is becoming common practice for companies to agree to assist the accompanying spouse/partner to find work in the foreign country. If this assistance does not eventuate, the unmet expectations can prompt cognition of a breach of contract, even violation.

- In one of the few studies that examine this issue, Guzzo et al.[43] found that expatriates' subjective perception of insufficiency in the support given while on assignment did influence their intention to quit the foreign assignment. Intention to leave the organization was found to be related to expatriates' perceived level of family-oriented support.

- The international assignment may commence with a high relational contract but it is not necessarily static. As the assignment progresses, situations such as culture shock, schooling concerns and illness are likely to cause frequent reassessment of the employment relationship.

- Where there is perceived violation, there may be a shift towards the transactional, with the person resolving to abide by the terms of the written contract (stay for the agreed period of time) but not be prepared to deliver beyond that – suggesting a link to performance.

- Incongruence between the perceptions of the parties to the contract arises partly because the evaluation of the psychological contract occurs at specific points in time, not when the agreement is originally formed.

- Highly mobile and effective international staff are likely to have strong commitment and loyalty to the multinational, but this would be accompanied by even greater emphasis on the relational and social elements of the psychological contract than that of single-assignment expatriates, making this group of strategically valuable employees extremely susceptible to perception of contract violation. In addition, they are likely to have exit options, as they are somewhat of a scarce resource and therefore are attractive to competitors.

Selection criteria

We now have a fuller understanding of the phenomenon called expatriate failure and the multifaceted nature of international assignments and why developing appropriate selection criteria has become a critical IHRM issue. Indeed, the 2002 GMAC-GRS survey found that locating suitable candidates is the top relocation challenge facing companies. It should be noted that selection is a two-way process between the individual and the organization. A prospective candidate may reject the expatriate assignment, either for individual reasons, such as family considerations, or for situational factors, such as the perceived toughness of a particular culture.

It is a challenge for those responsible for selecting staff for international assignments to determine appropriate selection criteria. Figure 4-5 illustrates the factors involved in expatriate selection, both in terms of the individual and the specifics of the situation concerned. It should be noted that these factors are inter-related. We base the following discussion around this figure.

Technical ability

Naturally, the person's ability to perform the required tasks is an important consideration. Technical and managerial skills are therefore an essential criterion. Indeed, research findings consistently indicate that multinationals place heavy reliance on relevant technical skills during the expatriate selection process.[44] For example, the ORC Worldwide 2002 survey mentioned earlier found that 72 per cent of responding firms selected assignees on the basis of skills or competencies for the

---

Figure 4-5   Factors in expatriate selection

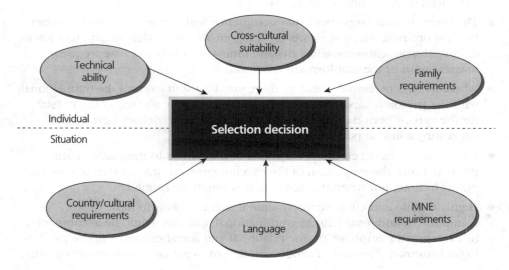

job. This is not surprising given that position filling is the most common reason for an international assignment. Reinforcing the emphasis on technical skills is the relative ease with which the multinational may assess the potential candidate's potential, as technical and managerial competence can be determined on the basis of past performance. Since expatriates are predominantly internal recruits, personnel evaluation records can be examined and checked with the candidate's past and present superiors. The dilemma, though, is that past performance may have little or no bearing on one's ability to achieve a task in a foreign cultural environment.

One should note here that technical ability (or lack thereof) does not emerge as a critical precursor to 'failure'. However, as discussed above, job-related aspects may be a component in the expatriate's intention to stay in the foreign location, or with the firm upon return home after successful completion of the assignment. The nature of the job itself (the situation in Figure 4-5) may counter the individual's technical ability to do the job, or interact with other factors to cause under-performance, even early recall. Given the role of expatriates in competence transfer, as we discussed in Chapter 3, technical skills are critical, but success depends on how the individual handles the situation. As a training officer in the Finnish multinational Kone Elevators[45] admitted:

> The difficulty in sending such persons abroad is that technical knowledge is not necessarily transferred in an efficient way. If the technical person concentrates too much on the project itself, stays for a short period of time and does not interact enough with local staff, the competence level of local personnel does not increase.

Cross-cultural suitability

As we have already discussed, the cultural environment in which expatriates operate is an important factor in determining successful performance. Apart from the obvious technical ability and managerial skills, expatriates require cross-cultural abilities that enable the person to operate in a new environment. There appears to be consensus that desirable attributes should include cultural empathy, adaptability, diplomacy, language ability, positive attitude, emotional stability and maturity. The research literature (especially the US literature) refers to 'the big five' personality characteristics: extroversion, agreeableness, conscientiousness, emotional stability and openness or intellect.[46]

In practice, although inter-cultural competence is recognized as important, it is difficult to precisely define what this comprises, let alone assess a candidate's suitability in this regard. One has to take into consideration aspects such as the individual's personality, attitude to foreigners and ability to relate to people from another cultural group. Multinationals may indicate that, for example, relational abilities are an important expatriate selection criterion, but few will assess a candidate's relational ability through a formal procedure such as judgment by senior managers or psychological tests. As we will discuss shortly, testing procedures are not necessarily the answer.

Family requirements

The contribution that the family, particularly the spouse, makes to the success of the overseas assignment is now well documented, as we mentioned above in relation to the impact of the accompanying spouse/partner on early return. Despite the importance of the accompanying spouse/partner, as Shaffer and

Harrison[47] point out, the focus has been on the expatriate. From the multinational's perspective, expatriate performance in the host location is the important factor. However, the interaction between expatriate, spouse/partner and family members' various adjustment experiences is now well documented.

It should be pointed out that the spouse (or accompanying partner) carries a heavy burden. Upon arrival in the country of assignment, the responsibility for settling the family into its new home falls on the spouse, who may have left behind a career, along with friends and social support networks (particularly relatives). Employment of servants may be expected – an experience for which Westerners from developed countries are seldom prepared. It is often not possible for the spouse/partner to work in the country of assignment. The well-being and education of the children also concern the spouse. Although the majority of spouses are female, accompanying male spouses/partners face similar problems of adjustment.[48] In fact, when one adds cultural adjustment problems to such a situation, it is perhaps not so surprising to find that some couples seek to return home prematurely.

Despite studies that emphasize the link between the favorable opinion of the spouse to the international assignment and expatriate adjustment, companies appear reluctant to include the spouse/partner in the selection process, treating it in a peripheral way. As a survey by Price Waterhouse[49] found:

> Compared to our 1995 survey, the number of companies which routinely interview an employee's spouse or partner as part of the selection process has increased slightly, from 9% to 11%. However, overall, fewer companies involve the spouse or partner in the selection process under any circumstances, rising from half in 1995 to two-thirds currently. Of the companies which do interview the spouse or partner, 12% interview them on their own. Given that more than a third of the companies believe the assignments that either failed, or had been ended prematurely, due to a spouse or partner's difficulties with adapting to life in the host location, it is perhaps a little surprising that companies are not attributing more importance to assessing their suitability.

The 2002 ORC Worldwide survey did not address the involvement of the spouse/partner in the selection process, although reports that assistance was provided to help the accompanying person cope with the international assignment. A similar story emerges from the GMAC-GRS 2002 Report.

Apart from the accompanying partner's career, there are family considerations that can cause a potential expatriate to decline the international assignment. Disruption to children's education is an important consideration, and the selected candidate may reject the offered assignment on the grounds that a move at this particular stage in his or her child's life is inappropriate. The care of ageing or invalid parents is another consideration (see IHRM in Action Case 4-1). While these two reasons have been noted in various studies, what has been somewhat overlooked is the issue of single parents. Given increasing divorce rates, this may become a critical factor in assignment selection and acceptance where the custody of children is involved. This is not necessarily an additional barrier for prospective female international managers only. An increasing number of males in the USA, for example, are being granted custody of the children of the marriage.[50] The associated legal constraints, such as obtaining the consent of the other parent to take the child (or children) out of the home country, and visiting/access rights, may prove to be a major barrier to the international mobility of both single mothers and single fathers.

Country/cultural requirements

As discussed in Chapter 1, international firms are usually required to demonstrate that an HCN is not available before the host government will issue the necessary work permit and entry visa for the desired PCN or TCN. In some cases, the multi-national may wish to use an expatriate and has selected a candidate for the international assignment, only to find the transfer blocked by the host government. Some countries, such as the USA, are changing their legislation to facilitate employment-related immigration,[51] which will make international transfers somewhat easier. As we will see in Chapter 9, the Social Charter allows for free movement of citizens of member countries within the European Union. It is therefore important that HR staff keep up-to-date with changing legislation in the countries in which the multinational is involved.

IHRM in Action Case 4-2 shows how one US multinational's careful planning allowed it to obtain the required number of PCN visas.

An important, related point is that generally a work permit is granted to the expatriate only. The accompanying spouse or partner may not be permitted to work in the host country. Increasingly, multinationals are finding that the inability of the spouse to work in the host country may cause the selected candidate to reject the offer of an international assignment. If the international assignment is accepted, the lack of a work permit for the accompanying spouse or partner may cause difficulties in adjustment and even contribute to failure. For these reasons, as reported above, some multinationals provide assistance in this regard.

Further, the host country may be an important determinant. Some regions and countries are considered 'hardship postings': remote areas away from major cities or modern facilities, or war-torn regions with high physical risk. Accompanying

IHRM in Action Case 4-2

Citibank plans for changing staffing needs

Banks, along with oil and construction companies, remain heavy users of PCN employees, because these industries require very specific (sometimes firm-specific) skills frequently not found in foreign locations. In the mid-1980s, Australia offered a once-only opportunity for foreign banks to enter the local market. Citibank already held a limited banking license that allowed it to operate in Australia as a merchant bank and finance company. A year before the licenses were to be awarded, Citibank sent one of its senior HR managers on a year-long assignment to Sydney to assess the staffing implications of an application to the Australian government for a banking license. First, an assessment was made as to how many PCN visas would be required. Then, a detailed summary was prepared for the Australian immigration department that demonstrated the history of Citibank's investment in training Australian nationals, with career examples of HCNs who were now employed by Citibank in Australia, in other foreign locations and in the USA. This proved to be a successful strategy: Citibank received one of the 16 licenses on offer and all of the PCN work permits it requested.

family members may be an additional responsibility that the multinational does not want to bear. There may be a reluctance to select females for certain Middle East or South East Asian regions. Indeed, some countries will not issue a work permit for a female. These aspects may result in the selection of HCNs rather than expatriates.

To overcome this problem, a group of more than 20 large multinationals (including Shell, British Airways, Unilever, PricewaterhouseCoopers and Siemens) has established an organization called 'Permits Foundation'[52] in an attempt to promote the improvement of work permit regulations for spouses of expatriates. It also aims to raise government awareness of the connection between work permits and employee mobility.

MNE requirements

As we examined in the previous chapter, situational factors have an influence on the selection decision. For instance, the MNE may consider the proportion of expatriates to local staff when making selection decisions, mainly as an outcome of its staffing philosophy. However, operations in particular countries may require the use of more PCNs and TCNs than would normally be the case, as multinationals operating in parts of Eastern Europe and China are discovering. This will affect the selection ratio, that is, PCN:TCN:HCN. Other situational factors include:

- The mode of operation involved. Selecting staff to work in an international joint venture may involve major input from the local partner and be constrained by the negotiated agreement on selection processes.[53]

- The duration and type of the assignment.[54] Family members tend not to accompany an expatriate when the assignment is for only 3–6 months, so family requirements may not be a strong factor in the selection decision.

- The amount of knowledge transfer inherent in the expatriate's job in the foreign operation. If the nature of the job is to train local staff, then the multinational may include training skills as a selection criterion.

Language

The ability to speak the local language is an aspect often linked with cross-cultural ability. However, we have chosen to stress language as situation-determined in terms of its importance as a factor in the selection decision. Language skills may be regarded as of critical importance for some expatriate positions, but lesser in others, although some would argue that knowledge of the host country's language is an important aspect of expatriate performance, regardless of the level of position.

Differences in language are recognized as a major barrier to effective cross-cultural communication.[55] Yet, in terms of the other selection criteria we have examined above, from the multinational's perspective, language is placed lower down the list of desirable attributes. For example, the ORC Worldwide survey results rank language ability as the fifth most important selection criterion. An explanation for this attitude may be drawn from a study of the foreign language needs of US multinationals. Through her interviews with people in nine companies of varying size and nature, Fixman[56] found that foreign language skills were rarely considered an important part of international business success. She comments: 'Language problems were largely viewed as mechanical and manageable problems that could be solved individually.'

Another component to language as a situation factor in the selection decision is the role of the common corporate language. As discussed previously, most multinationals adopt a common corporate language as a way of standardizing reporting systems and procedures. This is not, perhaps, an issue for PCN selection within multinationals from the Anglo-Saxon world (the USA, the UK, Canada, Australia and New Zealand), where the chosen company language remains the same as that of the home country. It becomes an expatriate selection issue, however, for multinationals from non-English-speaking countries that adopt English as the corporate language, unless the posting is to a country with a shared language. For instance, a Spanish multinational, using Spanish as the corporate language, selecting a PCN to head its new subsidiary in Mexico, does not face the same language issue as a Spanish multinational, with English as its corporate language, selecting a PCN to its US facility. For the latter, fluency in English is important. Lack of fluency in the corporate language, therefore, can be a selection barrier. Prospective candidates may be eliminated from the potential pool owing to a lack of at least competency in the common language.[57] Language ability may therefore limit the multinational's ability to select the most appropriate candidate.

The use of selection tests

Although there is a consensus among scholars and practitioners that personal characteristics (or traits) are important, there is considerable debate about how such personal characteristics can be reliably and accurately measured. Personality and psychological tests have been used in the selection process, but the effectiveness of such tests as predictors of cultural adjustment is questioned. For example, Torbiörn[58] comments that although desirable personality traits are specified and recommended, the tests or criteria to assess these traits are seldom convincingly validated. Likewise, Willis[59] states that if tests are used they should be selected with care and regard for reliability and validity because, although some tests may be useful in suggesting potential problems, there appears to be little correlation between test scores and performance. He further adds that most of the relevant tests have been devised in the USA and, therefore, may be culture-bound. Use of such tests without careful modification on non-American nationals adds another question mark to their reliability and validity as predictors of expatriate success. It is important that HRM staff in all locations are aware of the debate surrounding the use of selection tests, particularly the culture-bound nature of psychometric tests designed for PCNs.

Another constraint is that in some countries (the UK and Australia, for instance) there is controversy about the use of psychological tests.[60] There is also a different pattern of usage across countries – the use of such tests is very low in Germany.[61] The 1997–98 Price Waterhouse survey reported only 12 per cent used formal assessment centers and some companies 'indicated through their comments that they also use psychometric tests'. The majority of respondents (85 per cent) mainly assessed expatriate suitability through the traditional interview process. More recent surveys have not addressed this aspect of selection.

The difficulty of predicting success, then, seems to be related to the lack of valid and reliable screening devices to identify, with certainty, managers who will succeed in a foreign assignment. The crucial variables affecting the adjustment of the individual and family are not only difficult to identify or measure, but the complex relationship between personality factors and ability to adjust to another culture is not well understood.[62] Discussing this problem, Gertsen[63] points out that the use of personality traits to predict intercultural competence is further complicated by the fact that personality traits are not defined and evaluated in the same way in different cultures, stating:

> The most serious problem, however, is that attitudes do not always result in the implicitly expected behavior. If a person has very positive attitudes towards a culture but is unable to express this in his behavior, it has no effect.

Gertsen concludes that attitudes are relevant only to the extent that they determine a person's actual communicative behavior in another culture and that other personality traits are relevant in the same way.

Another drawback of expatriate selection based on traits or characteristics is the subjective nature of the scoring of abilities, especially those classified as personal and environmental characteristics. Nevertheless, models derived from this approach have value in that they provide some guidelines that can be applied during the selection process, rather than mere reliance on the potential manager's domestic record as a predictor.[64] One such model is that offered by Mendenhall and Oddou.[10,65] They propose a four-dimensional approach that attempts to link specific behavioral tendencies to probable overseas performance:

- The self-oriented dimension – the degree to which the expatriate expresses an adaptive concern for self-preservation, self-enjoyment and mental hygiene.
- The perceptual dimension – the expertise that the expatriate possesses in accurately understanding why host-nationals behave the way they do.
- The others-oriented dimension – the degree to which the expatriate is concerned about host-national co-workers and desire to affiliate with them.
- The cultural-toughness dimension – a mediating variable that recognizes that acculturation is affected by the degree to which the culture of the host country is incongruent with that of the home country.

The evaluation of the candidate's strengths and weaknesses on these four dimensions, Mendenhall and Oddou suggested, will focus appropriate attention on cross-cultural ability and behavior, thus complementing technical ability assessment.

Equal employment opportunity issues

In the recruitment and selection process, multinationals must address the issue of equal employment opportunity (EEO) for employees in all employment locations. This involves taking into consideration the increasingly conflicting national laws on employment. As Jain *et al.*[66] mention, mandatory retirement and hiring ages are illegal in some countries such as the USA and some other countries but remain a legal requirement in other countries.

Determining which law applies where, and which has precedence, is a problem without a specific solution. The USA has a comprehensive statute (Title VII of the Civil Rights Act of 1964) to cover many EEO situations. However, it should be noted that the US Supreme Court[67] has held that this act does not apply outside the territorial borders of the USA. The case involved an American citizen who claimed that he had been illegally discriminated against while working overseas for a US corporation. A naturalized citizen born in Lebanon, the plaintiff began working for Aramco Corporation in Texas in 1979 and was transferred by the company to work in Saudi Arabia in 1980, where he worked until 1984, when he was discharged. The Court rejected the person's claim that he had been harassed and ultimately discharged by Aramco Corporation on account of his race, religion and national origin. The decision has important implications for the status and protection of Americans working abroad for US firms.

Equal employment opportunity laws are expressions of social values with regard to employment and reflect the values of a society or country.[68] In parts of the Middle East, Africa, Asia and Latin America, women have tended to have a lower social status and are not universally employed. On the other hand, with the increasing rate of female entry into the workforce, many Western countries have introduced legislation to cover sex discrimination. Multinationals must be aware of legislation and ensure subsidiary compliance where appropriate in selecting expatriates. The selection procedures must be defended against illegality as our IHRM in Action Case 4-3 demonstrates.

Expatriate selection in practice: the role of the coffee machine

As we indicated at the beginning of the section on selection criteria, most multinationals admit that technical and/or managerial skills are the dominant, sometimes only, criteria used. We have suggested that reliance on technical skills is mainly due to the fact that most international assignments are filling a position. Of the factors outlined in Figure 4-5, technical ability is perhaps the easiest to measure. It is possible even to conclude that Figure 4-5 represents the ideal. Harris and Brewster[69] argue that expatriate selection, in reality, is an *ad hoc* process and they propose the 'coffee-machine' system, a term coined by a perhaps cynical expatriate these authors had interviewed. Harris and Brewster suggest that executives chatting around the coffee-machine (or water cooler) can start the selection process through a casual conversation about an assignment need confronting one of them. Another executive can volunteer the name of a potential expatriate, thus starting an informal short list of candidates. What happens next, according to Harris and Brewster, is that the multinational's processes are then activated to legitimize the decision that has, in effect, already been taken around the coffee-machine.

IHRM in Action Case 4-3

Observing local EEO laws

In 1993, one of the Hyatt hotels in Australia had to explain to the Equal Employment Opportunity Commissioner on national TV as to why it was circulating an internal memo that violated Australian Equal Employment (EE) legislation. The internal memo concerned was from a Japanese Hyatt hotel that had vacancies for two young single males. Under Australian EE law, these constitute age, marital status and sex discrimination, respectively, so the memo violated Australian law on three counts. The hotel's defence that such circulation of internal job vacancies was normal company practice was not acceptable. The EE Commissioner did recognize that special circumstances may have been behind the internal memo – that the positions were traineeships and that the persons would share accommodation in a male-only dormitory.

Source: '7.30 Report' current affairs program, Australian Broadcasting Corporation TV, 10 October 1993.

Harris and Brewster relate that this process was the most common form of selection process that they encountered in their study of UK firms. They then derived a typology of selection systems to explain variations found in the way expatriate selection is conducted, detailed in Table 4-2.

Harris and Brewster regard the coffee-machine scenario as an example of the informal/closed cell in their typology. However, one cannot generalize here. It is possible to find examples of formal, open selection processes. Harris and Brewster admit that the process can be influenced by the maturity of the multinational, its stage in the internationalization process and its size or industry. The type of position involved, the role of the HR function in the process and whether the multinational is reactive rather than proactive where international assignment selection is involved remain key factors in how selection processes work in multinationals.

Dual-career couples

So far, we have focused on selecting suitable candidates for international assignments. We will now consider an emerging constraint – the dual-career couple – on the available pool of candidates, thus hindering the recruitment and selection process. As an HR manager is quoted as saying:[70]

> Getting employees to move when their spouse has a job is a critical problem. It does restrict a lot of companies because you have so many more two-income families today.

Table 4-2	Harris and Brewster's selection typology

Formal	Informal
Open	
● Clearly defined criteria	● Less defined criteria
● Clearly defined measures	● Less defined measures
● Training for selectors	● Limited training for selectors
● Open advertising of vacancy (internal/external)	● No panel discussions
● Panel discussions	● Open advertising of vacancy
	● Recommendations
Closed	
● Clearly defined criteria	● Selectors' individual preferences determine selection criteria and measures
● Clearly defined measures	
● Training for selectors	
● Panel discussions	● No panel discussions
● Nominations only (networking/reputation)	● Nominations only (networking/reputation)

Source: H. Harris and C. Brewster, The Coffee-machine System: How International Selection Really Works, *International Journal of Human Resource Management*, Vol. 10, No. 3 (1999) p. 493. Reproduced with permission.

The rise in dual-career couples, along with the aging population and other family-related situations, combine to make more people immobile. Employees are prepared to state the grounds for refusal as 'family concerns'. That this has become more acceptable as a reason reflects a significant shift in thinking about the role of non-work aspects impinging on work-related matters.

The increase in the number of dual-career couples is a worldwide trend, one that is posing a dilemma for both companies and employees alike. This is not surprising given that accepting a traditional international assignment will impact upon the career of the potential candidate's spouse or partner. The ORC Worldwide 2002 survey focused on the issue of dual careers and international assignments. A major finding was that spousal or dual-career issues were the most common reasons for rejecting international assignments reported by North American and European firms, but were rarely cited by Asian firms. Rather, concern for children and aging parents were barriers to assignment acceptance for this group. Likewise, the GMAC-GRS 2002 survey cites spouse's career as a major factor in assignment refusal.

Multinationals are being forced to select from a diminishing pool of candidates who may be less qualified. This has strategic implications for staffing policies, and may be a reason why more TCNs are being utilized. As can be seen in the expatriate profile in Table 4-1, equal numbers (42 per cent each) of PCNs and TCNs currently are being used. While cost containment remains a major driver of localization (that is, replacing expatriates with HCNs), staff availability is also a factor.[71] Reflecting this global trend, the impact of the accompanying spouse/partner's career orientation upon the international assignment is an emerging area of research. It seems that career orientation not only affects the couple's willingness to move, but also may negatively affect performance and retention in the foreign location.[72]

Some multinationals are endeavoring to come up with solutions to the dual-career challenge. These can be divided into two categories: finding alternative arrangements and making the assignments more 'family friendly'.

Alternative assignment arrangements

These are linked to non-standard assignment categories outlined in Chapter 3.

Short-term assignments. In the ORC Worldwide 2002 survey, 72 per cent of responding firms used short-term assignments (compared with 26 per cent in a 1996 ORC survey) as an alternative means of satisfying the international assignment need.

Commuter assignments (sometimes referred to as 'commuter marriages'). The spouse/partner may decide to remain in the home country and the couple work out ways to maintain the relationship with the help of the firm. In a case known to the authors, when a major US multinational assigned a female expatriate to its Australian subsidiary for 18 months, her husband remained in Chicago. The multinational supported this arrangement through subsidized telephone bills and three return airline tickets. Alternatively, couples may move to jobs in adjoining countries, or within the same geographical region. For instance, one may work in Hong Kong (the original posting), the other in Bangkok. This makes commuting (relationship maintenance) easier than from the USA.[72] Multinationals adjust the compensation benefits to fit with the agreed arrangements. The ORC survey found that 46 per cent of responding firms had such arrangements (compared with 19 per cent in 1996).

Other arrangements.   Other arrangements included in the ORC 2002 report findings were:

- unaccompanied assignments   50%
- replacing assignments with business travel   57%
- virtual assignments   16%.

Only 23 per cent of respondents in a similar study by ORC Worldwide in 1995 reported the use of unaccompanied assignments.

As we discussed in Chapter 3, there has been little attention given to the advantages and disadvantages of these non-standard assignments in terms of the individual employees, their spouses/partners and the strategic objectives that prompt the use of international rather than local staff. Although these arrangements may have short-term benefits in overcoming reluctance to move, how effective they will be in encouraging dual-career couples to accept international assignments over time is yet to be determined.

Family-friendly policies

Inter-company networking.   Here the multinational attempts to place the accompanying spouse or partner in a suitable job with another multinational – sometimes in a reciprocal arrangement. To illustrate: a US multinational may enter into an agreement with a German multinational also operating in, say, China, that they find a position within their respective Chinese facilities for each other's accompanying partner (that is, 'you find my expatriate's spouse a job and work visa and I will do likewise for you'). Alternatively, a local supplier, distributor, or joint venture partner may agree to employ the accompanying spouse/partner.

Job-hunting assistance.   Here the multinational provides spouse/partner assistance with the employment search in the host country. This may be through employment agency fees, career counseling or simply work permit assistance. Some may provide a fact-finding trip to the host location before the actual assignment. The 2002 GMAC-GRS survey reports that 21 per cent of responding firms assisted in finding the accompanying spouse/partner employment and 15 per cent paid a job-finding fee.

Intra-company employment.   This is perhaps a logical but often a somewhat difficult solution. It means sending the couple to the same foreign facility, perhaps the same department. Not all multinationals are comfortable with the idea of having a husband and wife team in the same work location, nor do all couples wish it either. A large Australian multinational sent a couple into its Vietnamese operation, knowing that this would create a delicate situation – the wife reported directly to her husband. The selection decision was not undertaken lightly. HRM staff provided counseling before the assignment, and the situation was monitored carefully by headquarters.

On-assignment career support.   Motorola[73] is an example of how a multinational may assist spouses to maintain and even improve career skills through what

Motorola calls its Dual-Career Policy. This consists of a lump-sum payment for education expenses, professional association fees, seminar attendance, language training to upgrade work-related skills and employment agency fees. There are conditions attached, such as the spouse must have been employed before the assignment. Thus, if the spouse is unable to find suitable employment, the time can be spent on career development activities.

Education and training assistance was provided by 36 per cent of the responding firms in the GMAC-GRS 2002 survey. Other on-assignment assistance may help in establishing contacts and to pay for lost spousal income. The idea is to maintain skills so that the spouse may find work upon re-entry into the home country. These attempts demonstrate that creative thinking can assist multinationals overcome this potential barrier. It is worthy of note that 56 per cent of firms in the GMAC-GRS 2002 survey had policies that included provisions for spouses/partners (compared with 24 per cent in their 1999 survey). A total of 28 per cent indicated that they provided no assistance to expatriate spouses/partners. It is not possible to comment with authority on how effective the above assistance schemes are in terms of overcoming the dual-career barrier. However, it is clear that multinationals are attempting to address the issue and create solutions to what is a real barrier to mobility.

Are female expatriates different?

Our final issue in terms of selection for international assignments is related to gender. The typical expatriate tends to be male: 18 per cent in the GMAC-GRS 2002 survey were females, 14 per cent in the ORC 2002 survey. The authors of both of these surveys are keen to point out that the proportion of females is increasing. For example, the ORC report compares the 2002 situation to that of their 1992 survey, where only 5 per cent of expatriates were female. One can go further back to a 1984 article, in which Adler[74] reported a survey of international HR practices in over 600 US and Canadian companies that found that only 3 per cent of the 13 338 expatriates identified were female. She found that female expatriates tended to be employed by companies with over 1000 employees in the banking, electronics, petroleum and publishing industries. It has been argued that as the proportion of women in the domestic workforce continues to increase and as international experience becomes an essential criterion for career progression within multinationals, we will see more international managers who are female.

Over the past decade or so, researchers have attempted to discover why so few expatriates are female. Is it because they were unwilling to relocate? Is it attitudinal? Does it reflect a somewhat externalized belief that men in some cultures, such as certain Asian countries, do not like reporting to female managers, particularly foreign women and therefore women should not be posted overseas, creating what has been referred to as 'the glass border that supports the glass ceiling'.

Recent studies challenge some of the attitudes regarding the suitability of females for international assignments. For example, Stroh et al.[75] found that US and Canadian women are interested in and likely to accept international assignments, although there are variations between those with children and those without. However, the women in this study tended to believe that their companies were hesitant to ask them to accept an international assignment, although supervisors (whether male or female) did not necessarily share that belief. Further, performance of female expatriates was found initially to be affected by host-country prejudice regarding the role of women in certain countries – considered as culturally tough assignment locations. However, the longer the women were on such assignments, the less they perceived that prejudice was a barrier to effectiveness. Caligiuri and Tung,[76] in their study of female and male expatriates in a US-based multinational, found that females can perform equally as well as their male counterparts regardless of a country's attitude toward women in managerial positions.

Taking a different approach in her study of Austrian female expatriates, Fischlmayr[77] used the concepts of external and self-established barriers to explore why women are under-represented in international assignments. These are listed in Table 4-3.

Through 21 interviews with HR managers and female expatriates in Austrian multinationals from various industries and positions, Fischlmayr found that attitudes of HR directors were a major barrier to the selection of female expatriates, although self-established barriers were also very strong. Females in Austrian companies often had specifically to request an international assignment whereas their male colleagues were required to take international assignments. Further, some women regarded that their age was decisive in terms of others' perceptions and expectations about their behavior. The older the woman, the easier it is. Fischlmayr concludes that women are partly to blame for their under-representation.

Mayrhofer and Scullion[78] report on the experiences of male and female expatriates in the German clothing industry. They found that women were sent into a diverse number of countries, including those with an Islamic influence. Overall, there were few differences in the experiences of both gender groups, although female expatriates placed more value on integration of spouse/family issues prior to and during the assignment than did the males in the sample. Assignment lengths in this industry tended to be shorter and involved various forms of non-standard assignments and there were generally more female managers than perhaps found in other industries. More women than men were assigned for longer assignment terms and these authors conclude that the higher proportion of women in the industry appeared to make gender less of an issue. However, this did not apply at the top senior management positions where

Table 4-3	Barriers to females taking international assignments

External barriers	*Self-established barriers*
• HR managers reluctant to select female candidates	• Some women have limited willingness to relocate
• Culturally tough locations or regions preclude female expatriates	• The dual-career couple
• Those selecting expatriates have stereotypes in their minds that influence decisions	• Women are often a barrier to their own careers by behaving according to gender-based role models

Source: Based on the literature reviewed in I.C. Fischlmayr, Female Self-perception as Barrier to International Careers?, *International Journal of Human Resource Management*, Vol. 13, No. 5 (2002) pp. 773–783.

women were less represented. Mayrhofer and Scullion conclude that there are still barriers to female expatriates in terms of senior expatriate positions.

A further contribution comes from a study by Napier and Taylor[79] of female expatriates from various countries working in Japan, China and Turkey. The women fell into three categories: traditional expatriates, 'trailers' who were spouses/partners of male expatriates and 'independents' – professional women who could be called self-selected expatriates. Napier and Taylor found that gaining credibility with local clients was a major issue. Accommodating cultural differences, maintaining a social life and a need for appropriate interpersonal skills were important factors in coping with work demands. Networks became important for both business and social contexts. Being a minority (foreign females) meant higher visibility than they were used to and could be a positive in terms of getting access to key clients and customers.

What emerges as common across the various studies on female expatriates is that assignment location, level of organization support, spouse/partner satisfaction and inter-cultural experiences are important in terms of performance. The list of moderators is similar to those we discussed in general terms earlier in this chapter. What does appear to differentiate female and male expatriates is the degree to which these moderators affect individual performance and the value placed on cultural awareness training prior to the international assignment. The dual-career issue may prove to be a greater barrier for female mobility as males are more reluctant to accompany their spouse/partner.

Summary

This chapter has addressed key issues affecting recruitment and selection for international assignments. We have covered:

- Four myths related to the concept of a global manager – that there is a universal approach to management; that people can acquire multicultural adaptability and behaviors; that there are common characteristics successful international managers share; and that there are no impediments to mobility.

- The debate surrounding the definition and magnitude of expatriate failure.

- Cultural adjustment and other moderating factors affecting expatriate intent to stay and performance. These included duration of the assignment, willingness to move, work-related factors and the employment relationship.

- Individual and situational factors to be considered in the selection decision. Evaluation of the common criteria used revealed the difficulty of selecting the right candidate for an international assignment and the importance of including family considerations in the selection process.

- Dual-career couples as a barrier to staff mobility, and the techniques that multinationals are utilizing to overcome this constraint.

- Female expatriates and whether they face different issues to their male counterparts.

It is also clear that, while our appreciation of the issues surrounding expatriate recruitment and selection has deepened in the past 20 years, much remains to be explored. The field is dominated by US research into predominantly US samples of expatriates, although there has been an upsurge in interest from European academics and practitioners. Will the factors affecting the selection decision be similar for multinationals emerging from countries such as China and India? If more multinationals are to encourage subsidiary staff to consider international assignments as part of an intra-organizational network approach to management, we will need further understanding of how valid the issues discussed in this chapter are for all categories of staff from different country locations.

Another area that remains ignored is the selection of non-expatriates, that is, the international business travelers we discussed in Chapter 3. In our survey of current literature, there is a paucity of recognition of this group. The various consulting firm surveys conducted into relocation trends in 2002 that we draw on in this chapter indicate that more multinationals are resorting to replacing traditional assignments with business travel as a way of overcoming staff immobility. Likewise, there is a need for further work into the performance–selection link surrounding non-standard assignments, including commuter and virtual assignments.

It is apparent, though, that staff selection remains critical. Finding the right people to fill positions, particularly key managers – whether PCN, TCN or HCN – can determine international expansion. However, effective recruitment and selection are only the first step. As we will explore in the next chapter, maintaining and retaining productive staff are equally important.

Discussion questions and exercises

1 What is the difference between a global manager and a global mindset?

2 Should multinationals be concerned about expatriate failure? If so, why?

3 What are the most important factors involved in the selection decision?

4 Are female expatriates different?

5 Discuss the proposition that most expatriate selection decisions are made informally, as suggested by the 'coffee-machine' solution.

6 You are the President of a small but growing graphics software provider based in Silicon Valley in California. The company's main product is the provision of specialized computer-generated graphics for televised sporting events. You have just been awarded the contract to provide graphics for a European sports channel. This requires you to establish an office in Paris where the European client is based. The best available person to establish and manage the Paris office is Julia Moore, but she has indicated that to stay in Paris for more than 1 year will place a strain on her relationship with partner Rod Cook, who is the owner/manager of a successful computer software development firm. What solution can you come up with to overcome this barrier to mobility?

7 You are from Corporate Headquarters. As a member of the HR department, you are responsible for managing international assignments. You are to present a 10-minute summary of the key aspects of expatriate selection to a

regional meeting of subsidiary managers, none of whom have any experience in HR or in selecting expatriates. The corporate objective is to use intra-regional international assignments for cross-border project teamwork between their various operations within the region. What aspects of expatriate selection should you highlight in your presentation?

Further reading

H.C. Jain, P.J. Sloane and F.M. Horwitz, 2003. *Employment Equity and Affirmative Action: an International Comparison*, Armonk: New York: M.E. Sharpe.

J. Selmer, 2002. Practice Makes Perfect? International Experience and Expatriate Adjustment, *Management International Review*, Vol. 42, No. 1, pp. 71–87.

M. Linehan and J.S. Walsh, 2001. Key Issues in the Senior Female International Career Move: a Qualitative Study in a European Context, *British Journal of Management*, Vol. 12; pp. 85–95.

M.A. Shaffer and D.A. Harrison, 2001. Forgotten Partners of International Assignments: Development and Test of a Model of Spouse Adjustment, *Journal of Applied Psychology*, Vol. 86, No. 2, pp. 238–254.

M. Harvey and R.G. Richey, 2001. Global Supply Chain Management: the Selection of Globally Competent Managers, *Journal of International Management*, Vol. 7, pp. 105–128.

P.M. Caligiuri and R.L. Tung, 1999. Comparing the Success of Male and Female Expatriates from a US-based Multinational Company, *International Journal of Human Resource Management*, Vol. 10, No. 5, pp. 763–782.

C.A. Bartlett and S. Ghoshal, 1997. The Myth of the Generic Manager: New Personal Competencies for New Management Roles, *California Management Review*, Vol. 40, No. 1, pp. 92–116.

Notes and references

1 R.S. Schuler and V.L. Huber, *Personnel and Human Resource Management*, 5th edn, St. Paul, MN: West Publishing, 1993.

2 A.V. Phatak, *International Dimensions of Management*, 4th edn, Cincinnati, OH: South Western, 1995 p. 205. See also, M. Borg, *International Transfers of Managers in Multinational Corporations*, Uppsala: University of Uppsala, 1987.

3 F.T. Murray and A.H. Murray, Global Managers for Global Businesses, *Sloan Management Review*, Vol. 27, No. 2 (1986) pp. 75–80.

4 N. Forster, The Myth of the 'International Manager', *International Journal of Human Resource Management*, Vol. 11, No. 1 (2000) pp. 126–142.

5 Y. Baruch, No Such Thing as a Global Manager, *Business Horizons*, January–February (2002) pp. 36–42.

6 N. Forster, The Persistent Myth of High Expatriate Failure Rates. *International Journal of Human Resource Management*, Vol. 8, No. 4 (1997), p. 430.

7 Price Waterhouse, *International Assignments: European Policy and Practice 1997/1998*, 1997.

8 A.W.K. Harzing, The Persistent Myth of High Expatriate Failure Rates, *International Journal of Human Resource Management*, Vol. 6, No. 2 (1995), p. 458.

9 R.L. Tung, Selection and Training of Personnel for Overseas Assignments, *Columbia Journal of World Business*, Vol. 16, No. 1 (1981) pp. 68–78.

10 R.L. Tung, Selection and Training Procedures of U.S., European and Japanese Multinationals, *California Management Review*, Vol. 25, No. 1 (1982) pp. 57–71.

11 R.L. Tung, Human Resource Planning in Japanese Multinationals: a Model for US Firms? *Journal of International Business Studies*, Fall (1984), pp. 139–149.

12 C. Brewster, *The Management of Expatriates*, Human Resource Research Centre Monograph Series, No. 2, Bedford: Cranfield School of Management, 1988.

13 In a pilot study, Hamill investigated the IHRM practices and policies of seven British multinationals. He found that the failure rate among British expatriates was significantly lower (less than 5 per cent) than that reported for US multinationals: J. Hamill, Expatriate Policies in British Multinationals, *Journal of General Management*, Vol. 14, No. 4 (1989) pp. 19–33.

14 E. Marx, *International Human Resource Practices in Britain and Germany*, London: Anglo-German Foundation, 1996.

15 Organizational Resource Counselors, *Dual Careers and International Assignments Survey*, 2002. The organization changed its name to ORC Worldwide in 2003 according to its website, accessed July 2003.

16 I. Björkman and M. Gertsen, Corporate Expatriation: an Empirical Study of Scandinavian Firms, in *Proceedings of the Third Symposium on Cross-cultural Consumer and Business Studies*, Honolulu, December 1990. Danish firms did not respond to Tung's survey, but the Swedish and Norwegian firms did.

17 P.J. Dowling and D. Welch, International Human Resource Management: an Australian Perspective, *Asia-Pacific Journal of Management*, Vol. 6, No. 1 (1988) pp. 39–65. Although precise records were not kept, the four companies estimated failure rates of less than 5 percent.

18 For example, Enderwick and Hodgson explain that the absence of 'expatriate failure' in their study of New Zealand firms may be due to their early stages in internationalisation: P. Enderwick and D. Hodgson, Expatriate Management Practices of New Zealand Business, *International Journal of Human Resource Management*, Vol. 4, No. 2 (1993) pp. 407–423.

19 M.E. Mendenhall and G. Oddou, The Overseas Assignment: a Practical Look, *Business Horizons*, September–October (1988) pp. 78–84.

20 M. Mendenhall and G. Oddou, The Dimensions of Expatriate Acculturation: a Review, *Academy of Management Review*, Vol. 10 (1985) pp. 39–47.

21 Tanshin Funin: Bachelors in Exile, *Focus Japan*, December (1990) p. 4.

22 The Lonely Mother who Chose Death before Disgrace, *The Age*, 25 October (1992) p. 4.

23 GMAC Global Relocation Services/Windham International, *Global Relocation Trends 2000 Survey Report*, October 2000.

24 J. Selmer, B.P. Ebrahimi and L. Mingtao, Career Management of Business Expatriates from China, *International Business Review*, Vol. 11, No. 1, (2002) pp. 17–33.

25 For a review and assessment of the U-Curve, see J.S. Black and M. Mendenhall, The U-Curve Adjustment Hypothesis Revisited: a Review and Theoretical Framework, *Journal of International Business Studies*, Vol. 22, No. 2 (1991) pp. 225–247.

26 H. De Cieri, P.J. Dowling and K.F. Taylor, The Psychological Impact of Expatriate Relocation on Partners, *International Journal of Human Resource Management*, Vol. 2, No. 3 (1991) pp. 377–414.

27 M. Kauppinen, *Antecedents of Expatriate Adjustment: a Study of Finnish Managers in the United States*, Helsinki: Helsinki School of Economics Press, 1994.

28 J.S. Black and G.K. Stephens, The Influence of the Spouse on American Expatriate Adjustment and Intent to Stay in Pacific Rim Overseas Assignments, *Journal of Management*, Vol. 15, No. 4 (1989) pp. 529–544. See also Ref. 27 for support of this finding.

29 J.M. Brett and L.K. Stroh, Willingness to Relocate Internationally, *Human Resource Management*, Vol. 34, No. 3 (1995) pp. 405–424.

30 One US personnel director interviewed by the authors pointed out that attributing expatriate recall to 'failure of spouse to adjust' was at times a simplistic explanation. He postulated that, apart from the probability of the expatriate blaming his wife for his own failure to adjust, some astute spouses may see the expatriate's poor performance and trigger the early recall to limit damage to the expatriate's career.

31 H.B. Gregersen and J.S. Black, A Multifaceted Approach to Expatriate Retention in International Assignments, *Group & Organization Studies*, Vol. 15, No. 4 (1990) pp. 461–485.

32 M.S. Shaffer, D.A. Harrison and K.M. Gilley, Dimensions, Determinants and Differences in the Expatriate Adjustment Process, *Journal of International Business Studies*, Vol. 30, No. 3 (1999) pp. 557–581.

33 M.C. Bolino and D.C. Feldman, Increasing the Skill Utilization of Expatriates, *Human Resource Management*, Vol. 39, No. 4 (2000) pp. 367–379.

34 See, for example, M.Birdseye and J. Hill, Individual, Organizational/Work and Environmental Influences on Expatriate Turnover Tendencies: an Empirical Study, *Journal of International Business Studies*, Vol. 26, No. 4 (1995) pp. 787–813; and E. Naumann, Organizational Predictors of Expatriate Job Satisfaction, *Journal of International Business Studies*, Vol. 24, No. 1 (1993) pp. 61–79.

35 M. Kraimer, S.J. Wayne and R.A. Jaworski, Sources of Support and Expatriate Performance: the Mediating Role of Expatriate Adjustment, *Personnel Psychology*, Vol. 54 (2001) pp. 71–92.

36 This section is based on D. Welch, Globalisation of Staff Movements: Beyond Cultural Adjustment, *Management International Review*, Vol. 43, No. 2 (2003) pp. 149–169.

37 D.M. Rousseau and K.A. Wade-Benzoni, Linking Strategy and Human Resource Practices: How Employee and Customer Contracts are Created, *Human Resource Management*, Vol. 33, No. 3 (1994) pp. 463–489.

38 See also J. Hallier and P. James, Middle Managers and the Employee Psychological Contract: Agency, Protection and Advancement, *Journal of Management Studies*, Vol. 34 (1997) pp. 703–728.

39 D. Guest, Is the Psychological Contract Worth Taking Seriously? *Journal of Organizational Behaviour*, Vol. 19 (1998) pp. 649–664.

40 E.W. Morrison and S.L Robinson, When Employees Feel Betrayed: a Model of How Psychological Contract Violation Develops, *Academy of Management Review*, Vol. 22, No. 1 (1997) pp. 226–256.

41 N.J. Allen and J.P. Meyer, The Measurement and Antecedents of Affective, Continuance and Normative Commitment, *Journal of Occupational Psychology*, Vol. 63 (1990) pp. 1–18.

42 D.E. Morrison, Psychological Contracts and Change, *Human Resource Management*, Vol. 33, No. 3 (1994) p. 359.

43 R.A. Guzzo, K.A. Noonan and E. Elron, Expatriate Managers and the Psychological Contract, *Journal of Applied Psychology*, Vol. 79, No. 4 (1994) pp. 617–626.

44 A.L. Hixon, Why Corporations Make Haphazard Overseas Staffing Decisions, *Personnel Administrator*, Vol. 31, No. 3 (1986) pp. 91–94; M.E. Mendenhall, E. Dunbar and G. Oddou, Expatriate Selection, Training and Career-pathing: A Review and a Critique, *Human Resource Planning*, Vol. 26, No. 3 (1987) pp. 331–345; J. McEnery and G. DesHarnais, Culture Shock, *Training and Development Journal*, Vol. 44, No. 4 (1990) pp. 43–47; I. Björkman and M. Gertsen, Selecting and Training Scandinavian Expatriates: Determinants of Corporate Practice, *Scandinavian Journal of Management*, Vol. 9, No. 2 (1993) pp. 145–164; E. Marx, *International Human Resource Practices in Britain and Germany*; Price Waterhouse, *International Assignments: European Policy and Practice*, 1996.

45 R. Marschan-Piekkari, D. Welch and L. Welch, Adopting a Common Corporate Language: IHRM Implications, *International Journal of Human Resource Management*, Vol. 10, No. 3 (1999) p. 385.

46 See, for example, P. Caligiuri, The Big Five Personality Characteristics as Predictors of Expatriate's Desire to Terminate the Assignment and Supervisor-rated Performance, *Personnel Psychology*, Vol. 53 (2000) pp. 67–88.

47 M.A. Shaffer and D.A. Harrison, Forgotten Partners of International Assignments: Development and Test of a Model of Spouse Adjustment, *Journal of Applied Psychology*, Vol. 86, No. 2 (2001) pp. 238–254.

48 M. Harvey, The Executive Family: an Overlooked Variable in International Assignments, *Columbia Journal of World Business*, Spring (1985), pp. 84–93; see also A. Thompson, Australian Expatriate Wives and Business Success in South East Asia, *Euro-Asian Business Review*, Vol. 5, No. 2 (1986) pp. 14–18; J.E. Harris, Moving Managers Internationally: the Care and Feeding of Expatriates, *Human Resource Planning*, Vol. 12, No. 1 (1989) pp. 49–53.

49 J.S. Black and G.K. Stephens, The Influence of the Spouse on American Expatriate Adjustment and Intent to Stay in Pacific Rim Overseas Assignments, *Journal of Management*, Vol. 15, No. 4 (1989) p. 541; see also H. De Cieri, P.J. Dowling and K.F. Taylor, The Psychological Impact of Expatriate Relocation on Partners, *The International Journal of Human Resource Management*, Vol. 2, No. 3 (1991) pp. 377–414; and Refs 12 and 44.

50 R. Johnson, Daddy Dearest, *The Guardian*, 2 March (1998) p. G2:2.

51 C. Shusterman, A Welcome Change to Immigration Law, *Personnel Journal*, September (1991) pp. 44–48.

52 PricewaterhouseCoopers, *International Assignments: Global Policy and Practice Key Trends 2002*, PricewaterhouseCoopers, 2002, p. 18.

53 S.N. As-Saber, P.J. Dowling and P.W. Liesch, The Role of Human Resource Management in International Joint Ventures: a Study of Australian–Indian Joint Ventures, *International Journal of Human Resource Management*, Vol. 9, No. 5 (1998) pp. 751–766.

54 D. Welch and L. Welch, Linking Operation Mode Diversity and IHRM, *International Journal of Human Resource Management*, Vol. 5, No. 4 (1994) pp. 911–926.

55 D. Victor, *International Business Communication*, New York: Harper Collins, 1992.

56 C. Fixman, The Foreign Language Needs of U.S.-based Corporations, *Annals* AAPSS, Vol. 511, September (1990) p. 25.

57 R. Marschan-Piekkari, D. Welch and L. Welch, Adopting a Common Corporate Language, *International Journal of Human Resource Management*, Vol. 10, No. 3 (1999) pp. 377–390.

58 I. Torbiörn, *Living Abroad: Personal Adjustment and Personnel Policy in the Overseas Setting*, New York: Wiley, 1982.

59 H.L. Willis, Selection for Employment in Developing Countries, *Personnel Administrator*, Vol. 29, No. 7 (1984) p. 55.

60 See, for example, P. Sparrow and J-M. Hiltrop, *European Human Resource Management in Transition*, Hemel Hempstead, 1994; P.J. Dowling, Psychological Testing in Australia: an Overview and an Assessment, in *Australian Personnel Management: a Reader*, ed. G. Palmer, Sydney: Macmillan, 1988.

61 Marx found that only 4.4% of the Germany companies in her survey used such tests, compared with 15.2% in the UK firms; see Ref. 14.

62 See Ref. 44 (Hixon).

63 M. Gertsen, Expatriate Selection and Training, in *Proceedings of the Fifteenth Annual Conference of the European International Business Association*, ed. R. Luostarinen, Helsinki, December, 1989, p. 1257.

64 G.M. Baliga and J.C. Baker, Multinational Corporate Policies for Expatriate Managers: Selection, Training, Evaluation, *Advanced Management Journal*, Vol. 50, No. 4 (1985) pp. 31–38; see also J.S. Black, The Relationship of Personal Characteristics with the Adjustment of Japanese Expatriate Managers, *Management International Review*, Vol. 30, No. 2 (1990) pp. 119–134, for a review and discussion of cross-cultural adjustment.

65 For a review of the Type A literature, see V.A. Price, *Type A Behaviour Pattern: a Model for Research and Practice*, New York: Academic Press, 1982.

66 H.C. Jain, P.J. Sloane and F.M. Horwitz, *Employment Equity and Affirmative Action: an International Comparison*, Armonk: New York: M.E. Sharpe, 2003.

67 E.E.O.C. v. Arabian American Oil Co., 111 S. Ct. 1227 (1991). For an excellent commentary on this case, see G.L. Clark, The Geography of Civil Rights, *Environment and Planning D: Society and Space*, Vol. 10 (1992) pp. 119–121.

68 For a recent review, see Ref. 66.

69 H. Harris and C. Brewster, The Coffee-machine System: How International Selection Really Works, *The International Journal of Human Resource Management*, Vol. 10, No. 3 (1999) pp. 488–500.

70 PricewaterhouseCoopers, *International Assignments Global Policy and Practice Key Trends 2002*, PricewaterhouseCoopers, 2002, p. 19.

71 M.G. Harvey, The Impact of Dual-career Families on International Relocations, *Human Resource Management Review*, Vol. 5, No. 3 (1995) pp. 223–244.

72 G.K. Stephens and S. Black, The Impact of Spouse's Career-orientation on Managers during International Transfers, *Journal of Management Studies*, Vol. 28, No. 4 (1991) p. 425.

73 The Conference Board, *Managing Expatriates' Return*, Report No. 1148-98-RR, New York: Conference Board 1996.

74 N.J. Adler, Women in International Management: Where Are They? *California Management Review*, Vol. 26, No. 4 (1984) pp. 78–89.

75 L.K. Stroh, A. Varma and S.J. Valy-Durbin, Why Are Women Left at Home: Are They Unwilling to Go on International Assignments? *Journal of World Business*, Vol. 35, No. 3 (2000) pp. 241–255.

76 P.A. Caligiuri and R.L. Tung, Comparing the Success of Male and Female Expatriates from a US-based Multinational Company, *International Journal of Human Resource Management*, Vol. 10, No. 5 (1999) pp. 763–782.

77 I.C. Fischlmayr, Female Self-perception as Barrier to International Careers? *International Journal of Human Resource Management*, Vol. 13, No. 5 (2002) pp. 773–783.

78 W. Mayrhofer and H. Scullion, Female Expatriates in International Business: Empirical Evidence from the German Clothing Industry, *International Journal of Human Resource Management*, Vol. 13, No. 5 (2002) pp. 815–836.

79 N.K. Napier and S. Taylor, Experiences of Women Professionals Abroad: Comparisons Across Japan, China and Turkey, *International Journal of Human Resource Management*, Vol. 13, No. 5 (2002) pp. 837–851.

Training and development

Chapter objectives

Training aims to improve employees' current work skills and behavior, whereas development aims to increase abilities in relation to some future position or job. In this chapter, we examine how the international assignment is a vehicle for both training and development, as reflected in the reasons why international assignments continue to play a strategic role in international business operations. The role of training in preparing and supporting personnel on international assignments is also considered. We examine the following issues:

- The role of training in supporting expatriate adjustment and on-assignment performance.

- Components of effective pre-departure training programs such as cultural awareness, preliminary visits and language skills. Relocation assistance and training for trainers are also addressed.

- The effectiveness of pre-departure training.

- The developmental aspect of international assignments and its relation to international career paths.

- Training and developing international management teams.

Reflecting the general literature on this topic, the focus of the chapter is on the traditional, expatriate assignment. However, where possible, we will draw out training and development aspects relating to short-term assignments, non-standard assignments and international business travelers.

Introduction

In order to compete successfully in a global market, more firms are focusing on the role of human resources as a critical part of their core competence and source of competitive advantage. As Kamoche[1] comments: 'The human resource refers to the accumulated stock of knowledge, skills, and abilities that the individuals possess, which the firm has built up over time into an identifiable expertise.' Training and development activities are part of the way in which the multinational builds it stock of human resources. An indication of the importance of this is the increasing number of multinationals that have established their own 'universities' or 'schools'. Motorola, McDonald's and Disney universities are good examples of these in-house training centers. Several European, Japanese and Korean firms have similar arrangements, such as the Lufthansa Business School and the Ericsson Management Institute.

The international assignment in itself is an important training and development tool:

- Expatriates are trainers, as part of the transfer of knowledge and competence between the various units – a major rationale for the use of international assignments. Whether implicitly or explicitly stated, they are expected to assist the multinational train and develop HCNs, that is, train their replacements.

- Expatriates are also expected to ensure that systems and processes are adopted, and inevitably they will be engaged in showing how these systems and processes work, in addition to monitoring the effective performance of HCNs.

- One of the reasons for international assignments is management development. A move into another area – job rotation – is a useful way for employees to gain a broader perspective. It assists in developing capable people who form the required pool of global operators, as discussed in earlier chapters.

Therefore, the way in which the multinational anticipates and provides suitable training for international assignments is an important first step. This is reflected in the growth of interest in, and provision of, pre-departure training to prepare expatriates and accompanying family members for the international assignment.

Figure 5-1 is a schematic representation of the structure of this chapter. It shows the link between international recruitment and selection, which we covered in Chapter 4, and training and development activities. Most expatriates are internal hires, selected from within the multinational's existing operations, although, as indicated by the dotted arrow in Figure 5-1, some expatriates may be hired externally for an international assignment. We will now consider the various elements related to

Figure 5-1	International training and development

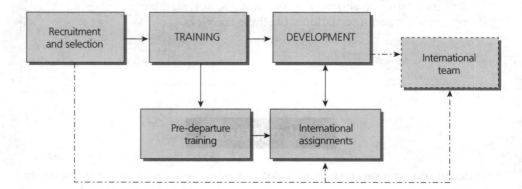

expatriate training and development in the context of managing and supporting international assignments.

The role of expatriate training

Given that the primary selection criterion is technical ability, it is not surprising to find that most of the literature is devoted to expatriate pre-departure training activities that are mainly concerned with developing cultural awareness. Attention to this aspect has been fueled by the reported link between expatriate failure rates and cultural adjustment discussed in Chapter 4. Therefore, once an employee has been selected for an expatriate position, pre-departure training is considered to be the next critical step in attempting to ensure the expatriate's effectiveness and success abroad, particularly where the destination country is considered culturally tough. In Figure 5-1, pre-departure training is indicated as a subset of general training. Effective cultural training, it is advocated, assists individuals to adjust more rapidly to the new culture. As Earley[2] points out, 'A major objective of intercultural training is to help people cope with unexpected events in a new culture.'

The limited, predominately US-based, research into this area reveals that a large number of US multinationals have been reluctant to provide even a basic level of pre-departure training, although this is slowly changing. Particular interest in the area began with Tung's study[3] on expatriation practices, including the use of pre-departure training programs. Her results showed that US multinationals tended to use training programs for expatriates less frequently than European and Japanese firms (32 compared with 69 and 57 per cent, respectively). The US attitude to the provision of pre-departure training appeared to persist through the 1980s. For example, a 1984 study of 1000 US multinationals found that only 25 per cent offered extensive pre-departure training programs[4] and a 1989 study of US firms found that only 13 per cent of respondents indicated that they would offer expatriates a pre-departure program.[5] Among the various reasons cited by firms in these studies was that top management did not believe that pre-departure training was necessary or effective.[6] So, although the potential benefits of cultural awareness training are widely acknowledged, such training was downgraded or not offered by a large number of US multinationals.[7]

The past decade has seen a change in attitude, due perhaps to cost considerations and also the growth of providers of pre-departure training that multinationals can access. For example, the 2002 survey of global relocation trends by GMAC Global Relocation Services (GRS) (in conjunction with the US National Foreign Trade Council and the SHRM Global Forum) referred to in Chapter 4 also covered pre-departure training trends. A total of 77 per cent of the 181 firms surveyed were US based. Cross-cultural training of at least 1 day's duration was provided by 64 per cent of responding firms. However, 76 per cent of this group indicated that attendance was optional. This is an improvement on the findings of a 1997 survey of European firms (including subsidiaries of non-European multinationals). Only 13 per cent of responding firms in this survey always provided expatriates with access to cultural awareness courses, although a further 47 per cent provided briefings for culturally 'challenging' postings (compared with 21 per cent in a 1995 survey).[8]

Previously, multinational firms placed less priority on providing pre-departure training for the spouse and family.[9] However, perhaps owing to increasing recognition of the interaction between expatriate performance and family adjustment, more multinationals are now extending their pre-departure training programs to include the spouse/partner and children. For example, in the GMAC-GRS 2002 survey, responses on the provision of pre-departure training reveal the majority include at least the accompanying spouse:

- whole family　　　　　　　33%
- expatriate and spouse　　　29%
- employee only　　　　　　2%
- none　　　　　　　　　　36%

In the 2002 survey of dual careers and international assignments by ORC Worldwide, also referred to in Chapter 4, the report's authors commented that provision of pre-departure training for accompanying spouses and partners continues to increase.

Components of effective pre-departure training programs

Studies indicate that the essential components of pre-departure training programs that contribute to a smooth transition to a foreign location include cultural awareness training, preliminary visits, language instruction and assistance with practical, day-to-day matters.[10] We will look at each of these in turn.

Cultural awareness programs

It is generally accepted that, to be effective, the expatriate employee must adapt to and not feel isolated from the host country. A well-designed, cultural awareness training program can be extremely beneficial, as it seeks to foster an appreciation of the host country's culture so that expatriates can behave accordingly, or at least develop appropriate coping patterns. As discussed in Chapter 4, without an understanding (or at least an acceptance) of the host country's culture in such a situation, the expatriate is likely to face some difficulty during the international assignment. Therefore, cultural awareness training remains the most common form of pre-departure training.

The components of cultural awareness programs vary according to country of assignment, duration, purpose of the transfer and the provider of such programs. As part of her study of expatriate management, Tung[11] identified five categories of pre-departure training, based on different learning processes, type of job, country of assignment and the time available. These were area studies programs that include environmental briefing and cultural orientation, culture assimilators, language training, sensitivity training and field experiences. To understand possible variations in expatriate training, Tung proposed a contingency framework for deciding the nature and level of rigor of training. The two determining factors were the degree of interaction required in the host culture and the similarity between the individual's native culture and the new culture. The related training elements in her framework involved the content of the training and the rigor of the training. Essentially, Tung argued that:

- If the expected interaction between the individual and members of the host culture was low, and the degree of dissimilarity between the individual's native culture and the host culture was low, then training should focus on task- and job-related issues rather than culture-related issues. The level of rigor necessary for effective training should be relatively low.

- If there was a high level of expected interaction with host nationals and a large dissimilarity between the cultures, then training should focus on cross-cultural skill development in addition to the new task. The level of rigor for such training should be moderate to high.

Tung's model specifies criteria for making training method decisions, such as degree of expected interaction and cultural similarity. One limitation of the model is that it does not assist the user to determine which specific training methods to use or what might constitute more or less rigorous training.

In 1997, Tung[12] revisited her earlier work, through a survey conducted in partnership with Arthur Andersen. She reported that her original recommendations held, although with some provisions:

- Training should be more orientated to life-long learning than 'one-shot' programs with an area-specific focus.
- There should be more emphasis on provision of foreign language training.
- There should be emphasis on the levels of communication competence, not just verbal communication, so the person becomes bicultural and bilingual, which allows an easier transition between one culture and another.
- Cross-cultural training assists in managing diversity.
- The preview of the expatriate position should be realistic, as this facilitates effective performance.

Mendenhall and Oddou[10] proposed a model that builds upon that of Tung's 1981 model, which was subsequently refined[13] (see Figure 5-2). These authors propose three dimensions: training methods, levels of training rigor and duration of the training relative to degree of interaction and culture novelty. These provide useful guidelines for determining an appropriate program. For example, if the expected level of interaction is low and the degree of similarity between the individual's home culture and the host culture is high, the length of the training should probably be less than 1 week. Methods such as area or cultural briefings via lectures, films or books would provide the appropriate level of training rigor.[14,15]

On the other hand, if the individual is going overseas for a period of 2–12 months and is expected to have some interaction with members of the host culture, the level of training rigor should be higher and its length longer (1–4 weeks). In addition to the information-giving approaches, training methods such as culture assimilators and role-plays may be appropriate.[16] If the individual is going to a fairly novel and different host culture and the expected degree of interaction is high, the level of cross-cultural training rigor should be high and training should last as long as 2 months. In addition to the less rigorous methods already discussed, sensitivity training, field experiences, and intercultural experiential workshops may be appropriate training methods in this situation.

Later, Black and Mendenhall[17] concluded that the earlier model, like that of Tung's, was primarily 'cultural' in nature, with little integration of the individual's new tasks and the new host culture. Black and Mendenhall therefore proposed what they described as an extensive theoretically based model using Bandura's social learning theory and prior cultural awareness training models. They take three aspects of social learning theory – attention, retention and reproduction – and show

how these are influenced by individual differences in expectations and motivation, and the incentives to apply learned behaviors in the foreign location. This approach recognizes that effective training is only the first step and that the expatriate's willingness and ability to act upon that training in the new environment are crucial to effective performance.

An obvious practical limitation of Black and Mendenhall's model is that insufficient time is often given as a reason why multinationals do not provide pre-departure training. It would therefore be difficult to develop appropriate pre-departure training programs in such cases. Other contextual and situational factors, such as cultural toughness, length of assignment and the nature/type of the job, may have a bearing on the content, method and processes involved in the cultural awareness training program. More importantly, monitoring and feedback should be recognized as important components of individual skill development, particularly as adjustment and performance are the desired outcomes of cultural awareness training.

Figure 5-3 draws together the components of the three models reviewed above. It stresses the importance of attention paid by the potential expatriate to the behaviors and probable outcomes of a cultural awareness training program, the individual's ability and willingness to retain learned behaviors and their reproduction as appropriate in the host location. Poor performance could be addressed by clarifying incentives for more effective reproduction of the required level of behavior or by providing additional cultural awareness training during the international assignment. Therefore, we combine adjustment and performance and link it to the performance

Figure 5-2	The Mendenhall, Dunbar and Oddou cross-cultural training model

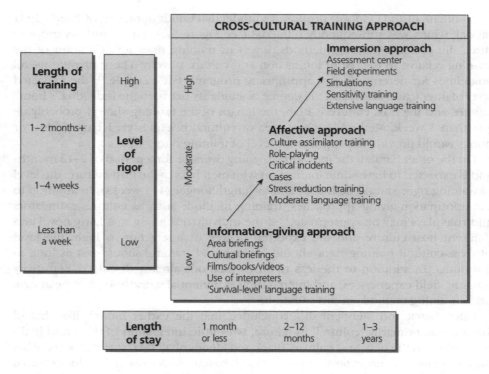

Source: M. Mendenhall, E. Dunbar, and G. Oddou, Expatriate Selection, Training and Career-pathing: a Review and Critique, *Human Resource Management*, Vol. 26 (1987) p. 338.

management system, whereas Black and Mendenhall have adjustment and performance as separate outcomes, with adjustment leading to performance. We argue that performance affects adjustment in many instances. Further, it seems important that adjustment and performance be linked to the multinational's performance management system, as will become clearer in Chapter 10, where we address performance management systems and issues.

Preliminary visits

One technique useful in orienting international employees is to send them on a preliminary trip to the host country. A well-planned trip overseas for the candidate and spouse provides a preview that allows them to assess their suitability for and interest in the assignment. Such a trip also serves to introduce expatriate candidates to the business context in the host location and helps encourage more informed pre-departure preparation. When used as part of a pre-departure training program, visits to the host location can assist in the initial adjustment process.

The 1997 European survey mentioned above reported that 53 per cent of firms always provided preliminary visits and a further 38 per cent indicated such use in certain circumstances. The average length of visit was about 1 week. The country of assignment was a determining factor. Visits were not provided if the country concerned was already known to the expatriate (perhaps from a previous visit either on firm-related business or as a tourist), or was perceived as culturally close (e.g. Zurich to Frankfurt or New York to Toronto). Unfortunately, the 2002 surveys by GMAC and ORC Worldwide do not deal with preliminary visits. However, a study of expatriates

---

Cultural awareness training and assignment performance

Figure 5-3

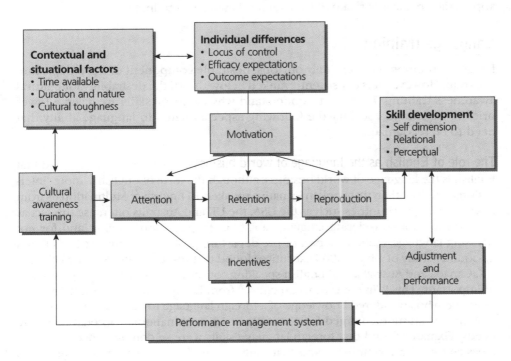

Source: Adapted from Tung,[11] Mendenhall *et al.*[13] and Black and Mendenhall.[7,17]

from Germany, the USA, Korea and Japan working in Singapore, and Singaporean repatriates and expatriates, did include preliminary visits as part of pre-departure training. Osman-Gani[18] reports that of these five groups, only the US expatriates rated preliminary visits as important, ranking them second behind cross-cultural training.

Obviously, the couple may reject the assignment on the basis of the preliminary visit. As one firm in the 1997 European study[19] is reported to have admitted: 'We do not provide pre-assignment visits where conditions are so poor that nobody would want to go.' Most firms that utilize preliminary visits, however, weigh cost against premature recall and underperformance risks. A potential problem is that the aim of the preliminary visit is often twofold – part of the selection decision and part of pre-departure training. The multinational could send mixed signals if it offers the preliminary visit as part of the selection process but the couple find upon arrival in the proposed country of assignment that they are expected to make decisions regarding suitable housing and schools. The couple may interpret such treatment as 'accepting the preliminary visit equals accepting the assignment', thus negating its role in the decision-making process. Where multinationals use the preliminary visit to allow the couple to make a more informed decision about accepting the overseas assignment, it should be used solely for that purpose. From the couple's perspective, when they have flown to the prospective location at the multinational's expense, it then may become more difficult to reject the assignment.

Combined with cultural awareness training, the preliminary visit is a useful component of a pre-departure program. Exposure to the expatriate community, if one exists in the proposed host location, can also be a positive outcome. Brewster and Pickard[20] found that an expatriate community has an influence on expatriate adjustment. Perhaps the welcome received from, and interaction with, current expatriates assist in developing a positive attitude to the assignment, confirming acceptance of the assignment, and even providing motivation to reproduce appropriate behaviors retained from cultural awareness training.

Language training

Language training is a seemingly obvious, desirable component of a pre-departure program. However, it is consistently ranked below that of the desirability for cultural awareness training. In trying to understand why language skills are given a lower priority we should consider the following aspects related to language ability that need to be recognized.

The role of English as the language of world business.   It is generally accepted that English is the language of world business, although the form of English is more 'international English' than that spoken by native speakers of English.[21] Multinationals from English-speaking countries such as the USA, the UK and Australia often use this fact as a reason for not considering language ability in the selection process, and for not stressing language training as part of pre-departure programs. Tung[12] reports that a 12-country study of almost 3000 executives found that respondents from the USA, the UK, Canada and Australia – all English-speaking countries – deemed language skills as unimportant. This is in contrast to executives from Europe, Asia and South America, however, who considered knowledge of a foreign language to be critical to success.

A similar attitude emerged from a study of US multinationals' foreign language needs. Fixman[22] found that foreign language skills were seldom included as part of cross-cultural understanding, and that language problems were largely viewed as mechanical and manageable problems that could easily be solved. As Pucik[23] comments, an exclusive reliance on English diminishes the multinational's linguistic capacity. The resultant lack of language competence has strategic and operational implications as it limits the multinational's ability to monitor competitors and process important information. For example, translation services, particularly those external to the firm, cannot make strategic inferences and firm-specific interpretations of language specific data. Fixman[24] raises the question of protecting important technology in international joint venture activities: 'It would seem that the less one understands of a partner's language, the less likely one is to detect theft of technology.' Perhaps more importantly, as Wright and Wright[25] in their study of British firms point out, to accept English as the *de facto* language of international business gives the advantage to the other person:

> The other speaker controls what is communicated and what is understood. The monolingual English speaker has less room to manoeuvre, no possibility of finding out more than he [or she] is given. His position forces him to be reactive rather than proactive in the relationship. What he says and understands is filtered through the other speaker's competence, over which he has no control.

Disregarding the importance of foreign language skills may reflect a degree of ethnocentrism. A study by Hall and Gudykunst[26] has shown that the lower the level of perceived ethnocentrism in an MNE, the more training it provides in cultural awareness and language training. It also reflects a degree of perhaps unconscious arrogance on the part of expatriates from English-speaking countries. However, more firms are including language training, as evidenced by recent surveys. For example, the ORC Worldwide 2002 survey revealed that provision of language training to spouses and partners, as part of pre-departure training programs, had markedly increased; 59 per cent of the responding firms provided language training prior to departure and 74 per cent provided language training while the person was on assignment. In fact, it was the most common form of spousal assistance while on assignment. Language fluency is seen to be a key to adjustment.

Perhaps as a result of the increased global competitive pressures, and growing awareness of its strategic and operational importance, more US multinationals are requesting that US business schools include foreign languages in their curricula and are giving hiring preference to graduates with foreign language skills. A similar trend is evident in the UK and in Australia.

Host-country language skills and adjustment. Clearly, the ability to speak a foreign language can improve the expatriate's effectiveness and negotiating ability. As Baliga and Baker[15] point out, it can improve managers' access to information regarding the host country's economy, government and market. Of course, the degree of fluency required may depend on the level and nature of the position that the expatriate holds in the foreign operation, and the amount of interaction with external stakeholders such as government officials, clients and trade officials, and with host-country nationals.

In a survey of 400 expatriates by Tung and Arthur Andersen,[27] the importance of language skills was identified as a critical component in assignment performance. Respondents indicated that ability to speak the local language, regardless of how different the culture was to their home country, was as important as cultural awareness in their ability to adapt and perform on assignment. Knowledge of the host-country language can assist expatriates and family members gain access to new social support structures outside of work and the expatriate community.

Language skills are therefore important in terms of task performance and cultural adjustment. Their continued omission from pre-departure training can be partly explained by the length of time it takes to acquire even a rudimentary level of language competence. Hiring language-competent staff to enlarge the 'language pool' from which potential expatriates may be drawn is one answer, but its success depends on up-to-date information being kept on all employees, and frequent language auditing to see whether language skills are maintained.[28]

Knowledge of the corporate language.   As previously mentioned, multinationals tend to adopt (either deliberately or by default) a common company language to facilitate reporting and other control mechanisms. Given its place in international business, often English becomes the common language within these multinationals and, as we identified in Chapter 3, expatriates can become language nodes, performing as communication conduits between subsidiary and headquarters, owing to their ability to speak the corporate language.

It also can give added power to their position in the subsidiary, as expatriates – particularly PCNs – often have access to information that those not fluent in the corporate language are denied. An expatriate fluent in the parent-company language and the language of the host subsidiary can perform a gate-keeping role, whatever the formal position the expatriate may hold. A PCN working in a middle management position in the Mexican subsidiary for the Finnish multinational Kone Elevators provides a good example of the power of language, particularly its gate-keeping potential. As Figure 5-4 illustrates, the expatriate was fluent in Finnish (the parent-country language), English (the corporate language) and Spanish (host-country language) – position 1 in Figure 5-4. The subsidiary manager at the time was not fluent in English, and had no knowledge of Finnish – position 2 in Figure 5-4. The expatriate became the language mediator between headquarters and Mexican subsidiary managers. His role as translator meant that the Finnish expatriate had access to sensitive information, placing him in a powerful gate-keeper role to an extent not usually found at his lower hierarchical position. Further, if the expatriate was absent from the office, some work was delayed until his return.

It will be recalled from the GE case, presented in Chapter 2, that Tungsram employees were transferred to GE plants in the USA for technical and operative

---

| **Figure 5-4** | The impact of language on power |

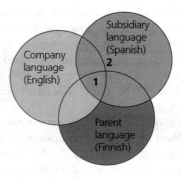

Source: Adapted from R. Marschan-Piekkari, D. Welch and L. Welch, In the Shadow: the Impact of Language on Structure, Power and Communication in the Multinational, *International Business Review*, Vol. 8, No. 4 (1999) p. 432.

training. Likewise, the Pepsi-Cola International Management Institute is an umbrella system for the delivery of training programs such as sales force management or production techniques for the manufacturing of Pepsi brands. Part of this approach is the 'Designate Program', which brings HCNs to the USA for a minimum of 18 months of training in the domestic US Pepsi system. Fiat, the Italian automobile manufacturer, uses staff transfers as part of its training program, with HCN recruits spending time at corporate headquarters. All of these training programs will be conducted in the corporate language. Fluency in the corporate language is, therefore, a prerequisite for international training assignments and may constrain the ability of subsidiary employees to attend and benefit from such training. Pre-departure training programs need to include both the language of the host country and the corporate language.

Practical assistance

Another component of a pre-departure training program is that of providing information that assists in relocation. Practical assistance makes an important contribution toward the adaptation of the expatriate and his or her family to their new environment. Being left to fend for oneself may result in a negative response toward the host country's culture, and/or contribute to a perceived violation of the psychological contract. Many multinationals now take advantage of relocation specialists to provide this practical assistance, for example, in finding suitable accommodation and schools. Further language training for the expatriate and family could be provided, particularly if such training was not possible before departure. Usually, during the assignment, host country HR staff will organize any further orientation programs and language training. However, it is important that corporate HRM staff liaise with the sending line manager in addition to the HR department in the foreign location to insure that practical assistance is provided.

Training for the training role

Expatriates are often used because of a lack of suitably trained staff in the host location. Consequently, expatriates often find themselves training HCNs as their replacements. The obvious question is how expatriates are prepared for this training role. Our review of extant literature indicates that this aspect has yet to be specifically addressed. We do know from the cross-cultural management literature that there are differences in the way people approach tasks and problems, and that this can have an impact on the learning process.[29] The ability to transfer knowledge and skills in a culturally sensitive manner perhaps should be an integral part of pre-departure training programs.

TCN and HCN expatriate training

Anecdotal evidence suggests that in some firms pre-departure training may not be provided to TCNs being transferred to another subsidiary, and for HCNs transferred into the parent country operations. Where it is provided, it may not be to the extent of that available to PCNs. As an Australian working in the Japanese subsidiary of a US multinational remarked: 'We [that is, TCNs] were third-class nationals in Japan. The Americans received cultural training about Japan before they left the US. We were just given our plane tickets.' This omission could create perceptions of inequitable treatment in situations where PCN and TCNs work in the same foreign location, and affect adjustment to the international assignment.

Not considering the need for HCNs transferred to the parent organization reflects an ethnocentric attitude.[30] As mentioned in Chapter 1, the approach taken by the Finnish telecommunications firm Nokia to adopt the terms 'expatriate' for those being sent out from the unit (whether parent or subsidiary) and 'inpatriate' for those coming into the unit (whether PCN, TCN or HCN) is one way for a multinational to signal that all who work internationally require management and support. In order to design and implement TCN and HCN pre-departure training, local management, particularly those in the HR department, need to be conscious of the demands of an international assignment – just as we have discussed in terms of corporate/headquarters HR staff. There perhaps needs also to be recognition and encouragement of this from headquarters, and monitoring to ensure that sufficient subsidiary resources are allocated for such training.

Provision of training for non-traditional expatriate assignments

In theory, all staff should be provided with the necessary level of pre-departure training given the demands of the international assignment. Cultural adjustment is inherent in international staff transfers. Pre-departure training should also be provided for employees on short-term assignments, on non-standard assignments such as commuting and to international business travelers – the non-expatriates discussed in Chapter 3. However, there is a paucity of information regarding pre-departure training for non-standard assignments.

Short-term and non-standard assignments.   Given the generally low level of provision of pre-departure training to traditional expatriates, it is not surprising to find that those on short-term and non-standard assignments receive little or no preparation before departure. The oversight may be due to lack of time, which is a standard reason for non-provision of pre-departure training.

This may be why multinationals are beginning to use modern technology to overcome time and resource constraints. For example, the GMAC-GRS 2002 survey referred to earlier asked respondents if they used CD-based and web-based cross-cultural programs. Only 21 per cent of responding firms used such facilities, of which:

- 60 per cent used CD and web-based programs as additional forms of support for in-person programs
- 41 per cent used CD and web-based programs as stand-alone alternatives
- 16 per cent indicated that CD and web-based programs were the only form of pre-departure training offered.

One firm explained that employees on short-term assignments were provided with access to web-based information, whereas longer term expatriates were provided with both in-person and web-based programs. The GMAC-GRS data revealed that firms with smaller expatriate populations (1–25 and 51–100) were more likely to use CD- or web-based cross-cultural training than did firms with over 100 expatriates.

International business travelers.   Non-expatriates, as we discussed in Chapter 3, tend to be a forgotten group, yet for many firms they may comprise the largest contingent of employees involved in international business. International business travelers are flying into and out of foreign operations performing a myriad of tasks, including training, for example, explaining new product development, or service or process, to HCN employees that will involve demonstrations, seminar presentations and other methods of information dissemination. Such internal company interaction usually will involve the use of the corporate language. Therefore, non-expatriates need to be aware that HCNs will differ in their level of competence. It is easy to equate intelligence with language fluency, perceiving lack of fluency as a sign of stupidity. Company briefings and training sessions will need to take into account local variances in how people conduct themselves in formal situations and approach the 'classroom' situation.

International business travelers may be providing new product information to foreign agents or distributors. These activities naturally involve cross-cultural interaction. Competence in the local language or at least an ability to work with and through interpreters may be required. The same applies to those conducting negotiations with host-government officials, prospective clients, suppliers and subcontractors.

All these activities are strategically important yet there is little in the literature regarding the provision of training for these roles. From the limited, mainly anec-dotal, information available, it would seem that non-expatriates learn on the job, and gradually acquire the knowledge and skills to function effectively in various coun-tries and situations.[31]

The effectiveness of pre-departure training

The objective of pre-departure training is to assist the expatriate to adjust to the demands of living and working in a foreign location. The questions are how effect-ive such training is and what components have been considered to be essential by those who have been provided pre-departure training.

The 2002 GMAC-GRS survey asked firms to indicate the value of cross-cultural preparation for expatriate success; 35 per cent indicated it was of great value, 45 per cent reported high value and 17 per cent considered it of medium value. However, the report's authors did not provide information on how the responding firms evaluated their training, how such training was provided and what was covered in their cross-cultural training.

Two recent academic studies have attempted to assess the effectiveness of pre-departure training. Eschbach *et al.*[32] report the results of a study of 79 US repatriates (returnees from international assignments, as explained in Chapter 7). They measured cognitive, affective and experiential cross-cultural training, and language training, provided by the company or self-initiated. The amount and type of training, based on the models of Tung and Black *et al.* described earlier in this chapter, was included. Expatriates with integrated cross-cultural training exhibited cultural proficiency earlier and appeared to have greater job satisfaction than those with lesser training. Repatriates commented that there was a need for accurate, up-to-date cultural and language training for expatriates and spouses and many considered that preliminary visits should be used.

The second study was a meta-analysis of the cross-cultural training literature.[33] The conclusion reached was that the effectiveness of cross-cultural training was somewhat weaker than expected, owing to:

● Limited data as few organizations systematically evaluate or validate the effectiveness of their training programs or make them available to the public.

- The use of a mixture of different training methods, making evaluation of which method is most effective difficult to isolate.
- The large diversity in cultures that expatriates face.
- The interaction between individual differences between expatriates and the work environment they face. What works for one person may not work for another. Hence the effects of cross-cultural training can be as diverse as the countries to which expatriates are assigned.

The authors add that traditional training methods may underestimate the complexity of international business life, where expatriate managers are required to perform complex jobs across multiple cultural contexts, sometimes on the same day or even within the hour. Training programs that capture this reality are difficult to find and many existing cross-cultural training programs have yet to prove their utility.[34]

Developing staff through international assignments

International assignments have long been recognized as an important mechanism for developing international expertise, as discussed in Chapter 3. The expected outcomes are:

- *Management development*. Individuals gain international experience, which assists in career progression, whereas the multinational gains through having a pool of experienced international operators on which to draw for future international assignments.
- *Organizational development*. International assignments also provide a multinational with a way of accumulating a stock of knowledge, skills and abilities upon which it can base its future growth. A global mindset is an important side benefit, as key personnel take a broader view. Further, as discussed previously, expatriates are agents of direct control and socialization, and assist in the transfer of knowledge and competence.

We shall now consider these outcomes, first from the perspective of the individual and then from the multinational's viewpoint.

Individual development

An international assignment can be compared with job rotation, a management development tool that seeks to provide certain employees with opportunities to enhance their abilities by exposing them to a range of jobs, tasks and challenges. It is therefore not surprising to find an implicit assumption that an international assignment has *per se* management development potential. Along with expected financial gain, perceived career advancement is often a primary motive for accepting international assignments.

However, there is a paucity of research that demonstrates the link between an international assignment and career advancement. Two exceptions are studies by Feldman and Thomas[35] and Naumann.[36] While these studies confirm career expectations as motives, the expatriates involved were taken from those currently on assignment. Over a decade later, there remains a need for research that establishes career paths as a direct consequence of international assignments.

There are two possible explanations for this lack of interest in the career outcomes of international assignments:

- Companies and academics have been somewhat preoccupied with the process of expatriation from the organization's perspective. It is important to understand the roles played by the various international HRM activities so that proper management and support for expatriates can be provided to reduce underperformance and improve cost-effectiveness.

- Surveys consistently report that expatriates consider career progression as a primary motive for accepting international assignments. Such a consistency of response – that is, career advancement as a reason for accepting an overseas assignment – has masked the issue of whether these career expectations are, indeed, met. In other words, we know why people accept international assignments, but we do not have a clear picture of when and how these expectations are met, and the consequences to both the individual and the multinational if the expected career outcomes are not met. The discussion of the employment relationship in Chapter 4 raised the possibility of violation of the psychological contract and weakening commitment as possible outcomes of unmet career expectations.

It is possible to trace the typical assignment and identify critical decision points that may have career-related outcomes for a particular individual. Figure 5-5 attempts to illustrate a sequence that may be common to expatriates (that is, PCNs, TCNs as well as HCNs who accept assignments to the parent operations). For ease of discussion, we will simply refer to the sending unit or subsidiary as 'parent'.

Figure 5-5 follows the stages of expatriation from recruitment and selection to completion of the particular assignment. The numerals are positioned at what have been identified as critical decision points. For example, Decision Point 1 occurs during recruitment and selection for a specific assignment, where the expatriate either applies, or is informally selected, for an international assignment. Further

---

Expatriate career decision points

Figure 5-5

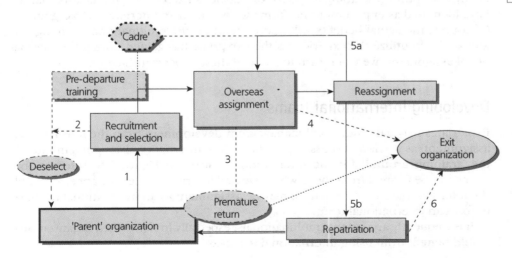

Source: D. Welch, Expatriation and Career Development in the Changing Global Workscape, Paper presented at the 23rd Annual EIBA Conference, Stuttgart, 14–16 December 1997.

information about the host location during the recruitment and selection process (including pre-departure training if that is available), or family considerations, may prompt the potential candidate to withdraw at this point. Hence Decision Point 2 is 'deselect'. There may be some career considerations as to whether a voluntary withdrawal at this point would have a negative consequence upon the person's future. Such a perception may influence the individual's decision to accept rather than reject the assignment.

As discussed earlier in terms of adjustment and performance, the expatriate may decide to leave the international assignment (as indicated in Decision Point 3 – Premature return). The individual then is assigned a position back in the 'parent' operation. The premature return may or may not have career advancement consequences. Alternatively, as indicated by Decision Point 4, the expatriate may decide to exit the organization – prompted by a perceived violation of the psychological contract, or perhaps as a result of another job offer that is perceived to be better in terms of the person's career. This may be with a domestic firm back in the home country or with another foreign multinational.

Decision Point 5 – Reassignment – either can be back into the 'parent' organization or the person may accept another international assignment. Those who elect to take a consecutive international assignment may, upon subsequent reassignment, return to the 'parent' operation, or become part of what is often referred to as the international 'cadre' or team. As we will discuss in Chapter 7, reassignment (or repatriation) back into the 'parent' operation is a common ending to an international assignment and may or may not be to a position that leads to career advancement. There is a suggestion that turnover among repatriates may be as a consequence of a perceived lack of career advancement on the basis of the international experience. Decision Point 6 can be relevant at this stage, as indicated by the dotted arrow connecting 'Repatriation' with 'Exit organization'.

These decision points are based upon the issues that we have discussed in the preceding chapters and also upon the suggestions in the literature regarding the management development potential of international assignments. How individuals react at each point may vary according to the perceived value of the assignment. It may depend on whether the perceived benefits outweigh the costs in terms of family disruption (including a spouse or partner's career) and the factors that we have identified as important to performance while on an international assignment. Of course, the actual benefits will also depend on the multinational's willingness and ability to utilize the experiences the expatriate has gained during the international assignment. We will return to some of these aspects in Chapter 7.

Developing international teams

Expatriates may gain individual management development from the international assignment, as we have discussed previously. The international assignment often is the 'training ground' for the international 'cadre' in Figure 5-6. International teams can be formed from those who have had international experience, although the international assignment itself may be assignment to an international team, or to form an international team.

It is frequently argued that multinationals, especially in networked organizations, would benefit from using international teams as:

● a mechanism for fostering innovation, organizational learning and the transfer of knowledge

- a means of breaking down functional and national boundaries, enhancing horizontal communication and information flows
- a way of encouraging diverse inputs into decisions, problem-solving and strategic assessments
- a way of developing a global perspective
- a way of developing shared values, thus assisting in the use of informal, normative control through socialization.

Research and development and international projects are common situations where teamwork is utilized and forms the basis of much of the literature on multinational teams, a sub-set of which is the virtual team, where members are geographically dispersed (see Figure 5-6).

To a certain extent, international assignments achieve team-building by exposing employees to various parts of the global organization. Consequently, expatriates develop local networks that often persist after completion of the assignment. These predominantly informal networks can later be activated for work situations, such as providing membership of project teams. Take the following hypothetical example. Günther, an engineer from the German subsidiary, spent two years assisting the construction of the Chinese factory, during which time he worked with Arnie, the project manager from the US parent company. A year after the Chinese project was completed, Arnie was placed in charge of building a similar factory in India. He immediately asks for Günther to be assigned as part of the project team, in addition to two Chinese engineers who had impressed Arnie during his time in China. Thus, Arnie's informal network influences the proposed composition of his project team. In addition, Arnie has identified potential international operators – Günther from the German subsidiary and the two HCNs with whom he worked in China.

Developing international teams through international assignments   **Figure 5-6**

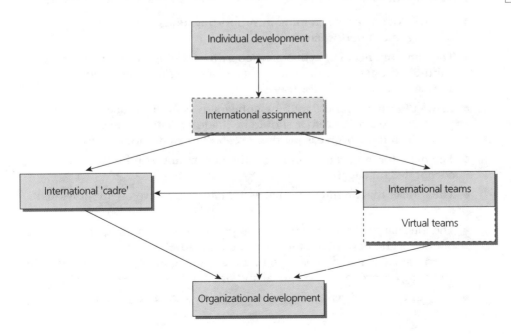

Not everyone will wish to become part of an international 'cadre' but, to create an effective global pool of international operators, many multinationals are conscious that they need to provide international experience to many levels of managers, regardless of nationality. A small cadre comprised only of PCNs may defeat the purpose of having a team of experienced employees who are capable of operating in multiple environments on various types of tasks and jobs.

While the international assignment plays an important role in both management and organizational development, its effectiveness depends on the individuals concerned, the type of multinational and contextual factors. For example, Caligiuri and Di Santo[37] argue that certain personality characteristics that have been identified as expatriate predictors of success cannot be developed through international assignments. In other words, individual characteristics such as dogmatic or authoritarian tendencies are not likely to be altered through an expatriate experience. However, Caligiuri and Di Santo do suggest that individuals can learn to be more sensitive to the challenges of working in another country, that is, become culturally aware. This knowledge and experience would prove valuable when working in an international team comprised of colleagues from other nationalities.

The multinational needs to be able to provide the resources and support for those working in international teams such as R&D projects. Managers supervising international teams, for example, will need to understand processes such as group dynamics, especially how national cultures affect group functioning. Those who have previous experience of international assignments and teams will be better placed than those who have not. Perhaps this is why some multinationals are placing greater stress on the need for international experience and are prepared to use expatriates despite the cost and difficulties often associated with international assignments.

Summary

This chapter has concentrated on the issues relating to training and developing expatriates for international assignments. In the process, we have discussed:

- The role of expatriate training in supporting adjustment and on-assignment performance.

- The components of effective pre-departure training programs such as cultural awareness, preliminary visits, language skills, relocation assistance and training for trainers.

- How cultural awareness training appears to assist in adjustment and performance and therefore should be made available to all categories of staff selected for overseas postings, regardless of duration and location.

- The need for language training for the host country and in the relevant corporate language.

- The impact that an international assignment may have on an individual's career.

- The international assignment as an important way of training international operators and developing the international 'cadre'. In this sense, an international assignment is both training (gaining international experience and competence) and managerial and organizational development.

- How international assignments are connected to the creation of international teams.

Discussion questions and exercises

1 What are some of the challenges faced in training expatriate managers?

2 You are the Group HR director for a small company that has begun to use international assignments. You are considering using an external consulting firm to provide pre-departure training for employees, as you do not have the resources to provide this 'in-house'. What components will you need covered? How will you measure the effectiveness of the pre-departure training program provided by this external consultant?

3 How does an international assignment assist in developing a 'cadre' of international operators? Why is it necessary to have such a 'cadre'?

4 Why do some multinationals appear reluctant to provide basic pre-departure training?

5 Consider the hypothetical case of Arnie and his preferred team members for the proposed Indian project. What factors are likely to facilitate and inhibit his ability to form this team?

Further reading

D.M. Schweiger, T. Atamer and R. Calori, 2003. Transnational Project Teams and Networks: Making the Multinational Organization More Effective, *Journal of World Business*, Vol. 38, No. 2, pp. 127–140.

T.R. Kayworth and D.E. Leidner, 2001/2002. Leadership Effectiveness in Global Virtual Teams, *Journal of Management Information Systems*, Vol. 18, No. 3, pp. 7–40.

M.A. Morris and C. Robie, 2001. A Meta-analysis of the Effects of Cross-cultural Training on Expatriate Performance and Adjustment, *International Journal of Training and Development*, Vol. 5, No. 2, pp. 112–125.

P.C. Earley and E. Mosakowski, 2000. Creating Hybrid Team Cultures: an Empirical Test of Transnational Team Functioning, *Academy of Management Journal*, Vol. 43, No. 1, pp. 26–49.

M. Osman-Gani, 2000. Developing Expatriates for the Asia-Pacific Region: a Comparative Analysis of Multinational Enterprise Managers from Five Countries Across Three Continents, *Human Resource Development Quarterly*, Vol. 11, No. 3, pp. 213–235.

J. Selmer, 2000. A Quantitative Needs Assessment Technique for Cross-cultural Work Adjustment Training, *Human Resource Development Quarterly*, Vol. 11, No. 3, pp. 269–281.

L.A. Peterson, 1997. International HRD: What We Know and Don't Know, *Human Resource Development Quarterly*, Vol. 8, No. 1, pp. 63–79.

Notes and references

1 K. Kamoche, Strategic Human Resource Management with a Resource-capability View of the Firm, *Journal of Management Studies*, Vol. 33, No. 2 (1996) p. 216.

2 P.C. Earley, Intercultural Training for Managers: a Comparison, *Academy of Management Journal*, Vol. 30, No. 4 (1987) p. 686.

3 R. Tung, Selection and Training Procedures of U.S., European, and Japanese Multinationals, *California Management Review*, Vol. 25, No. 1 (1982) pp. 57–71. Tung also asked those respondents who reported no formal training programs to give reasons for omitting these programs. Again, differences were found between the three regions. The US companies cited a trend toward employment of local nationals (45 per cent), the temporary nature of such assignments (28 per cent), the doubtful effectiveness of such training programs (20 per cent) and lack of time (4 per cent). The reasons given by European multinationals were the temporary nature of such assignments (30 per cent), lack of time (30 per cent), a trend toward employment of local nationals (20 per cent) and the doubtful effectiveness of such programs. Responses from the Japanese companies were lack of time (63 per cent) and doubtful effectiveness of such programs (37 per cent).

4 J.C. Baker, Foreign Language and Departure Training in U.S. Multinational Firms, *Personnel Administrator*, July (1984) pp. 68–70.

5   D. Feldman, Relocation Practices, *Personnel,* Vol. 66, No. 11 (1989) pp. 22–25; see also J. McEnery and G. DesHarnais, Culture Shock, *Training and Development Journal,* April (1990) pp. 43–47.

6   M. Mendenhall and G. Oddou, The Dimensions of Expatriate Acculturation, *Academy of Management Review,* Vol. 10 (1985) pp. 39–47; Y. Zeira, Overlooked Personnel Problems in Multinational Corporations, *Columbia Journal of World Business,* Vol. 10, No. 2 (1975) pp. 96–103.

7   J.S. Black and M. Mendenhall, Cross-cultural Training Effectiveness: a Review and a Theoretical Framework for Future Research, *Academy of Management Review,* Vol. 15, No. 1 (1990) pp. 113–136.

8   Price Waterhouse, *International Assignments: European Policy and Practice.* Price Waterhouse, 1997–98.

9   K. Barham and M. Devine, *The Quest for the International Manager: a Survey of Global Human Resource Strategies,* Ashridge Management Research Group, Special Report No. 2098, London: The Economist Intelligence Unit, 1990; see also, D. Welch, Determinants of International Human Resource Management Approaches and Activities: A Suggested Framework, *Journal of Management Studies,* Vol. 31, No. 2 (1994) pp. 139–164.

10 See, for example, M. Mendenhall and G. Oddou, Acculturation Profiles of Expatriate Managers: Implications for Cross-cultural Training Programs, *Columbia Journal of World Business,* Winter (1986) pp. 73–79.

11 R. Tung, Selecting and Training of Personnel for Overseas Assignments, *Columbia Journal of World Business,* Vol. 16 (1981) pp. 68–78.

12 R.L. Tung, A Contingency Framework of Selection and Training of Expatriates Revisited, *Human Resource Management Review,* Vol. 8, No. 1 (1998) 23–37.

13 M. Mendenhall, E. Dunbar and G. Oddou, Expatriate Selection, Training and Career-pathing: a Review and Critique, *Human Resource Management,* Vol. 26 (1987) pp. 331–345.

14 Earley advocates the use of both documentary and interpersonal methods to prepare managers for intercultural assignments: P. Earley, International Training for Managers: a Comparison of Documentary and Interpersonal Methods, *Academy of Management Journal,* Vol. 30 (1987) pp. 685–698.

15 Baliga and Baker suggest that the expatriate receive training that concentrates on the assigned region's culture, history, politics, economy, religion, and social and business practices. They argue that only with precise knowledge of the varied components of their host culture can the expatriate and family grasp how and why people behave and react as they do: G. Baliga and J.C. Baker, Multinational Corporate Policies for Expatriate Managers: Selection, Training, and Evaluation, *Advanced Management Journal,* Autumn (1985), pp. 31–38.

16 For further information on the use of cultural assimilators, see R.W. Brislin, A Culture General Assimilator: Preparation for Various Types of Sojourns, *International Journal of Intercultural Relations,* Vol. 10 (1986) pp. 215–234; K. Cushner, Assessing the Impact of a Culture General Assimilator, *International Journal of Intercultural Relations,* Vol. 13 (1989) pp. 125–146.

17 J.S. Black and M. Mendenhall, A Practical But Theory-based Framework for Selecting Cross-cultural Training Methods, *Human Resource Management,* Vol. 28, No. 4 (1989) pp. 511–539. See also J.S. Black and M.E. Mendenhall, A Practical but Theory-based Framework for Selecting Cross-cultural Training Methods, in *Readings and Cases in International Human Resource Management,* ed. M. Mendenhall and G. Oddou, Boston, MA: PWS-Kent, 1991.

18 A.M. Osman-Gani, Developing Expatriates for the Asia-Pacific Region: a Comparative Analysis of Multinational Enterprise Managers from Five Countries Across Three Continents, *Human Resource Development Quarterly,* Vol. 11, No. 3 (2000) pp. 213–235.

19 Price Waterhouse, *International Assignments: European Policy and Practice,* Price Waterhouse, 1997–98, p. 35.

20 C. Brewster and J. Pickard, Evaluating Expatriate Training, *International Studies of Management and Organization,* Vol. 24, No. 3 (1994) pp. 18–35.

21 C. Wright and S. Wright, Do Languages Really Matter? The Relationship Between International Business Success and a Commitment to Foreign Language Use, *Journal of Industrial Affairs,* Vol. 3, No. 1 (1994) pp. 3–14. These authors suggest that international English is perhaps a better term than 'poor' or 'broken' English.

22 C. Fixman, The Foreign Language Needs of U.S.-based Corporations, *Annals AAPSS,* Vol. 511, September (1990).

23 V. Pucik, Strategic Human Resource Management in a Multinational Firm, in *Strategic Management of Multinational Corporations: the Essentials,* ed. H.V. Wortzel and L.H. Wortzel, New York: Wiley, 1985.

24 C. Fixman, The Foreign Language Needs of U.S.-based Corporations, *Annals AAPSS*, Vol. 511, September (1990), p. 36.

25 C. Wright and S. Wright, Do Languages Really Matter? The Relationship Between International Business Success and a Commitment to Foreign Language Use, *Journal of Industrial Affairs*, Vol. 3, No. 1 (1994), p. 5.

26 P.H. Hall and W.B. Gudykunst, The Relationship of Perceived Ethnocentrism in Corporate Cultures to the Selection, Training, and Success of International Employees, *International Journal of Intercultural Relations,* Vol. 13 (1989) pp. 183–201.

27 R.L. Tung and Arthur Andersen, *Exploring International Assignees' Viewpoints: a Study of the Expatriation/Repatriation Process*, Chicago: Arthur Andersen International Executive Services, 1997.

28 R. Marschan, D. Welch and L. Welch, Language: the Forgotten Factor in Multinational Management, *European Management Journal*, Vol. 15, No. 5 (1997) pp. 591–597; see also Ref. 22.

29 See, for example, H. Park, S.D. Hwang and J.K. Harrison, Sources and Consequences of Communication Problems in Foreign Subsidiaries: the Case of United States Firms in South Korea, *International Business Review*, Vol. 5, No. 1 (1996) pp. 79–98; A. Rao and K. Hashimoto, Intercultural Influence: a Study of Japanese Expatriate Managers in Canada, *Journal of International Business Studies*, Vol. 27, No. 3 (1996) pp. 443–466.

30 M. Harvey, 'Inpatriation' Training: the Next Challenge for International Human Resource Management, *International Journal of Intercultural Relations*, Vol. 21, No. 3 (1997) pp. 393–428.

31 An exception is an article by R.S. DeFrank, R. Konopaske and J.M. Ivancevich, Executive Travel Stress: Perils of the Road Warrior, *Academy of Management Executive*, Vol. 14, No. 2 (2000) pp. 58–71. However, the authors devote only one paragraph to host-culture issues.

32 D.M. Eschbach, G.E. Parker and P.A. Stoeberl, American Repatriate Employees' Retrospective Assessments of the Effects of Cross-cultural Training on their Adaptation to International Assignments, *International Journal of Human Resource Management*, Vol. 12, No. 2 (2001) pp. 270–287.

33 M.A. Morris and C. Robie, A Meta-analysis of the Effects of Cross-cultural Training on Expatriate Performance and Adjustment, *International Journal of Training and Development*, Vol. 5, No. 2 (2001) pp. 112–125. The authors define meta-analysis as 'a method developed in the late 1970s to summarize and integrate research findings from multiple articles ... to resolve conflicting findings of multiple studies on the same topic by combining their results in a systematic fashion', pp. 113–114.

34 J. Selmer, I. Torbiön, and C.T. de Leon, Sequential Cross-cultural Training for Expatriate Business Managers: Pre-departure and Post-arrival, *International Journal of Human Resource Management*, Vol. 9, No. 5 (1998) pp. 831–840.

35 D.C. Feldman and D.C. Thomas, Career Issues Facing Expatriate Managers, *Journal of International Business Studies*, Vol. 23, No. 2 (1992) pp. 271–294.

36 E. Naumann, A Conceptual Model of Expatriate Turnover, *Journal of International Business Studies*, Vol. 23, No. 3 (1992) pp. 449–531.

37 P. Caligiuri and V. Di Santo, Global Competence: What is It, and Can It be Developed Through Global Assignments? *Human Resource Planning*, Vol. 24, No. 3 (2001) pp. 27–35.

Compensation*

Chapter objectives

In the introductory chapter we described IHR managers as
grappling with complex issues. International managers must
(1) manage more activities from a broader perspective, (2) be more
involved in the lives of their far-flung employees, (3) balance the
needs of PCNs, HCNs and TCNs, (4) control exposure to financial
and political risks and (5) be increasingly aware of and responsive
to host-country and regional influences. All of these issues and
concerns are brought out in a discussion of compensation issues.
In this chapter we:

- Examine the complexities that arise when firms move from
  compensation at the domestic level to compensation in an
  International context.

- Detail the key components of an international compensation
  program.

- Outline the two main approaches to international compensation
  and the advantages and disadvantages of each approach.

- Examine the special problem areas of taxation, valid
  international living cost data and the problem of managing
  TCN compensation.

- Examine the recent developments and global compensation
  issues.

Introduction

Global compensation managers (that is, everyone involved at any level in pay-related
decisions) increasingly deal with two areas of focus. They must manage highly

*The contribution of Allen D. Engle Sr. (Eastern Kentucky University, USA) to the writing of this
chapter is gratefully acknowledged.

complex and turbulent local details while concurrently building and maintaining a unified, strategic pattern of compensation policies, practices and values.

For multinationals successfully to manage compensation and benefits requires knowledge of employment and taxation law, customs, environment and employment practices of many foreign countries, familiarity with currency fluctuations and the effect of inflation on compensation and an understanding of why and when special allowances must be supplied and which allowances are necessary in what countries – all within the context of shifting political, economic and social conditions. The level of local knowledge needed in many of these areas requires specialist advice and many multinationals retain the services of consulting firms which may offer a broad range of services or provide highly specialized services relevant to HRM in a multinational context.[1]

HR managers spend a great deal of time developing effective compensation and benefit programs for international employees because they are high-cost employees. An article in the *Employee Benefits Journal*[2] on developing expatriate remuneration packages reported that a US expatriate in Tokyo would cost US $230 000 per annum with the following compensation package (all figures in US dollars):

Cash premiums: $45 080
Relocation assistance: $51 750
Itemized reimbursements (benefits-in-kind): $41 860
Taxation: $91 310
Total: $230 000

Because of the complexity and expense, much of the discussion in this chapter addresses PCN compensation. However, issues relevant to TCNs and HCNs are also described because they are becoming more important to the success of many multinationals.[3] For example, in most Western countries a driver may be considered a luxury, available only to CEOs. In developing economies, a driver is economical in terms of cost, effectiveness and safety. Apart from the expectation that managers use drivers, parking is frequently chaotic in developing countries (especially in large cities) and the driver also performs the function of a parking attendant. In some developing countries it is common for the police to arrest drivers involved in traffic accidents and leave them in detention while responsibility and damages are assessed. Such a risk is unacceptable to most firms. Many multinationals do not allow their expatriate employees to drive at all in some developing countries and provide local drivers for both the expatriate and spouse.

Indeed, expatriate compensation – long the preoccupation of global HR executives – is increasingly seen more as a component of a more balanced, albeit complex, system of worldwide pay.[4] National and regional differences in the meaning, practice and tradition of pay remain significant sources of variation in the international firm. Yet these contextual sources of complexity must be balanced with strategic intent and administrative economy.[5] Rather than seeing pay as an ethnocentric extension of an essentially domestic strategy, pay systems are increasingly becoming truly global – with truly global objectives.[6]

Objectives of international compensation

When developing international compensation policies, a firm seeks to satisfy several objectives. First, the policy should be consistent with the overall strategy, structure and business needs of the multinational. Second, the policy must work to attract and retain staff in the areas where the multinational has the greatest needs and opportunities. Hence the policy must be competitive and recognize factors such as incentive for foreign service, tax equalization and reimbursement for reasonable costs. Third, the policy should facilitate the transfer of international employees in the most cost-effective manner for the firm. Fourth, the policy must give due consideration to equity and ease of administration.

The international employee will also have a number of objectives that need to be achieved from the firm's compensation policy. First, the employee will expect the policy to offer financial protection in terms of benefits, social security and living costs in the foreign location. Second, the employee will expect a foreign assignment to offer opportunities for financial advancement through income and/or savings. Third, the employee will expect issues such as housing, education of children and recreation to be addressed in the policy. (The employee will also have expectations in terms of career advancement and repatriation, as discussed in Chapters 3, 5 and 7.)

If we contrast the objectives of the multinational and the employee, we see, of course, the potential for many complexities and possible problems, as some of these objectives cannot be maximized on both sides. The 'war stories' about problems in international compensation that we see in HR practitioner magazines are testimony to these complexities and problems. However, if we take away the specialist jargon and allow for the international context, are the competing objectives of the firm and the employee *fundamentally* different from that which exists in a domestic environment? We think not. We agree with the broad thrust of an article by Milkovich and Bloom,[7] which argues that firms must rethink the traditional view that local conditions dominate international compensation strategy. We will return to these issues at the end of the chapter after we have covered some of the technical aspects and complexities of compensation in an international context.

Key components of an international compensation program

The area of international compensation is complex primarily because multinationals must cater to three categories of employees: PCNs, TCNs and HCNs. In this section, we discuss key components of international compensation as follows:

Base salary

The term base salary acquires a somewhat different meaning when employees go abroad. In a domestic context, base salary denotes the amount of cash compensation serving as a benchmark for other compensation elements (such as bonuses and benefits). For expatriates, it is the primary component of a package of allowances, many of which are directly related to base salary (e.g. foreign service premium, cost-of-living allowance, housing allowance) and also the basis for in-service benefits and pension contributions. It may be paid in home or local-country currency. The base salary is the foundation block for international compensation whether the employee is a PCN or TCN. Major differences can occur in the employee's package depending on whether the base salary is linked to the home country of the PCN or TCN, or whether an international rate is paid. (We will return to this issue later in the chapter.)

Foreign service inducement/hardship premium

Parent-country nationals often receive a salary premium as an inducement to accept a foreign assignment or as compensation for any hardship caused by the transfer. Under such circumstances, the definition of hardship, eligibility for the premium and amount and timing of payment must be addressed. In cases in which hardship is determined, US firms often refer to the US Department of State's *Hardship Post Differentials Guidelines* to determine an appropriate level of payment. As Ruff and Jackson[8] have noted, however, making international comparisons of the cost of living is problematic. It is important to note, though, that these payments are more commonly paid to PCNs than TCNs. Foreign service inducements, if used, are usually made in the form of a percentage of salary, usually 5–40 per cent of base pay. Such payments vary, depending upon the assignment, actual hardship, tax consequences and length of assignment. In addition, differentials may be considered; for example, a host country's work week may be longer than that of the home country, and a differential payment may be made in lieu of overtime, which is not normally paid to PCNs or TCNs.

Allowances

Issues concerning allowances can be very challenging to a firm establishing an overall compensation policy, partly because of the various forms of allowances that exist. The *cost-of-living allowance* (COLA), which typically receives the most attention, involves a payment to compensate for differences in expenditures between the home country and the foreign country (to account for inflation differentials, for example). Often this allowance is difficult to determine, so companies may use the services of organizations such as Organization Resource Counselors, Inc. (a US-based firm) or Employment Conditions Abroad (based in Britain). These firms specialize in providing COLA information on a global basis, regularly updated, to their clients. The COLA may also include payments for housing and utilities, personal income tax or discretionary items.[8]

The provision of a *housing allowance* implies that employees should be entitled to maintain their home-country living standards (or, in some cases, receive accommodation that is equivalent to that provided for similar foreign employees and peers). Such allowances are often paid on either an assessed or an actual basis. Other alternatives include company-provided housing, either mandatory or optional, a fixed housing allowance or assessment of a portion of income, out of which actual housing costs are paid. Housing issues are often addressed on a case-by-case basis, but as a firm internationalizes, formal policies become more necessary and efficient. Financial assistance and/or protection in connection with the sale or leasing of an expatriate's former residence are offered by many multinationals. Those in the banking and finance industry tend to be the most generous, offering assistance in sale or leasing, payment of closing costs, payment of leasing management fees, rent protection and equity protection. Again, TCNs receive these benefits less frequently than PCNs.

There is also a provision for *home leave allowances*. Many employers cover the expense of one or more trips back to the home country each year. The purpose of paying for such trips is to give expatriates the opportunity to renew family and business ties, thereby helping them to avoid adjustment problems when they are repatriated. Although firms traditionally have restricted the use of leave allowances to travel home, some firms give expatriates the option of applying the allowances to foreign travel rather than returning home. Firms allowing use of home leave allowances for foreign travel need to be aware that expatriate employees with limited international experience who opt for foreign travel rather than returning home may become more homesick than other expatriates who return home for a 'reality check' with fellow employees and friends.[9]

Education allowances for expatriates' children are also an integral part of any international compensation policy. Allowances for education can cover items such as tuition, language class tuition, enrolment fees, books and supplies, transportation, room and board and uniforms. (Outside the USA, it is common for high-school students to wear uniforms.) The level of education provided for, the adequacy of local schools and transportation of dependents who are being educated in other locations may present problems for multinationals. PCNs and TCNs usually receive the same treatment concerning educational expenses. The cost of local or boarding school for dependent children is typically covered by the employer, although there may be restrictions, depending on the availability of good local schools and on their fees. Attendance at a university may also be provided for when deemed necessary.

Relocation allowances usually cover moving, shipping and storage charges, temporary living expenses, subsidies regarding appliance or car purchases (or sales) and down payments or lease-related charges. Allowances regarding perquisites (cars, club memberships, servants[10] and so on) may also need to be considered (usually for more senior positions, but this varies according to location). These allowances are often contingent upon tax-equalization policies and practices in both the home and the host countries.

Increasingly, as indicated in Chapter 4, many multinational firms are also offering *spouse assistance* to help guard against or offset income lost by an expatriate's spouse as a result of relocating abroad. Although some firms may pay an allowance to make up for a spouse's lost income, US firms are beginning to focus on providing spouses with employment opportunities abroad, either by offering job-search assistance or employment in the firm's foreign office (subject to a work visa being available).

To summarize, multinationals generally pay allowances in order to encourage employees to take international assignments and to keep employees 'whole' relative to home standards. We will present more about this concept later in the chapter. In terms of housing, companies usually pay a tax-equalized housing allowance in order to discourage the purchase of housing and/or to compensate for higher housing costs. This allowance is adjusted periodically based on estimates of both local and foreign housing costs.

Benefits

The complexity inherent in international benefits often brings more difficulties than when dealing with compensation. Pension plans are very difficult to deal with country-to-country, as national practices vary considerably. Transportability of pension plans, medical coverage and social security benefits are very difficult to normalize. Therefore, firms need to address many issues when considering benefits, including:

● Whether or not to maintain expatriates in home-country programs, particularly if the firm does not receive a tax deduction for it.

- Whether firms have the option of enrolling expatriates in host-country benefit programs and/or making up any difference in coverage.
- Whether expatriates should receive home-country or host-country social security benefits.

Most US PCNs typically remain under their home country's benefit plan. In some countries, expatriates cannot opt out of local social security programs. In such circumstances, the firm normally pays for these additional costs. European PCNs and TCNs enjoy portable social security benefits within the European Union. Laws governing private benefit practices differ from country to country, and firm practices also vary. Not surprisingly, multinationals have generally done a good job of planning for the retirement needs of their PCN employees, but this is generally less the case for TCNs.[11] There are many reasons for this: TCNs may have little or no home-country social security coverage; they may have spent many years in countries that do not permit currency transfers of accrued benefit payments; or they may spend their final year or two of employment in a country where final average salary is in a currency that relates unfavorably to their home-country currency. How their benefits are calculated and what type of retirement plan applies to them may make the difference between a comfortable retirement in a country of their choice and a forced penurious retirement elsewhere.

In addition to the already discussed benefits, multinationals also provide vacations and special leave. Included as part of the employee's regular vacation, annual home leave usually provides airfares for families to return to their home countries. Rest and rehabilitation leave, based on the conditions of the host country, also provides the employee's family with free airfares to a more comfortable location near the host country. In addition to rest and rehabilitation leave, emergency provisions are available in case of a death or illness in the family. Employees in hardship locations often receive additional leave expense payments and rest and rehabilitation periods.

Approaches to international compensation

There are two main options in the area of international compensation – the *Going Rate Approach* (also referred to as the Market Rate Approach) and the *Balance Sheet Approach* (sometimes known as the Build-up Approach). In this section we describe each approach and discuss the advantages and disadvantage inherent in each approach.[12]

The Going Rate Approach

The key characteristics of this approach are summarized in Table 6-1. With this approach, the base salary for international transfer is linked to the salary structure in the host country. The multinational usually obtains information from local compensation surveys and must decide whether local nationals (HCNs), expatriates of the same nationality or expatriates of all nationalities will be the reference point in terms of benchmarking. For example, a Japanese bank operating in New York would need to decide whether its reference point would be local US salaries, other Japanese competitors in New York or all foreign banks operating in New York. With the Going Rate Approach, if the location is in a low-pay county, the multinational usually supplements base pay with additional benefits and payments.

There are advantages and disadvantages of the Going Rate Approach, summarized in Table 6-2. The advantages are as follows: there is equality with local nationals (very effective in attracting PCNs or TCNs to a location that pays higher salaries than those received in the home country); the approach is simple and easy for expatriates to understand; expatriates are able to identify with the host country; and there is often equity amongst expatriates of different nationalities.

There are also disadvantages with the Going Rate Approach. First, there can be variation between assignments for the same employee. This is most obvious when we compare an assignment in an advanced economy with one in a developing country, but also between assignments in various advanced economies where differences in managerial salaries and the effect of local taxation can significantly influence an employee's compensation level using the Going Rate Approach. Not surprisingly, individual employees are very sensitive to this issue. Second, there can be variation between expatriates of the same nationality in different locations. A strict interpretation of the Going Rate Approach can lead to rivalry for assignments to locations which are financially attractive and little interest in locations considered to be financially unattractive. Finally, the Going Rate Approach can pose problems upon repatriation when the employee's salary reverts to a home-country level that is below that of the host country. This is a problem not only for firms in developing countries, but also for firms from many countries where local managerial salaries are well below those in the USA, which is the world market leader in managerial salaries.[13] For example, a survey by Towers Perrin[14] of total compensation for CEOs around the world reported the following results by country (all figures in US dollars):

- USA: $1 932 580
- Argentina: $879 068

Going Rate Approach	Table 6-1

- Based on local market rates
- Relies on survey comparisons among:
  - Local nationals (HCNs)
  - Expatriates of same nationality
  - Expatriates of all nationalities
- Compensation based on the selected survey comparison
- Base pay and benefits may be supplemented by additional payments for low-pay countries

Advantages and disadvantages of the Going Rate Approach	Table 6-2

Advantages	Disadvantages
• Equality with local nationals • Simplicity • Identification with host country • Equity amongst different nationalities	• Variation between assignments for same employee • Variation between expatriates of same nationality in different countries • Potential re-entry problems

- Mexico: $866 831
- Canada: $787 060
- China (Hong Kong SAR): $736 599
- Belgium: $696 697
- UK: $668 526
- Singapore: $645 740
- Venezuela: $635 045
- The Netherlands: $604 854
- Italy: $600 319
- Australia: $546 914

The Balance Sheet Approach

The key characteristics of this approach (which is the most widely used approach for international compensation) are summarized in Table 6-3. The basic objective is to 'keep the expatriate whole'[15] (that is, maintaining relativity to PCN colleagues and compensating for the costs of an international assignment) through maintenance of home-country living standard plus a financial inducement to make the package attractive. The approach links the base salary for PCNs and TCNs to the salary structure of the relevant home country. For example, a US executive taking up an international position would have his or her compensation package built upon the US base-salary level rather than that applicable to the host country. The key assumption of this approach is that foreign assignees should not suffer a material loss due to their transfer, and this is accomplished through the utilization of what is generally referred to as the *Balance-sheet Approach*. According to Reynolds:[16]

> The balance sheet approach to international compensation is a system designed to equalize the purchasing power of employees at comparable position levels living overseas and in the home country, and to provide incentives to offset qualitative differences between assignment locations.

There are four major categories of outlays incurred by expatriates that are incorporated in the Balance Sheet Approach:

1 *Goods and services* – home-country outlays for items such as food, personal care, clothing, household furnishings, recreation, transportation, and medical care.
2 *Housing* – the major costs associated with housing in the host country.

Table 6-3	The Balance Sheet Approach

- Basic objective is maintenance of home-country living standard plus financial inducement
- Home-country pay and benefits are the foundations of this approach
- Adjustments to home package to balance additional expenditure in host country
- Financial incentives (expatriate/hardship premium) added to make the package attractive
- Most common system in usage by multinational firms

3 *Income taxes* – parent-country and host-country income taxes.

4 *Reserve* – contributions to savings, payments for benefits, pension contributions, investments, education expenses, social security taxes, etc.

Where costs associated with the host-country assignment exceed equivalent costs in the parent country, these costs are met by both the firm and the expatriate to ensure that parent-country equivalent purchasing power is achieved.

Table 6-4 shows a typical spreadsheet for an expatriate assignment using the Balance Sheet Approach. In this example, an Australian expatriate is assigned to a country called New Euphoria which has a Cost-of-Living Index of 150 relative to Australia and an exchange rate of 1.5 relative to the Australian dollar. In addition to a foreign service premium, a hardship allowance is also payable for this location. Housing is provided by the firm, and a notional cost for this is recognized by a 7 per cent deduction from the package, along with a notional tax deduction (we discuss taxation later in the chapter). The expatriate can see from this spreadsheet what components are offered in the package and how the package will be split between Australian currency and New Euphoria currency.

There are advantages and disadvantages of the Balance Sheet Approach, summarized in Table 6-5. There are three main advantages. First, the Balance Sheet Approach provides equity between foreign assignments and between expatriates of the same nationality. Second, as will be discussed further in Chapter 7, repatriation of expatriates is facilitated by this emphasis on equity with the parent country as expatriate compensation remains anchored to the compensation system in the parent country. Third, this approach is easy to communicate, as Table 6-4 illustrates.

Expatriate compensation worksheet — Table 6-4

Employee	Brian Smith
Position	Marketing Manager
Country	New Euphoria
Reason for change	New Assignment
Effective date of change	1 February 2004

Item	Amount A$ p.a.	Paid in Australian dollars A$ p.a.	Paid in local currency NE$ p.a.
Base salary	155 000	77 500	116 250
Cost of living allowance	38 800		58 200
Overseas service premium (20%)	36 400	36 400	
Hardship allowance (20%)	36 400	36 400	
Housing deduction (7%)	−10 850	−10 850	
Tax deduction	−75 175	−75 175	
TOTAL	180 575	64 275	174 450

COLA Index = 150
Exchange rate = 1.5   Authorized/Date

There are two main disadvantages of the Balance Sheet Approach. First, this approach can result in considerable disparities – both between expatriates of different nationalities and between PCNs and HCNs. Problems arise when international staff are paid different amounts for performing the same (or a very similar) job in the host location, according to their different home base salary. For example, in the Singapore regional headquarters of a US bank, a US PCN and a New Zealand TCN may perform the same banking duties but the American will receive a higher salary than the New Zealander because of the differences in US and New Zealand base-salary levels. As noted above, differences in base-salary levels can also cause difficulties between expatriates and HCNs. Traditionally, this has referred to the problem of highly paid PCNs being resented by local HCN employees because these 'foreigners' are perceived as being excessively compensated (and because they are blocking career opportunities for locals).

However, feelings of resentment and inequity can also run in the other direction. For instance, as indicated above, the USA has the highest level of managerial compensation in the world. Thus, a firm which establishes a subsidiary in the USA (or acquires a US business) may find that if it uses a Balance Sheet Approach, its expatriates may be substantially underpaid compared with local American employees. Although the logic of the balance sheet states that being tied to the home country assists in repatriation because the expatriate identifies with the home country, research in equity theory[17] suggests that employees do not always assess compensation issues in a detached and rational way.[18] As we discussed in Chapter 4, perceived insufficiency of support may be interpreted as a violation of the psychological contract and have a negative impact on expatriate adjustment and performance.

The issue of base-salary differences is also a concern for US employees working for foreign firms operating in the USA. Many non-US multinationals are reluctant to pay high US salaries to US employees who are offered international assignments (as HCNs into the firm's home-country operations, or as TCNs). US employees are equally reluctant to accept the lower salaries paid in the firm's home country. Hence the Balance Sheet Approach not only can produce disparities, but also may act as a barrier to staff acceptance of international assignments.

A second problem with the Balance Sheet Approach is that although it is both elegant and simple as a concept, it can become complex to administer. Complexities particularly arise in the areas of tightly integrated private and government fund transfers or, put more plainly, taxes and pensions.

Table 6-5	Advantages and disadvantages of the Balance Sheet Approach

Advantages	*Disadvantages*

• Equity
   – Between assignments
   – Between expatriates of the same nationality
 • Facilitates expatriate re-entry
 • Easy to communicate to employees
	• Can result in great disparities
	   – Between expatriates of different nationalities
	   – Between expatriates and local nationals
	 • Can be complex to administer

Taxation

This aspect of international compensation is probably the one that causes the most concern to HR practitioners and expatriates (both PCNs and TCNs), as taxation generally evokes emotional responses. No one enjoys paying taxes, and this issue can be very time consuming for both the firm and the expatriate. To illustrate the potential problems, an assignment abroad can mean that a US expatriate is taxed both in the country of assignment and in the USA. This dual tax cost, combined with all of the other expatriate costs, makes some US multinationals think twice about making use of expatriates. It is important to note that Section 911 of the US Internal Revenue Service (IRS) Code contains provisions permitting a substantial deduction on foreign-earned income, but US expatriates must file with the IRS and usually also with the host-country tax office during their period of foreign service. This requirement is more onerous than for some other nationalities who may not be required to declare their total global income to their home-country taxation authority.

Multinationals generally select one of the following approaches to handling international taxation:

- *Tax equalization* – firms withhold an amount equal to the home-country tax obligation of the PCN, and pay all taxes in the host country.

- *Tax protection* – The employee pays up to the amount of taxes he or she would pay on compensation in the home country. In such a situation, the employee is entitled to any windfall received if total taxes are less in the foreign country than in the home country. In her review of global compensation, Stuart[19] adds two other approaches: (1) *ad hoc* (each expatriate is handled differently, depending upon the individual package agreed to with the firm); and (2) *laissez-faire* (employees are 'on their own' in conforming to host-country and home-country taxation laws and practices). However, neither of these approaches is recommended and we shall focus on tax equalization and tax protection, as these are the most common approaches.

Tax equalization is by far the more common taxation policy used by multinationals.[19] Thus, for a PCN, tax payments equal to the liability of a home-country taxpayer with the same income and family status are imposed on the employee's salary and bonus. Any additional premiums or allowances are typically paid by the firm, tax-free to the employee. As multinationals operate in more and more countries, they are subject to widely discrepant income tax rates. It is also important to note that just focusing on income tax can be misleading, as the shares of both personal and corporate taxes are rising in the OECD countries.[20] For example, if we look at total tax revenues as a percentage of GDP, the 'top five' highest taxation countries are Sweden, Denmark, Finland, France and Belgium. The United States is 25th with the other large advanced economies towards the bottom of the list (Japan, 26th; Britain, 16th; and Germany, 12th).[20] A review of selected maximum federal marginal tax rates is given in Table 6-6.

Many multinationals have responded to this complexity and diversity across countries by retaining the services of international accounting firms to provide advice and prepare host-country and home-country tax returns for their expatriates. Increasingly, firms are also outsourcing the provisions of further aspects of the total expatriate compensation packages including a variety of destination services in lieu of providing payment in a package.[22] When multinationals plan compensation packages, they need to consider the extent to which specific practices can be modified in each country to provide the most tax-effective, appropriate rewards for

PCNs, HCNs and TCNs within the framework of the overall compensation policy of the firm.

As one international HRM manager noted, the difficulties in international compensation 'are not compensation so much as benefits'. Pension plans are very difficult to compare or equalize across nations, as cultural practices vary endlessly. Transportability of pension plans, medical coverage and social security benefits are very difficult to normalize.[23] Therefore, companies need to address many issues when considering benefits, including:

● Whether or not to maintain expatriates in home-country programs, particularly if the company does not receive a tax deduction for it.

● Whether companies have the option of enrolling expatriates in host-country benefit programs and/or making up any difference in coverage.

● Whether host-country legislation regarding termination affects benefit entitlement.

Table 6-6	Maximum marginal federal tax rates

Country	Maximum marginal rate (%)
Argentina	35
Australia	48.5
Belgium	55
Brazil	27.5
Canada	29
China (Hong Kong SAR)	15
China (Shanghai)	45
France	53.5
Germany	51
Italy	46
Japan	37
Malaysia	29
Mexico	40
New Zealand	39
Singapore	28
South Africa	42
South Korea	40
Spain	39.6
Sweden	25
Switzerland	11.5
Taiwan	40
Thailand	37
The Netherlands	52
UK	40
USA	39.6
Venezuela	34

Source: Adapted from Towers Perrin, Worldwide Total Remuneration 2001–2002.[21]

- Whether expatriates should receive home-country or host-country social security benefits.

- Whether benefits should be maintained on a home-country or host-country basis, who is responsible for the cost, whether other benefits should be used to offset any shortfall in coverage and whether home-country benefit programs should be exported to local nationals in foreign countries.

Differences in national sovereignty are also at work in the area of mandated public and private pension schemes, what many nations refer to as 'social security' programs. Table 6-7 highlights the differences in mandated degree of contribution

Social security contributions by employers and employees	Table 6-7

Country	Employer contribution rate (%)	Employee contribution rate (%)	Total contribution rate (%)
Argentina	7.81	11.00	18.81
Australia	0.00[a]	0.00[a]	0.00[a]
Belgium	11.21	8.65	19.86
Brazil	20.00	11.00	31.00
Canada	4.30	4.30	8.60
China (Hong Kong SAR)	5.00	5.00	10.00
China (Shanghai)	43.50	16.00	59.50
France	_[b]	_[b]	_[b]
Germany	12.80	12.80	25.60
Italy	30.94	9.89	40.83
Japan	8.68	8.68	17.36
Malaysia	1.75	0.50	2.25
Mexico	29.00	4.00	33.00
New Zealand	0.00[a]	0.00[a]	0.00[a]
Singapore	16.00	20.00	36.00
South Africa	0.00[a]	0.00[a]	0.00[a]
South Korea	6.20	6.20	12.40
Spain	30.60	6.35	36.95
Sweden	22.91	7.00	29.91
Switzerland	5.05	5.05	10.10
Taiwan	5.00	1.00	6.00
Thailand	3.00	3.00	6.00
The Netherlands	0.00[a]	29.40	29.40
UK	11.90	10.00	21.90
USA	6.20	6.20	12.40
Venezuela	9.00	4.00	13.00

[a] When the contributions are at zero, they are funded out of the General Tax Revenue and range from zero to very high values.
[b] Varies.
Source: Adapted from Towers Perrin, Worldwide Total Remuneration 2001–2002.[24]

(ranging from a low of zero to a high of nearly 60 per cent) and the mix of employer–employee contributions.

For many international firms, expatriate assignments are likely to increase in distance, number and duration over an employee's career, and more and more firms may create cadres of permanent international assignees – called 'globals' by some firms. The inherent complexity and dynamism of culturally embedded and politically volatile national tax and pension processes promise to tax the resources, time and attention of international human resource managers for the foreseeable future. Seamless networks of global firms, their specialist consultants and local and regional public and private interest are a goal, not yet a reality.

International living costs data

Obtaining up-to-date information on international living costs is a constant issue for multinationals. As we noted at the beginning of this chapter, the level of local knowledge required in many areas of international HRM requires specialist advice. Consequently, many multinationals retain the services of consulting firms that may offer a broad range of services or provide highly specialized services relevant to HRM in a multinational context. With regard to international living costs, a number of consulting firms offer regular surveys calculating a cost-of-living index that can be updated in terms of currency exchange rates. A recent survey of living costs[25] in selected cities ranked the 10 most expensive cities as Tokyo, Moscow, Osaka, Hong Kong, Beijing, Geneva, London, Seoul, Zurich and New York. The first US city in the index was New York, ranked as the 10th most expensive city. The least expensive city was Asuncion (Paraguay).

Multinationals using the Balance Sheet Approach must constantly update compensation packages with new data on living costs, which is an on-going administrative requirement. This is an important issue to expatriate employees and forms the basis of many complaints if updating substantially lags behind any rise in living costs. Multinationals must also be able to respond to unexpected events such as the currency and stock market crash that suddenly unfolded in a number of Asian countries in late 1997. Some countries such as Indonesia faced a devaluation of their currency (the Ruphiah) by over 50 per cent against the US dollar in a matter of weeks. This action had a dramatic impact on prices and the cost of living. There is also much debate about what should be in the 'basket of goods' which consulting firms use as the basis for calculating living costs around the world. For example, the Swiss Bank UBS uses the 'Big Mac Index' to measure the living costs around the world.[26] According to Table 6-8, it takes more than 3 hours for the average worker in Nairobi to earn enough for a Big Mac. In Los Angeles, Miami, Chicago and Tokyo, the global burger can be bought for a mere 10 minutes' effort.[28]

It is also possible to take a wider view and focus on *business costs* rather than living costs for expatriates, because the multinational firm is interested in the overall cost of doing business in a particular country as well as the more micro issue of expatriate living costs. *The Economist* Intelligence Unit[29] calculates such indices, which measure the relative costs of doing business in different economies by compiling statistics relating to wages, costs for expatriate staff, air travel and subsistence, corporation taxes, perceived corruption levels, office and industrial rents and road transport. Generally the developed countries tend to rank as more expensive than developing countries because their wage costs are higher.

Differentiating between PCNs and TCNs

As we have indicated, one of the outcomes of the Balance Sheet Approach is to produce differentiation between expatriate employees of different nationalities because of the use of nationality to determine the relevant home-country base salary. In effect, this is a differentiation between PCNs and TCNs. Many TCNs have a great deal of international experience because they often move from country to country in the employ of one multinational (or several) headquartered in a country other than their own (for example, an Indian banker may work in the Singapore branch of a US bank). As Reynolds[30] has observed, there is no doubt that paying TCNs according to their home-country base salary can be less expensive than paying all expatriates on a PCN scale (particularly if the multinational is headquartered in a country such as the USA or Germany, which have both high managerial salaries and a strong currency), but justifying these differences can be very difficult. Nonetheless, it is common practice for multinationals to use a home-country Balance Sheet Approach for TCNs. Evidently, the reduction in expenses outweighs the difficulty of justifying any pay differentials. However, as firms expand internationally, it is likely that TCN employees will become more valuable and firms may need to rethink their approach to compensating TCNs.

Range of working times required to buy one Big Mac	Table 6-8

City	Minutes
Los Angeles, Miami, Chicago, Tokyo	10
New York	12
Hong Kong	13
Zurich, Toronto, Montreal	14
Basle, Luxembourg, Dublin, Frankfurt, Vienna	15
Geneva, Copenhagen, Amsterdam, Berlin, London	16
Lugano	17
Oslo, Brussels, Taipei	18
Auckland, Helsinki, Stockholm, Sydney, Paris	19
Madrid, Milan, Athens, Singapore	21
Vilnius	62
Jakarta	67
Mexico City	75
Caracas	76
Bucharest, Lima	79
Kiev	84
Bogota	93
Bombay	112
Karachi	132
Nairobi	185

Note: price of one Big Mac divided by weighted average hourly pay across 13 occupations.
Source: UBS, Prices and Earning 2003.[27]

As a starting point, multinational firms need to match their compensation policies with their staffing policies and general HR philosophy. If, for example, a firm has an ethnocentric staffing policy, its compensation policy should be one of keeping the expatriate whole (that is, maintaining relativity to PCN colleagues plus compensating for the costs of international service). If, however, the staffing policy follows a geocentric approach (that is, staffing a position with the 'best person,' regardless of nationality), there may be no clear 'home' for the TCN, and the firm will need to consider establishing a system of international base pay for key managers paid in a major reserve currency such as the US dollar or the Euro. This system allows firms to deal with considerable variations in base salaries for managers.

Some tentative conclusions: patterns in complexity

It may be that international compensation administration is more complex than its domestic counterpart, but not radically different in pattern or form. Recent developments in the study of global pay issues may be seen to operate at three distinct levels: the basic level of cultural values and assumptions; the level of pay strategy, practices and systems design; and the level of pay administration and form[31] (see Figure 6-1).

At the level of cultural values, a debate is ongoing between advocates of pay systems that value competitive individualism and result in 'hierarchical' pay systems with

| **Figure 6-1** | Patterns for international pay |

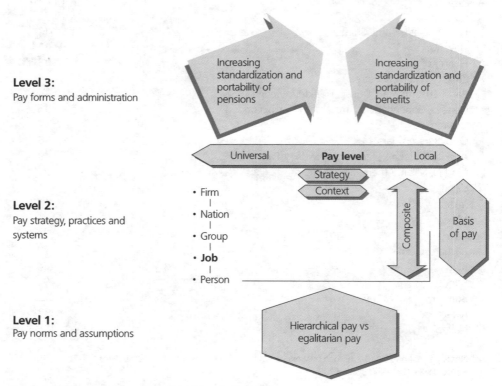

Level 3:
Pay forms and administration

Level 2:
Pay strategy, practices and systems

Level 1:
Pay norms and assumptions

Reprinted with permission. Copyright Allen D. Engle, Sr.

large pay differentials for executives, market-sensitive professions and other 'critical' employee groups[32] and the advocates of pay systems that value cooperative collectivism and result in more 'egalitarian' pay systems with smaller pay differentials and more shared group or firm-wide reward practices.[32] Multinational firms that violate corporate or local norms in one location in order to respond to local norms in a second location do so at their own risk.[33] This debate is enlivened by a global reaction to hierarchical pay systems as an exported 'best practice' from the USA in the light of recent CEO pay scandals as reported in the global media. These US-based pay scandals have set off a global reaction – often reinforcing local norms and values.[34]

At the level of pay strategy and attendant practices and systems design, increased complexity may be understood using a horizontal and a vertical axis. Horizontally, 'universal' pay systems may be preferred by corporate pay planners rather than dealing with myriad 'local' systems. Ease of administration and the standardization of practices are attractive and can contribute to simplicity in global assignments, resolving disputes related to perceived inequities or policy inconsistencies, etc. However, local or regional 'host contexts' and/or firm strategy may influence firms to compromise these global preferences and strategically align pay practices more or less in conformance with local or regional requirements. Strategic necessity and contextual requirements may incrementally grudgingly 'move' pay practices away from a universalized and towards a more localized character.[35]

Vertically, a number of levels of analysis have emerged to supplement or augment job-based pay. Firms may provide a *person* with personal 'choice' in pay and pay for his/her competencies.[36] Alternately, a firm may pay at the traditional *job* level, realizing that even standard jobs may vary tremendously across geographic regions. Firms may pay at the task *group* or plant level of aggregation.[37] Finally, firms may provide 'customized' pay at the *national* level, or provide standardized 'core' pay for all employees in the global *firm*.[38] Increasingly, we may combine pay packages across these vertical levels of analysis and pay for a combination of personal, job, group, national or corporate purposes.[38,39] These composite pay systems are more complex, but they are also more flexible and responsive to diverse employee demands and changing global business conditions.

At the level of pay form and administration, an increased standardization and portability of benefit programs and pension plans is in evidence.[40] Ironically, both centralized EU policies and decentralized US market forces have directed public and private benefit and pension providers to look for ways to provide standardized, portable medical insurance and pension packages in ways that were unimaginable 10 years ago. However, administrative burdens still exist owing to ongoing national differences in tax treatments and the role of public versus private sources for these forms of pay.

Summary

In this chapter, we have examined the complexities arising when firms move from compensation at the domestic level to compensation in an international context. It is evident from our review that compensation policy becomes a much less precise process than is the case in the domestic HR context. To demonstrate this complexity, we have:

● Detailed the key components of an international compensation program.

- Outlined the two main approaches to international compensation (the Going Rate and the Balance Sheet) and the advantages and disadvantages of each approach.
- Outlined special problem areas such as taxation, obtaining valid international living costs data, and the problems of managing TCN compensation.
- Presented a model of global pay that highlights the complexity and yet familiarity of pay practices in the global context. It is this combination of pay decisions based on strategic global standardization and sensitivity to changing local and regional conditions that characterizes the state of international pay practices.

Providing a strategic yet sensitive balance can only be achieved by creating and maintaining professional networks, comprised of home office and local affiliate HR practitioners, outsourcing selected activities through specialist consultants, and a close cooperation with local and regional governments and other key local institutions.

Discussion questions and exercises

1 What should be the main objectives for a multinational firm with regard to its compensation policies?
2 Describe the main differences in the Going Rate and Balance Sheet approaches to international compensation.
3 What are the key differences in salary compensation for PCNs and TCNs? Do these differences matter?
4 What are the main points multinational firms must consider when deciding how to provide benefits?
5 Why is it important for multinational firms to understand the compensation practices of other countries?
6 Explain how balancing the interests of global and local, occupational and functional perspectives might play out in a compensation decision scenario.

Further reading

Towers Perrin, 2003. Benefit Policies for Internationally Mobile Employees, a Survey by Towers Perrin. See also the Towers Perrin website (www.towers.com) for further information.
P.J. Dowling, K.B. Lowe, J. Milliman and H.D. Cieri, 2002. International Compensation Practices: a Ten-country Comparative Analysis, *Asia Pacific Journal of Human Resources*, Vol. 40, No. 1, pp. 55–80.
N.B. Krupp, 2002. Global Compensation Planning – Establishing and Maintaining a Competitive Edge in the International Marketplace, *Compensation and Benefits Management*, Vol. 18, Issue 2, pp. 54–56.
GMAC, 2002. Global Relocation Trends 2002 Survey Report, GMAC Global Relocation Services, accessed through Society for Human Resource Management Global Website (www.shrmglobal.org).
G. Parker and E.S. Janush, 2001. Developing Expatriate Remuneration Packages, *Employee Benefits Journal*, June, pp. 3–5.
R.S. Schuler and N. Rogovsky, 1998. Understanding Compensation Practice Variations Across Firms: the Impact of National Culture, *Journal of International Business Studies*, Vol. 29, No. 1, pp. 159–177.

J. Bonache and Z. Fernandez, 1997. Expatriate Compensation and its Link to the Subsidiary Strategic Role: a Theoretical Analysis, *International Journal of Human Resource Management*, Vol. 8, No. 4, pp. 457–475.

Notes and references

1 For example, specialized firms such as P-E International in the UK provide a survey of Worldwide Living Costs, and PricewaterhouseCoopers offer a worldwide consulting service called 'Global Human Resource Solutions', which covers a broad range of international HR issues.

2 G. Parker and E.S. Janush, Developing Expatriate Remuneration Packages, *Employee Benefits Journal*, June (2001) pp. 3–5.

3 C. Reynolds, *2000 Guide to Global Compensation and Benefits*, San Diego, CA: Harcourt Professional Publishing, 2000, pp. 3, 15–16.

4 Reynolds, *2000 Guide to Global Compensation and Benefits*, San Diego, CA: Harcourt Professional Publishing, 2000, Ch. 5 and 28.

5 See K. Lowe, J. Milliman, H. DeCeiri and P. Dowling, International Compensation Practices: a Ten-country Comparative Analysis, *Human Resource Management*, Vol. 41, No. 1 (2002) pp. 45–66; S. Overman, In Sync: Harmonizing Your Global Compensation Plans May Be Done More 'In Spirit' Than to the Letter, *HR Magazine*, Vol. 45, No. 3 (2000) pp. 86–92; K. Bensky, Developing a Workable Global Rewards System, *Workspan*, Vol. 45, No. 10 (2002), pp. 44–48.

6 M. Bloom and G.T. Milkovich, A SHRM Perspective on International Compensation and Rewards Systems, in *Research in Personnel and Human Resource Management, Supplement 4*, Greenwich, CT: JAI Press, 1999, pp. 283–303; V. Pucik, Human Resources in the Future: an Obstacle or a Champion of Globalization? *Human Resource Management*, Vol. 36, No. 1 (1997) pp. 163–167.

7 G.T. Milkovich and M. Bloom, Rethinking International Compensation, *Compensation and Benefits Review*, Vol. 30, No. 1 (1998) pp. 15–23.

8 H.J. Ruff and G.I. Jackson, Methodological Problems in International Comparisons of the Cost of Living, *Journal of International Business Studies*, Vol. 5, No. 2 (1974) pp. 57–67.

9 The experience of the authors in their research on expatriates and their families is that for some expatriates (particularly expatriates with little international experience), using home leave allowances for foreign travel can intensify feelings of homesickness. Without the benefit of returning home to mix with employees and friends, it is possible to idealize what they remember of their experience at work and home and fail to come to a measured judgment of what is good and bad in both their host and home environments. Some spouses commented that their first home leave was beneficial in helping them to adjust to the host location. Being treated by family and friends as a visitor in their hometown made them identify with the host location as 'home', and they returned with a more positive attitude. Thus, in general, we would take the view that home leave allowances should normally be used for the purpose they are provided – to give employees and their families the opportunity to renew family and business ties, thereby helping them to avoid adjustment problems when they are repatriated.

10 It is common in Asia and many developing countries in other regions for expatriates and local business people to employ maids and cooks in their houses. As stated in an earlier note when discussing employment of drivers, it may be expected that an expatriate would employ servants and not to do so would be judged negatively as this would be depriving local people of employment. Not surprisingly, this is one benefit which expatriate spouses miss when they return to their home country.

11 Trends in Expatriate Compensation, *Bulletin to Management*, 18 October (1990) p. 336.

12 The material in the tables describing the two main approaches to international compensation is based on various sources – the research and consulting experience of the first author and various discussions on this topic with a range of HR managers and consultants in Australia and the USA.

13 In interviews conducted by the first author with senior management of Australian firms operating internationally, repatriation difficulties was one of the major reasons cited for not following a Going Rate Approach with Australian expatriates.

14 Towers Perrin, *Worldwide Total Remuneration 2001–2002*, p. 20. Total compensation included basic salary, variable bonus, compulsory company contributions, voluntary company contributions, perquisites and long-term incentives. See also the Towers Perrin website (www.towers.com) for further information.

15 See B.W. Teague, *Compensating Key Personnel Overseas*, New York: The Conference Board, 1972, and J.J. Martoccho, *Strategic Compensation*, 3rd edn, Upper Saddle River, NJ: Pearson/Prentice-Hall, 2004, for more detailed discussions of the concept of keeping the expatriate 'whole'.

16 This discussion of the Balance Sheet Approach follows the presentation in Chapter 5 of C. Reynolds, *2000 Guide to Global Compensation and Benefits*, San Diego, CA: Harcourt Professional Publishing, 2000.

17 See Chapter 3 of T.J. Bergmann, V.G. Scarpello and F.S. Hills, *Compensation Decision Making*, 3rd edn, Fort Worth, TX: Dryden Press, 1998, for a review of equity theory applied to compensation.

18 For example, the first author has interviewed a number of Australian expatriates working in the USA. In all cases they were compensated using a balance sheet approach and in all cases each expatriate commented on the effect which a lower Australian base salary had on the overall level of their salary package relative to local US employees. Most were earning substantially less than local US senior managers and some were earning less than their local subordinates.

19 Stuart, Global Payroll – A Taxing Problem, *Personnel Journal*, October (1991) pp. 80–90.

20 Tax Burdens, *The Economist*, 2 November (2000) (accessed online on 18 July 2003).

21 Towers Perrin, *Worldwide Total Remuneration 2001–2002*, p. 32. See also the Towers Perrin website (www.towers.com) for further information.

22 GMAC, *Global Relocation Trends 2002 Survey Report* GMAC Global Relocation Services, 2002. Accessed through Society for Human Resource Management Global Website (www.shrmglobal.org).

23 R.S. Schuler and P.J. Dowling, *Survey of SHRM/I Members*, New York: Stern School of Business, New York University, 1988.

24 Ref. 21, p. 34.

25 *Finfacts Worldwide 2003 Cost of Living Survey City Rankings*, Mercer Human Resource. (accessed 20 July 2003). For further reading see http://www.finfacts.ie.

26 F.W. Williams, Price of a Big Mac: 10 minutes in Miami, three hours in Nairobi, *Financial Times*, 21 August (2003).

27 Accessed from http://www.ubs.com/e/ubs_ch/bb_ch/market_information.Referenz.0002.File.dat/3.9_PL_e.pdf.

28 For more details, see www.ubs.com/economicresearch.

29 Reported in *The Economist*, 24 January (1998) p. 110.

30 C. Reynolds, Cost-effective Compensation, *Topics in Total Compensation*, Vol. 2, No. 1 (1988) p. 320.

31 See E. Schein, *Organizational Culture and Leadership*, San Francisco: Jossey-Bass, 1985.

32 G.T. Milkovich and J. Newman, *Compensation*, 7th edn, Boston: McGraw-Hill/Irwin, 2002, pp. 73–74; 82–83.

33 H. Timmons, Pay Debated at British Bank's Meeting. *New York Times*, 31 May (2003).

34 C. Bartlett, S. Ghoshal and J. Birkinshaw, *Transnational Management: Text, Cases and Readings in Cross-border Management*, 4th edn, Boston: McGraw-Hill/Irwin, 2004, pp. 12–13.

35 M. Bloom, G.T. Milkovich and A. Mitra, International Compensation: Learning From How Managers Respond to Variations in Local Host Contexts, in press. Also see A. Mitra, M. Bloom and G.T. Milkovich, Crossing a Raging River: Seeking Far-Reaching Solutions to Global Pay Challenges. *World at Work Journal*, vol. 11, No. 2 (2002) pp. 6–17.

36 J.B. Boudreau, P.M. Ramstad and P.J. Dowling, Global Talentship: Toward a Decision Science Connecting Talent to Global Strategic Success, in *Advances in Global Leadership*, Vol. 3, ed. W.H. Mobley and P.W. Dorfman, Oxford: Elsevier Science, 2003, pp. 63–99. Also see A. Engle, M. Mendenhall, R. Powers and Y. Stedham, Conceptualizing the Global Competency Cube: a Transnational Model of Human Resource, *Journal of European Industrial Training*, Vol. 25, No. 7 (2001) pp. 346–353.

37 E.E. Lawler III *Rewarding Excellence*. San Francisco: Jossey-Bass, 2000; C. Garvey, Steer Teams With the Right Pay. *HR Magazine*, Vol. 47, No. 5 (2002) pp. 71–78.

38 G.T. Milkovich and M. Bloom, Rethinking International Compensation, *Compensation and Benefits Review*, Vol. 30, No. 1 (1998) pp. 15–23.

39 A. Engle and M. Mendenhall, Transnational Roles and Transnational Rewards: Global Integration in Executive Compensation, *Proceedings of the 7th Conference on International Human Resource Management*, Limerick University, Limerick, Ireland, June 2003, CD-Rom Reference No. 53.

40 P. Sparrow, International Rewards Systems: to Converge or Not to Converge? In *International HRM: Contemporary Issues in Europe*, ed. C. Brewster and H. Harris, London: Routledge, 1999, pp. 102–119. Also see R. Subramanian and T. Singh, Spanning the Globe with Deferred Compensation, *World at Work Journal*, Vol. 11, No. 2 (2002) pp. 18–25; A. Werdel and V. Diamond, Navigating Stock Options in Europe: Steering Clear of Tax and Legal Pitfalls. *Workspan*, Vol. 45, No. 8 (2002) pp. 28–31; On the Public Agenda; Awareness of the Age Dilemma, an interview with J. Klein, *World at Work Journal*, Vol. 10, No. 4 (2001) pp. 19–24; C. deAenlle, Scaling Back Expat Packages, *International Herald Tribune Online*, 26 July (2003) www.iht.com/articles/104174.htm.

CHAPTER

7

Re-entry and career issues

Chapter objectives

Whereas the preceding chapters concentrated on the management and support of international assignments, this chapter deals with what could be called the post-assignment stage. Re-entry, though, raises issues for both the expatriate and the multinational, some of which may be connected to events that occurred during the international assignment. We treat this stage as part of the international assignment. We examine:

- the process of re-entry or repatriation
- job-related issues
- social factors, including family factors that affect re-entry and work adjustment
- multinational responses to repatriate concerns
- return on investment (ROI) and knowledge transfer
- designing a repatriation programme.

Introduction

It is evident from the preceding chapters that there have been considerable advances in our understanding and knowledge of the issues surrounding the management and support of expatriates in terms of recruitment and selection, pre-departure training and compensation. As Figure 7-1 indicates, the expatriation process also includes repatriation: the activity of bringing the expatriate back to the home country.

Although it is now more widely recognized by managers and academics that repatriation needs careful managing, attention to this aspect of international assignments has been somewhat belated. In fact, an assessment of the literature reveals that repatriation continues to be of lesser importance than the other stages of the expatriation process.

Re-entry into the home country presents new challenges. The repatriate (returning person) may be coping with what has been termed **re-entry shock**, or reverse culture shock. Whereas people frequently expect life in a new country to be different, they may be less prepared for homecoming to present problems of adjustment. As a consequence, it can be a traumatic experience for some,[1,2] even more than what was encountered in the foreign location. From the multinational's perspective, repatriation is frequently considered as the final stage in the expatriation process (as indicated in Figure 7-1), but the multinational's ability to attract future expatriates is affected by the manner in which it handles repatriation.[2,3]

In this chapter, we focus on the key factors associated with re-entry, including how the repatriation process is handled by the individual and the receiving work unit and family adjustment. We will also explore how repatriation affects the successful 'closure' of the foreign assignment, its impact on future career paths within the multinational and the effect on staff mobility. The reasons for the international assignment and its outcomes are assessed, that is, how the multinational recoups its investment in human capital and the process of knowledge and competence transfer upon re-entry. It should be noted that what is written about the re-entry process centers on the traditional expatriate assignment, based predominantly on experiences of repatriated PCNs.

The repatriation process

Typically, on completion of the international assignment, the multinational brings the expatriate back to the home country, although not all international assignments end with a transfer home. Some expatriates may agree to become part of the multinational's international team of managers – as indicated by the dotted arrow in Figure 7-1 – and thus have consecutive overseas assignments. In the event that one of these consecutive assignments involves the expatriate returning to the home-country operations, it will be treated as 'just another posting' rather than re-entry or repatriation. For example, John Citizen is moved from his home base in the US parent operations to Japan for 2 years. He then spends 4 years in China, followed by 1 year in headquarters in the USA before moving on to another position in the English operations. That 1-year period spent at headquarters is not treated as re-entry back into the home-country operations. In contrast, Mary Smith has spent 3 years working in China and is repatriated back to the USA into a defined position at headquarters.

At some point, members of the international team or 'cadre' will face repatriation although, as it often occurs at the retirement-from-work life stage, there will be different concerns that need to be addressed, as will be discussed later in this chapter.

| **Figure 7-1** | Expatriation includes repatriation |

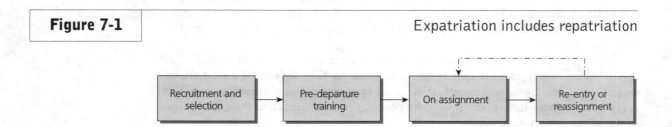

It is possible to divide repatriation into four related phases, as illustrated in Figure 7-2.

1 *Preparation* involves developing plans for the future and gathering information about the new position. The firm may provide a checklist of items to be considered before the return home (such as closure of bank accounts and settling bills) or a thorough preparation of employee and family for the transfer home. However, there is little evidence in the literature that preparation for repatriation is seen by the multinational to be as important as pre-departure training.[2] At best, there may be some inclusion of repatriation issues in the pre-departure training provided to the expatriate.

2 *Physical relocation* refers to removing personal effects, breaking ties with colleagues and friends and travelling to the next posting, usually the home country. Most multinationals use removal firms or relocation consultants to handle the physical relocation, for both the movement out and the return home of the employee and family, and this may be formalized in their HR policies. According to Forster,[4] comprehensive and personalized relocation assistance reduces the amount of uncertainty, stress and disruption experienced by the repatriate and family.

3 *Transition* means settling into temporary accommodation where necessary, making arrangements for housing and schooling and carrying out other administrative tasks (such as renewing driver's license, applying for medical insurance, opening bank account). Some companies hire relocation consultants to assist in this phase also.

4 *Readjustment* involves coping with such aspects as company changes, reverse culture shock and career demands.

Of the four phases identified in Figure 7-2, the readjustment phase is the one that seems to be the least understood and most poorly handled (highlighted by shading of that phase). For example, in 1996, Harzing conducted a comprehensive survey of 287 subsidiaries of nearly 100 different multinationals. She reports that

---

The repatriation process   **Figure 7-2**

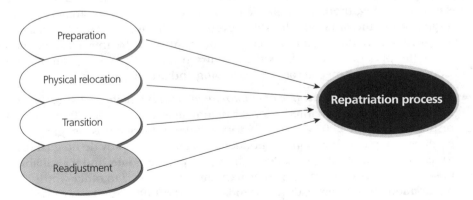

Source: Adapted from D. Welch, T. Adams, B. Betchley and M. Howard, The View from the Other Side: the Handling of Repatriation and Other Expatriation Activities by the Royal Australian Air Force, in *Proceedings of the Academy of International Business Southeast Asia Conference*, ed. O. Yau and B. Stening, Brisbane, June 1992.

52 per cent of sampled firms experienced repatriate re-entry problems.[5] The 2002 GMAC-GRS[6] global survey of 181 multinationals (referred to in previous chapters) reports that responding firms admitted a 44 per cent expatriate turnover rate, half of whom left their firms within the first year of re-entry. One respondent stated: 'Employees with international experience are more likely to leave the company.' It should be remembered that 39 per cent of the multinationals in the 2002 GMAC-GRS survey did not know their expatriate attrition rate. The percentage of exiting employees could be higher.

Given the reasons why international assignments are used and the various roles that are assigned to expatriates – as discussed in Chapter 3 – it seems important to understand why re-entry is problematic yet of seemingly lesser importance to researchers and practitioners than other stages of the international assignment. To this end, we now examine factors that may contribute to re-entry problems, considering the process first from the individual's perspective, and then from the multinational's viewpoint.

Individual reactions to re-entry

As with cross-cultural adjustment, the re-entry process is a complex interaction of several factors. It is possible to group the major factors that have been identified as moderators of re-entry readjustment into two categories: job-related factors and social factors.

Job-related factors

These center around future employment prospects as a consequence of the international assignment, value being placed on the person's international experience, coping with new role demands and the loss of status and financial benefits upon re-entry. We shall examine these factors in turn.

Career anxiety.   When surveyed, expatriates consistently list two motivators for accepting an international assignment: career advancement and financial gain.[7–9] It is not surprising, then, that a prime factor in re-entry is career anxiety. This can emerge prior to the physical relocation, even before Phase 1 in Figure 7-2, and can affect productivity during the last couple of months of the international assignment as the person contemplates the re-entry process. So, what prompts career anxiety? The causes range across the following and are often inter-related:

● *No post-assignment guarantee of employment*. This is becoming the reality for the majority of those on international assignments. For example, 70 per cent of respondents in the 2002 GMAC-GRS survey did not provide post-assignment employment guarantees. One respondent explained: 'We provide no guarantee for employment. We do guarantee to bring the person home, and if a suitable position is not readily available, they have three months.'[10] In other words, repatriation more often leads to redundancy, as the 1990s trend away from re-entry job guarantees continues. A 1998 survey by Price Waterhouse (now PricewaterhouseCoopers) survey[11] reported a decrease in post-assignment job guarantees from 69 per cent in their 1995 survey to 46 per cent in 1998.

Studies that break down general trends into regions and countries reveal some differences. The Tung–Arthur Andersen 1997 survey of 49 North American firms reported that the majority (almost 60 per cent) did not guarantee a position at home upon successful completion of the overseas assignment.[7] In her study of international HR practices in German and UK firms, Marx[12] found that the majority of German firms offered a guaranteed job upon return from the foreign assignment, whereas the majority of UK firms admitted that they were not able to offer jobs upon repatriation. Marx suggests that Continental European firms may have to provide such guarantees in order to attract expatriates. However, a respondent in the 2002 GMAC-GRS survey explained that: 'Our approach depends on the base [sending] country. Europeans have a labour contract, and the US does not.'[10] Given the lack of job security, it is not surprising that career anxiety commences prior to homecoming, and acts as a readjustment moderator upon re-entry if career outcomes are not realized.

- *A fear that the period overseas has caused a loss of visibility and isolation* – as captured in the phrase, 'out of sight, out of mind'.[5,13] Again, this fear can commence towards the end of the international assignment as the person begins to consider the re-entry process, and depends on various elements: the amount of contact that the person has had with the home organization, the position level concerned and whether the person is aware well in advance of the type of re-entry job awaiting in the home country. Lack of information may increase the level of anxiety, leaving the person with a decided impression that the company has not planned adequately, or that a mediocre or makeshift job awaits.[14] If there is no post-assignment job guarantee, the anxiety level will be understandably high.

- *Changes in the home workplace.* Anxiety can be exacerbated by informal communication from home-based colleagues about organizational changes. It may be that the multinational is in the process of a major restructuring, the aftermath of a merger or acquisition, or sale of divisions or business units. These changes are usually accompanied by job shedding. Knowledge of such changes and potential or real job loss naturally will add to the level of anxiety, particularly if the expatriate does not have a guaranteed job upon repatriation.

  Another issue here is that restructuring can affect the host-country operations – such as closure of a plant, dissolving of a joint venture or merging of operations post-acquisition. This may leave the expatriate stranded, or force an early repatriation which has not been planned.[15] If similar changes are also occurring in the home country, then availability of suitable positions will have been reduced. One repatriate who was placed in such a position explains:[16]

  > The division I worked for was reorganized, and the subsidiary I worked for was placed under stringent cost-cutting guidelines, which forced me to return earlier than anticipated. My re-entry was very cold, with little support in finding a job since previous management had been fired.

Work adjustment.   Black *et al.*[17] argue that work adjustment has an important impact on a person's intent to stay with the organization. Career anxiety is one moderating factor, but others may also lead to readjustment problems.

- *The employment relationship.* An individual's career expectations may be based on clear messages sent by top management to the effect that an international assignment is a condition for career progression. That is, verbal or written statements such as, 'We are an international company and we need internationally oriented people who have worked in our overseas facilities.' These pronouncements can be made in the context of the need for a global orientation or mindset where a definite link is made between international experience and global managers.

Perceptions regarding expected career outcomes also are influenced by comments made by HR or line managers during the recruitment and selection stage. For example, the line manager may suggest to a younger employee: 'You should volunteer for that international assignment. It would be a smart career move at this stage in your life.' If others have been promoted upon repatriation, it may be perceived to be the 'norm', thus reinforcing the perception that international assignments lead to promotion upon re-entry.

For these reasons, the person believes promotion should follow based on successful performance while abroad and, if the re-entry position does not eventuate within a reasonable timeframe, then career anxiety is justified. Moreover, unmet expectations or unfulfilled promises, as we discussed in terms of the employment relationship in Chapter 4, can provoke intense feelings of betrayal and violation of the psychological contract. This reaction emerged in a recent study by Lazarova and Caligiuri[18] of 58 repatriates from four North American-based companies. Their results suggest that repatriation support practices are positively related to perceptions of organizational support, and these affect repatriates' intention to stay or leave the organization. The psychological contract is a moderator of re-entry readjustment as well as on-assignment adjustment and performance. The repatriate may believe that the performance overseas warrants promotion: that signals were given by the organization that effective performance in the international assignment would result in career advancement. When the expected promotion does not eventuate, the repatriate may feel there is no option but to leave the organization.

The difficulty, as will be remembered from Chapter 4, is that the psychological contract concerns both perceptions and expectations, complicated by the fact that the company representative making statements about career outcomes prior to the international assignment is not necessarily the person who is responsible for re-entry decisions about job placement and promotion.

- *Re-entry position.* It would seem for some that promotion is a primary issue as the following comment from a repatriate reveals:[16]

> Get a promotion before the return! You are forgotten while overseas, and you start all over on the return. The promotions go to people who have been in a position for extended periods; nothing done overseas counts in this company.

Fears surrounding future employment and career development can materialize. Peers are promoted ahead of the repatriated manager, and the repatriate sometimes is placed in a position that is, in effect, a demotion. The situation may be exacerbated if the repatriate had held a senior position in the foreign location and now finds himself (or herself) at a less senior level. As a consequence, the re-entry position is frequently judged by whether it matches the repatriate's career expectation, particularly when the international assignment has caused considerable family disruption, such as a forced break in the career of the accompanying partner or difficulties experienced with the education of the children involved. Put simply, the repatriate wants the 'end to justify the means', so that the family unit is fully compensated for the sacrifices it has made in expectation of career advancement.

A question put to responding firms in the GMAC-GRS 2002 survey concerned the career impact of international experience. Firms were asked to compare the careers of expatriates with those of employees without international experience, with the following results:

– expatriates were promoted faster – 36 per cent
– expatriates obtained new positions in the company more easily – 33 per cent
– expatriates changed employers more often – 23 per cent
– not sure about the career link to international experience – 35 per cent
  (note: respondents provided multiple answers).

The report's authors make the following comment:

> We find it disturbing that each year, a high percentage of respondents are not sure about the impact that an international assignment has on an expatriate's career. How can one make a convincing case for accepting an assignment if one cannot determine the impact that the assignment will have on an expatriate's career?

Stroh[19] found that the best predictors of repatriate turnover were whether the company had a career development plan and whether the company was undergoing turbulence, such as downsizing. She argues that there are more likely to be lower rates of repatriate turnover in organizations that planned for the repatriation of their employees and that provided career development planning for them.

● *Devaluing the overseas experience*. Career progression is important but to be promoted upon re-entry signifies that international experience is important and valued by the organization. Consider the following comments made by expatriates from various countries:

> I think that our corporation can benefit from the experience I gained abroad, but no one asked me for any information. It is as if I never went [US repatriate].[20]

> You gain a lot of experience, but it is dismissed here [Australian repatriate].[21]

> The job I returned to was not satisfactory … I felt strongly overqualified and it took three-quarters of a year before I got a relevant job [Norwegian repatriate].[22]

> When I came home, I was assigned to a newly created, undefined staff job, where I had no friends, no contacts and no access to management [US repatriate].[23]

> The problem is when one comes back from an international assignment it may happen that there is no position for the person to return to. Sometimes it is necessary to be a supplementary person in a department and one has to wait for a job. That is not very nice to come back to [British repatriate].[24]

As these comments reveal, the re-entry position may be a less challenging job with reduced responsibility and status than that held either during the international assignment, or prior to the period overseas, in 'holding' positions such as a task force or project team or in temporary positions engaged in duties that do not appear to exploit their newly gained international expertise.[16,25–27] For some, the return position is frequently a lateral move rather than a promotion.[28,29] The positions do not seem to be related, or draw upon, experiences and skills that the person may have acquired during the international assignment – that is, giving the impression that such experience is devalued.

Furthering the sense of the devaluing of international experience are the reactions of work colleagues. Suggestions can be met with xenophobic responses[30] – along the lines of 'you are at home now', or 'it won't work here'. Some repatriates report a general lack of interest. For example, Stroh *et al.*[23] quote an interviewee: 'Returning repatriates should be warned about the extreme lack of interest Americans usually show in anything outside their own world'.

Coping with new role demands. Along with career issues, a mismatch of expectations affects the repatriate's perception of the role associated with network position. A role is the organized set of behaviors that are assigned to a particular position. Although an individual may affect how a role is interpreted and performed, the role itself is predetermined, usually defined in the job description.[31] Effective role behavior is an interaction between the concept of the role, the interpretation of expectations, the person's ambitions, and the norms inherent in the role. Figure 7-3 illustrates the elements of the repatriate's role as a focus for a discussion of the readjustment issues related to role behavior.

Readjustment problems may occur because, although the repatriate is attempting to function back in the home country, his or her role conception remains influenced by that of the foreign assignment. The message being sent (denoted by the direction

Figure 7-3   The repatriate's role

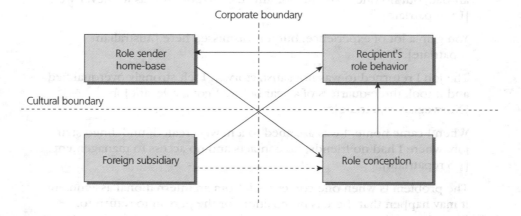

Source: Adapted from I. Torbiörn, The Structure of Managerial Roles in Cross-cultural Settings, *International Studies of Management and Organization*, Vol. 15, No. 1 (1985).

of the arrow in Figure 7-3) by the home company (the role sender) has crossed the cultural boundary. The person has been operating for some time in the foreign location, and consequently may have made significant changes to his or her role behavior.[32] For example, an American working in Indonesia may have altered his managerial style and be more authoritarian based on messages sent by the foreign subsidiary; or it could be that the time in the Indonesian subsidiary has reinforced an authoritarian tendency. Conflict is likely to occur if the repatriate does not resume the managerial behavior appropriate to the US context upon return.

Torbiörn[33] contends that as long as the repatriate's 'identity and basic values are still bound up in the culture of the home country, the strain of adjusting to conditions at home will be slight'. However, while the repatriate may retain the role conception, and the cultural norms regarding behavior appropriate to that role, the foreign subsidiary's influence may linger, as indicated by the dotted arrow in Figure 7-3, and what is communicated to the home company, in the form of role behavior, will not conform to the home company's expectations. As shown by the broken line between the role sender and role recipient boxes at the top of Figure 7-3, there is a 'corporate boundary' to be crossed in the communication of the role conception between the role recipient (the repatriate) and the role sender (the home company). The role sender, however, may not recognize the cultural and corporate boundaries that affect the repatriate's role conception and role behavior, and thus unwittingly contribute to readjustment problems.

While research in this area is limited, in their study of 125 repatriate managers from four large US multinationals, Black and Gregersen[34] found that role clarity, rather than role conflict, was significantly related to work adjustment. Discussing these findings, the authors explain that role conflict may be an important factor in expatriate assignments owing to conflicting role signals between home office and the foreign subsidiary, whereas role conflict upon return most likely stems from conflicting job signals from different individuals within the home operation. They add: 'While there are advantages in providing jobs that are clear and free from role conflicts, it is perhaps more important for firms to provide clear jobs upon repatriation'. In other words, role clarity emerges as an aspect of healthy repatriation.

A further contribution to our understanding of repatriate readjustment comes from Gregersen and Black's finding regarding role discretion.[35] Role discretion refers to the freedom to adjust the work role to fit the individual, making it easier for the person to utilize past, familiar behavior, thus reducing the level of uncertainty in the new job that assists adjustment. They found that, for their sample, role discretion had a positive impact upon adjustment, a finding that appears to confirm earlier studies on the relationship between role discretion, role clarity and work adjustment.[33,35] In a later survey of Finnish repatriates, Gregersen found fairly consistent results in terms of role clarity and role discretion with those of American repatriates. He comments:[36]

> The consistent results between American and Finnish managers suggest
> that greater role discretion upon repatriation seems to facilitate repatriation
> adjustment. In addition, the importance of role clarity to work adjustment
> suggests that Finnish and American firms may want to provide clearer jobs
> upon repatriation.

However, it would appear that, for North American companies at least, role clarity and role discretion remain a repatriation issue. It emerged as important in Baughn's survey of US repatriates.[37] The category 'reduced responsibility and autonomy on the job' was ranked second, after 'career advancement', as a major concern upon repatriation for respondents in the Tung–Arthur Andersen survey mentioned earlier. These findings lend added support to the importance of role clarity, role conflict and role discretion in work adjustment after re-entry.[17]

Further, the above studies suggest that the corporate boundary in Figure 7-3 may be stronger than the 'cultural boundary', in terms of the repatriate role. Limited support for this conclusion comes from the results of a study by Forster,[4] who surveyed 124 employees recently repatriated back to the UK. Analysis of the responses indicated five predictors for repatriation maladjustment (in ranked order):

- length of time abroad
- unrealistic expectations of job opportunities in the home company
- downward job mobility
- reduced work status
- negative perceptions of the help and support provided by employers during and after repatriation.

Job-related factors were found to be more important than non-work and family factors.

A point that is not directly addressed, but may help to explain the inter-relationships between the variables found significant in the above studies, is that the period overseas does alter the person. The experiences of living and working in another country can affect the person's self-efficacy (the degree to which an individual believes that he or she can execute a set of behaviors). In addition, the expatriate position commonly involves a more demanding job position. Learning how to cope successfully with the various challenges encountered during the foreign assignment may give the person more self-confidence, along with a broader perspective.[38] These changes may be subtle for some people; for others they can be profound, and may be influenced by factors such as length of time spent abroad, country of assignment, and individual differences such as age and personality. As a result, the reverse culture shock experienced by the repatriate may be as much a function of the degree to which the person has altered as the changes that have occurred in the home country, as indicated in Figure 7-4.

The period of time spent overseas is an important aspect. The longer the person is away from the home country, the more likely there will be readjustment problems

---

Figure 7-4   The readjustment challenge

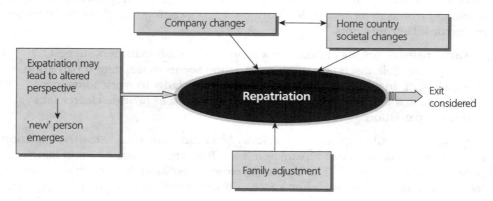

upon return.[37,39] Another contributing factor may be the length of time that the repatriate is kept in a so-called 'holding pattern'. This may be acceptable as an interim measure, but the longer repatriates are treated as temporary, the more likely they are to become anxious about the future, and have less commitment to the home work unit and the parent organization.[2]

Other workplace changes may affect readjustment. The repatriate often encounters changes in the formal and informal information channels in the home organization, particularly if there has been widespread restructuring and downsizing. Technological advances in the multinational may render the repatriate's functional skills and knowledge outdated. A Norwegian repatriate described his reaction: 'Everything had changed ... I had inadequate technological knowledge on, for instance, PC systems'.[22] Unless there was sufficient contact with the expatriate during the international assignment, the person will be unprepared for these changes. When coupled with other job-related problems, these changes make work adjustment a difficult process.

Loss of status and pay.   Usually, at least for PCNs, the international assignment is a form of promotion. It carries greater autonomy, a broader area of responsibility (because of the smaller size of the overseas subsidiary) and, at the top management level, a prominent role in the local community. The result is higher status. Some expatriates use the term *kingpin* to describe their positions overseas. Upon return, the repatriate is expected to resume his or her position within the home company, with the loss of status and autonomy. In effect, the repatriate is treated as just another company executive. This shift may cause readjustment problems. For example, a repatriate can find that, whereas in the foreign operation he was the key decision-maker, now he has to seek permission from a superior. One Australian repatriate described this feeling: 'Over there, you are the big fish in the small pond. Back home, you return to being the small fish in a big pond.'[40]

Compounding the problem is the loss of expatriate premiums. As Conway states, 'More commonly, employees are brought home to resume life on a scale that may be significantly less comfortable than what they had grown used to abroad. Pay is usually lower in absolute terms'.[41] A similar finding is reported by the Tung–Arthur Andersen survey referred to earlier. However, in their study of 21 US firms, Napier and Petersen[42] found that most of the repatriates in their sample felt that their personal finances were better *after* the assignment than *before*, even though they were not as favourable as before the overseas assignment. Napier and Petersen explain that the total compensation package received while on assignment was greater than before, thus allowing the person to return to the US with increased savings.

Another contributing factor is that the returning manager may no longer be able to afford to buy a home similar to the one sold a few years before. A US study suggests that the current practice of providing expatriates with better housing than they had at home may contribute to repatriation problems. That is, a drop in the standard of housing conditions has a negative impact on the adjustment of US repatriates.[14] This creates somewhat of a dilemma for US HR managers. As we discussed in Chapter 4, the amount of support provided for the expatriate and family is critical to adjustment and intent to stay in the foreign location, but may have a negative effect on re-entry.

Social factors

The familiar surrounds of the home environment may ease the transition, or at least the cultural adjustment will not be as demanding as that confronted in the foreign country. However, the international experience can distance the repatriate, and his or her family, socially and psychologically. If the expatriate position gave the person a high profile, involving interaction with the social and economic elite, the return home may bring with it some measure of social disappointment, thus reinforcing the *kingpin* syndrome. The financial loss of the compensation premium, housing subsidy and related benefits can exacerbate these feelings.

It must be stressed here that, where spouses, partners and children are involved, each family member is experiencing his or her own readjustment problems. For some returnees, re-entry is a shock. It is as if they had pressed the 'pause' button as they flew out of the country, and expected life at home to remain in the 'freeze frame'. Re-entry reminds them that life is not static. Others may have, as a coping behavior in the foreign location, glamorized life back home, and now have to come to terms with reality, to accept the negative as well as the positive aspects of home. For example, the foreign country may have appeared more expensive in relative terms, but upon repatriation, the family is confronted with a higher level of inflation in the home country than was previously the case. Conversely, life at home may now seem dull and unexciting in contrast, and the family unit may begin to glamorize the life they left behind in the foreign location. These reactions can be compounded if the family income has been reduced upon repatriation. Of course, the income level depends on whether spouses/partners worked while in the foreign location, and how quickly they find suitable jobs upon repatriation.

Naturally, impressions generated about changes in the home country may depend on how effectively the family has been able to keep up-to-date with events back home. One could expect that the coverage by satellite television news channels such as CNN and BBC World, and global-oriented newspapers, make it easier for US and UK expatriates to follow their home events than those coming from smaller countries such as Australia or Norway. The Internet has the potential to provide an avenue for expatriates to stay in touch, although this depends on the availability of, and access to, television cable networks, computer facilities and Internet connections in the foreign location.

Re-establishing social networks can also be difficult, especially if the family has been repatriated to a different state or town in the home country. Families who return to their previous domestic locations often find that friends have moved away. Repatriated spouses may find their friends have re-entered the workforce and are no longer available for social activities. There can be a sense of loss as the level of attention and support from the multinational is withdrawn: 'The phone does not ring. We went from a very close [expatriate] community to here where everyone is very busy with their own lives.'[43] Many repatriates report that people show little interest in hearing about their expatriate experiences, which can make conversation uncomfortable.[44,45] As one US repatriate relates: 'It was very difficult discussing my experiences with my co-workers and friends because Americans refuse to accept that life somewhere else could be as good or better than in the USA.'[46]

Children may also find re-entry difficult. Coming back to school, attempting to regain acceptance into peer groups and being out-of-touch with current slang, sport and fashion can cause problems. However, there are few reported studies in the literature that focus on children's repatriation. An exception is a study of 40 Japanese children that found the children faced difficulties reintegrating into both their peer groups and the Japanese educational system.[47] One can speculate, though, that the more difficult the re-entry process for the children, the greater is the 'spill-over' effect for the repatriate.

Effect on partner's career.   Partners encounter difficulties in re-entering the workforce, particularly if the partner has not been able to work outside the home prior to, or during, the foreign assignment, but now desires to find outside employment, either as part of a re-entry coping strategy or owing to altered family circumstances. Negative experiences during the job search may affect the partner's self-worth, compounding the readjustment process, and even causing tension in the relationship. For those who held positions prior to the overseas assignment, difficulties in re-entering the workforce may depend on occupation,[48] length of time abroad, unemployment levels in the home country and personal characteristics such as age and gender.[14]

There is a dearth of research into the effects of the foreign assignment and repatriation upon the partner's career, and many questions surrounding this issue remain unexplored:

- Do new employers consider the value of the time overseas to 'compensate' for the forced career disruption? One study reported: 'being a trailing spouse during the expatriate's international assignment constitutes a damaging gap in their employment history'.[49]

- Have those partners who were able to work during the foreign assignment found employment in career-related jobs, and been able to progress upon repatriation?

- Do male 'trailing' partners face different challenges upon repatriation than do females? In one of the few reported studies into dual-career expatriates, Harvey[50] found a difference between female expatriate managers' expectations prior to and after expatriation, exposing the need for support for the male trailing partner. The overseas assignment was the focus of Harvey's study, but one could assume that the same results would hold true upon repatriation. More recently, Linehan and Scullion[24] looked at the repatriation process of female expatriates working in various European companies but did not consider the career aspect of the accompanying spouse/partner.

Readjustment of the expatriate, whether male- or female-led, may be linked with concerns about the effect that the foreign assignment might have on the partner's career. Given that dual-career couples are on the increase, and that more females expect overseas assignments, the issue of the partner's career is likely to become a major factor determining staff availability for future overseas assignments. A 2002 global survey by ORC Worldwide[51] found that job-search assistance (20 per cent), CV/résumé preparation (20 per cent) and career counselling (18 per cent) were the most common forms of spousal assistance upon re-entry. The report's authors comment:

> Surprisingly, the provision of these three important support mechanisms has decreased since the previous increase in the 1996 survey. Taking into account the increased recognition of the dual career issues and their significance for successful assignments leading to the growth in pre-assignment and on-assignment spousal assistance, this decrease in the support on repatriation was unexpected.

Our analysis has revealed how various factors influence re-entry and readjustment at the individual level. As can be seen from the IHRM in Action Case 7-1, these moderating factors can combine to create a somewhat volatile situation that may lead to the repatriate's exit from the multinational.

Re-entry problems

John Handel had been back in his hometown for 2 months after an exciting 3 years working in the Japanese subsidiary of a US multinational. As he sat in his empty office looking out at the city skyline, John reviewed his situation. Well, he had to admit, for him it had been an exciting and challenging time as his position there as finance manager had been a promotion. More importantly, it had brought him in contact with different work approaches and procedures and he had interacted with American expatriates from headquarters as well as local Japanese. Even though his previous position had been in the Asia-Pacific Regional Office, it had not provided him with the same exposure as he enjoyed in Japan. John knew that he had gained valuable experience and self-confidence as a result.

It had not been all excitement, though, for the family. Anne, his wife, did not complain but John knew that she faced a difficult time because of his international assignment. One reason was because his two teenaged children had to attend the International School located at a considerable distance from the Japanese subsidiary, which meant they only came 'home' each weekend. It made life particularly lonely for Anne, as she was not working in Japan. She did admit that she often missed her work as a pathologist. Anne was having trouble back home finding employment as her previous department in a local medical school had been closed down owing to reduced government funding.

Both children enjoyed the international environment at the school, and had adjusted better than John had hoped. Coming back to Australia, though, was proving to be traumatic. His elder son had not been accepted into his chosen university course owing to non-recognition of the accreditation of the International School – or at least that was what Peter claimed. His younger son, Jason, was not adjusting easily either.

Dinner last night had not been a happy occasion, but tonight will be worse, John knew. How was he going to explain that the family had made such sacrifices to further his career that was now going nowhere? His repatriated position back to the Regional Office was badly timed, to say the least. Headquarters in the States had decided to reorganize the entire global operation and, as a result, the Regional Office was to be upgraded to a Regional Headquarters, and relocated in Japan. John knew that it made sound business sense as most of the Asian-Pacific activity was centred around the Japanese facility and its South-East Asian and Chinese markets. To retain its regional headquarters in Australia on the grounds of sentiment was unthinkable in such a highly competitive industry. 'But where does that leave me? All the work is being transferred northwards. My position will now be filled by someone from either headquarters or, more probably, from Japan. My boss made that quite clear. I could not have asked the family to move back anyway,' thought John. The situation was compounded by the news today that several of his colleagues in the regional office had been made redundant. 'My acceptance of the international assignment has been career suicide – and not just for me,' John thought. 'I will have to see if there are positions available elsewhere if I am going to be able to face Anne and the boys tonight. Surely another company will value my international experience.'

This case is based on a real incident. The names of the people concerned have been changed to respect confidentiality and anonymity.

Multinational responses

The above sections have considered the re-entry and career issues from the perspective of the individual repatriate. We shall now examine the issues from the viewpoint of the multinational. Early studies into the issue of repatriation indicated that it was somewhat neglected by multinationals. For example, Mendenhall et al.[52] concluded that US human resource professionals may be unaware of the challenges facing repatriated managers. Commenting on the results of his 1989 study Harvey[44] noted that:

> Even though many executives have experienced difficulties upon repatriation, [US] multinational companies have seemingly not addressed the issues related to repatriation with the same level of interest as preparing executives for expatriation.

A 1997 survey found that only 27 per cent of responding firms indicated that they held re-entry sessions to discuss issues, such as career objectives, performance and plan for re-entry. The majority of these firms indicated that they waited up to 90 days before initiating such sessions.[53] There would seem to have been some progress lately: 73 per cent of responding firms in the 2002 GMAC-GRS survey held re-entry discussions with expatriates, although this was down from the 83 per cent figure indicated in 2001. Of those who held re-entry discussions, 53 per cent said these were informal, 38 per cent held formal sessions and 10 per cent did not know. The timing of these re-entry discussions also varies, though the majority held them while the expatriates were on assignment.

The GMAC-GRS survey did not report on spousal or family involvement in re-entry discussions, but these aspects were raised in the ORC Worldwide 2002 Report. As mentioned earlier in this chapter, job search assistance, résumé preparation and career counselling were the most common forms of assistance. However, the report does not indicate if this was negotiated before or during the international assignment or upon re-entry, and if it was part of a re-entry discussion.

Managing the process of repatriation should be of concern to multinationals that desire to maximize the benefits of international assignments and create a large internal labour market. A well-designed repatriation process is important in achieving these objectives, for three main reasons: staff availability, return on investment and knowledge transfer. These are now discussed.

Staff availability

The way in which the multinational handles repatriation has an impact on staff availability for current and future needs. Re-entry positions signal the importance given to international experience. If the repatriate is promoted or given a position that obviously capitalizes on international experience, other members of the multinational interpret international assignments as a positive career move. On the other hand, if the multinational does not reward expatriate performance, tolerates a high turnover among repatriates or is seen to terminate a repatriate's employment upon re-entry, then the workforce may interpret the acceptance of an international assignment as a high-risk decision in terms of future career progression within the organization. The multinational's ability to attract high-calibre staff for international assignments is thereby lessened, and this can have a negative effect on the multinational's activities in the long term.

Return on investment (ROI)

Expatriates are expensive. Where possible, multinationals try to localize positions through the employment of HCNs but, as we have discussed elsewhere, not all positions can or should be localized. The alternative, which more companies are utilizing, or experimenting with, is a short-term or non-standard assignment to replace the traditional expatriate form. Cost containment is the driver here along with staff immobility. For example, 80 per cent of firms in a 2002 global survey by PricewaterhouseCoopers[54] identified cost reduction as important or very important in the evolution of international assignment practices. However, faced with the business reality that expatriates will always be with us, the question is how to ensure that the organization reaps the benefits of international assignments regardless of duration and form. Black and Gregersen[14] calculate that a US multinational spends around one million dollars on each expatriate over the duration of a foreign assignment. They argue that, if approximately one in four repatriates exits the firm within 1 year of repatriation:

> It represents a substantial financial and human capital loss to the firm, especially if the skills, knowledge, and experience that the individual gains are important to the firm and scarce in the internal or external labour markets.

Getting a return on this investment would appear to be an important objective, but not easy to achieve. First, there is a matter of definition. Respondents in the GMAC-GRS 2002 survey were asked if ROI could be defined as 'accomplishing the assignment objectives at the expected cost'. A total of 96 per cent of respondents agreed with this definition. They were then asked to rate expatriate assignments in terms of ROI: 30 per cent rated it as good or excellent, 38 per cent as average and 32 per cent as fair or poor. Difficulties encountered in attempts to measure ROI were:

- receiving feedback from the business unit concerned
- tracking international assignments in a systematic way
- no formal planning
- a lack of objective measures
- too many decisions being made without realizing the costs relating to the international assignment.

Second, ROI concentrates on the international assignment period, and can be substituted by a cost–benefit analysis to justify a decision to replace expatriates with HCNs, rather than considering gains that accrue to the organization through repatriated staff. It is difficult to measure intellectual capital gains – improvements in the stock of knowledge and competence that result from a successful repatriation process. We will return to some of these aspects when we examine performance management in Chapter 10.

Knowledge transfer

A common theme in current international business that is stressed by company managers is the need for cross-fertilization of ideas and practices that assist in developing and maintaining competitive advantage. International assignments are a primary method of achieving this objective. As the PricewaterhouseCoopers 2002[55] report concludes:

> Organizations need to make sure that their business strategies are supported by sound mobility strategies … The need to move key employees

around the business, regardless of national boundaries, will be increasingly vital to the success of a global organization.

Given the roles played by expatriates, along with their cost, it is reasonable to expect that multinationals would endeavor to retain key staff and to extract and build upon their international experience. However, as we have seen in our examination of re-entry and career issues, a relatively high turnover of repatriate staff seems acceptable. That 39 per cent of responding firms in the 2002 GMAC-GRS survey do not know the attrition rate is evidence of this. One GMAC-GRS respondent commented: 'There is a high level of investment with a low value on the experience'.[56] More telling is the continuing trend not to guarantee post-assignment positions so that the organization has greater flexibility over employment levels.

We can draw several conclusions regarding repatriate attrition rates. First, despite the rhetoric, knowledge transfer is treated as a one-way activity. Expatriates are sent on international assignments and effectiveness is determined on the performance of their ascribed roles and work responsibilities. Any transfer of knowledge and competence occurs there in the host location, and remains there. Expatriates return to their home base and are reassigned or resign. Consider the following comments about international assignment objectives volunteered by responding firms in the 2002 GMAC-GRS survey.[57]

- The primary reason for an expatriate assignment is to go into a country and train someone who is local to do a specific job function and then return home.
- Work is project oriented. We send expatriates to complete projects and leave.
- Expatriates develop local management talent.
- Our main reason for sending expatriates is to supplement national staff capacity, provide training and coaching and provide professional expertise.
- We view these as developmental assignments to broaden employee experience.

There is no mention about an international assignment being part of transferring knowledge and competence around the organization, or even as a two-way process. The point here is that while performing their tasks in the host location, expatriates develop skills and gain experience, knowledge and network relationships that can then be used upon repatriation in some way or another. For example, a project manager working in Russia can report, on re-entry to his UK home base, technical problems encountered and solutions that were developed to overcome these problems, thus sharing the experience. However, not all of the knowledge about that project is explicit. Much will remain tacit and person-bound. What is codified and made explicit often is retained within the project team, even though some of the information and knowledge could be applicable to other projects or types of business concerning Russia, such as important contacts, management styles and some technical solutions.

HCNs transferred to headquarters for developmental reasons, for example, may benefit through such exposure but the experience will remain person-bound if the home unit does not allow the repatriated HCN opportunities to share knowledge and information. Contacts at headquarters can be used for personal advantage. A similar case can be made for TCNs transferred back from another subsidiary. The aims of cross-fertilization of ideas and best practices given to justify cross-border movement of staff require the right environment to facilitate sharing of information and knowledge. The 'not-invented-here' mindset (or xenophobia) can operate to devalue repatriate contributions.

The trend towards not providing post-assignment position guarantees suggests that multinationals accept loss of experience, knowledge and competence; that repatriates effectively forced to leave the organization will take with them what could be vital and valuable, allowing competing firms to reap the benefits of a substantial investment in human capital. As Downes and Thomas[58] found, multinationals that valued international experience were rewarded by loyal employees who contributed to the intellectual capital base of their companies. Unfortunately, that repatriates become an underutilized resource has been a consistent finding in studies and surveys examining repatriation (see, for example, Refs 7, 10 and 18).

Designing a repatriation program

Although there is no simple, quick solution, preparing the repatriate and family for re-entry appears to have some value. The potential for mismatch of expectations regarding the future may be addressed as part of pre-re-entry training before the return, and discussed during re-entry counselling sessions (sometimes referred to as debriefing) between the receiving organization in the home country and the repatriate. In today's parlance, such sessions would enable both parties to 'take a reality check'.

What should be covered in formal repatriation programs? Table 7-1 is an amalgam of the lists suggested by respondents in the various surveys referred to above.

Some companies assign the expatriate a **mentor** (also referred to as a company contact, sponsor or 'godfather'). The mentor is usually in a more senior position than the expatriate, from the sending work unit, and knows the expatriate personally. The rationale behind the use of a mentor is to alleviate the 'out-of-sight, out-of-mind' feeling discussed earlier through the provision of information (such as workplace changes) on a regular basis, so that the expatriate is more prepared for conditions faced upon re-entry. A mentor should also ensure that the expatriate is not forgotten when important decisions are made regarding positions and promotions.

Table 7-1	Topics covered by a repatriation program

- Preparation, physical relocation and transition information (what the company will help with)
- Financial and tax assistance (including benefit and tax changes; loss of overseas allowance)
- Re-entry position and career-path assistance
- Reverse culture shock (including family disorientation)
- School systems and children's education and adaptation
- Workplace changes (such as corporate culture, structure, decentralization)
- Stress management, communication-related training
- Establishing networking opportunities
- Help in forming new social contacts

A survey of re-entry practices in 152 multinational companies from the USA, Europe and Asia[49] found that 26 per cent of respondents provided mentors for their expatriates, although this was related to various organizational factors:

- Size of expatriate workforce: firms with more than 250 expatriates were more likely to assign mentors (43 per cent) than those with 55–100 expatriates (15 per cent).

- Which work unit was responsible for the expatriate: mentors are more likely if corporate HR formulates expatriate policy (in 35 per cent of cases) and when the expatriate is managed by a separate international assignments unit (in 41 per cent of cases) rather than at the divisional level (18 per cent).

- Nationality of responding company: 35 per cent of Continental European firms reported the use of mentors compared with 20 per cent in US firms. This result compares with findings from a study of European-based multinationals: over a quarter used a career mentor/sponsor system, with a further 19 per cent indicating that such a scheme would be introduced in the future.

Linehan and Scullion[24] found that 40 of the 50 females in their study had experienced mentoring relationships, and believed that their management positions were partially due to that relationship. The mentors provided contact and support from the home organization, which also facilitated re-entry and reduced the 'out-of-sight, out-of-mind' syndrome. Their experiences led them to adopt mentoring roles in their new domestic positions.

It is reasonable to suggest that the practice of mentoring, to be effective, has to be managed. For example, what happens when the mentor retires or leaves the firm – two likely events in a multinational undergoing radical restructuring? Who monitors the mentor's performance? Recent surveys have not specifically covered the practice of mentoring, although 12 per cent of responding firms in the 2002 GMAC-GRS survey indicated they used mentors. Firms in a 1997/98 Price Waterhouse survey[59] defined mentoring duties to include:

- Maintaining contact with the expatriate throughout the assignment.

- Ensuring that expatriates are kept up-to-date with developments in the home country.

- Ensuring that expatriates are retained in existing management development programmes.

- Mentors are responsible for assisting expatriates with the repatriation process, including helping them with a repatriation position.

It may be that having a mentor assists the expatriate to adjust during the foreign assignment but, by itself, does not necessarily help re-entry. Stroh[60] concludes that her study: 'did not show that having a mentoring programme would make an independent contribution to repatriate retention rate', although there was a suggested link between assignment of a mentor, career development, and repatriate retention. In other words, an effective mentor is likely to alert the firm of the imminent return of the repatriate and thus affect the re-entry position, or the practice is part of a managed repatriation program.

Although recognition of the importance of repatriation programmes is increasing, and companies are experimenting with other measures such as mentors, other avenues could be explored, such as using repatriates as an important information source. Inviting repatriates to assist in developing repatriation programs may contribute to relevant and effective policies. It may also have a desirable side-effect upon readjustment, simply by giving participating repatriates a sense that they are not an underutilized resource, and that the firm recognizes they can make a valuable contribution to the expatriation process. It is, naturally, important that wherever possible the multinational ensures equity of treatment between PCN, TCN and HCN expatriates.

Summary

This chapter has been concerned with the repatriation process. We have covered:

- The repatriation process. One may conclude that in re-entry, the broader socio-cultural context of the home country takes a backstage position – unlike in the expatriation adjustment phase, where the foreign culture can be overwhelming.[14] Cultural novelty has been found to affect adjustment and, for the majority of repatriates, coming home to the familiar culture may assist in readjustment. Indeed, given the more profound effect that job-related factors appear to have, **re-entry shock** is perhaps a more accurate term to describe the readjustment process experienced upon repatriation.

- Job-related issues centered on career issues upon re-entry. Factors that affected career anxiety were no post-assignment guarantee of employment, fear that the period overseas had caused a loss of visibility, changes in the home workplace that affect re-entry positions and the employment relationship. The re-entry position was an important indicator of future career progression and the value placed on international experience. Coping with new role demands was another factor in readjustment, along with loss of status and pay.

- Social factors explored were loss of social standing – the kingpin syndrome – and the accompanying loss of the expatriate lifestyle. Family readjustment was also important. A specific aspect was the effect of the international assignment upon the spouse/partner's career, such as being re-employed and having international experience recognized.

- Multinational responses to repatriates' concerns focused on re-entry procedures. We looked at how repatriation affected staff availability, whether companies were measuring and obtaining a return on investment through international assignments and the contribution of repatriates to knowledge transfer.

- Designing effective repatriation programs, including the use of mentors.

Although the focus of this chapter has been repatriation in the general sense, the issue of career expatriates should be raised. The repatriation literature reviewed in preparation for this chapter makes little mention of the process of managing the return of those who have been part of the international team of managers (or cadre) – those who have worked outside their home countries for lengthy periods of time. For this strategically important group of employees, at some point repatriation may coincide with retirement. One is left with the impression that those who return to retire in their home country are no longer of concern to their firms. However, one could expect that these individuals would require special counselling to assist not only the transition back to the home country, but also from work to retirement.

Viewing repatriation as part of the expatriation process, as suggested in Figure 7-1, should remind those responsible for expatriation management of the need to prepare repatriates for re-entry and to recognize the value of the international experience to both parties.

Discussion questions and exercises

1 What factors contribute to re-entry shock?

2 How can multinationals assist dual career couples' repatriation?

3 What are the elements of a good mentoring system?

4 What aspects would you include in a pre-repatriation program?

5 You have been asked to accept an international assignment that involves working in Nigeria for 2 years. Following the general trend, your employer will not provide a post-assignment job guarantee. You realize that the probability of unemployment when the assignment is finished is rather high. Why would you accept the international assignment?

6 Discuss the case presented in IHRM in Action Case 7-1. What steps should the HR department concerned have taken to assist in John's repatriation?

Further reading

M. Linehan and H. Scullion, 2002. Repatriation of European Female Corporate Executives: an Empirical Study, *International Journal of Human Resource Management*, Vol. 13, No. 2, pp. 259–260.

M. Lazarova and P. Caligiuri, 2001. Retaining Repatriates: the Role of Organizational Support Practices, *Journal of World Business*, Vol. 36, No. 4, pp. 389–401.

M. Bolino and D.C. Feldman, 2000. Increasing the Skill Utilization of Expatriates, *Human Resource Management*, Vol. 39, No. 4, pp. 367–379.

M. Downes and A.S. Thomas, 1999. Managing Overseas Assignments to Build Organizational Knowledge, *Human Resource Planning*, Vol. 22, No. 4, pp. 31–48.

L.K. Stroh, H.B. Gregersen and J.S. Black, 1998. Closing the Gap: Expectations Versus Reality Among Repatriates, *Journal of World Business*, Vol. 33, No. 2, pp. 111–124.

J.S. Black, H.B. Gregersen and M.E. Mendenhall, 1992. Toward a Theoretical Framework of Repatriation Adjustment, *Journal of International Business Studies*, Vol. 23, No. 4, pp. 737–760.

Notes and references

1 R. Moran, Coping with Re-entry Shock, *International Management*, December (1989) p. 67.

2 M.G. Harvey, Repatriation of Corporate Executives: an Empirical Study, *Journal of International Business Studies*, Vol. 20, No. 1 (1989) pp. 131–144.

3 D. Welch, Determinants of International Human Resource Management Approaches and Activities: a Suggested Framework, *Journal of Management Studies*, Vol. 31, No. 2 (1994) pp. 139–164.

4 N. Forster, The Forgotten Employees? The Experiences of Expatriate Staff Returning to the UK, *International Journal of Human Resource Management*, Vol. 5, No. 2 (1994) p. 408.

5 A.W. Harzing, *Environment, Strategy, Structure, Control Mechanisms, and Human Resource Management in Multinational Companies*, Company Report, University of Limburg, 1996.

6 GMAC-Global Relocation Services, US National Foreign Trade Council and SHRM Global Forum, *Global Relocation Trends 2002 Survey Report*, 2002.

7 R.L. Tung and Arthur Andersen, *Exploring International Assignees' Viewpoints: a study of the Expatriation/Repatriation Process*, Chicago: Arthur Andersen, International Executive Services, 1997.

8   D.E. Welch, Globalisation of Staff Movements: Beyond Cultural Adjustment, *Management International Review*, Vol. 43, No. 2 (2003) pp. 149–169.

9   D.C. Feldman and D.C. Thomas, Career Issues Facing Expatriate Managers, *Journal of International Business Studies*, Vol. 23, No. 2 (1992) pp. 271–294.

10   Ref. 6, p. 51.

11   Price Waterhouse Europe, *International Assignments: European Policy and Practice*, Price Waterhouse International Assignment Services Europe, 1997.

12   E. Marx, *International Human Resource Practices in Britain and Germany*, London: Anglo-German Foundation for the Study of Industrial Society, 1996.

13   D. Osborn, The International Mobility of French Managers, *European Management Journal*, Vol. 15, No. 5 (1997) pp. 584–590.

14   S. Black and H.B. Gregersen, When Yankee Comes Home: Factors Related to Expatriate and Spouse Repatriation Adjustment, *Journal of International Business Studies*, Vol. 22, No. 4 (1991) pp. 671–694.

15   M. Bolino and D.C. Feldman, Increasing the Skill Utilization of Expatriates, *Human Resource Management*, Vol. 39, No. 4 (2000) pp. 367–379.

16   L.K. Stroh, H.B. Gregersen and J.S. Black, Closing the Gap: Expectations Versus Reality Among Repatriates, *Journal of World Business*, Vol. 33, No. 2 (1998) p. 119.

17   J.S. Black, H.B. Gregersen and M.E. Mendenhall, Toward a Theoretical Framework of Repatriation Adjustment, *Journal of International Business Studies*, Vol. 23, No. 4, (1992) pp. 737–760.

18   M. Lazarova and P. Caligiuri, Retaining Repatriates: the Role of Organizational Support Practices, *Journal of World Business*, Vol. 36, No. 4 (2001) pp. 389–401.

19   L.K. Stroh, Predicting Turnover among Repatriates: Can Organizations Affect Retention Rates? *International Journal of Human Resource Management*, Vol. 6, No. 2 (1995) p. 450.

20   Ref. 18, p. 395.

21   Ref. 3, p. 148.

22   A.J. Jensen and J. Ottesen, International Human Resource Management in Norwegian Companies, Siviløkonom Thesis, Norwegian School of Management, Oslo, 1996, p. 92.

23   Ref. 16, p. 120.

24   M. Linehan and H. Scullion, Repatriation of European Female Corporate Executives: an Empirical Study, *International Journal of Human Resource Management*, Vol. 13, No. 2 (2002) pp. 259–260.

25   R.L. Tung, Career Issues in International Assignments, *Academy of Management Executive*, Vol. 2, No. 3 (1988) pp. 241–244.

26   H.B. Gregersen, Commitments to a Parent Company and a Local Work Unit during Repatriation, *Personnel Psychology*, Vol. 45, No. 1 (1992), pp. 29–54.

27   R.L. Tung, A Contingency Framework Revisited, *Human Resource Management Review*, Vol. 8, No. 1 (1998) pp. 23–37.

28   R.L. Tung and E.L. Miller, Managing in the Twenty-first Century: the Need for Global Orientation, *Management International Review*, Vol. 30, No. 1 (1990) pp. 5–18.

29   D. Allen and S. Alvarez, Empowering Expatriates and Organizations to Improve Repatriation Effectiveness, *Human Resource Planning*, Vol. 21, No. 4 (1998) pp. 29–39.

30   M.R. Hammer, W. Hart and R. Rogan, Can You Go Home Again? An Analysis of the Repatriation of Corporate Managers and Spouses, *Management International Review*, Vol. 38, No. 1 (1998) pp. 67–86.

31   H. Mintzberg, *The Nature of Managerial Work*, Englewood Cliffs, NJ: Prentice-Hall, 1973, p. 54.

32   L. Gomez-Mejia and D.B. Balkin, The Determinants of Managerial Satisfaction with the Expatriation and Repatriation Process, *Journal of Management Development*, Vol. 6, No. 1 (1987) pp. 7–17.

33   I. Torbiörn, The Structure of Managerial Roles in Cross-cultural Settings, *International Studies of Management and Organization*, Vol. 15, No. 1 (1985) p. 69.

34   Ref. 14, p. 688.

35   H.B. Gregersen and J.S. Black, A Multifaceted Approach to Expatriate Retention in International Assignments, *Group and Organization Studies*, Vol. 15, No. 4 (1990) pp. 461–485; also Torbiörn (1985).

36   H.B. Gregersen, Coming Home to the Arctic Cold: Finnish Expatriate and Spouse Repatriation Adjustment and Work-related Outcomes, paper presented at the Academy of International Business Meeting, Brussels, November 1992, p. 23.

37   C. Baughn, Personal and Organizational Factors Associated with Effective Repatriation, in *Expatriate Management: New Ideas for International Business*, ed. J. Selmar, Westport, CT: Quorum Books, 1995.

38 N.K. Napier and R.B. Peterson, Expatriate Re-entry: What Do Expatriates Have to Say? *Human Resource Planning,* Vol. 14, No. 1 (1991) pp. 19–28.
39 Ref. 14, p. 686.
40 D.E. Welch, The Personnel Variable in International Operations: A Study of Expatriate Management in Australian Companies. Unpublished Ph.D. thesis, Monash University, Australia, 1990.
41 M. Conway, "Reducing Expatriate Failure Rates", *Personnel Administrator*, Vol. 29, No. 7 (1984) pp. 31–38.
42 Ref. 38, p. 24.
43 H. De Cieri, P.J. Dowling and K.F. Taylor, The Psychological Impact of Expatriate Relocation on Partners, *International Journal of Human Resource Management*, Vol. 2, No. 3 (1991) p. 403.
44 M.G. Harvey, The Other Side of Foreign Assignments: Dealing with the Repatriation Dilemma, *Columbia Journal of World Business*, Vol. 17, No. 1 (1982) pp. 52–59.
45 R. Savich and W. Rodgers, Assignment Overseas: Easing the Transition Before and After, *Personnel*, August (1988) pp. 44–48.
46 Ref. 37, p. 224.
47 W. Enloe and P. Lewin, Issues of Integration Abroad and Readjustment to Japan of Japanese Returnees, *International Journal of Intercultural Relations*, Vol. 11 (1987) pp. 223–248.
48 G.K. Stevens and S. Black, The Impact of Spouse's Career Orientation on Managers During International Transfers, *Journal of Management Studies*, Vol. 28, No. 4 (1991) pp. 417–428.
49 The Conference Board, *Managing Expatriates Return: A Research Report*, New York: Report No. 1148-96-RR (1997) p. 16.
50 M.G. Harvey, Dual-career Expatriates: Expectations, Adjustment and Satisfaction with International Relocation, *Journal of International Business Studies*, Vol. 28, No. 3 (1997) pp. 627–658.
51 Organization Resources Counselors (now ORC Worldwide), *Dual Careers and International Assignments Survey*, ORC, 2002, p. 7.
52 M. Mendenhall, E. Dunbar and G. Oddou, Expatriate Selection, Training and Career-pathing: a Review and a Critique, *Human Resource Planning*, Vol. 26, No. 3 (1987) pp. 331–345.
53 Ref. 49, p. 28.
54 PricewaterhouseCoopers, *International Assignments: Global Policy and Practice Key Trends*, 2002.
55 Ref. 54, p. 28.
56 Ref. 6, p. 56.
57 Ref. 6, p. 40.
58 M. Downes and A.S. Thomas, Managing Overseas Assignments to Build Organizational Knowledge, *Human Resource Planning*, Vol. 22, No. 4 (1999) pp. 31–48.
59 Ref. 11, p. 32.
60 Ref. 19, p. 454.

Global HR issues

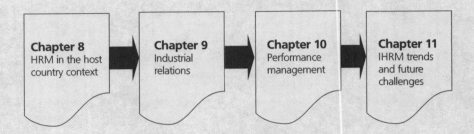

| Chapter 8
HRM in the host
country context | Chapter 9
Industrial
relations | Chapter 10
Performance
management | Chapter 11
IHRM trends
and future
challenges |

International human resource management involves more than managing and supporting international assignments. Part III is therefore concerned with various themes pertaining to global HR issues. Chapter 8 covers HRM in the host-country context. We first examine the question of whether the multinational can standardize its work practices or if factors in host countries force adaptations and the implications for HRM. Factors such as host-country culture, mode of operation, firm size, maturity and international experience and subsidiary mandate are identified and discussed. We also look at HR practices for retaining, developing and retrenching local staff and the HR implications of standardizing communication through the adoption of a common corporate language; and the monitoring HR practices used by foreign subcontractors.

Chapter 9 examines issues relating to industrial relations that need to be taken into consideration by multinational firms. It covers the interaction between the multinational and trade unions, recent trends and issues in the global workforce context and the impact of regional economic zones such as the European Union.

Chapter 10 examines the strategic role of performance management. It considers multinational performance management at the global and local levels and the link between control and performance. The various factors influencing the performance of expatriate and non-expatriate employees is then addressed. The chapter concludes with a discussion of individual performance appraisal in the international context, including issues surrounding HCN appraisal.

Chapter 11 looks at trends and future challenges and also theoretical developments that link strategy and IHRM. This chapter concludes not only Part III, but draws the three Parts together as a way of finalising the book.

HRM in the host country context

Chapter objectives

Discussion of international HRM issues generally tends to be biased in the direction of expatriate management, particularly that of parent-country nationals, partly owing to their strategic importance. In this chapter, we attempt to redress the balance by examining HRM issues in subsidiary operations. We cover the following aspects:

- Factors that influence standardization or adaptation of work practices and the role of HR, including host-country culture and workplace environment, mode of operation, firm size, maturity and international experience and subsidiary mandate.

- Retaining, developing and retrenching local staff.

- HR implications of language standardization: HCN selection, training and promotion on the basis of language skills.

- Monitoring HR practices used by foreign subcontractors.

Introduction

In Chapter 2, we covered the internationalization process and the range of responses to the managerial challenges encountered in international business operations. Control and coordination issues are paramount and underlie many of the decisions taken by headquarters management. As Laurent[1] has noted:

> In order to build, maintain and develop their corporate identity, multinational organizations need to strive for consistency in their ways of managing people on a worldwide basis. Yet, and in order to be effective locally, they also need to adapt those ways to the specific cultural requirements of different societies. While the global nature of the business may call for increased consistency, the variety of cultural environments may be calling for differentiation.

Laurent proposed that, in practice, this would require states of minds and mind-sets that allow five conditions to be met:

1 An explicit recognition by the parent organization that its own particular ways of managing human resources reflect some assumptions and values of its home culture.

2 An explicit recognition by the parent organization that its particular ways are neither universally better nor worse than others but are different and likely to exhibit strengths and weaknesses, particularly abroad.

3 An explicit recognition by the parent organization that its foreign subsidiaries may have other preferred ways of managing people that are neither intrinsically better nor worse, but could possibly be more effective locally.

4 Willingness by headquarters staff not only to acknowledge cultural differences, but also to take active steps to ensure these are discussed and incorporated where appropriate.

5 The building of a genuine belief by all parties involved that more creative and effective ways of managing people could be developed as a result of cross-cultural learning.

Implicit in Laurent's analysis is the 'think global, act local' mantra that has driven much of multinational management thinking over the past decade. The idea of a global mindset is compelling. The message is to encourage all employees to appreciate 'the bigger picture' – to recognize interdependencies and inter-relationships between units, and between units and headquarters, so that resource sharing and knowledge transfer occurs for the benefit of the corporate 'whole'.

Hence the need for consistency of, and conformity to, corporate goals and objectives is driven from the center, accompanied by an underlying presumption that it is possible to achieve unity of purpose through all employees worldwide adopting corporate values, codes of conduct and prescribed work practices. It is reflected in headquarters predispositions, as we reviewed in Chapter 3, when looking at staff placement in subsidiary operations: whom to place in key positions and what positions can and should be localized. Even in mature multinationals, what has been termed 'lingering ethnocentrism' is evident in the way in which the parent company approaches subsidiary management, particularly in the use of control mechanisms. At the same time, effective multinational management requires sensitivity to various host-country requirements regarding employment, such as hiring, reward and promotion practices, and respect for local customs. How to accomplish this, however, is complicated by the nature of the relationship between units and the 'parent', the level of equity involved and factors within host-country environments that facilitate or constrain the transfer of global management practices and business processes.

In this chapter, we will explore how a multinational's HR practices in host-country contexts are shaped by the interaction between the various parties involved and the trade-offs that occur in order to manage people in a multi-national context. Again, we recognize that current thinking on these issues has been shaped by investigation of larger multinationals and their relationship with a network of diverse subsidiaries, but much is germane to all firms operating internationally.

Standardization and adaptation of work practices

A multinational's approach to its subsidiary operations centers around what processes, procedures and practices can be and should be transferred, and to what degree they require adaptation, if any, to be effectively implemented at the local level. Transferring technology, systems and know-how are seen as significant aspects, and the role of people in the process is a critical part. As discussed in Chapter 4, expatriates frequently are used to oversee the successful implementation of appropriate work practices, and there is a link between the number of expatriates and the transfer of multinational work practices. At some point, however, multinational management replaces expatriates with local staff with the expectation that these work practices will continue as planned. This approach is based on assumptions that appropriate behavior will have been instilled in the local workforce through training programs and hiring practices, and that the multinational's way of operating has been accepted in the manner intended. In this way, the multinational's corporate culture will operate as a subtle, informal control mechanism – a substitution of direct supervision.

However, this depends on receptivity of the local workforce to adhere to corporate norms of behavior, the effectiveness of expatriates as agents of socialization and whether cost considerations have led the multinational to localize management prematurely. Further, transplanting methods and techniques that have been successful in one environment can be inappropriate in another. Thus, the standardization–adaptation choice that confronts the multinational in other areas of its operations applies to the management of the global workforce. Factors that influence standardization are host-country culture and workplace environment, the mode of operation involved, the size and maturity of the firm and the relative importance of the subsidiary. We shall briefly consider these factors.

Host-country culture and workplace environment

In Chapter 1 we identified national culture as a moderating variable in international HRM. We explained how members of a group or society share a distinct way of life with common values, attitudes and behaviors that are transmitted over time in a gradual, yet dynamic, process. Values and attitudes towards behavior are affected by culture, as shown in Figure 8-1. Work behavior is culturally determined to the extent that it is contained in role definition and expectations. When it comes to multinational management, we distinguish between national culture of the parent company, national culture of the subsidiary unit and the way in which corporate culture acts as a potential unifying force. For a multinational with subsidiary operations in 70 countries, establishing a common corporate culture may be important for cohesion, but whether corporate culture can supersede or supplant other 'cultures' is a subject of much debate, as we discussed in Chapter 2.[2] However, managerial attitudes towards subsidiary management may include a firm belief in the power of a strong corporate culture and expectations that employees internalize or 'buy into' corporate values. Often, though, what is meant by corporate culture translates as universal work practices, that is, common practices rather than common values as a unifying force within a multinational, indicated by the double-headed arrow between corporate culture and standardization of behavior in Figure 8-1. Standardization of work practices involves behavior modification through corporate training programs, staff rotation, rewards and promotion, most of which fall into the ambit of the human resource function. These activities concentrate on developing and maintaining corporate-defined behavioral standards and processes that ensure their adherence. A corporate code of conduct is a good example of this. Corporate identity is important and it is possible to generate a sense of pride and belongingness that enables unity of purpose to be achieved. Subsidiary staff may have strong identity with the local unit, but the challenge is to foster employee identification with the global level.[3]

Alongside this is the issue of effectiveness of standardization. Is it possible to impose work practices that are influenced by one culture upon employees who have been socialized into another way of behaving within their work environment? People may be prepared to adopt certain work behaviors to retain their employment, but that does not necessarily mean that they ascribe to the corporate values that shape required behavioral outcomes. For example, Taylor[4] found that Chinese working in Japanese plants in China perceived team briefings and other such forums as a new form of rhetoric, replacing nationalist and Communist party propaganda of the past, and consequently were considered of little value by workers and managers. Likewise, Liberman and Torbiörn,[5] in their study of eight European subsidiaries of a global firm, found variations in the degree to which employees adopted corporate norms. In some countries, employees were agreeable towards the wearing of company clothing emblazoned with its logo, as such action did not challenge their national culture. In one subsidiary, however, there was great resistance to the implementation of performance assessment for non-managerial positions as it went against existing practice. Liberman and Torbiörn concluded that practices could be applied – that is, standardized – if they did not disagree with local norms. Further, commonalities were more likely to be found at top management level. This is perhaps not surprising given that top management is more heavily influenced by corporate objectives and strategic direction. Top-level managers experience more interaction with their peers from other

---

Figure 8-1   The linkage between culture and behavior

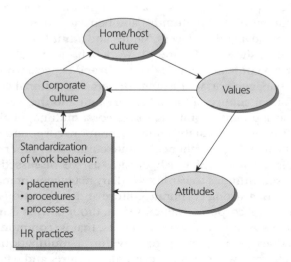

Source: Adapted from N. Adler, *International Dimensions of Organizational Behaviour*, 3rd edn, Cincinnati OH: South-Western College Publishing, 1997, p. 16.

subsidiaries (for example, through attendance at regional and corporate meetings) and with managers from headquarters.

There are also indications that cultural distance will have a bearing on the degree to which work practices require adaptation. That is, one can expect hiring practices to be more similar in the Anglo-Saxon countries (USA, Canada and Australia) than between the USA and India. However, as more multinationals set up operations in countries previously closed to foreign direct investment on a large scale, one can expect some convergence of HR practices, given the way in which we have observed such convergence in other countries.

An important factor is the presence of expatriates and their ability to encourage and impose appropriate work behavior. A study by As-Saber *et al.*[6] found that there was a clear preference for using HCNs in key positions by multinationals operating in India. The authors suggest that a major reason for HCN preference was the belief that the right Indian will know more than an expatriate manager could learn in years on the job. As will be recalled from Chapter 3, localization of HR staff positions is more likely to ensure that local customs and host-government employment regulations are followed, although this also acts as a divergent force. Khilji[7] found that, although foreign multinationals in Pakistan had formulated policies, implementation was low 'because managers brought up and trained in a hierarchical and centralized set-up resist sharing power and involving employees in decision making'. This was despite a host-country expectation that multinationals would transfer their best practices and act as a positive force in the introduction of what was regarded as desirable Western management styles. However, the multinationals in Khilji's study had taken a polycentric approach, with HCNs in key positions, including that of HR manager.

Mode of operation

A multinational's ability to impose standardized work practices is not only affected by cultural differences that may create resistance to change from subsidiary staff. As Bae and Lawler[8] conclude from their study of international and local firms in Korea, 'HRM strategy is not solely determined by national cultural differences. There is some latitude for management to make choices.' Figure 8-2 demonstrates the factors that influence standardization of work practices, including mode of operation.

One managerial choice is the form of operation that the multinational uses. Entering via an acquisition may provide the multinational with market advantages, but its ability to transfer technical knowledge, systems and HR practices may be restricted. Plant and equipment may need upgrading along with the skills of the workforce that the purchaser inherits. This is particularly the case with what has been termed a **brownfield** – where the multinational acquires an existing local firm as part of the establishment of a local operation, but the multinational effectively replaces many of the resources and capabilities.[9] The local company requires considerable investment and restructuring to make it operable, and this will include human resources, with a high demand on expatriates initially. Investment in training programs has been a critical factor. This type of acquisition is more common in emerging markets, such as those of Eastern Europe.

A study by Buckley *et al.*[10] provides two examples of how mode of operation can inhibit or facilitate standardization. In late 1978, the Chinese government announced an open-door policy and commenced economic reforms aimed at moving the country from a centrally planned to a market economy. Western firms that entered China early were more or less forced to enter into joint ventures with State Owned Enterprises (SOEs), whereas those entering later have been able to establish wholly owned operations. One case in Buckley *et al.*'s study is Shanghai Bell – a joint venture formed in 1983 between a Belgian telecommunications firm (now Alcatel Bell), the Belgian government and the Chinese Postal and Telecommunications Industries Corporation (PTIC). There was a gradual transfer of relevant technology by the Belgian firm, with a long-term reliance on Belgian expatriates. The Belgian firm had limited control over the Chinese employees in the joint venture and was constrained by its partner's expectations and differing goals.

The second case was different. The US telecommunications firm Motorola established a wholly owned operation in Tianjin, China, in 1992. Changing conditions in China meant that Motorola could effectively build a 'transplant factory': importing production equipment, organizational processes and practices from either the parent or other subsidiaries in its global network. This enabled Motorola to integrate the Chinese operation into the broader corporate network, and to localize management. These have been supported by HR initiatives such as a special management training program (CAMP – China Accelerated Management Program[11]), English language training and transfer of Chinese employees into the US operations. Motorola has been able to transfer its processes and systems, such as Six Sigma quality control, bringing its technology, knowledge and work practices, supported by HR activities, into the new facilities in China relatively quickly.

Ownership and control therefore are factors that need to be taken into consideration when looking at how multinationals handle the standardization of work practices. The autonomy to implement processes and procedures is naturally higher in wholly owned subsidiaries whereas the question of control over the international joint venture (IJV) remains a concern for multinational firms. Elements such as complementarities between IJV partners and the degree of interdependence between the IJV and other parts of the multinational have been found to be important influences on effective IJV operation and transfer of work practices.

Figure 8-2   Factors influencing standardization of work practices

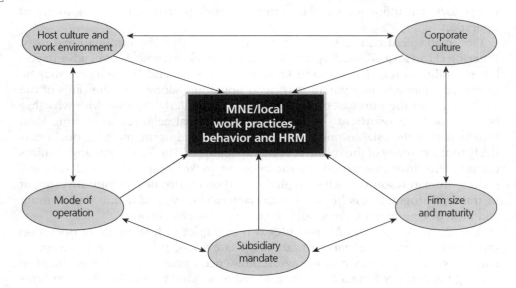

For example, Yan's[12] study of 87 IJVs operating in China revealed the importance of a strategic objective for the IJV in determining work practices. Those firms pursuing a strategic position in China were more likely to seek to diffuse task-related work practices compared with those who were more short-term. Yan concluded that task-related influence in an IJV plays an important role in directly shaping HRM practices.

It is not surprising that firms that take a longer-term view seek to influence the work practices and operations of the IJV. It takes time and considerable effort to integrate local IJV managers into the 'global family', as illustrated in the case of Hindustan Lever presented in IHRM in Action Case 8-1.

Another mode of operation is that of a **management contract**. We briefly explained this mode in Chapter 2 as where the multinational operates an international entity on a contract basis rather than through an equity arrangement. The

---

IHRM in Action Case 8-1

Unilever's Indian experience

Unilever, the consumer goods multinational, was created through the merger in 1929 of the British firm Lever Brothers and the Dutch firm Margarine Unie. In 2003, it was operating in 88 countries worldwide, employing 265 000 people. It is controlled by two holding companies: Unilever plc (English) and Unilever NV (The Netherlands), but operates as a single company. Its two Chairmen head the Executive Committee of the Board. Its website Homepage describes the company as a multi-local multinational, with a stress on local operations; 90% of managers are locally recruited and trained. In 2000, the company restructured. It now operates as two global divisions: Foods, and Home and Personal Care, with 10 regional groups reporting to their respective global divisional executive directors. Both global divisions have their own executive boards.

Unilever has been operating in India for over 60 years through a 51% owned local entity, Hindustan Lever. Unilever endeavours to establish a strong sense of corporate identity, referred to as 'Unileverization'. It has been rather successful in India – to the extent that there is a popular saying: 'You can take the person out of Hindustan Lever, but you can't take Hindustan Lever out of

the person.' Values such as thrift and simplicity are advocated from the top. According to the company, every Unilever management trainee begins his or her career by spending 6–8 weeks in a rural village which ensures they connect with consumers. Its managers have been drawn from graduates of India's top business schools and developed through its in-house training program. Cultivating its own talent that is familiar with the Indian way of doing business, combined with loyalty to Unilever's worldwide approach to managing, has made Hindustan Lever staff attractive to foreign and local competitors. There has been active poaching of its management staff. For example, in 1997, in a newspaper interview, the Hindustan Lever Chairman was asked about the effects of the arrival of more foreign multinationals in India. He commented that Hindustan Lever has had to make adjustments: 'We have significantly increased our salaries at various levels.' Keki Dadiseth, former Chairman of Hindustan Lever, now heads the Home and Personal Care Global Division, Unilever Headquarters.

Source: Based on information obtained from Unilever's website and Miriam Jordan, Role Model for the New Multi-nationals, *Financial Times* India Survey, June 24 (1997) p. 19.

managing company (the multinational) undertakes the usual management functions, provides the skills, expertise and resources, and trains the local employees (HCNs). For example, the multinational may have built under a project contract an airport facility in a less developed country (a turnkey operation). Through a separate contract, it may then provide the management expertise to run the airport. The terms of the contract may contain specific conditions relating to the use and training of HCNs ultimately to manage the airport.

Although management contracts may not be as common as other contractual forms such as a joint venture, they often are a lucrative and effective way of operating internationally. Host governments have seen the management contract as a way of countering the negative impacts of foreign direct investment, especially foreign control of local operations and the import of inappropriate technology. Locals own the facility, while foreign managers run it. This may give the multinational considerable power over resources, sourcing of materials and components and day-to-day operations. In other words, they run the show without having to provide any equity or carry the risks associated with foreign direct investment. There has been little research into the specifics of this mode of operation. Early work in the 1970s and 1980s identified the HRM implications of the management contract, but there has been a paucity of academic work since these early studies emanating predominantly from UK scholars.[13]

By nature, the management contract involves the heavy use of expatriate staff, for various lengths of time. The early British studies demonstrated that external recruitment for the majority of management staff increased the likelihood of the contract failing. The purpose, of course, is to buy management expertise that expatriates bring to the situation. There is a large component of training of HCNs involved. Management may not have the same degree of discretionary power that full ownership brings. The US hotel chain Holiday Inn had a 10-year contract with a Tibetan hotel. The expatriate managers were precluded from giving incentives to or disciplining its staff. This created some difficulties when hotel employees took their breaks at the same time – which happened to be when guests arrived expecting lunch.[14] Although not without implementation difficulties, management contracts are used extensively in the hotel industry.

Hence mode of operation has an impact on the multinational's ability to transfer work and HR practices. Of course, there are other modes, such as franchising and licensing, utilized by firms that we have not dealt with here. These modes will likewise have specific HR impacts, depending in part on the type of arrangement entered into with the client firm. For example, there is often a training component in a licensing arrangement. This may be undertaken with the licensee in the foreign market, or personnel from the licensee firm may attend training in the licensor's home operation.

Firm size, maturity and international experience

Key factors influencing international operations are the size and maturity of the multinational. Motorola's experience in China reflects its large size and the fact that it had a wealth of international experience upon which Motorola management could draw when considering entering a transitional economy such as China. A smaller multinational, a relative newcomer to international business, may not have the same level of ability or resources, and an alternative mode of operation such as a joint venture would be an attractive proposition. However, as mentioned earlier, studies of Sino–foreign joint ventures demonstrate that this mode of operation is not without its HR challenges, and that the experiences of Shanghai Bell are not uncommon. As Warner explains, 'the shift from the older [management and HR] practices has only been partial, especially in larger enterprises, whether state-owned enterprises or even Sino–foreign joint ventures'.[15] This is mainly because multinationals have a stronger association with government partners in China and tend to be somewhat locked into maintaining management practices that are a legacy of pre-reform days.

Subsidiary mandate

Linked to the issue of size and maturity of the multinational is the position of the subsidiary in relation to the rest of the organization and its mandated role – what is expected of it in terms of contribution to global activities. Recently, there has been considerable interest in looking at the role of the subsidiary, particularly in the context of large networked multinationals. In Chapter 2, we considered such organizations from a structural perspective as a consequence of international growth. The perspective was that of the center or parent company. Studies have examined how subsidiaries' roles and positions alter over time, related to subsidiary initiative-taking, power and resource relationships, host-country environment, the predisposition of top management and the active championing of subsidiary managers.[16] This line of scientific inquiry has been helpful in focusing attention on the roles of various subsidiaries, that subsidiaries may be both initiators and producers of critical competences and capabilities that contribute to competitive advantage. Centers of excellence at the subsidiary level can be viewed as an indication of how some multinationals are recognizing that levels of expertise differ across the organization and that not all innovation and 'best practice' originates from the center, that is, from headquarters. General Electric's establishment of a center of excellence in Hungary is an example. This action affected the subsidiary's mandate, changing it from being a miniature replica of the parent to being strategically independent or a product specialist.[17]

However, the difficulties in transferring knowledge and competence from the subsidiary level – whether from a designated 'center of excellence' or not – to the rest of the network are similar to the difficulties that we discussed in the context of headquarter to subsidiary transfer. The 'sticky' nature of knowledge, for example, applies regardless of its origins, but the designated role of the subsidiary and the standing of its management are critical in determining the spread and adoption of subsidiary-initiated practices. A major barrier can be what Birkinshaw and Ridderstråle[18] describe as 'the corporate immune system'. Subsidiary initiatives often are met with significant resistance analogous to the way the human body neutralizes or rejects foreign matter. Individuals within the organization resist change, or support low-risk projects, and are wary of ideas that challenge their own power base.

Staff movements across subsidiary operations are one way to break down these barriers and produce corporate rather than subsidiary champions who are prepared to disseminate information about subsidiary initiatives and capabilities and recommend adoption in other parts of the organization where appropriate. Tregaskis,[19] in her study of R&D centers, reports how one firm found personal relationships built up by visits by key staff to other units facilitated information sharing and the eventual adoption of new products by other subsidiaries. Face-to-face meetings were important in building trust and exchanges of tacit knowledge. Another mechanism is the use of project teams where members are drawn from various business and functional units.

Global or local work practices and HRM

Our analysis of HR and workplace standardization versus adaptation reflects the convergence–divergence debate. Forces for standardization are mainly internal to the multinational driven by the need for control and to sustain competitive advantage. Host governments, though, may encourage standardization through the transfer of 'foreign' work practices and processes and management techniques if such moves are aligned with political and economic imperatives. Forces for adaptation come from external constraints that the multinational confronts in its various markets. Therefore, it is not a case of 'either–or', but rather managing people across borders contains elements of both standardization and adaptation, and multinational transfer of managerial and HR practices both influence and inhibit convergence.[20] A key factor here is time. Organizations, like societies, are not static. China is a case in point. As Björkman and Fan[21] point out, early entrants into China localized their HRM practices; however, 'during the 1990s there seems to have been a trend towards introducing more "Western" HRM policies in China'.

There are many cases where multinationals have successfully replicated work practices in their foreign subsidiaries through intensive training programs designed and implemented by headquarters. This is particularly true regarding technical training for operating employees in areas where certain skills and work practices are regarded as strategically essential. Japanese multinationals such as Nissan and Honda have been able to train substantial numbers of HCNs in their US, UK and European subsidiaries with reasonable success (see, for example, Ref. 22 and 23). The conduct or delivery of training programs may have been modified to cater for local differences, but the outcome is similar.

As Huo *et al.*[24] conclude from their study of personnel selection processes across 10 countries:

> While the recruiting practices used in different countries are inching toward global convergence, we expect national cultures to continue affecting the hiring practices ... As such, human resource managers still need to be culturally sensitive when devising the recruitment systems in various cultural environments. After all, the 'best international resource management practices' ought to be the ones *best* adapted to cultural and national differences.

Retaining, developing and retrenching staff

Consider the following scenario. A multinational, as part of its cost leadership strategy, decides to build a production facility in country X where labor costs are low. It then finds it needs to invest heavily in training local employees, thereby automatically increasing the cost of that labor (the paradox referred to as 'the expense of cheap labor'). Not only does the unit cost of labor rise over time, but also trained employees may well become attractive to its foreign and local competitors in country X, who simply offer higher wages to lure them away. If this 'poaching' of HCNs is successful, the multinational discovers that its competitors reap the training benefits while it receives little return for its investment in human capital. Further, poached employees have to be replaced and trained, thus increasing labor costs. This scenario is played out time and time again, in different countries as multinationals seek cost advantages.

Cost considerations produce what has been referred to as mobile factories as multinationals move in and out of countries as changing circumstances dictate. A good example is that of the US-based data technology company Seagate.[25] It closed one of its Irish plants in 1997 despite having only been in operation for 1 year. Seagate repaid the Irish government the $16 million it had received in grants to establish the Irish plant. Instead, it increased the size of its Malaysian plant to capitalize on the fall in value of the Malaysian currency, the ringgit. At the time Seagate had 30 per cent of the world disk drive market, employing 108 000 people worldwide.

Unit labor costs are not the only factor. Skilled labor is also a consideration and markets that provide a large pool of highly skilled, yet relatively cheap labor are doubly attractive. India is one such market. Despite a recent slump due to the collapse of the 'dotcom' boom, the information technology industry in India has been regarded as attractive owing to its workforce composition – highly educated, skilled programmers and software engineers who earn a fraction of the salaries of their US counterparts. To capitalize on this cost advantage, US firms such as IBM, Hewlett-Packard and Electronic Data Systems have outsourced software development to Indian suppliers.[26] Other multinationals, such as General Electric, have used the availability of a highly educated yet relatively cheap labor force to establish their call centers in various parts of India. Local staff employed in these call centers are trained to speak English with accents and idioms so that US, UK and Australian customers are often unaware that their 'local' call has been diverted to a call center in India.

Another aspect in the Chinese context is the role played by network connections called *guanxi*: dyadic personal relationships between people. Tung and Worm[27] explain that although these relationships bear similarities to the Western practice of networking, there are differences: *guanxi* are contingent upon conditions such as asymmetry, reciprocity and necessity. These authors stress the importance of *guanxi* for successful business operations in China but recognize the difficulties that this poses for Western executives. They suggest that hiring practices for key positions should take into account prospective Chinese employees' *guanxi*. The difficulty is being able to assess whether prospective employees have the right *guanxi*.

When hiring Chinese nationals for executive jobs (because of their communication skills, local contacts and understanding of the domestic market[28]), many multinationals have found that Chinese managers lack decision-making skills and are wary of taking personal initiatives. Along with job-related skills, corporate management training programs are required that provide HRM skills appropriate to the Chinese context, and skills for problem solving in high-pressure situations.[29]

Mode of operation again is a consideration for HCN employment. One of the attractions of an IJV is the assumption that a more experienced local partner can assist in identifying a suitable workforce. The IJV may perhaps even use the existing human resources (its internal labor market) of the local partner, if this pool of labor is considered to be sufficient in terms of skill and productivity levels. However, this can lead to unexpected labor costs if the local partner regards the joint venture operation as a convenient way of redeploying surplus employees who may not have the skills required. The multinational then has to invest heavily in the training of HCN staff in the IJV, leading to escalating training costs perhaps not 'factored in' to the original market entry decision. The risk of poaching again is high. However, multinationals will weigh labor availability and cost against strategic imperatives. A presence in China and India may be a more powerful push than the potential loss of skilled labor.

Retaining and developing staff

Multinationals find that they need to invest in training employees to use equipment, operate systems and the like. What actions can these firms take to gain the benefits of this investment in human capital? Obviously, it is not easy to prevent employees from leaving the operation. Poaching of skilled employees is a business reality. Shanghai Bell was an early entrant into the Chinese market and became the 'academy for the industry', experiencing high staff turnover to both Chinese and foreign-owned competitors.[10] In post-reform China, employees have tended to change jobs frequently in pursuit of higher wages rather than skills development.[30] To a certain extent, this may be traced back to the employment system that existed prior to reforms associated with the transition to a market economy. Guaranteed continuation of employment, along with various welfare and benefits offered to employees, such as accommodation, medical treatment, childcare and pensions, has been referred to as the 'iron rice bowl'. In exchange for job security, employees had little freedom to move to another work unit – that is, they were unable to quit or transfer jobs and were locked into a dependency relationship with their enterprises. Managers were deprived of their right to fire or lay off unqualified or non-productive employees.[31]

The changing Chinese work environment means more mobile employees. The experience of the Shangri-La Hotel is a case in point. It reportedly lost 89 per cent of its employees in 1993.[32] The hotel had invested considerable time and money into training employees in aspects such as English language fluency, service orientation and hotel etiquette – all of which made these employees attractive to competitors and they were easily lured away with offers of higher pay. Management were able to reduce turnover to 40 per cent by providing improved housing near to the hotel, more training opportunities and career development.

Although companies operating in China are endeavouring to reduce their attrition rates, through the provision of additional benefits and staff development programs, Chinese employees are recognizing compensation differentials and that is having an impact upon job attitudes. For example, a study[33] of 180 employees working in various joint venture hotels with foreign partners from Hong Kong, Japan, Taiwan, the UK and Singapore found that local employees compared their salaries with that of expatriates, rather than with locals working in other organizations in China. This provoked a heightened sense of salary injustice; however local employees' intention to quit was not affected either by the cultural origin of the expatriates or by the comparison with expatriate salaries.

A fair environment and good management practices are emerging as essential in retaining Chinese employees, rather than above-market compensation alone. Goodall and Roberts,[34] in their study of a European oil company operating in China, cite the example of one employee who found that being part of a wider organizational network was an incentive to stay with the multinational:

> I've been offered more pay to go to Exxon, but I've been here four years. I started as support staff and worked hard to build trust, learn about the [company] culture, build a network … The management know me and trust me to do the job. If I leave I have to learn a new culture, prove you're good.

It is not just China where there is a high turnover of subsidiary staff. Firms operating in Russia have faced similar issues, as a study by Camiah and Hollinshead[35] highlights. Demand for Russians with foreign language skills and experience working in Western companies is high and such individuals can generally move freely between jobs. Khatri *et al*.[36] report similar job-hopping behaviors in Singapore and other Asian countries.

Retrenchment

This is the reverse side of the employment coin. Strategic decisions taken at corporate headquarters such as plant rationalization can result in the closure of host-country operations, as multinationals divest and withdraw or de-internationalize.[37] For example, the US automobile manufacturer Ford Motor Corporation closed 5 of its 11 plants in Europe, resulting in job losses. The English car-assembly plant had been in operation for almost 71 years.[38] Some staff were retained in the R&D (engine design) center in England, but job losses are an inevitable outcome of such actions. The Seagate plant closure in Ireland mentioned above resulted in the loss of 1400 jobs.

Of course, the multinational's ability to carry out retrenchments will be determined by the host-country environment. For example, once hired, it is not easy to dismiss employees under Indian labor law.[39] The Industrial Dispute Act provides strict rules for layoffs and dismissals. Consequently, dismissals and layoffs are difficult, and such actions can be contested through a petition to the government and can lead to a time-consuming process of negotiation.[40] The closure of a host-country operation can cause a political backlash from local trade unions, retrenched staff and host government ministers, particularly in developed countries, as we will discuss in the next chapter.

Partial retrenchments are also difficult. Often, decisions will be made at headquarters that a certain percentage of jobs must be cut worldwide and subsidiary HR staff are expected to translate figures into redundancies. For example, in 2002, the US investment bank Credit Suisse First Boston announced that it would be cutting up to 7% of its global workforce – resulting in 1750 redundancies. Such announcements cause low morale while subsidiary staff wait to see whose jobs will be lost. The recent downturn in the telecommunications industry saw a similar round of job losses, with both Nokia (Finland) and Ericsson (Sweden) reducing staff in certain divisions worldwide.[41]

A further aspect is the aftermath of a merger or acquisition as the new management integrates the operations into the existing organization. There is inevitably some overlap of departments, functions and services that need addressing. Efficiency demands some streamlining and employee redundancy results. Multinationals can use voluntary redundancy and natural attrition to achieve some of the necessary cutbacks in employee numbers. In some cases, employees can be proactive, and exit the organization on their own initiative, which can mean that the organization loses key staff, skills and knowledge. Cognizant of such dangers, when Deutsche Bank (Germany) acquired Bankers Trust (US), it reportedly set aside US $400 million in what was referred to as retention money to tie key executives to the new organization.[42]

Retrenchment is not confined to subsidiary closures. The decision to shift operations to lower labor cost locations can affect parent-country operations. This applies to the outsourcing of administrative activities in addition to manufacturing operations. For example, the UK telecommunications company BT (British Telecom) announced in March 2003 that it will transfer its call center operations to India, at the cost of 2000 UK jobs.[43] Not surprisingly, the announcement met with angry responses from UK employees, including the threat of strike action. Similarly, the UK firm R. Griggs announced in November 2002 that it was closing its British factories and moving production of its famous shoes – Dr Martens – to China. This would involve the loss of 1000 jobs.[44]

Consequently, global and subsidiary HR staff can become involved in situations involving strike activity, boycotts and political pressure. Some multinationals outsource retrenchment to consultants. The use of consultants may not be possible in all countries, nor is it always desirable to use outsiders to handle sensitive situations. HR staff may be called upon to deal with the consequences of staff retrenchment for those who remain employed, such as low morale and so-called 'survivor guilt'.

HR implications of language standardization

In Chapter 2, we introduced the concept of language standardization. Typically, multinationals adopt a common language, usually English, for corporate reporting and information dissemination. Language standardization assists in informal communication through the development of intra-organizational networks, and fosters a sense of belonging to a global 'family', thus enhancing corporate identity. However, as Marschan-Piekkari *et al*. point out:[45] 'Companies do not have languages, people do'. Language standardization therefore puts pressure on employees to become competent in the corporate language as there is an implicit message regarding career development, given that promotion may be determined by corporate language fluency. Company information regarding HR matters such as internal job vacancies and promotions are disseminated in the common language via in-house newsletters and intranet bulletins. Perceptions about the importance of fluency in the common language are reinforced through training and development programs, where presenters and participants are from other subsidiary operations and headquarters and the language of instruction is the corporate language, as discussed in Chapter 5. As English has become the *lingua franca* of international business, fluency in the corporate language tends to be fluency in English, although some European multinationals operate a dual system. For example, Nestlé uses both French and English as its company languages.

What the limited research into language standardization is revealing is the range of critical HR challenges that result from this managerial decision. Top management tend to be fluent in the corporate language as much of their day-to-day activities involve communication that necessitates interaction with others outside their home base. Of course, as English is the corporate language within English-speaking multinationals such as Motorola, fluency in English only becomes an issue when a US top manager confronts a subsidiary manager from a non-English-speaking country whose level of fluency may not be the same as that of a manager from the Canadian operation. Subsidiary managers who become comfortable in operating in English may cease to recognize that language is a barrier for others. Therefore, the use of a common language may only bind the organization together at the top management level.

For subsidiary staff, English can be a selection criterion. However, this assumes that there is a suitable pool of candidates in the host country who are fluent in the corporate language. A survey by *Business Week*[46] in 2001 of the proportion of Europeans who said they spoke English revealed a significant difference across countries:

- The Netherlands   80%
- Germany   55%

- France   40%
- Italy   39%
- Spain   36%.

Where the pool of potential employees with good English skills is limited, competition may be intense and push up labor costs, combined with a high attrition rate of these desirable employees. In Europe, people competent in English command salaries 25–35 per cent higher and usually higher level positions than those who are not English speakers.[47] The current attraction of India over China for IT and business process outsourcing is partly due to the size of its English-speaking population.

The business reality for multinationals entering foreign markets through a merger or acquisition, or where IJV staff have been redeployed from the local partner's operation, is that buying-in English language skills through the hiring process is not an option. Much of the workforce is inherited, comprised of local staff who often lack the required level of English competency. Some will need to become fluent in order to operate new processes and understand instructions that may not be translated into the local language. The US firm Otis Elevators is a case in point. It uses English as its common corporate language. It also has established centers of excellence. Engineering diagrams and instructions for manufacturing processes developed in its French center are sent to the Chinese factory in English. When documentation is given to employees and middle management at the shop floor, problems have arisen as lack of competence in English led to misinterpretations of technical information and diagrams.[48] Center of excellence staff send out documents in the corporate language as information is generally forwarded to a number of other subsidiary operations. It is generally left to subsidiary management to decide if, and by whom, document translation is undertaken.

HR staff may also re-translate information to ensure the message is communicated as intended. For instance, HR staff in the Australian subsidiary of the Swedish telecommunications firm Ericsson would check for what they called 'Swenglish'. Documents translated from Swedish into English – the company language – sometimes would contain peculiar words and phrases that made little sense to Australians, so HR staff would rewrite such documents.[49]

Introducing the corporate language for global reporting purposes, global and regional meetings and information gathering and dissemination will have a great impact on employees, particularly those in lower positions. As indicated in Figure 8-3, existing employees who seek a career with the multinational are faced with a choice: not to learn the corporate language and therefore remain local and at a lower position, or to acquire the level of competence in the common corporate language which will provide access to enhanced training options, international assignments and career progression. The Swedish–Swiss multinational ABB uses English as its corporate language. Chinese employees in its joint ventures are offered English language training. ABB pays the full cost of lessons to those at the managerial level and 70% of the cost for all other employees. Performance appraisal of joint venture staff includes facility in English, and employees are encouraged to speak English during management meetings and have 'English only' days. These actions encourage English language skills and ensure a competent pool of employees is available from which potential expatriates may be drawn.[50] A clear link between language fluency and promotion within the local subsidiary and opportunities for international assignments may be one way to assist in keeping key employees, so that the multinational obtains a return on its investment in human capital.

At the subsidiary level, several options are available to handle language standardization. In their study of this issue within the Finnish elevator company, KONE, Marschan-Piekkari *et al.*[51] found that subsidiary managers could be passive or active in their approach to the requirement to operate in English. Some chose to ignore the directive to provide language training for their subsidiary staff, despite having a budget to do so. As an HR manager at KONE's global training center in Finland admitted:

> There are subsidiaries, particularly in southern Europe, where local management tries to restrict information communication at organizational levels below them and in a way monopolize the contacts with the rest of KONE. In such units, little is invested in local common language training.

Decentralization can permit such action unless the multinational monitors the development of language training at the subsidiary level. After all, information is power and language fluency provides people with an opportunity to gate-keep.

Other subsidiary managers were proactive. Recognizing that English language fluency prohibited their staff from attending global training programs in Finland, the German and Austrian subsidiaries combined for training purposes, using the shared German language rather than English as the language of instruction. Apart from knowledge sharing and competence training, this had added benefits in terms of employees from these operations having the opportunities to get to know others outside their own country, creating a network of personal relationships. Similarly, the Spanish and Italian units found that they could provide more training to their employees by sharing their budgets and offering programs in shared locations using Spanish/Italian.

Figure 8-3	HR implications of language standardization

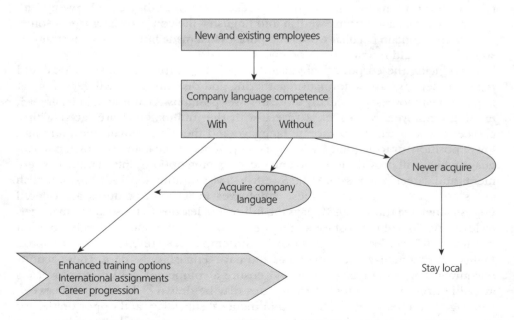

Source: R. Marschan-Piekkari, D. Welch and L. Welch, *International Journal of Human Resource Management*, Vol. 10, No. 3 (1999) p. 384. Reproduced with permission of the Editor.

Subsidiary action therefore created what Marschan-Piekkari *et al.* term a 'shadow structure', with subsidiaries grouped by language clusters, behind the formal regional matrix structure.[52] As can be seen from Figure 8-4, language standardization also created its own hierarchy: Finns were at the apex, speaking the parent-country language (Finnish) and the corporate language (English). The second layer were English-as-a-first language employees from the UK, US and Australian subsidiary operations and those in South-East Asia such as Hong Kong. Employees from the Spanish-speaking group felt most distant from the rest of KONE.

As we discussed in Chapter 3, expatriates become 'language nodes' – particularly those who become fluent in the host-country language in addition to the corporate language. As such, they provide subsidiary staff with access to information in their own language so that the language barrier is overcome.

Shadow structure of KONE based on language   **Figure 8-4**

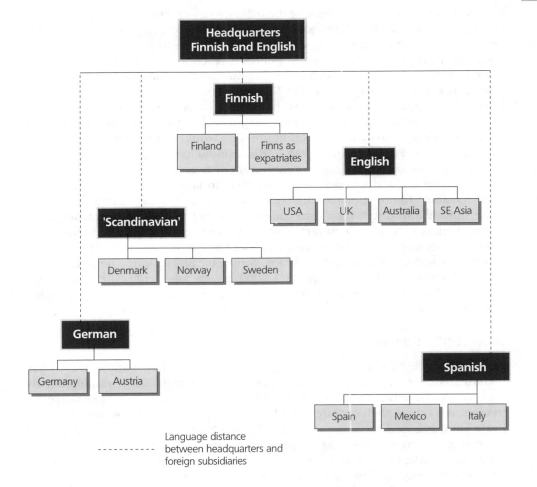

Source: R. Marschan-Piekkari, D. Welch and L. Welch, In The Shadow: The Impact of Language on Structure, Power and Communication in the Multinational, *International Business Review*, Vol. 8, No. 4 (1999) p. 434. Reproduced with permission of the Editor.

Monitoring the HR practices of host country subcontractors

An issue that has been somewhat overlooked in the IHRM literature is the need to monitor the HR practices used in host-country subcontracting firms. Many multinationals, particularly in the textile, clothing and footwear (TCF) industries, and other consumer goods industries such as electrical goods, do not establish their own manufacturing operations, nor do they select to operate through an international joint venture. Rather, they outsource the activity under contract to local or foreign-owned firms who produce the products – hence the term international subcontracting. Given the highly competitive nature of these industries, multinationals operate through subcontracting in developing markets where labor costs are lower.

Adherence to a code of conduct

A critical issue is the management of the extended international supply chain and ensuring that quality standards are met. However, particularly for multinationals with well-known brands, such as Nike, Levi Strauss, Benetton, Reebok and Adidas, the major management challenge has been the reaction of its Western consumers to employment practices used by its subcontractors in countries such as India, China, Turkey, Indonesia, El Salvador, Honduras, the Dominican Republic and the Philippines. Various multinationals have been accused of condoning work practices such as the use of child labor, long working hours for minimal pay and unsafe working environments – conditions that would not be permitted in their home countries. Public uproar in the 1990s resulted in various actions by governments, the United Nations and non-government organizations (NGOs) to try to enforce codes of conduct upon subcontracting firms through their multinational partners. Some multinationals, with corporate reputations and valuable brands at stake, quickly introduced their own codes of conduct, which subcontracting firms had to sign as part of the contract. These codes of conduct included acceptable working conditions, non-use of child labor and minimum wages. Violation of the codes of conduct became grounds for contract cancellation. There is now a universal standard, similar to the ISO 9000 quality standard, called the Social Accountability 8000, whose principles are drawn from UN human rights conventions. We discuss these issues in more detail in Chapter 11.

Monitoring mechanisms

While the code of conduct approach initially appeared to handle the public relations issue, ongoing enforcement has proven difficult. Large multinationals such as Nike have the resources to assign expatriate staff as production managers to countries where they operate via subcontracting.[53] The clothing firm The Gap has a country-based investigator in Honduras who monitors implementation of the company's code of conduct at different locations.[54] Companies also have staff from headquarters and/or from regional centers, to make inspection visits to subcontractors' factories. These visits are either announced or unannounced. External agents can be hired to make such visits. In addition, companies can have auditors, such as PricewaterhouseCoopers, monitor subcontractors' adherence to codes of conduct. However, a report by the United Nations International Labor

Organization[55] into business ethics in the TCF industries explains that the logistics involved in such monitoring activities are considerable and few companies have the personnel this requires. Further, most companies rely on local buying agents and quality control representatives to act as work practices monitors as well, although few are suitably trained in labor legislation, occupational health and safety and other work practices covered in a code of conduct. Despite the legal contract, the code of conduct often is viewed as a moral undertaking rather than a genuine method of supervision.

The US Department of Labor[56] monitors products entering the country for adherence to acceptable work practices. Officials visit plants exporting goods to the USA and check if US multinationals are monitoring and auditing their international subcontractors for workplace compliance to codes of conduct. The Department notes that the closer the relationship between a US multinational and its supplier, the greater is the ability of the US company to influence labor standards in the production process. In fact, some multinationals are unaware of the actual length of their supply chain. They may sign a code of conduct agreement with a suitable subcontracting firm, assuming that this is the producer when, in fact, that subcontractor further subcontracts to other local firms. An example of the distance between retailer and actual producers is that of the US retailer JC Penny. It sources its apparel from Renzo, a US-based importer. Renzo uses a Philippines agent, Robillard, who is required to sign up to JC Penny's code of conduct. Robillard uses several contractors in the Philippines, one of which is Castleberry, which does the cutting, finishing and packing. Castleberry contracts sewing to about 30 plants under supervision. Some of the fine sewing is contracted out to home workers. In these circumstances, monitoring adherence to a code of conduct is complicated. A survey in 1998 by Swiss auditors Société Générale de Surveillance found that about 30% of its cases in China involved further subcontracting to smaller factories with lower safety standards.

Another complicating factor is that the international contractor may be foreign-owned, and its management expatriates are imposing their own work practices upon the HCN workforce. This can produce a volatile situation for the multinational, as Nike found in Vietnam. Its subcontractors were South Korean and Taiwanese firms, whose expatriate managers were considered harsh by the Vietnamese workers. We highlighted a clash between a South Korean manager and Vietnam workers in the IHRM in Action Case 3-1 in Chapter 3. Apparently, similar clashes occurred in these subcontracting firms. Soon Nike found itself caught up in a political situation with Vietnamese and international press attention brought to bear on its Vietnamese contractors.[57]

A role for HR?

Large multinationals find it challenging to ensure adherence to a code of conduct within their own subsidiary operations. It is not surprising, therefore, to find it problematic in situations where activities are outsourced to firms. The situation with international subcontractors is not dissimilar to that encountered with other contractual modes such as franchising, licensing and IJVs. With joint ventures, much depends on whether the local joint venture partner controls the day-to-day operations of the IJV, and how many staff the multinational is able to place in the IJV to oversee adherence to its code of conduct relating to work practices such as health and safety and compliance to local labor laws and regulations.

There is a role for HR managers. They can become involved by:

- Drawing up and reviewing codes of conduct.
- Conducting a cost–benefit analysis to see how viable it would be to have an expatriate stationed in the country concerned to oversee international subcontractors' compliance.
- Championing the need to train local buyers and agents in elements of the code of conduct so that they can monitor subcontractors' adherence to workplace practices and quality checks.
- Being a member of the team who conducts periodic visits to international subcontractors.
- Overseeing external monitors and auditors where used. This will include checks to see whether the visits have been announced in advance or are surprise visits. Has the external agent spoken to workers as well as to managers? Have they local language skills, or was an interpreter used?
- Checking that performance and rewards systems take into consideration compliance to codes of conduct.

Summary

This chapter has focused on issues relating to HRM and work practices in the host-country context. We chose four main areas to examine:

- The standardization versus adaptation debate as it relates to subsidiary operations. We identified four inter-related factors that influence the multinational's ability to impose or transfer its preferred work and HR practices:
  - The host-country culture and workplace environment. We looked at the interplay between values, attitudes and work behavior and the role of corporate culture in assisting work outcomes.
  - Mode of operation. Managerial discretion to introduce its own practices is higher in wholly owned subsidiary operations than in IJVs. Acquisitions may be constrained by the inherited workforce. We also looked at management contracts as a mode of operation that may influence standardization of work practices in foreign operations.
  - Firm size, maturity and level of international experience. Firms such as Motorola can draw upon experience and resources to an extent not possible for smaller and less-experienced international players.
  - Subsidiary mandate. The position of the subsidiary in the intraorganizational network and level of interdependence between units for resources can assist in the transfer of 'best practice'.
- Retaining, developing and retrenching local staff. Aspects such as the paradox of cheap labor, the skill level of the local workforce and training were examined, along with poaching of staff and job-hopping. Although our examples are drawn from Chinese and Indian situations, these issues are not confined to these two countries.

We also looked at the impact of strategic decisions on subsidiary operations – such as plant closures and rationalization – that result in employee retrenchments at the subsidiary and in the home-country operations.

- The HR implications of language standardization. The decision to use a corporate language – usually English – has implications for subsidiary staff in areas such as selection for positions, attendance at company training programs and promotion.

- Monitoring the HR practices used by international subcontractors. This discussion opened up a somewhat contentious issue for multinationals who are expected to monitor the work practices employed by international subcontractors. Mechanisms used to monitor adherence by these firms to multinationals' codes of conduct include using internal agents, such as expatriates or 'flying' visits by headquarters or regional staff, external agents such as local buyers and auditors.

It should be noted in conclusion that there is a wealth of literature covering comparative management and HR systems.[58] We drew a little on this literature to highlight general HR issues in the host context that multinational firms confront and deal with. However, it was not our intention to cover in detail specific host-country cultures and management practices as that is outside the scope of this book. Our aim has been to raise issues relating to IHRM in the multinational context from the perspective of the subsidiary.

Discussion questions and exercises

1 What work practices can be standardized?

2 How does a management contract allow a multinational to transfer its work practices into a foreign operation?

3 How does a subsidiary's mandate affect its ability to transfer ideas and work practices to other parts of the global network?

4 You are the HR director of a medium-sized firm manufacturing children's clothing. Management has decided that, to maintain competitiveness given the flood of cheaper imports coming into your country, the company has to manufacture offshore. However, it lacks the resources for an equity arrangement and decides to use international subcontracting agreements with a large Chinese manufacturer. You have been asked to undertake a cost–benefit analysis of the alternative mechanisms available to ensure adherence to your newly devised code of conduct. What should be included in such an analysis?

5 What contributes to the poaching of subsidiary employees? What steps can be taken to try and retain key employees?

6 Language standardization requires subsidiary employees to become competent in the corporate language if they seek a career within the multinational. Discuss ways in which employees can be disadvantaged by a lack of corporate language competence.

Further reading

W.M. Danis, 2003. Differences in Values, Practices and Systems Among Hungarian Managers and Western Expatriates: An Organizing Framework and Typology, *Journal of World Business*, Vol. 38, No. 3, pp. 224–244.

C.J. Zhu and P.J. Dowling, 2002. Staffing Practices in Transition: Some Empirical Evidence from China, *International Journal of Human Resource Management*, Vol. 13, No. 4, pp. 569–597.

C. Zhu and P.J. Dowling, 2000. Managing human resources in state-owned enterprises in transnational economies: a case study in the People's Republic of China. *Research and Practice in Human Resource Management*, Vol. 8, No. 1, pp. 63–92.

P.S. Budhwar and P.R. Sparrow, 2002. An Integrative Framework for Understanding Cross-national Human Resource Management Practices, *Human Resource Management Review*, Vol. 12, pp. 377–403.

J. Birkinshaw and N. Hood (eds), 1998. *Multinational Corporate Evolution and Subsidiary Development*. London: Macmillan.

Notes and references

1   A. Laurent, The Cross-Cultural Puzzle of International Human Resource Management, *Human Resource Management*, Vol. 25 (1986) pp. 91–102.

2   See, for example, M. Alvesson and P.O. Berg, *Corporate Culture and Organizational Symbolism*, Berlin: Walter de Gruyter, 1992; D. Welch and L. Welch, Being Flexible and Accommodating Diversity: the Challenge for Multinational Management, *European Management Journal*, Vol. 15, No. 6 (1997) pp. 677–685.

3   C. Reade, Dual Identification in Multinational Corporations: Local Managers and Their Psychological Attachment to the Subsidiary Versus the Global Organization, *International Journal of Human Resource Management*, Vol. 12, No. 3 (2001) pp. 405–424.

4   B. Taylor, Patterns of Control within Japanese Manufacturing Plants in China: Doubts about Japanization in Asia, *Journal of Management Studies*, Vol. 36, No. 6 (1999) pp. 853–873.

5   L. Liberman and I. Torbiörn, Variances in Staff-related Management Practices at Eight European Country Subsidiaries of a Global Firm, *International Journal of Human Resource Management*, Vol. 11, No. 1 (2000) pp. 37–59.

6   S.N. As-Saber, P.J. Dowling and P.W. Liesch, The Role of Human Resource Management in International Joint Ventures: a Study of Australian–Indian Joint Ventures, *International Journal of Human Resource Management*, Vol. 9, No. 5 (1998) pp. 751–766.

7   S.E. Khilji, Modes of convergence and divergence: an Integrative View of Multinational Practices in Pakistan, *International Journal of Human Resource Management*, Vol. 13, No. 2 (2002) pp. 232–253.

8   J. Bae and J.J. Lawler, Organizational and HRM Strategies in Korea: Impact on Firm Performance in an Emerging Economy, *Academy of Management Journal*, Vol. 43, No. 3 (2000) pp. 502–517.

9   K.E. Meyer and S. Estrin, Brownfield Entry in Emerging Markets, *Journal of International Business Studies*, Vol. 32, No. 3 (2001) pp. 575–584.

10 P.J. Buckley, J. Clegg and H. Tan, The Art of Knowledge Transfer: Secondary and Reverse Transfer in China's Telecommunications Manufacturing Industry, *Management International Review*, Vol. 43, Special Issue 2 (2003) pp. 67–93.

11 Company website information, December 2002 (www.motorola.com).

12 Y. Yan, A Comparative Study of Human Resource Management Practices in International Joint Ventures: the Impact of National Origin, *International Journal of Human Resource Management*, Vol. 14, No. 4 (2003) pp. 487–510.

13 UK research conducted by M. Brooke, J. Holly and R. Ellison of the University of Manchester Institute of Science and Technology (UMIST). See, for example, J. Holly, Management Contracts in *Handbook of International Trade*, ed. M.Z. Brooke and P.J. Buckley, Issue 2, Kluwer: Brentford, 1982.

14 D.J. Yang, Rare Air and Yak Burgers, *Business Review Weekly*, 10 August (1987).

15 M. Warner, Management–labour relations in the new Chinese economy, *Human Resource Management Journal*, Vol. 7, No. 4 (1997) pp. 30–43.

16 See, for example, J. Birkinshaw and N. Hood, Multinational Subsidiary Evolution: Capability and Charter Change in Foreign-owned Subsidiary Companies, *Academy of Management Review*, Vol. 23, No. 4 (1998) pp. 773–795.

17 See, for example, E. Delany, Strategic Development of the Multinational Subsidiary Through Subsidiary Initiative-taking, *Long Range Planning*, Vol. 33 (2000) pp. 220–244; Y. Kim, Different Subsidiary Roles and International Human Resource Management: an Exploratory Study of Australian Subsidiaries in Asia, *Journal of Asia-Pacific Business*, Vol. 4, No. 4 (2002) pp. 39–60.

18 J. Birkinshaw and J Ridderstråle, Fighting the Corporate Immune System: a Process Study of Subsidiary Initiatives in Multinational Corporations, *International Business Review*, Vol. 8, No. 2 (1999) p. 154.

19 O. Tregaskis, Learning Networks, Power and Legitimacy in Multinational Subsidiaries, *International Journal of Human Resource Management*, Vol. 14, No. 3 (2003) pp. 431–447.

20 J. Quintanilla and A. Ferner, Multinationals and Human Resource Management: Between Global Convergence and National Identity, *International Journal of Human Resource Management*, Vol. 14, No. 3 (2003) pp. 363–368.

21 I. Björkman and X. Fan, Human Resource Management and the Performance of Western Firms in China, *International Journal of Human Resource Management*, Vol. 13, No. 6 (2002) p. 855.

22 S. Beechler and J.Z. Yang, The Transfer of Japanese-style Management to American Subsidiaries: Contingencies, Constraints and Competencies, *Journal of International Business Studies*, Vol. 25, No. 3 (1994) pp. 467–491.

23 J.P. Giusti, D.R. Baker and P.J. Graybash, Satellites Dish Out Global Training, *Personnel Journal*, June (1991) pp. 80–84.

24 Y.P. Huo, H.J. Huang and N.K. Napier, Divergence or Convergence: a Cross-national Comparison of Personnel Selection Practices, *Asia Pacific Journal of Human Resources*, Vol. 40, No. 1 (2002) p. 52.

25 J.M. Brown, Asian Turmoil Hits Irish Plant, *Financial Times*, 13/14 December (1997) p. 2.

26 J. Shankar, Growth Surge Drives Subcontinent Boom, *The Australian*, 17 June (2003) p. 34.

27 R.L. Tung and V. Worm, Network Capitalism: the Role of Human Resources in Penetrating the China Market, *International Journal of Human Resource Management*, Vol. 12, No. 4 (2001) pp. 517–534.

28 T.L. Kamis, Education for the PRC Executive. *The China Business Review*, July–August (1996) pp. 36–39.

29 S. Melvin, 1996. Training the Troops. *The China Business Review*, March–April (1996) pp. 22–28.

30 C.J. Zhu, Human Resource Development in China During the Transition to a New Economic System, *Asia Pacific Journal of Human Resources*, Vol. 35, No. 3 (1997) pp. 19–44.

31 C.J. Zhu and P.J. Dowling, Staffing Practices in Transition: Some Empirical Evidence from China, *International Journal of Human Resource Management*, Vol. 13, No. 4 (2002) pp. 569–597.

32 E. Weldon and W. Vanhonacker, Operating a Foreign-invested Enterprise in China: Challenges for Managers and Management Researchers, *Journal of World Business*, Vol. 34, No. 1 (1999) pp. 94–107.

33 K. Leung, Z. Wang and P.B. Smith, Job Attitudes and Organizational Justice in Joint Venture Hotels in China: the Role of Expatriate Managers, *International Journal of Human Resource Management*, Vol. 12, No. 6 (2001) pp. 926–945.

34 K. Goodall and J. Roberts, Only Connect: Teamwork in the Multinational, *Journal of World Business*, Vol. 38, No. 2 (2003) pp. 150–164.

35 N. Camiah and G. Hollinshead, Assessing the Potential for Effective Cross-cultural Working Between 'New' Russian Managers and Western Expatriates, *Journal of World Business*, Vol. 38, No. 3 (2003) pp. 245–261.

36 N. Khatri, Chong Tze Fern and P. Budhwar, Explaining Employee Turnover in an Asian Context, *Human Resource Management Journal*, Vol. 11, No. 1 (2001) pp. 54–74.

37 G.R.G. Benito and L.S. Welch, De-internationalisation, *Management International Review*, Vol. 37, Special Issue No. 2 (1997) pp. 7–25.

38 Ford in Europe, *Historical Time Line*, Cologne, 3 March 2003; company website (www.ford.com), News Release section.

39 An Indian Tiger, *The Economist*, 9 April, (1994) p. 15; India's Businesses: Blinking in the Sunlight, *The Economist*, 9 April (1994) pp. 76–78.

40 Pricewaterhouse, *Doing Business in India*, Calcutta: Price Waterhouse, 1993.

41 Jobs Under the Axe, *Australian Financial Review*, 12–13 October (2002) pp. 22–23; Nokia to Axe 400 Staff in R&D Refocus, *The Australian*, 3 April (2001) p. 35.

42 T. Corrigan, $400 m Set Aside for Gold Handcuffs, *Financial Times*, 1 December (1998) p. 24.

43 BT Opens Indian Call Centres, BBC News On-line UK Edition, 7 March 2003.

44 China Prices Put Paid to Doc Martens' Northants Factories, *Business Weekly*, 1 November 2002 (on-line version).

45   R. Marschan-Piekkari, D. Welch and L. Welch, Adopting a Common Corporate Language: IHRM Implications, *International Journal of Human Resource Management*, Vol. 10, No. 3 (1999) pp. 377–390.

46   Should Everyone Speak English, *Business Week, European Edition*, 12 August (2001) p. 40.

47   Ref. 46, p.36.

48   A. Liu, R. Wong and P. Hamill, Otis Elevators, MBA Group Assignment, Melbourne, 2003.

49   HR manager of Australian subsidiary, presentation to MBA students, Melbourne, 29 April 2000. One of the students commented that, as an expatriate top manager in the Australian subsidiary of a German firm, he always sought the original German version and made corrections before distributing material to his Australian staff. He agreed that this was necessary to avoid misunderstandings and to preserve managerial professionalism.

50   ABB staff discussions, Mt Eliza Business School, Beijing, MBA class, November 2002.

51   R. Marschan, D.E. Welch and L.S. Welch, Language: the Forgotten Factor in Multinational Management, *European Management Journal*, Vol. 15, No. 5 (1997) pp. 591–598.

52   R. Marschan-Piekkari, D. Welch and L. Welch, In the Shadow: the Impact of Language on Structure, Power and Communication in the Multinational, *International Business Review*, Vol. 8, No. 4 (1999) pp. 421–440.

53   T. Saywell, Staying Alert, *Far Eastern Economic Review*, 29 January 1998.

54   US Department of Labor, Bureau of International Labor Affairs, www.dol.gov/ilab/media/reports/iclp/apprel/3e.htm.

55   J-P Sajhau, Business Ethics in the Textile, Clothing and Footwear (TFC) Industries, Sector Publications, Part 8, International Labour Organization, SAP 2.60/WP.1110, 28 September 2000. On-line copy obtained August 2003.

56   US Department of Labor website, www.dol.gov.

57   K. Huckshorn, Nike and Vietnam: a Labour Case Study, *Initiative for Policy Dialogue*, www.1.gsb.columbia.edu/ipd/j_nike_bk.html, 7 August 2003.

58   G.R. Tonks and P.J. Dowling, The Case of the Bougainville Mine: Success and Failure in the Management of a Multinational Corporation, *Journal of the Australian and New Zealand Academy of Management*, Vol. 8, No. 1 (2002) pp. 70–85.

Industrial relations*

Chapter objectives

The focus of the preceding chapters has been on managing and supporting international assignments, post-assignment and the issues in subsidiary operations. In this chapter we:

- Discuss key issues in industrial relations and the policies and practices of multinationals.

- Examine the potential constraints that trade unions may have on multinationals.

- Outline key concerns for trade unions.

- Discuss recent trends and issues in the global workforce context.

- Discuss the formation of regional economic zones such as the European Union.

Introduction

Before we examine the key issues in industrial relations as they relate to multinational firms, we need to consider some general points about the field of international industrial relations.[1] First, it is important to realize that it is difficult to compare industrial relations systems and behavior across national boundaries; an industrial relations concept may change considerably when translated from one industrial relations context to another.[2] The concept of collective bargaining, for example, in the USA is understood to mean negotiations between a local trade union and management; in Sweden and Germany the term refers to negotiations between an

* The contributions of Ali Niazi (University of Canberra) and Helen De Cieri (Monash University) to the writing of this chapter are gratefully acknowledged.

employers' organization and a trade union at the industry level. Cross-national differences also emerge as to the objectives of the collective bargaining process and the enforceability of collective agreements. Many European unions view the collective bargaining process as an ongoing class struggle between labor and capital, whereas in the USA union leaders tend toward a pragmatic economic view of collective bargaining rather than an ideological view. Second, it is generally recognized in the international industrial relations field that no industrial relations system can be understood without an appreciation of its historical origin.[3] As Schregle[4] has observed,

> A comparative study of industrial relations shows that industrial relations phenomena are a very faithful expression of the society in which they operate, of its characteristic features and of the power relationships between different interest groups. Industrial relations cannot be understood without an understanding of the way in which rules are established and implemented and decisions are made in the society concerned.

An interesting example of the effect of historical differences may be seen in the structure of trade unions in various countries. Poole[5] has identified several factors that may underlie these historical differences:

- the mode of technology and industrial organization at critical stages of union development
- methods of union regulation by government
- ideological divisions within the trade union movement
- the influence of religious organizations on trade union development
- managerial strategies for labor relations in large corporations.

As Table 9-1 shows, union structures differ considerably among Western countries. These include industrial unions, which represent all grades of employees in an

Table 9-1	Trade union structure in leading western industrial societies
Australia	General, craft, industrial, white-collar
Belgium	Industrial, professional, religious, public sector
Canada	Industrial, craft, conglomerate
Denmark	General, craft, white-collar
Finland	Industrial, white-collar, professional and technical
Japan	Enterprise
Norway	Industrial, craft
Sweden	Industrial, craft, white-collar and professional
Switzerland	Industrial, craft, religious, white-collar
The Netherlands	Religious, conglomerate, white-collar
UK	General, craft, industrial, white-collar, public sector
USA	Industrial, craft, conglomerate, white-collar
West Germany	Industrial, white-collar

Source: M. Poole, *Industrial Relations: Origins and Patterns of National Diversity*, London: Routledge & Kegan Paul, 1986, p. 79

industry; craft unions, which are based on skilled occupational groupings across industries; conglomerate unions, which represent members in more than one industry; and general unions, which are open to almost all employees in a given country. These differences in union structures have had a major influence on the collective bargaining process in Western countries. Some changes in union structure are evident over time; for example, enterprise unions are increasingly evident in industrialised nations. Enterprise unions are common in Asia-Pacific nations, although there are national variations in their functions, and in the proportion of enterprise unions to total unions.

The less one knows about how a structure came to develop in a distinctive way, the less likely one is to understand it. As Prahalad and Doz[6] note, the lack of familiarity of multinational managers with local industrial and political conditions has sometimes needlessly worsened a conflict that a local firm would have been likely to resolve. Increasingly, multinationals are recognizing this shortcoming and admitting that industrial relations policies must be flexible enough to adapt to local requirements. This is evidently an enduring approach, even in firms that follow a non-union labor relations strategy where possible, as IHRM in Action Case 9-1 points out.

IHRM in Action Case 9-1

Advice for companies going global

The key to expanding successfully overseas is to become one with the culture of the location, even if it means unionization of employees, Michael R. Quinlan, chairman and chief executive officer of McDonald's Corp., tells conferees at a meeting of the Human Resources Management Association of Chicago.

After opening fast-food restaurants in 53 nations, McDonald's has learned that it must follow the established practices of a foreign country to succeed there, Quinlan says. For example, a number of European countries and Australia have very strict unionization standards, and operations there are unionized as a condition of doing business. Acknowledging that McDonald's has had some 'horrible union fights around the world,' Quinlan advises employers considering expansion into other nations to 'do it their way, not your way'.

The main implication of dealing with unions is the increased cost of wages and benefits, according to Quinlan. Still, he adds that he does not feel that unionization has interfered with employees' loyalty to McDonald's, or to the company's philosophy of service and employee motivation. Declaring that unions do not 'bring much to the equation' of the employee–employer relationship, Quinlan says McDonald's is 'basically a non-union company' and intends to stay that way.

Another source of difficulty for McDonald's in its expansion overseas lies in the fact that fast-food restaurants are unfamiliar in most nations. Opening the first McDonald's inside the Communist bloc, in Yugoslavia, took 12 years, Quinlan notes. He also points out that the company's policy is to staff its restaurants, from crew through management, only with nationals – for the 3300 foreign outlets, the corporation employs only 35 expatriate US citizens, and its goal is to have 100 per cent local employees within 5 years.

Source: The Bureau of National Affairs, *Bulletin to Management*, March 7 (1991) pp. 66–67 (P.O. Box 40949, Washington, DC 20016-0949).

Key issues in international industrial relations

The focus of this chapter is on the industrial relations strategies adopted by multinationals rather than the more general topic of comparative industrial relations.[7–10] A central question for industrial relations in an international context is that of the orientation of multinational firms to organized labor.

Industrial relations policies and practices of multinational firms

Because national differences in economic, political and legal systems produce markedly different industrial relations systems across countries, multinationals generally delegate the management of industrial relations to their foreign subsidiaries. However, a policy of decentralization does not keep corporate headquarters from exercising some coordination over industrial relations strategy. Generally, corporate headquarters will become involved in or oversee labor agreements made by foreign subsidiaries because these agreements may affect the international plans of the firm and/or create precedents for negotiations in other countries. Further, Marginson *et al.* found that the majority of the firms in their study monitored labor performance across units in different countries.[11,12] Comparison of performance data across national units of the firm creates the potential for decisions on issues such as unit location, capital investment and rationalization of production capacity. The use of comparisons would be expected to be greatest where units in different countries undertake similar operations.

Much of the literature on the industrial relations practices of multinationals tends to be at a more cross-national or comparative level. There is, however, some research on industrial relations practices at the firm level. Empirical research has identified a number of differences in multinational approaches to industrial relations. Indeed, a number of studies have examined differences in the propensity of multinational headquarters to intervene in, or to centralize control over, matters such as industrial relations in host locations. Multinational headquarters involvement in industrial relations is influenced by several factors, as detailed below.

The degree of inter-subsidiary production integration.   According to Hamill,[13] a high degree of integration was found to be the most important factor leading to the centralization of the industrial relations function within the firms studied. Industrial relations throughout a system become of direct importance to corporate headquarters when transnational sourcing patterns have been developed, that is, when a subsidiary in one country relies on another foreign subsidiary as a source of components or as a user of its output.[11,14] In this context, a coordinated industrial relations policy is one of the key factors in a successful global production strategy.[15] One example of the development of an international policy for industrial relations can be seen in the introduction of employee involvement across Ford's operations.[16]

Nationality of ownership of the subsidiary.   There is evidence of differences between European and US firms in terms of headquarters involvement in industrial relations.[17] A number of studies have revealed that US firms tend to exercise greater centralized control over labor relations than do British or other European firms.[18] US firms tend to place greater emphasis on formal management controls and a close reporting system (particularly within the area of financial control) to ensure that planning targets are met. In his review of empirical research of this area, Bean[9] showed that foreign-owned multinationals in Britain prefer single-employer bargaining (rather than involving an employer association), and are more likely than British firms to assert managerial prerogative on matters of labor utilization. Further, Hamill[13] found US-owned subsidiaries to be much more centralized in labor relations decision making than British-owned. Hamill attributed this difference in management procedures to the more integrated nature of US firms, the greater divergence between British and US labor relations systems than between British and other European systems, and the more ethnocentric managerial style of US firms.

International human resource management approach. In earlier chapters, we discussed the various international human resource management approaches utilized by multinationals; these have implications for international industrial relations. Interestingly, an ethnocentric predisposition is more likely to be associated with various forms of industrial relations conflict.[19] Conversely, it has been shown that more geocentric firms will bear more influence on host-country industrial relations systems, owing to their greater propensity to participate in local events.[12]

MNE prior experience in industrial relations. European firms have tended to deal with industrial unions at industry level (frequently via employer associations) rather than at firm level. The opposite is more typical for US firms. In the USA, employer associations have not played a key role in the industrial relations system, and firm-based industrial relations policies are the norm.[8,20]

Subsidiary characteristics. Research has identified a number of subsidiary characteristics to be relevant to centralization of industrial relations. First, subsidiaries that are formed through acquisition of well-established indigenous firms tend to be given much more autonomy over industrial relations than are greenfield sites set up by a multinational firm.[13] Second, according to Enderwick, greater intervention would be expected when the subsidiary is of key strategic importance to the firm and the subsidiary is young.[21] Third, where the parent firm is a significant source of operating or investment funds for the subsidiary, that is, where the subsidiary is more dependent on headquarters for resources, there will tend to be increased corporate involvement in industrial relations and human resource management.[22] Finally, poor subsidiary performance tends to be accompanied by increased corporate involvement in industrial relations. Where poor performance is due to industrial relations problems, multinationals tend to attempt to introduce parent-country industrial relations practices aimed at reducing industrial unrest or increasing productivity.[13]

Characteristics of the home product market. An important factor is the extent of the home product market (discussed in some depth in Chapter 1).[9] If domestic sales are large relative to overseas operations (as is the case with many US firms), it is more likely that overseas operations will be regarded by the parent firm as an extension of domestic operations. This is not the case for many European firms, whose international operations represent the major part of their business. Lack of a large home market is a strong incentive to adapt to host-country institutions and norms. There is evidence of recent change in the European context: since the implementation of the Single European Market in 1993, there has been growth in large European-scale companies (formed via acquisition or joint ventures) that centralize management organization and strategic decision-making. However, processes of operational decentralization with regard to industrial relations are also evident.[23]

Management attitudes towards unions.

An additional important factor is that of management attitudes or ideology concerning unions.[24] Knowledge of management attitudes concerning unions may provide a more complete explanation of multinational industrial relations behavior than could be obtained by relying solely on a rational economic model. Thus, management attitudes should also be considered in any explanation of managerial behavior along with such factors as market forces and strategic choices. This is of particular relevance to US firms, since union avoidance appears to be deeply rooted in the value systems of American managers.[25]

As Figure 9-1 shows, Denmark has the highest level of union membership, the USA has the second lowest and France has the lowest in the Western world.[26] Hence French and US managers may be less likely to have extensive experience with unions than managers in many other countries. Worldwide trade union membership has fallen over the past decade, although the decline is not universal. This decline in union density in many countries may be explained by economic factors such as reduced public sector employment, reduced employment in manufacturing industries as a share in total employment and increased competition; it is also suggested to be associated with decentralization of industrial relations to business unit level, changes in governance and legislative changes. Drops in union density in central and eastern Europe may be explained by political and economic changes associated with the dissolution of the Soviet bloc and the end of compulsory union membership. Union membership decline is also linked to the introduction of new forms of work organization, globalization of production and changes in workforce structure.[27]

| **Figure 9-1** | Percentage of those in employment who were trade-union members, 2001 |

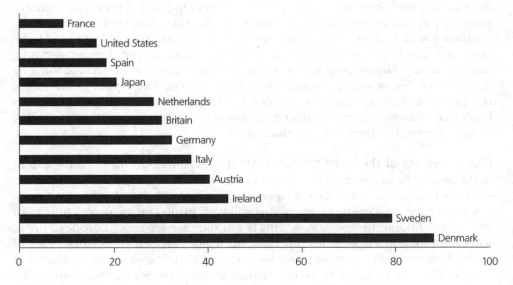

Source: Adapted from data obtained from the European Foundation for the Improvement of Living and Working Conditions; www.eurofound.eu.int.

Although there are several problems inherent in data collection for a cross-national comparison of union-density rates, several theories have been suggested to explain the variations among countries. Such theories consider economic factors such as wages, prices and unemployment levels, social factors such as public support for unions and political factors. In addition, studies indicate that the strategies utilized by labor, management and governments are particularly important.[5,9,28]

Another key issue in international industrial relations is industrial disputes. Hamill[29] examined strike-proneness of multinational subsidiaries and indigenous firms in Britain across three industries. Strike proneness was measured via three variables – strike frequency, strike size and strike duration. There was no difference across the two groups of firms with regard to strike frequency, but multinational subsidiaries did experience larger and longer strikes than local firms. Hamill suggests that this difference indicates that foreign-owned firms may be under less financial pressure to settle a strike quickly than local firms – possibly because they can switch production out of the country.

Overall, it is evident that international industrial relations are influenced by a broad range of factors. Commenting on the overall results of his research, Hamill[30] concluded that

> general statements cannot be applied to the organization of the labor
> relations function within MNEs. Rather, different MNEs adopt different labor
> relations strategies in relation to the environmental factors peculiar to each
> firm. In other words, it is the type of multinational under consideration which
> is important rather than multinationality itself.

Trade unions and international industrial relations

Trade unions may limit the strategic choices of multinationals in three ways: (1) by influencing wage levels to the extent that cost structures may become uncompetitive; (2) by constraining the ability of multinationals to vary employment levels at will; and (3) by hindering or preventing global integration of the operations of multinationals.[31] We shall briefly examine each of these potential constraints.

Influencing wage levels

Although the importance of labor costs relative to other costs is decreasing, labor costs still play an important part in determining cost competitiveness in most industries. The influence of unions on wage levels is, therefore, important. Multinationals that fail to manage their wage levels successfully will suffer labor cost disadvantages that may narrow their strategic options.

Constraining the ability of multinationals to vary employment levels at will

For many multinationals operating in Western Europe, Japan and Australia, the inability to vary employment levels at will may be a more serious problem than wage levels. Many countries now have legislation that limits considerably the ability of firms to carry out plant closure, redundancy or layoff programs unless it can be shown that structural conditions make these employment losses unavoidable.

Frequently, the process of showing the need for these programs is long and drawn-out. Plant closure or redundancy legislation in many countries also frequently specifies that firms must compensate redundant employees through specified formulae such as 2 weeks' pay for each year of service. In many countries, payments for involuntary terminations are substantial, especially in comparison with those in the USA.

Trade unions may influence this process in two ways: by lobbying their own national governments to introduce redundancy legislation, and by encouraging regulation of multinationals by international organizations such as the Organization for Economic Cooperation and Development (OECD). (Later in this chapter we describe the *Badger* case, which forced Raytheon finally to accept responsibility for severance payments to employees made redundant by the closing down of its Belgian subsidiary.) Multinational managers who do not take these restrictions into account in their strategic planning may well find their options severely limited. In fact, recent evidence shows that multinationals are beginning to consider the ability to dismiss employees to be one of the priorities when making investment location decisions.[32]

Hindering or preventing global integration of the operations of multinationals

In recognition of these constraints, many multinationals make a conscious decision not to integrate and rationalize their operations to the most efficient degree, because to do so could cause industrial and political problems. Prahalad and Doz[6] cite General Motors as an example of this 'sub-optimization of integration'. GM was alleged in the early 1980s to have undertaken substantial investments in Germany (matching its new investments in Austria and Spain) at the demand of the German metalworkers' union (one of the largest industrial unions in the Western world) in order to foster good industrial relations in Germany. One observer of the world auto industry suggested that car manufacturers were sub-optimizing their manufacturing networks partly to placate trade unions and partly to provide redundancy in sources to prevent localized social strife from paralysing their network. This sub-optimization led to unit manufacturing costs in Europe that were 15 per cent higher, on average, than an economically optimal network would have achieved. Prahalad and Doz drew the following conclusion from this example:[33]

> Union influence thus not only delays the rationalization and integration of MNEs' manufacturing networks and increases the cost of such adjustments (not so much in the visible severance payments and 'golden handshake' provisions as through the economic losses incurred in the meantime), but also, at least in such industries as automobiles, permanently reduces the efficiency of the integrated MNC network. Therefore, treating labor relations as incidental and relegating them to the specialists in the various countries is inappropriate. In the same way as government policies need to be integrated into strategic choices, so do labor relations.

The response of trade unions to multinationals

Trade union leaders have long seen the growth of multinationals as a threat to the bargaining power of labor because of the considerable power and influence of large multinational firms. While it is recognized that multinationals are 'neither uniformly anti-union nor omnipotent and monolithic bureaucracies',[34] their potential for lobbying power and flexibility across national borders creates difficulties for employees and trade unions endeavouring to develop countervailing power. There are several ways in which multinationals have an impact upon trade union and employee interests. Kennedy[8] has identified the following seven characteristics of MNEs as the source of trade union concern about multinationals:

- Formidable financial resources. This includes the ability to absorb losses in a particular foreign subsidiary that is in dispute with a national union and still show an overall profit on worldwide operations. Union bargaining power may be threatened or weakened by the broader financial resources of a multinational. This is particularly evident where a multinational has adopted a practice of transnational sourcing and cross-subsidization of products or components across different countries. 'The economic pressure which a nationally based union can exert upon a multinational is certainly less than would be the case if the company's operations were confined to one country.'[35]

- Alternative sources of supply. This may take the form of an explicit 'dual sourcing' policy to reduce the vulnerability of the multinational to a strike by any national union. Also, temporary switching of production in order to defeat industrial action has been utilized to some extent, for example, in the automotive industry.[35]

- The ability to move production facilities to other countries. A reported concern of employees and trade unions is that job security may be threatened if a multinational seeks to produce abroad what could have, or previously has, been manufactured domestically. National relative advantages provide MNEs with choice as to location of units. Within the EU, for example, evidence suggests that multinational management is locating skill-intensive activities in countries with national policies promoting training and with relatively high labor costs. Conversely, semi-skilled, routinized activities are being located in countries with lower labor costs.[11] Threats by multinationals, whether real or perceived, to reorganize production factors internationally, with the accompanying risk of plant closure or rationalization, will have an impact on management–labor negotiations at a national level. However, technical and economic investments would reduce a multinational's propensity to relocate facilities.

- A remote locus of authority (i.e. the corporate head office management of a multinational firm). Although many multinationals report decentralization and local responsiveness of HRM and industrial relations, trade unions and works councils have reported that the multinational decision-making structure is opaque and the division of authority obscured. Further, employee representatives may not be adequately aware of the overall MNE organizational strategy and activities.[36]

- Production facilities in many industries. As Vernon[37] has noted, most multinationals operate in many product lines.

- Superior knowledge and expertise in industrial relations.

- The capacity to stage an 'investment strike,' whereby the multinational refuses to invest any additional funds in a plant, thus ensuring that the plant will become obsolete and economically non-competitive.

Another issue reported by trade unions is their claim that they have difficulty accessing decision-makers located outside the host country and obtaining financial information. For example, according to Martinez Lucio and Weston:[38]

> Misinformation has been central to the management strategy of using potential investment or disinvestment in seeking changes in certain organizations. ... For example, in companies such as Heinz, Ford, Gillette and General Motors, workers have established that they had on occasions been misinformed by management as to the nature of working practices in other plants.

The response of labor unions to multinationals has been threefold: to form international trade secretariats (ITSs), to lobby for restrictive national legislation and to try to achieve regulation of multinationals by international organizations.

International trade secretariats (ITSs)

There are 15 ITSs, which function as loose confederations to provide worldwide links for the national unions in a particular trade or industry (e.g. metals, transport and chemicals). The secretariats have mainly operated to facilitate the exchange of information.[39] One of the fastest growing of the ITSs is the European Regional Organization of the International Federation of Commercial, Clerical, Professional and Technical Employees (generally known by its initials, Euro-FIET) which is focused on the service sector.[40] The long-term goal of each ITS is to achieve transnational bargaining with each of the multinationals in its industry. Each ITS has followed a similar program to achieve the goal of transnational bargaining.[41] The elements of this program are (1) research and information, (2) calling company conferences, (3) establishing company councils, (4) company-wide union–management discussions and (5) coordinated bargaining. Overall, the ITSs have met with limited success, the reasons for which Northrup[42] attributes to (1) the generally good wages and working conditions offered by multinationals, (2) strong resistance from multinational firm management, (3) conflicts within the labor movement and (4) differing laws and customs in the industrial relations field.

Lobbying for restrictive national legislation

On a political level, trade unions have for many years lobbied for restrictive national legislation in the USA and Europe. The motivation for trade unions to pursue restrictive national legislation is based on a desire to prevent the export of jobs via multinational investment policies. For example, in the USA, the AFL-CIO has lobbied strongly in this area.[8,43] A major difficulty for unions when pursuing this strategy is the reality of conflicting national economic interests. In times of economic downturn, this factor may become an insurmountable barrier for trade union officials. To date, these attempts have been largely unsuccessful and, with the increasing internationalization of business, it is difficult to see how governments will be persuaded to legislate in this area.

Regulation of multinationals by international organizations

Attempts by trade unions to exert influence over multinationals via international organizations have met with some success. Through trade union federations such as the European Trade Union Confederation (ETUC) and the International Confederation of Free Trade Unions (ICFTU), the labor movement has been able to lobby the International Labor Organization (ILO), the United Nations Conference on Trade and Development (UNCTAD),[44] the Organization for Economic Cooperation and Development (OECD) and the European Union (EU). The ILO has identified a number of workplace-related principles that should be respected by all nations: freedom of association, the right to organize and collectively bargain, abolition of forced labor and non-discrimination in employment. In 1977 the ILO adopted a code of conduct for multinationals (Tripartite Declaration of Principles Concerning MNEs and Social Policy).[45] The ILO code of conduct, which was originally proposed in 1975, was influential in the drafting of the OECD guidelines for multinationals, which were approved in 1976. These voluntary guidelines cover disclosure of information, competition, financing, taxation, employment and industrial relations and science and technology.[46–48]

A key section of these guidelines is the *umbrella* or *chapeau clause* (the latter is the more common term in the literature) that precedes the guidelines themselves. This clause states that multinationals should adhere to the guidelines 'within the framework of law, regulations and prevailing labor relations and employment practices, in each of the countries in which they operate'. Campbell and Rowan[47] state that employers have understood the chapeau clause to mean compliance with local law supersedes the guidelines, while labor unions have interpreted this clause to mean that the guidelines are a 'supplement' to national law. The implication of the latter interpretation is significant: a firm could still be in violation of the OECD guidelines even though its activities have complied with national law and practice. Given the ambiguity of the chapeau clause and the fact that the OECD guidelines are voluntary, it is likely that this issue will remain controversial.

There is also some controversy in the literature as to the effectiveness of the OECD guidelines in regulating multinational behavior.[49] This lack of agreement centers on assessments of the various challenges to the guidelines. The best known of these challenges is the *Badger* case. The Badger Company was a subsidiary of Raytheon, a US-based multinational. In 1976 the Badger Company decided to close its Belgian subsidiary, and a dispute arose concerning termination payments.[50] Since Badger (Belgium) NV had filed for bankruptcy, the Belgian labor unions argued that Raytheon should assume the subsidiary's financial obligations. Raytheon refused, and the case was brought before the OECD by the Belgian government and the International Federation of Commercial, Clerical, Professional and Technical Employees (FIET), an international trade secretariat. The Committee on International Investments and MNEs (CIIME) of the OECD indicated that paragraph six of the guidelines (concerned with plant closures) implied a 'shared responsibility' by the subsidiary and the parent in the event of a plant closing. Following this clarification by the CIIME and a scaling down of initial demands, Badger executives and Belgian government officials negotiated a settlement of this case.

Blanpain[51] concludes that the *Badger* case made clear the responsibility of the parent company for the financial liability of its subsidiary, but that this responsibility is not unqualified. As to whether the *Badger* case proved the 'effectiveness' of the OECD guidelines, Jain[52] and Campbell and Rowan[47] point out that the Belgian unions devoted considerable resources to make this a test case and had assistance from both American unions (which, through the AFL-CIO, lobbied the US Department of State) and the Belgian government in their negotiations with the OECD and Badger executives. Liebhaberg[53] is more specific in his assessment:

Despite an outcome which those in favor of supervision consider to be positive, the Badger case is a clear demonstration of one of the weaknesses in the OECD's instrument, namely that it does not represent any sort of formal undertaking on the part of the twenty-four member states which are signatories to it. The social forces of each separate country must apply pressure on their respective governments if they want the guidelines applied.

A recent development with the OECD guidelines (which are addressed by 36 OECD and non-OECD governments) has been the follow-up procedures. The system of National Contact Points promotes observance of the guidelines by MNEs operating in or from the governments' territories. It appears that this system is now having some influence on MNE behavior in the industrial relations area. As the Chair of the 2002 Annual Meeting of the National Contact Points noted:[54]

> Evidence so far suggests that the guidelines are making a difference. Many companies have publicly acknowledged that they use the guidelines as a benchmark for good behavior. The guidelines are being used to help prevent misunderstandings and promote mutual confidence and predictability between the business community and home and host societies. About twenty specific instances where there are questions about whether or not a company has observed the guidelines in a particular business situation have been considered so far.

Recognizing the limitations of voluntary codes of conduct, European trade unions have also lobbied the Commission of the European Union to regulate the activities of multinationals.[36,55] Unlike the OECD, the Commission of the EU can translate guidelines into law, and has developed a number of proposals concerning disclosure of information to make multinationals more 'transparent.'[56–58] These are discussed in more detail in the next section.

Regional integration: the European Union (EU)

Regional integration such as the development of the EU has brought significant implications for industrial relations.[59] In the Treaty of Rome (1957), some consideration was given to social policy issues related to the creation of the European Community. In the EU, the terms 'social policy' or 'social dimension' are used to cover a number of issues including in particular labor law and working conditions, aspects of employment and vocational training, social security and pensions. There have been a number of significant developments in EU social policy over the past four decades. The Social Charter of the Council of Europe came into effect in 1965. In 1987, the major objective of the implementation of the Single European Act was to establish the Single European Market (SEM) on 31 December 1992, in order to enhance the free movement of goods, money and people within the SEM. The social dimension aims to achieve a large labor market by eliminating the barriers that restrict the freedom of movement and the right of domicile within the SEM. The European Community Charter of the Fundamental Social Rights of Workers (often referred to simply as the Social Charter) was introduced in 1989, and has guided the development of social policy in the 1990s.[60] Naturally, the social dimension has been the subject of much debate: proponents defend the social dimension as a means of achieving social justice and equal treatment for EU citizens, while critics see it as a kind of 'social engineering'.[61]

At the signing of the Treaty on European Union in Maastricht in February 1992, Britain was allowed to opt out of the social policy agreements. The other 11 member states were party to a protocol (the Social Policy Protocol), which allows them to agree their own directives without Britain's participation.[62] With the election of the Blair Labour government in Britain in 1997, this anomaly was resolved when all members of the EU signed the Treaty of Amsterdam on 17 June 1997. This means that there now exists a single coherent legal basis for action by the EU Member States with regard to social policy.

The Social Chapter in the Treaty of Amsterdam opens with a general statement of objectives.[63] Its first Article (Article 117 of the EC Treaty), drawn largely from Article 1 of the Maastricht Social Agreement, begins with a reference to fundamental social rights such as those in the European Social Charter of 1961 and the Social Charter of 1989. It then sets out the objectives for the EU: to support and complement the activities of the Member States in a number of listed areas. These include improvement of working conditions and of the working environment in the interest of workers' health and safety, information and consultation of workers, integration of persons excluded from the labor market and equality of opportunity, and at work, between men and women. However, the Treaty excludes matters of pay, the right of association and the right to strike or to lock out. The European Commission department responsible for social policy is known as Directorate-General Employment and Social Affairs. Table 9-2 summarizes the six Directorates of DG Employment and Social Affairs and the different areas of social policy covered by each Directorate.

Multinationals are often accused of doing research and development in developed countries and operating out of low cost countries. A recent press release by the EU listing the top 100 Best Workplaces in the EU in 2003 provides some evidence that this pattern may be changing to some extent in Europe (see Table 9-3). Of these 100, the top ten companies were from all over Europe.[64] The global software giant Microsoft was listed as one of the top 10 best workplaces in multiple countries (Belgium, France, Germany and Ireland).[64]

Disclosure of information and European Works Councils

The EU has introduced a range of Directives related to the social dimension. Of the Directives concerned with multinationals, the most contentious has been the Vredeling Directive (associated with Henk Vredeling, a former Dutch member of the EU Commission).[65] The Seventh (Vredeling) Directive's requirement of disclosure of company information to unions faced strong opposition led by the then conservative British government and employer representatives. They argued that employee involvement in consultation and decision-making should be voluntary. The European Works Councils (EWC) Directive was approved on 22 September 1994 and implemented 2 years later. Under the terms of the Treaty of Amsterdam, this Directive applies to all EU Member States. This is the first pan-European legislation that regulates collective relationships between multinationals and employees. The Directive requires EWCs to be established in multinationals with at least 1000 employees, having 100 or more employees in each of two Member States. According to Chesters, more than 1000 multinationals, including around 200 US-based firms, are affected by the EWC Directive.[19,66] The Directive is designed to provide coverage to all employees, whether unionized or not. The EWC Directive aims to enhance employees' rights to information and consultation in general, and to provide rights to information regarding international corporate decisions that would significantly affect workers' interests.[57,67] Partly in response to the EWC

Table 9-2	The Six Directorates

Introduction

Based in Brussels and Luxembourg, the Directorate-General (DG) Employment and Social Affairs is the European Commission department responsible for social policy. It is made up of six Directorates responsible for different areas of social policy.

Directorate General

Directorate A: Employment Strategy and European Social Fund (ESF) Policy Development and Coordination, is responsible for employment policies, labor market policies, employment services (EURES) and local development and readaption.

Directorate B: National Employment and Social Inclusion, Monitoring and ESF Operations I, is responsible for policy development of the European Social Fund, information on the Fund, assessment of the political impact of the Fund, the Community Initiatives, technical assistance and innovation studies and adaptation to industrial change.

Directorate C: National Employment and Social Inclusion, Monitoring and ESF Operations II, is responsible for the operation of the European Social Fund in the Member States.

Directorate D: Adaptability, Social Dialogue and Social Rights, is responsible for relations with the social partners and organization of the social dialogue, industrial relations and labor law, coordination of social security for migrant workers, migration policy and promotion of free movement for workers, equal opportunities for women and men and family policy.

Directorate E: Social Protection and Social Integration, is responsible for analysis of and research on the social situation, social security and actions in the social field and integration of disabled people. It also deals with external relations, international organizations, information and publications on behalf of the whole DG.

Directorate F: Management of Resources, is responsible for management of human resources and training, financial management, system audits in the Member States, ex-post controls and management of information sources.

Directorate G: Horizontal and International Issues, is responsible for those units with broad crosscutting policy or service remits that extend across the whole DG and the Commission generally. Some of the most typical and pressing issues include equality of women and men, enlargement and international cooperation, knowledge society, information and communication and evaluation.

Source: http://europa.eu.int/comm/dgs/employment_social/organigram/g_en.htm

Directive, firms such as General Motors and Heinz have subsidized visits of worker representatives to other plants and provided information and forums for discussion at the European level.[38]

Obviously, all firms operating in the EU will need to become familiar with EU Directives and keep abreast of changes. While harmonization of labor laws can be seen as the ultimate objective, Michon[68] argues that the notion of a European social community does not mean a unification of all social conditions and benefits or, for that matter, of all social systems. However, the EU does aim to establish minimal standards for social conditions that will safeguard the fundamental rights of workers. A recent study on EWCs by Gilman and Marginson[69] summarized these somewhat conflicting trends in the following way:

	Top 10 best workplaces in the EU, 2003[a]	**Table 9-3**

Company	Location
Asda	UK
Caja Madrid	Spain
Cloetta Fazer	Finland
Ferrari Maserati Group	Italy
Janssen-Cilag	Greece
MBNA	Ireland
Microsoft	Belgium, France, Germany, Ireland
Unimerco	Denmark
VX Company	The Netherlands
Winterheller Software	Austria

[a] Listed in alphabetical order.
Source: Adapted from the 27 March 2003 Press Release from the European Union (http://europa.eu.int).

The salience of both country and sector influences on the provisions of EWC agreements places a question mark against the perspective that sees EWCs as primarily international extensions of national structures of information and consultation. The influence of national systems of industrial relations on the provisions of EWC agreements is important, but the similarities within particular sectors, which cross national borders, reflects a more general process of 'converging divergences' (Katz and Darbishire, 2000) under which growing divergence in industrial relations arrangements and practice within national systems is occurring alongside increased cross-border convergence of practices within given sectors.

Pan-European pensions

The EU Council of Ministers has approved the pension funds Directive that sets standards for the prudential supervision of pension plans in the EU. The Member States will need to implement the Directive by the middle of 2005. The Directive covers employer-sponsored, separately funded pension plans.[70] The Directive provides pension funds with a coherent framework to operate within the internal market and allows European companies and citizens the opportunity to benefit from more efficient pan-European pension funds. Once implemented, the Directive will ensure a high level of protection for both members and beneficiaries of pension funds.[70] The Directive refers to the pension plan providers as 'Institutions for Occupational Retirement Provision' (IORP) who will be subject to detailed rules of operation, including requirements to inform members and beneficiaries properly of the terms and status of the plan, prudently calculate promised benefits and cover them with sufficient assets and give supervisory authorities the necessary powers to monitor and supervise the plans.[70]

The Directive allows institutions to accept sponsorship and run a pension scheme for companies located in any of the Member States. Currently, occupational pension providers mostly operate in the Member State in which they are established. As a result, companies with operations in the current 15 Member States are forced to use the services of 15 different providers to provide pension benefits, resulting in costs associated with redundancy of operations estimated at €40 million per year per company.[71] The Directive allows for 'mutual recognition of Member States' supervisory regimes'.[71] This enables an IORP to manage the plans of firms located in other Member States whilst applying the rules of the Member State in which it is established. This ensures continued application of the social and labor legislation of the host Member States.[71]

The greatest barrier to implementation of the pan-European pensions is the taxation differences among Member States. The consulting firm Mercer HR states in a report analysing the viability of pan-European pensions that 'The Directive does not attempt to cover taxation issues which may need a separate and more prolonged process though the EU legislative institutions.'[72] Many Member countries' tax laws do not recognize contributions to foreign pension plans. This creates unfavourable tax circumstances for employees working outside their home countries and contributing to pension plans in their host countries. While the EU has indicated that these laws may run foul of EU rules, changing the tax policies of the Member States will be a challenging task.[73] In a recent newsletter addressing pan-European pensions, AON Consulting concluded that 'Recent European Court of Justice decisions are encouraging and may open the way to wider availability of tax relief on cross-border pension contributions, but there is a way to go yet before all the barriers are down.'[74] AON also warned that if the current shift toward defined contribution plans continues, the issue of pan-European pension funds might become debatable.[74]

The issue of social 'dumping'

One of the concerns related to the formation of the SEM was its impact on jobs. There was alarm that those Member States that have relatively low social security costs would have a competitive edge and that firms would locate in those Member States that have lower labor costs. The counter-alarm was that states with low-cost labor would have to increase their labor costs, to the detriment of their competitiveness.[75] There are two industrial relations issues here: the movement of work from one region to another, and its effect on employment levels; and the need for trade union solidarity to prevent workers in one region from accepting pay cuts to attract investment, at the expense of workers in another region. There is some, although not as much as was expected, evidence of 'social dumping' in the EU.[76] It is likely that this issue will be a contentious one in Europe for some time and multinationals need to be aware of this debate when doing business in Europe.[77]

The impact of the digital economy

Processes of knowledge acquisition used by MNEs are an emerging issue in the USA where local technology workers are increasingly being paid their normal salaries to train people from overseas eventually to do their jobs, as discussed in Chapter 8. These newly trained professionals then replace their trainers. This is in part an unintended consequence of the US non-immigrant visa programme – particularly the L-1 classification that allows companies to transfer workers from overseas offices to the USA for as long as 7 years. Importantly, this visa classification allows companies to pay these workers their home-country wage.[78] For example, an Indian worker gets paid roughly one sixth of the average US programmer's salary, which is about US$60 per hour in wages and benefits.[78] Another important current issue is the widening of the digital divide. The obstacles to communication due to delay and distance have been reduced by the digital convergence of information and communication technologies (ICT). The use of networking and the Internet is creating a far greater access to information than ever before which is disrupting established economic relations.[79]

The effect of these developments on the structure of markets and organizations and established patterns of economic behavior will be profound. The creation and loss of jobs, the content and quality of work, the location of work, the nature of the employment contract, the skills required and how often they can be obtained, the organization of work and the functioning and effectiveness of worker and employer organizations are all affected by the emerging era of digital globalization. While the networking economy has opened new opportunities for job creation, this does not necessarily mean an increase in knowledge or skill requirements. Unskilled jobs, de-skilling and skill polarization in the networking economy also exist.[79] Only 15 per cent of the world's population (living mostly in industrialized countries) has access to ICT.[80] This leaves a majority of the world's population technologically disconnected. As noted by the International Labor Organization, 'The digital divide exists not only *between* societies but *within* societies.' Internet usage is stratified and is much more common among younger rather than older people, men rather than women, urban rather than rural dwellers, and people with higher levels of education and income.[80] The ILO also noted that:

> In spite of the challenges this dynamic poses, the ICT revolution presents an unusually vast mix of risks and opportunities extending to every area of the world of work. While the technological forces in play are powerful and irreversible, other forces, such as social policy and institutional innovation, could make ICT into a manageable revolution. All countries need to address the threats and opportunities of the communications revolution: a passive stance invites marginalization.

Summary

The literature reviewed in this chapter and the discussion surrounding the formation of regional economic zones such as the European Union and the Asia Pacific Economic Cooperation (APEC)[81] support the conclusion that transnational collective bargaining has yet to be attained by trade unions.[55,82] As Enderwick[83] has stated:

> The international operations of MNEs do create considerable impediments in effectively segmenting labor groups by national boundaries and stratifying groups within and between nations. Combining recognition of the overt segmentation effects of

international business with an understanding of the dynamics of direct investment yields the conclusion that general multinational collective bargaining is likely to remain a remote possibility.

Enderwick argues that trade unions should opt for less ambitious strategies in dealing with multinationals, such as (1) strengthening national union involvement in plant-based and company-based bargaining, (2) supporting research on the vulnerability of selective multinationals and (3) consolidating the activities of company-based ITSs. Despite setbacks, especially with the regional economic integration issues discussed in this chapter, it is likely that trade unions and the ILO will pursue these strategies and continue to lobby where possible for the regulation of multinationals via the European Commission and the United Nations.

Recent research on multinationals and industrial relations has provided useful information on the issues and challenges related to this aspect of international HRM.[11] Further research is needed on how multinationals view developments in international industrial relations and whether these developments will influence the overall business strategy of the firm. Further research is also needed on how global firms implement industrial relations policy in various countries.

Discussion questions and exercises

1 Why is it important to understand the historical origins of national industrial relations systems?

2 In what ways can trade unions constrain the strategic choices of multinationals?

3 Identify four characteristics of multinationals that give trade unions cause for concern.

4 How have trade unions responded to multinationals? Have these responses been successful?

5 What is 'social dumping,' and why should unions be concerned about it?

Further reading

R.D. Lansbury, J. Kitay and N. Wailes, 2003. The Impact of Globalisation on Employment Relations: Some Research Propositions, *Asia Pacific Journal of Human Resources*, Vol. 41, No. 1, pp. 62–74. *World Labour Report 2003*, Geneva: International Labour Office, 2003.

T. Edwards and A. Ferner, 2002. The Renewed 'American Challenge': a review of employment practice in US multinationals, *Industrial Relations Journal*, Vol. 33, No. 2.

S. Frenkel and S. Kuruvilla, 2002. Logics of Action, Globalisation, and Changing Employment Relations in China, India, Malaysia and the Philippines, *Industrial and Labour Relations Review*, Vol. 55, No. 3, pp. 387–412.

M. Poole, R. Lansbury and N. Wailes, 2001. A Comparative Analysis of Developments in Industrial Democracy, *Industrial Relations*, Vol. 40, No. 3, pp. 490–522

R.N. Block, K. Roberts, C. Ozeki and M.J. Roomkin, 2001. Models of International Labour Standards, *Industrial Relations*, Vol. 40, No. 2, pp. 258–286

Katz, H. and O. Darbishire, 2000. *Converging Divergencies*, Ithaca, NY: ILR Press.

Notes and references

1 These introductory comments are drawn from J. Schregle, Comparative Industrial Relations: Pitfalls and Potential, *International Labour Review*, Vol. 120, No. 1 (1981) pp. 15–30.

2 This point is also referred to as the *emic–etic* problem. See Chapter 1 for a detailed discussion of this point.

3 O. Kahn-Freund, *Labour Relations: Heritage and Adjustment*, Oxford: Oxford University Press, 1979. Also see R.B. Peterson and J. Sargent, Union and Employer Confederation Views on Current Labour Relations in 21 Industrialized Nations, *Relations Industrielles*, Vol. 52, No. 1 (1997) pp. 39–59.

4 Ref. 1, p. 28.

5 M. Poole, *Industrial Relations: Origins and Patterns of National Diversity*, London: Routledge, 1986.

6 C.K. Prahalad and Y.L. Doz. *The Multinational Mission: Balancing Local Demands and Global Vision*, New York: The Free Press, 1987.

7 For general reviews of the comparative industrial relations literature, see Refs 8–10.

8 T. Kennedy, *European Labour Relations*, Lexington, MA: Lexington Books, 1980.

9 R. Bean, *Comparative Industrial Relations: an Introduction to Cross-national Perspectives*, New York: St. Martin's Press, 1985.

10 M. Poole, in *Industrial Relations; International and Comparative Industrial Relations*, ed. G.J. Bamber and R.D. Lansbury, Sydney: Allen and Unwin, 1987.

11 P. Marginson, P. Armstrong, P.K. Edwards and J. Purcell, Extending Beyond Borders: Multinational Companies and the International Management of Labour, *International Journal of Human Resource Management*, Vol. 6, No. 3 (1995) pp. 702–719.

12 M. Martinez Lucio and S. Weston, New Management Practices in a Multinational Corporation: the Restructuring of Worker Representation and Rights, *Industrial Relations Journal*, Vol. 25 (1994) pp. 110–121.

13 J. Hamill, Labour Relations Decision-making within Multinational Corporations, *Industrial Relations Journal*, Vol. 15, No. 2 (1984) pp. 30–34.

14 S.H. Robock and K. Simmonds, *International Business and Multinational Enterprises*, 4th edn. Homewood, IL: Irwin, 1989.

15 D.F. Hefler, Global Sourcing: Offshore Investment Strategy for the 1980s, *Journal of Business Strategy*, Vol. 2, No. 1 (1981) pp. 7–12.

16 K. Starkey and A. McKinlay, *Strategy and the Human Resource. Ford and the Search for Competitive Advantage*, Oxford: Blackwell, 1993.

17 B.C. Roberts and J. May, The Response of Multinational Enterprises to International Trade Union Pressures, *British Journal of Industrial Relations*, Vol. 12 (1974) pp. 403–416; R. Hyman and A. Ferner (1992), cited in Ref. 9.

18 J. La Palombara and S. Blank, *Multinational Corporations and National Elites: a Study of Tensions*, New York: The Conference Board, 1976; A.B. Sim, Decentralized Management of Subsidiaries and Their Performance: a Comparative Study of American, British and Japanese Subsidiaries in Malaysia, *Management International Review*, Vol. 17, No. 2 (1977) pp. 45–51; Y.K. Shetty, Managing the Multinational Corporation: European and American Styles, *Management International Review*, Vol. 19, No. 3 (1979) pp. 39–48.

19 P. Marginson, European Integration and Transnational Management–Union Relations in the Enterprise, *British Journal of Industrial Relations*, Vol. 30, No. 4 (1992) pp. 529–545.

20 D. Bok, Reflections on the Distinctive Character of American Labour Law, *Harvard Law Review*, Vol. 84 (1971) pp. 1394–1463; J.P. Windmuller and A. Gladstone (eds), *Employers Associations and Industrial Relations: a Comparative Study*, Oxford: Clarendon Press, 1984.

21 P. Enderwick, The Labour Utilization Practices of Multinationals and Obstacles to Multinational Collective Bargaining, *Journal of Industrial Relations*, Vol. 26, No. 3 (1984) pp. 354–364.

22 P.M. Rosenzweig and N. Nohria, Influences on Human Resource Management Practices in Multinational Corporations, *Journal of International Business Studies*, Vol. 25, No. 2 (1994) pp. 229–251.

23 P. Marginson, A. Buitendam, C. Deutschmann and P. Perulli, The emergence of the Euro-company: Towards a European Industrial Relations? *Industrial Relations Journal*, Vol. 24, No. 3 (1993) pp. 182–190; P. Marginson and K. Sisson, The Structure of Transnational Capital in Europe: The Emerging Euro-company and its Implications for Industrial Relations, in *New Frontiers in European Industrial Relations*, ed. R. Hyman and A. Ferner, Oxford: Blackwell, 1994.

24 For a lucid discussion of the importance of understanding ideology, see G.C. Lodge, Ideological Implications of Changes in Human Resource Management, in *HRM Trends and Challenges*, ed. D.R.E. Walton and P.R. Lawrence, Boston: Harvard Business School Press, 1985.

25 T.A. Kochan, R.B. McKersie and P. Cappelli, Strategic Choice and Industrial Relations Theory, *Industrial Relations*, Vol. 23, No. 1 (1984) pp. 16–39.

26 European Foundation for the Improvement of Living and Working Conditions, www.eurofound.eu.int, 2003.

27 See V. Frazee, Trade Union Membership is Declining Globally, *Workforce*, Vol. 3, No. 2 (1998) p.8; *World Labour Report 1997–98. Industrial Relations, Democracy and Social Stability*, Geneva: ILO, 1997; W. Groot and A. van den Berg, Why Union Density has Declined, *European Journal of Political Economy*, Vol. 10, No. 4 (1994) pp. 749–763.

28 J. Visser, Trade Unionism in Western Europe: Present Situation and Prospects, *Labour and Society*, Vol. 13, No. 2 (1988) pp. 125–182.

29 J. Hamill, Multinational Corporations and Industrial Relations in the UK, *Employee Relations*, Vol. 6, No. 5 (1984) pp. 12–16.

30 Ref. 13, p. 34.

31 This section is based in part on Chapter 5, The Impact of Organized Labour, in Ref. 6.

32 For example, the decision by Hoover to shift some of its production from France to Scotland in the early 1990s appeared to be influenced by the ease with which the employer could implement layoffs. See D. Goodhart, Ground Rules for the Firing Squad, *Financial Times*, 15 February (1993) p. 8.

33 Ref. 6, p. 102.

34 M. Allen, Worldly Wisdom, *New Statesman and Society*, Vol. 6 (1993) p. xii.

35 Ref. 9, p. 191.

36 B. Mahnkopf and E. Altvater, Transmission Belts of Transnational Competition? Trade Unions and Collective Bargaining in the Context of European Integration, *European Journal of Industrial Relations*, Vol. 1, No. 1 (1995) pp. 101–117.

37 R. Vernon, *Storm over the Multinationals: the Real Issues*, Cambridge, MA: Harvard University Press, 1977.

38 M. Martinez Lucio and S. Weston, Trade Unions and Networking in the Context of Change: Evaluating the Outcomes of Decentralization in Industrial Relations, *Economic and Industrial Democracy*, Vol. 16 (1995) p. 244.

39 For a detailed analysis of ITSs, see R. Neuhaus, *International Trade Secretariats: Objectives, Organization, Activities*, 2nd edn, Bonn: Friedrich-Ebert Stiftung, 1982. For an overview of international labor politics and organizations, see T. Boswell and D. Stevis, Globalisation and International Labour Organizing: a World-system Perspective, *Work and Occupations*, Vol. 24, No. 3 (1997) pp. 288–308.

40 For further information on the FIET, see their web page, http://www.eiro.eurofound.ie/.

41 N. Willatt, *Multinational Unions*, London: Financial Times, 1974.

42 H.R. Northrup, Why Multinational Bargaining Neither Exists Nor is Desirable, *Labour Law Journal*, Vol. 29, No. 6 (1978) pp. 330–342. Also see J. Gallagher, Solidarity Forever, *New Statesman and Society*, (1997) p. 10.

43 R.B. Helfgott, American Unions and Multinational Enterprises: a Case of Misplaced Emphasis, *Columbia Journal of World Business*, Vol. 18, No. 2 (1983) pp. 81–6.

44 Up to 1993 there was a specialized UN agency known as the United Nations Centre on Transnational Corporations (UNCTC), which had published a number of reports on MNEs (see, for example, *Transborder Data Flows: Transnational Corporations and Remote-sensing Data*, New York, 1984; and *Transnational Corporations and International Trade: Selected Issues*, New York, 1985). Since 1993, the responsibilities of the UNCTC have been assigned to UNCTAD. For further information, see the UNCTAD web site at www.unicc.org/unctad/en/aboutorg/inbrief.htm. See Boswell and Stevis[39] for more information on these international organizations.

45 See B. Leonard, An Interview with Anthony Freeman of the ILO, *HR Magazine*, Vol. 42, No. 8 (1997) pp. 104–109. For coverage of the ongoing debate on international labor standards and globalization, see E. Lee, Globalisation and Labour Standards: a Review of Issues, *Management International Review*, Vol. 136, No. 2 (1997) pp. 173–189; R.N. Block, K. Roberts, C. Ozeki and M.J. Roomkin, Models of International Labour Standards *Industrial Relations*, Vol. 40, No. 2 (2001) pp. 258–286.

46 For a detailed description and analysis of the OECD Guidelines for Multinational Enterprises, see Refs 47 and 48.

47 D.C. Campbell and R.L. Rowan, *Multinational Enterprises and the OECD Industrial Relations Guidelines*, Industrial Research Unit, Philadelphia: Wharton School, University of Pennsylvania, 1983.

48 R. Blanpain, *The OECD Guidelines for Multinational Enterprises and Labour Relations, 1982–1984: Experiences and Review*, Deventer, The Netherlands: Kluwer, 1985.

49 J. Rojot, The 1984 Revision of the OECD Guidelines for Multinational Enterprises, *British Journal of Industrial Relations*, Vol. 23, No. 3 (1985) pp. 379–397.

50 For a detailed account of this case, see R. Blanpain, *The Badger Case and the OECD Guidelines for Multinational Enterprises*, Deventer, The Netherlands: Kluwer, 1977.

51 R. Blanpain, *The OECD Guidelines for Multinational Enterprises and Labour Relations, 1976–1979: Experience and Review*, Deventer, The Netherlands: Kluwer, 1979.

52 H.C. Jain, Disinvestment and the Multinational Employer – a Case History from Belgium, *Personnel Journal*, Vol. 59, No. 3 (1980) pp. 201–205.

53 B. Liebhaberg, *Industrial Relations and Multinational Corporations in Europe*, London: Cower, 1980, p. 85.

54 OECD Guidelines to Multinational Enterprises: 2002 Annual Meeting of the National Contact Points, Report by the Chair, Meeting held on 18 June 2002, p. 30; http://www.oecd.org/dataoecd/24/4/1956371.pdf.

55 C.S. Jensen, J.S. Madsen and J. Due, A Role for a Pan-European Trade Union Movement? Possibilities in European IR-regulation, *Industrial Relations Journal*, Vol. 26, No. 1 (1995) pp. 4–18.

56 G.W. Latta and J.R. Bellace, Making the Corporation Transparent: Prelude to Multinational Bargaining, *Columbia Journal of World Business*, Vol. 18, No. 2 (1983) pp. 73–80.

57 J.T. Addison and W.S. Siebert, Recent Developments in Social Policy in the New European Union, *Industrial and Labour Relations Review*, Vol. 48, No. 1 (1994) pp. 5–27.

58 N. Donnelly and C. Rees, *Industrial Relations and Multinational Companies in the European Community: the Work of the International Companies Network*, Warwick Papers in Industrial Relations No. 54, Warwick: Warwick Business School, 1995.

59 See, for example, P. Teague, EC Social Policy and European Human Resource Management, in *Policy and Practice in European Human Resource Management*, ed. C. Brewster and A. Hegewisch, London: Routledge, 1994; L. Ulman, B. Eichengreen and W.T. Dickens (eds), *Labour and an Integrated Europe*, Washington, D.C: Brookings Institution, 1993.

60 Commission of the European Communities, *Community Charter of the Fundamental Social Rights of Workers*, Luxembourg: Office for Official Publications of the European Communities, 1990.

61 See, for example, J. Lodge, Social Europe: Fostering a People's Europe? in *European Community and the Challenge of the Future*, ed. J. Lodge, London: Pinter, 1989; J. Addison and S. Siebert, The Social Charter of the European Community: Evolution and Controversies, *Industrial and Labour Relations Review*, Vol. 44, No. 4 (1991) pp. 597–625; M. Hall, Industrial Relations and the Social Dimension of European Integration: Before and After Maastricht, in *New Frontiers in European Industrial Relations*, ed. R. Hyman and A. Ferner, Oxford: Blackwell, 1994.

62 J. Pickard, Maastricht Deal Worries the Multinationals, *PM Plus*, January (1992) p. 4; B. Fitzpatrick, Community Social Law After Maastricht, *Industrial Law Journal*, Vol. 21, No. 3 (1992) pp. 199–213; B. Bercusson and J.J. Van Dijk, The Implementation of the Protocol and Agreement on Social Policy of the Treaty on European Union, *The International Journal of Comparative Labour Law and Industrial Relations*, Vol. 11, No. 1 (1995) pp. 3–30.

63 The Treaty of Amsterdam revised the Treaties on which the European Union was founded. For further information see http://europa.eu.int/abc/obj/amst/en/index.htm and http://www.europarl.eu.int/basicdoc/en/default.htm.

64 European Union Press Release, 27 March 2003, 1800 h, http://europa.eu.int.

65 For a detailed analysis of the Vredeling Directive, see D. Van Den Bulcke, Decision Making in Multinational Enterprises and the Information and Consultation of Employees: the Proposed Vredeling Directive of the EC Commission, *International Studies of Management and Organization*, Vol. 14, No. 1 (1984) pp. 36–60.

66 See A. Chesters, What You Need to Know About Works Councils, *Workforce*, July (1997) pp. 22–23. Also see New Legislation on EWCs and Collective Bargaining, *European Industrial Relations Review*, December (1996) pp. 15–16; M. Gold and M. Hall, Statutory European Works Councils: the Final Countdown?, *Industrial Relations Journal*, Vol. 25, No. 3 (1994) pp. 177–186.

67 P. Knutsen, Corporatist Tendencies in the Euro-Polity: The EU Directive of 22 September 1994, on European Works Councils, *Economic and Industrial Democracy*, Vol. 18, No. 2 (1997) pp. 289–323.

68 F. Michon, The 'European Social Community': a Common Model and Its National Variations? Segmentation Effects, Societal Effects, *Labour and Society*, Vol. 15, No. 2 (1990) pp. 215–236. Also see E. Szyszczak, Future Directions in European Union Social Policy Law, *Industrial Law Journal*, Vol. 24, No. 1 (1995) pp. 19–32.

69 M. Gilman and P. Marginson, Negotiating European Works Councils: Contours of Constrained Choice *Industrial Relations Journal*, Vol. 33, No. 1 (2002) pp. 36–51

70 Worldwide Pay and Benefits Headlines, Towers Perrin, July 2003, www.towers.com.

71 M. Minehan, New Directive Moves EU Closer to Pan-European Pensions, Strategic Human Resource Management Global Online, www.shrmglobal.org, June 2003.

72 Mercer – Pan-European Pensions: Fact or Fiction? http://www.mercerhr.com, July 2003.

73 EU Commentary on Pension Funds Directive, http://europa.eu.int, July 2003.

74 AON Newsletter on Pan-European Pensions, http://www.aon.com, July 2003.

75 W. Nicoll and T.C. Salmon, *Understanding the European Community*, Hertfordshire: Philip Allan, 1990, p. 191.

76 C.L. Erickson and S. Kuruvilla, Labour Costs and the Social Dumping Debate in the European Union, *Industrial and Labour Relations Review*, Vol. 48, No. 1 (1994) pp. 28–47.

77 For further reading, see M. Muller-Camen, P. Almond, P. Gunnigle, J. Quintanilla and A. Tempel, Between Home and Host Country: Multinationals and Employment Relations in Europe, *Industrial Relations Journal*, Vol. 32, No. 5 (2001) pp. 435–448.

78 R. Konrad, Visa Plans Cost Jobs, Tech Workers Assert, *International Herald Tribune*, 21 August 2003.

79 Digital Divide is Wide and Getting Wider. Vast Swathes of the Globe are Technologically Disconnected, International Labor Organization, Press Kit, January 2001, http://ilo.org.

80 The Digital Divide, Department of Communication, International Labour Organization, 2001, http://ilo.org.

81 M. Zanko, Change and Diversity: HRM Issues and Trends in the Asia-Pacific Region, *Asia Pacific Journal of Human Resources*, Vol. 41, No. 1 (2003) pp. 75–87.

82 See H. Ramsey, Solidarity at Last? International Trade Unionism Approaching The Millennium, *Economic and Industrial Democracy*, Vol. 18, No. 4 (1997) pp. 503–537.

83 Ref. 21, p. 357.

Performance management*

Chapter objectives

The aim of this chapter is to draw together the relevant literature on performance management in the international context as it relates to IHRM. The focus is on identifying those aspects that require a substantial modification of traditional performance management (especially appraisal criteria and processes) that are imposed by international operations. We specifically address the following aspects:

- multinational performance management at the global and local level: considering aspects such as non-comparable data, the volatility of the global environment, the effect of distance and level of subsidiary maturity

- performance management as part of a multinational's control system

- factors associated with expatriate performance, including compensation package, task and role, headquarters' support, host environment factors and cultural adjustment

- performance management of expatriates and non-expatriates, and for those on non-standard assignments such as commuter and virtual

- issues related to the performance appraisal of international employees.

Introduction

Perhaps one of the most challenging aspects for a firm operating internationally is how to manage the performance of its various overseas facilities. As we discussed in

* The significant contribution of Marilyn Fenwick (Monash University, Australia) to the writing of this chapter is gratefully acknowledged.

| Figure 10-1 | Basic components of performance management |

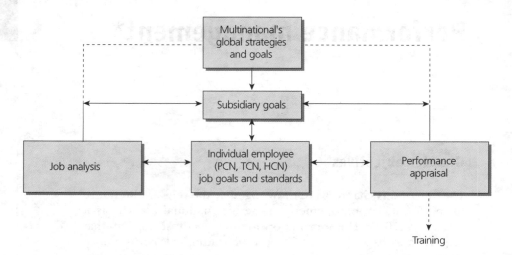

Source: Adapted from M. Tahvanainen and D. Welch, Expatriate Job Performance Management: a Review and a Critique, in *New Challenges for European and International Business*, ed. R. Schiattarella, Proceedings of the 21st Annual Meeting of the European International Business Academy, Urbino, December 1995.

Chapter 2, control matters become more complex as the geographical spread, product and operation mode become more diverse. Staffing decisions are only part of the picture. The multinational requires an effective system for managing the performance of its global operations that assists strategic cohesion and competitiveness but, at the same time, does not impose burdensome reporting procedures that impinge upon local responsiveness. Monitoring performance and ensuring conformance to agreed standards are important elements of a multinational's managerial control system.

In this chapter, we differentiate between 'performance management' and 'performance appraisal'. **Performance management** is a process that enables the multinational to evaluate and continuously improve individual, subsidiary unit and corporate performance, against clearly defined, pre-set goals and targets. Figure 10-1 illustrates the basic components of international performance management. It provides a convenient starting point for our exploration of the link between the multinational's internationalization strategies, its goals for individual units in terms of contribution to global profitability and the performance management of individual employees, whether PCN, TCN or HCN. This link is important as an individual's performance is appraised (or evaluated) according to expectations of appropriate outcomes and behavior that contribute to organizational goal attainment.

Multinational performance management

While its general strategic position may be international, multinational, global or transnational[1] (depending on its size, industry, geographic dispersal, etc.), a multinational makes strategic choices based on economic and political imperatives.

Within this context, as indicated in Figure 10-1, the multinational has specific expectations for each of its foreign subsidiaries, in terms of market performance and contribution to total profits and competitiveness. When evaluating subsidiary performance against these expectations, however, it is important to recognize various constraints that may affect goal attainment. These include the following.

Whole versus part

By its very nature, a multinational is a single entity that faces a global environment, which means that it simultaneously confronts differing national environments. Integration and control imperatives often place the multinational in the position where it decides that the good of the whole is more important than one subsidiary's short-term profitability. An example provided by Pucik[2] is where a multinational establishes an operation in a particular market where its main global competitor has a dominant position. The objective of entering the market is to challenge the competitor's cash flow with aggressive pricing policies. Pucik explains that:

> The balance sheet of this particular subsidiary might be continually in the red, but this strategy, by tying up the competitor's resources, may allow substantially higher returns in another market. The difficulties in quantifying such a global strategy in terms of the usual return-on-investment objectives are obvious.

Another situation is where the multinational establishes a joint venture in a particular market in order to have a presence there, even though it has low expectations in the short term and may provide minimum resources to the venture. Therefore, the consequences of such global decisions for subsidiary management must be taken into consideration for performance appraisal.

Non-comparable data

Frequently, the data obtained from subsidiaries may be neither interpretable nor reliable, as the following examples illustrate:[3]

> Sales in Brazil may be skyrocketing, but there are reports that the Brazilian government may impose tough new exchange controls within a year, thus making it impossible for the multinational to repatriate profits. Does this mean that the MNE is performing effectively? Is the subsidiary performing effectively?

> Sales in Peru may be booming, but headquarters management was unaware that under Peruvian accounting rules, sales on consignment are counted as firm sales. How should the headquarters accounting system handle these sales relative to sales from other subsidiaries, which do not consider sales on consignment as firm sales?

As Garland *et al.*[3] explain, physical measures of performance may be easier to interpret than in the above examples, but difficulties may still arise. For instance, notions of what constitutes adequate quality control checks can vary widely from one country to another, import tariffs can distort pricing schedules, or a dock strike in one country can unexpectedly delay supply of necessary components to a manufacturing plant in another country. Further, local labor laws may require full employment at plants that are producing at below capacity. These factors can make an objective appraisal of subsidiary performance problematic and may complicate the appraisal of individual subsidiary managers.

Volatility of the global environment

The turbulence of the global environment requires that long-term goals be flexible in order to respond to potential market contingencies. According to Pucik,[4] an inflexible approach may mean that subsidiaries could be pursuing strategies that no longer fit the new environment. Consider, for example, the impact on international business of major events in the past decade or so, such as the collapse of communist rule in the late 1980s in Eastern Europe and the former Soviet Union, the adoption of the Euro as the single currency by most of the European Union countries, Chinese market reforms, the rise of international terrorism and the Severe Acute Respiratory Syndrome (SARS) epidemic.

Each of these events has had profound implications for the global and local strategies of multinationals. Because subsidiaries operate under such volatility and fluctuation, they must tailor long-term goals to the specific situation in a given market. Problems arise when subsidiary managers perceive that goals and deadlines set by a distant headquarters strategy team are unrealistic and inflexible, owing to a failure to take into account local conditions that change as a result of a volatile environment. Obviously, involving regional and subsidiary managers in strategic planning assists in overcoming this perception.

Separation by time and distance

Judgments concerning the congruence between the multinational and local subsidiary activities are further complicated by the physical distances involved, time-zone differences, the frequency of contact between the corporate head-office staff and subsidiary management and the cost of the reporting system.[4] Developments in sophisticated worldwide communications systems, such as fax machines, video telephone conferences and e-mail, do not fully substitute 'face-to-face' contacts between subsidiary managers and corporate staff. In some areas, the telecommunications system may be so overloaded, or underdeveloped, that reliable telephone, fax services and Internet connections cannot be assumed. It is often necessary to meet personally with a manager to understand fully the problems that managers must deal with. For this reason, many multinational corporate managers spend a considerable amount of time traveling in order to meet expatriate and local managers in foreign locations. It is then possible for HR corporate staff, when designing performance management systems, to take account of country-specific factors.

Variable levels of maturity

According to Pucik,[4] without the supporting infrastructure of the parent, market development in foreign subsidiaries is generally slower and more difficult to achieve than at home, where established brands can support new products and new business areas can be cross-subsidized by other divisions. As a result, more time may be needed to achieve results than is customary in a domestic market and this fact ought to be recognized in the performance management process. Further, variations in customs and work practices between the parent country and the foreign subsidiary need to be considered. For example,[3]

One does not fire a Mexican manager because worker productivity is half the American average. In Mexico, that would mean that this manager is working at a level three or four times as high as the average Mexican industrial plant. Here we need relevant comparative data, not absolute numbers; our harassed Mexican manager has to live with Mexican constraints, not European or American ones and these can be very different. The way we measure worker productivity is exactly the same, but the numbers come out differently because of that environmental difference.

In summary, there are a number of significant constraints that must be considered when appraising the performance of a foreign subsidiary. Because this appraisal is primarily based on strategic factors, it affects the appraisal and success of the subsidiary's chief executive (or managing director) most directly.

Control and performance management

Although it is not often described as such, performance management is a part of a multinational's control system. It will be recalled from the discussion of control mechanisms in Chapter 2 (see Figure 2-10) that performance targets were listed as part of formal control. Through formal control mechanisms and communication through the feedback and appraisal aspects, performance management also contributes to shaping corporate culture, both formally and informally,[5] thereby acting as an informal control mechanism as well as part of the bureaucratic control system. Figure 10-2 illustrates the performance–behavior–outcomes linkage. It is through formal and informal control mechanisms that the multinational achieves the consistency, coordination and compliance of desired behavior and outcomes to implement its global strategy. These behaviors and outcomes are expected at all levels and areas – both at subsidiary level and at headquarters.

In a sense, by adopting a performance management approach, multinationals are drawing on a number of human resource management functions to realize performance goals set during the performance appraisal process. Its proponents argue, somewhat convincingly, that effective performance management is beneficial to both the individual and the firm. As Tahvanianen[6] points out, strong goal setting

---

MNE control and performance   **Figure 10-2**

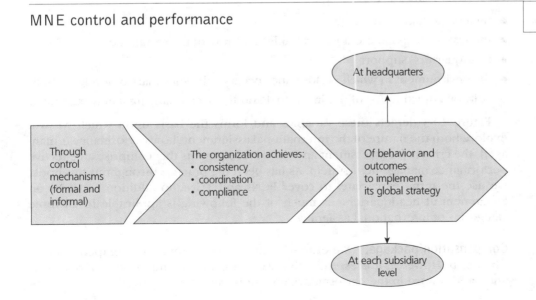

and appraisal are key elements of an individual performance management system that also may include training and development and performance-related pay.

Performance management of international employees

Having considered the broader context, we now turn our attention to individual performance management. Consistent with our general approach, we use the term 'expatriate' to cover PCNs, TCNs and those HCNs on assignment to headquarters. However, in this chapter, we also address performance management issues relating to non-expatriates (international business travelers). Given the broad scope and the fact that often issues are common to both expatriates and non-expatriates, we have decided to use the term 'international employees' when all these various groups are involved.

As discussed in Chapter 3, international assignments vary in terms of the duration and scope of physical relocation required. That is, from traditional expatriate assignments when expatriates and, usually, their family members relocate, to virtual assignments, where no physical relocation by employees or their families is required. When attempting to manage the performance of staff working across the multinational, it is essential to consider all these variables in relation to the nature of the international assignment. The following sections also identify some performance management issues associated with expatriate and non-expatriate international assignments.

Expatriate performance management

As noted in Chapters 3 and 4, expatriation remains a key dimension of multinational enterprise and performance. When attempting to determine expatriate performance, it is important to consider the impact of the following variables and their inter-relationship:

● the compensation package
● the task – the assignment task variables and role of the expatriate
● headquarters' support
● the environment in which performance occurs – the subsidiary or foreign facility
● cultural adjustment – of the individual and the accompanying family members.

Figure 10-3 depicts these variables and forms the basis upon which we will explore both the nature of the international assignment, how performance is managed, the criteria for assessment and the other elements that comprise an effective performance management system. As has been the practice throughout this book, we use the term 'expatriate' to cover PCNs and TCNs, in addition to HCNs on assignment at headquarters, as much of the following is applicable to all three categories of international assignees.

Compensation package. We examined the issues surrounding compensation in Chapter 6. However, it is essential that we recognize the importance of remuneration and reward in the performance equation. Perceived financial benefits, along

Variables affecting expatriate performance | **Figure 10-3** |

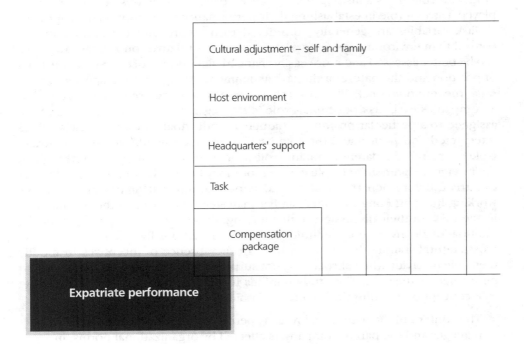

with the career progression potential associated with an overseas assignment, are often important motives for accepting the posting. If these expectations are not realized during the assignment, the level of motivation and commitment is likely to decrease, thus affecting performance.

Task.   As outlined earlier, expatriates are assigned to foreign operations to fulfill specific tasks. Hays[7] identified four such tasks:

- The **chief executive officer**, or subsidiary manager, who oversees and directs the entire foreign operation.
- The **structure reproducer** carries the assignment of building or reproducing in a foreign subsidiary a structure similar to that which he or she knows from another part of the company. He or she could be building a marketing framework, implementing an accounting and financial reporting system or establishing a production plant, for example.
- The **troubleshooter** is the individual who is sent to a foreign subsidiary to analyse and solve a particular operational problem.
- The **operative** is the individual whose assignment is to perform functional job tasks in an existing operational structure, in generally lower level, supervisory positions.

In her study of expatriate performance management in the Finnish multinational Nokia Telecommunications, Tahvanainen[6] identified five categories of top managers, middle managers, business establishers, project employees and R&D project personnel. There were clear differences in the way performance management was approached within these groups. For example, middle managers played a moderate role in establishing performance goals, whereas business establishers played a strong role in establishing their performance goals and job descriptions.

Task variables are generally considered to be more under a multinational's control than environmental factors. Because of this relative control, task variables can be better assessed and more easily changed, depending, of course, on the level of position and the nature of the task assignment. Along with the specifics of the task, the multinational, like any other organization, determines the role that accompanies each task position. A role is the organized set of behaviors that are assigned to a particular position. Although an individual may affect how a role is interpreted and performed, the role itself is predetermined.[8] For the expatriate (role recipient), the parent company (role sender) predetermines his or her role in the foreign assignment and role expectations may be clearly communicated to the expatriate before departure. Black and Porter[9] found that American expatriates working in Hong Kong exhibited similar managerial behavior to those remaining in the USA. In their discussion of this finding, these authors suggest that the US multinationals involved communicated role expectations by omitting to provide cross-cultural training before departure. In the absence of incentives to modify their role behavior when abroad, it is not surprising that the expatriates concerned performed as they did. This study reminds us that the transmission of expatriate role conception is culturally bound. As Torbiörn[10] explains:

> The content of the managerial role, as perceived by both the individual manager and the parent company, is affected by organizational norms, in terms of parent-company expectations of the manager and by the set of cultural norms that the manager holds in relation to other cultural and organizational norms that may be represented by other role senders. Organizational and cultural norms thus interactively determine the role content of the manager.

The difficulty that this presents for the expatriate manager is that the role is defined in one country, but performed in another. That is, the cultural norms regarding the set of behaviors that define 'a manager in the USA' may not be the same as those considered appropriate for a manager's role in Indonesia.

Communication of role conception from the multinational to the expatriate is indicated by the solid arrows in Figures 10-4 and 10-5. Role conception is also communicated to the role recipient by host-country stakeholders (e.g. subsidiary employees, host-government officials, customers, suppliers) as shown by the dotted arrows. This, however, crosses a cultural boundary. Role behavior provides the feedback loop, again at two levels: the parent- and the host-country stakeholders. Trying to perform to differing expectations may cause role conflict. If the PCN manager adapts his or her role behavior according to the role conception communicated in the host environment, it may conflict with that predetermined at headquarters. Janssens' study[11] of expatriate performance indicated that role conflict is likely to result in situations where the international manager has an understanding of the host-country culture and realizes that the use of headquarters' procedures or actions may lead to ineffective management. She postulates that the higher the degree of intercultural interaction, the more problems the expatriate has with role conflict.

From the perspective of headquarters, commitment to the parent is perceived as important, given the part that the PCN plays in transferring know-how and 'the

PCN role conception

Figure 10-4

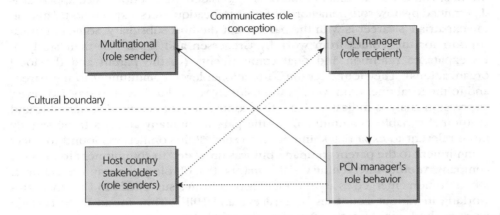

Source: Adapted from I. Torbiörn, The Structure of Managerial Roles in Cross-cultural Settings, *International Studies of Management and Organization*, Vol. 15, No 1 (1985) p. 60.

TCN role conception

Figure 10-5

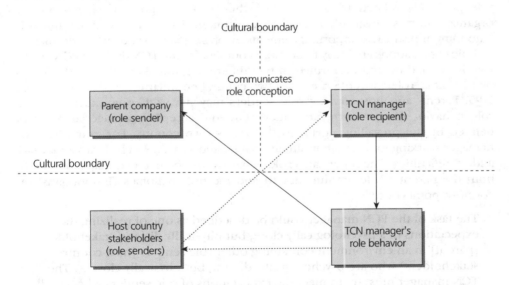

Source: Adapted from I. Torbiörn, The Structure of Managerial Roles in Cross-cultural Settings, *International Studies of Management and Organization*, Vol. 15, No. 1 (1985) p. 60.

company way of doing things' into the subsidiary. This helps to explain the preference for using headquarters' standards in expatriate performance appraisal as a control mechanism.[11] If the PCN is perceived to identify too closely with host-subsidiary concerns, he or she may be recalled (the term 'going native' is often used to describe this perception). Some multinationals will restrict the length of stay to not more than 3 years to contain the possibility of PCN identification with local concerns. Because of the importance given to the parent as role sender in performance appraisal, a PCN may elect to ignore role communication sent from the host-country stakeholders if he or she considers that performance appraisal is determined by how role behavior conforms to headquarters' expectation. After all, the expatriate's career is with the parent, not the host subsidiary. Some empirical support for this comes from work by Gregersen and Black[12] in their study of US expatriate retention and dual commitments (to the parent and the local organizations). They found, at the correlational level, commitment to the parent and to the local operation were both positively related to intent to stay. However, 'regression analysis indicated that when controlling for certain demographic and attitudinal variables, commitment to the parent company appears to be slightly more relevant to expatriates' intention to stay'. Role conflict was found to affect commitment to the parent company, but was unrelated to commitment to the host company. Another intervening variable may be that of role autonomy. For example, job discretion emerged as an important aspect from a survey of 115 US expatriates working in various countries by Birdseye and Hill.[13] They found that: 'Foreign work methods may be more structured than their American counterparts (perhaps more procedures and protocols) and that individuals have less discretion in how they approach tasks and problems.' These authors conclude that individuals are likely to blame this lack of discretion on the organization, the job and the location – in that order. A similar finding emerged from a study of US domestic and international relocation by Feldman and Tompson.[14] The degree of change in job duties was positively related to adjustment, whereas the degree of change in the organization was negatively related to adjustment. Hence role conflict and role autonomy appear to be important elements in job satisfaction and task performance.

Role expectations are likely to be more complex for the TCN than the PCN, as the role is defined by and performed in two different countries to that of the TCN's own. That is, role conception crosses two cultural boundaries, as shown in Figure 10-5. Parent- and host-country role senders may have differing expectations of role behavior that, in turn, are different to the accepted managerial behavior defined by the prevailing norms in the TCN's own country. For example, a US manager working for a Dutch multinational posted as a TCN in Indonesia may face added difficulties. The American's role behavior may be deemed inappropriate by both the parent (Dutch multinational) and the host nationals (Indonesians). As Torbiörn points out:[10]

> The task of the PCN manager could be described as one of realizing the expectations of a psychologically close, but physically distant, stakeholder [parent] in an environment containing other role senders [host-country stakeholders] who are psychologically distant, but physically close … The TCN manager must try to meet the expectations of role senders who are all psychologically distant in a context that is also psychologically distant.

However, as will be recalled from the discussion of the rationale for using TCNs, often the country of assignment is perceived by headquarters as culturally close (that is, a German multinational decides to transfer a Canadian rather than a German to the USA). Whether cultural closeness lessens the potential for TCN role conflict situations has yet to be empirically investigated.[15]

As there are very few studies that specifically examine TCN performance management issues,[16] we can only assume that many of the aspects relating to PCNs discussed above will apply to the TCN situation. An American manager working in Indonesia, for instance, whether as a PCN or TCN, may encounter lack of job discretion – with perhaps the same effect in terms of performance – depending on the strength of other intervening variables. For example, differing role senders may exacerbate the situation through conflicting role expectations.

The preceding discussion demonstrates the importance of considering the role that accompanies each task position. Given that task performance is a core component of expatriate appraisal, it is also necessary to recognize that it does not occur in isolation. Many individuals and firms rank job ability as the primary ingredient relating to their expected probability of success in the international assignment, as discussed in Chapter 4. Certain types of tasks, however, require significantly more interaction with host-country stakeholders. Hence the task variables should not be evaluated in isolation from the subsidiary environment context.

Another factor relating to task variables that warrants consideration is the similarity of the job to which the individual is assigned abroad to the job he or she held domestically. Some types of tasks require an individual to operate within a given structure, whereas other tasks demand the creation of the structure. Individuals vary greatly in their ability to conceive and implement a system and their tolerance for lack of structure and ambiguity. Some multinationals have experienced failure abroad because they assumed that an individual could be effective in setting up a structure, such as a marketing system, based on evidence of good performance within the existing marketing structure in the domestic corporation.[17]

Headquarters' support. The expatriate assignment differs from a domestic relocation as it involves the transfer of the individual and accompanying family members into a foreign environment, outside their normal cultural comfort zones. The individual's primary motivation for accepting the assignment may be career or financially orientated, but this is often mixed with a genuine feeling of loyalty and commitment to the sending organization. As mentioned previously, the process of adjustment to the foreign location typically produces, to varying degrees, a range of emotional and psychological reactions to unfamiliar situations encountered over the period of the stay in the host country. The level of headquarters' support provided to the individual and the family is an important performance variable.

Host environment. The environment has an impact on any job, but it becomes of primary importance with regard to expatriate management. According to Gregersen *et al.*,[18] the international context – with its differing societal, legal, economic, technical and physical demands – can be a major determinant of expatriate performance. Consequently, expatriate performance should be placed within its international and also its organizational context. Therefore, the five major constraints identified above in terms of multinational strategy and goal setting for the subsidiary are important considerations for expatriate performance management.

The type of operation to which the expatriate is assigned is important. For instance, it may be relatively easier to perform in a wholly owned subsidiary than in a joint venture with a state-owned enterprise in China. Conflicting goals between the parent companies are a common problem within international joint ventures and can make the expatriate's job more difficult. An expatriate IJV manager may have difficulty trying to serve two masters and experience a high level of uncertainty regarding the effect of differing goal expectations for the IJV upon his or her performance appraisal. Similarly, the stage of the international business will influence the success of the expatriate. An expatriate overseeing the establishment of a new facility in a foreign country, especially in a developing or emerging market, will face different challenges and constraints to one who is posted into a mature operation.

Cultural adjustment.   The process of cultural adjustment may be a critical determinant of expatriate job performance, as we discussed in the context of 'expatriate failure' in Chapter 4. Indeed, much of the literature reviewed in our discussion of the cause of expatriate 'failure' covers the process of adjustment. It is likely that expatriates and their families will have some difficulty adjusting to a new environment and this will impact on the manager's work performance. The dilemma is that adjustment to a foreign culture is multifaceted and individuals vary in terms of their reaction and coping behaviors. Determining the relevance of adjustment to the new environment when assessing expatriate work performance may be problematic. The five variables – compensation package, task, headquarters' support, host environment and cultural adjustment – reviewed above and shown in Figure 10-3, are not mutually exclusive, but interact in a way that has significant implications for the appraisal of international employees' performance. Designers and users of performance management systems need to be conscious of and responsive to, the impact of these variables.

A contextual model of expatriate performance management

One of the few studies that examined expatriate performance management, as opposed to those that focused solely on appraisal, is that conducted by Tahvanainen.[19] Taking a grounded theory approach, using qualitative case methodology, Tahvanainen explored the international, domestic and organizational context in which expatriate performance management occurred within the Finnish multinational Nokia Telecommunications. From this study, Tahvanainen developed a comprehensive model that illustrates the interrelationships between the various elements discussed so far in this chapter. The model (see Figure 10-6) illustrates how performance appraisal (through goal setting) is both an outcome of the company strategies and goals and an important source of information on which other performance management activities, such as training and development and performance-related pay, are based.

As illustrated in Figure 10-6, the organizational context is comprised of the nature of the job, the organizational structure, a standard performance appraisal system, top management support, size of the receiving unit (subsidiary) and the style and skills of the manager and subsidiary employees. The mediating effect of any of these elements varies according to the strength of its interaction with other elements. In Nokia, for example, the organizational structure emerged as important. Like some of its Nordic counterparts, Nokia adopted a global matrix form that prevails at the top management level of the multinational as an overarching structure. However, in some divisions and particularly at lower organizational levels, a traditional line management organization remains. The multinational also used project teams. Tahvanainen found that employees within these different organizational configurations were managed differently. For example, expatriates in line positions were evaluated by their host-country managers, whereas product managers, who reported through the matrix structure, were evaluated by host- and home-country superiors. As Tahvanainen points out, the matrix structure can, in fact, resolve inherent conflict between differing expectations, as the two superiors appraising an expatriate's performance are, in the normal course of their work, required to recognize commonality of global and area goals in other areas besides employee performance.

Another aspect of the model shown in Figure 10-6 is that clarification of performance expectations is an important element linking company strategies and

Contextual model of expatriate performance management   **Figure 10-6**

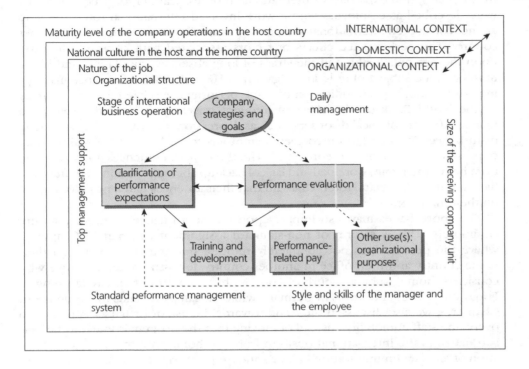

Source: M. Tahvanainen, *Expatriate Performance Management: the Case of Nokia Telecommunications*, Helsinki: Helsinki School of Economics, 1998. Reproduced with permission of the author.

goals with performance appraisal. Individual goal setting does not always occur within all job categories but performance expectations may be conveyed in informal ways. Likewise, a concept – daily management – is added as a critical component of the organizational context. For example, expatriates working in customer project operations tended to rely more on guidance, performance review, feedback and coaching on an ongoing informal basis rather than Nokia's standardized performance management system. The model also indicates, through the use of dotted lines and arrows connecting the various elements, that performance management varies across job categories and expatriate situations and the extent to which data collected through the performance management system is utilized.

A somewhat surprising finding of the Nokia study was the seeming irrelevance of national culture as a contingency variable. While the Finnish culture indirectly affected expatriate performance management, it was not evident as a powerful factor that influenced general expatriate performance management. Tahvanainen explains that this finding may reflect the implementation of a standard, global performance appraisal system within Nokia, rather than extending an existing domestic system to expatriates. Another explanation is that, in general, Nokia expatriates either did not report to HCN managers, or only to PCN managers, so their performance was evaluated in the Finnish context. For these reasons and in recognition that the framework is limited by its empirical grounding in a single case study, Tahvanainen includes national context in her contextual model.

Performance management of non-expatriates

In Chapter 3, non-expatriates (international business traveler, or 'frequent flyer') were described as employees whose work involved international travel but who are not considered international assignees because they do not relocate to another country. The performance effects of factors associated with constant air travel upon the person's health and the stress of long absences from family and home have been the subject of little investigation in HR or IHRM performance management literature.[20] As an indication of some performance-related factors, a survey by the World Bank on the effect of frequent travel upon its staff revealed an increase in psychological disorders, such as depression, nervous anxiety and sleep disturbance: 'We first attributed these symptoms to jet lag, but we realised that other significant factors were involved. The three main influences are separation from home and family, workload and lack of back-up abroad'.[21] Among 500 frequent fliers surveyed by Hyatt Hotel, 18% said that their absences had a negative impact on their marriages.[21,22]

The above issues may also impact upon the performance of another group: commuters. This is a form of non-standard assignment outlined in Chapter 3 where the person does not completely relocate but commutes between their home country and their office in another country, for instance an executive who considers 'home' to be a suburb of London, but who, from Monday morning to Friday night, lives and works in Germany while the family remains in London.[23] In Chapter 3, we also discussed the trend towards the use of virtual assignments to overcome staff immobility. Instead of moving into the host environment, the person manages the international position from the home country using a combination of regular communication link-ups and frequent trips to the foreign location.

As yet, little is really known about the implications of such international business travel, whether as part of a non-standard assignment or as a component of a specific job, on individual performance. However, it is possible to suggest some performance management challenges:

● How to determine performance criteria and goals related to the effective conduct of non-standard assignments, especially virtual assignees. As indicated in Figure 10-1, goal setting is an important component of the performance management process. This requires the link between each employee's performance and the achievement of the multinational's strategic goals and objectives to be clearly established and understood. However, as the role conceptions in Figures 10-4 and 10-5 show, shared conceptions of roles and expectations are complicated by the numbers of cultures and organizational contexts involved. With virtual assignees, monitoring and evaluating a physically and geographically distant group of employees are problematic. It is 'management by remote control'. In addition, the virtual assignee may be faced with dual goals – that of the domestic-located job and the virtual work group. Therefore, the perennial challenge of effectively communicating the strategic links between the assignee's performance and organizational strategy is likely to be magnified.[24]

● The goal-setting element of the performance management process is generally advocated as a highly participative process between supervisor and employee.[25] As with the traditional expatriate assignment, work conducted through non-standard assignments and international travel is still conducted across cultural and national boundaries and thereby subject to cultural differences in norms about acceptable or preferred levels of participation.

- Isolating the international dimensions of job performance might not be as straightforward as in traditional expatriate assignments. It may depend on the quality of the goals set and how individual performance levels are determined.

- Outstanding performance, underperformance or failure in non-expatriate and non-standard assignments will challenge the performance appraisal process.

- As we shall explore in a later section of this chapter, regular feedback on progress towards those goals is most usually provided through the performance appraisal activity. Performance feedback for assignees will only be relevant if it reflects the international contexts in which they are performing.[26] Those enduring concerns of who conducts performance appraisals, how and based on what performance data, may be intensified when they involve increasing numbers of others outside head office with whom the assignee is working.

- One key function of performance appraisal feedback is that it provides opportunities to improve performance by identifying performance gaps that might be eliminated with training and development. Cross-cultural awareness and competence training will still be relevant for non-expatriates. However, a detailed analysis of other pre-departure and ongoing training that might be required for non-expatriate assignments is yet to be conducted.

- Employee expectations about rewards for performance and as elements of their working conditions, together with motivation, are important aspects of individual performance. In multinationals, the management of links between performance and rewards is already complex, owing to the specialized local knowledge required across multiple employment and legal environments. The challenges for IHRM are to determine what to reward when dealing with non-expatriate assignments and the way in which compensation for each type of international assignment fits with global compensation strategy.

- The impact of non-standard assignments on host-country national co-workers should also be considered – particularly in terms of the impact on these staff of international business travelers and commuters who 'drop in, drop out'.

Performance appraisal of international employees

Now that we have an understanding of the variables likely to influence performance, including the nature of the international assignment being performed, we can discuss the criteria by which performance is to be appraised (or evaluated – the terms are used interchangeably in the relevant literature). We note that the focus on expatriate management is also reflected in the literature about the performance appraisal of international staff and much of the following discussion reflects that emphasis. However, aspects of expatriate performance appraisal are also relevant to the appraisal of non-expatriates and these, along with the aspects that distinguish between the two categories of international staff, will be highlighted.

As will be recalled from Figure 10-1, individual performance management involves job analysis, job goals and standards and performance appraisal. Traditionally, it comprises a formal process of goal setting, performance appraisal and feedback. Data from this process are often used to determine pay and promotion, and training and development requirements. Company goals influence the individual's job analysis and job description, against which job goals and standards are established and measured. There are differences in the way in which this process is handled within companies. For example, in Germany and Sweden it is common for employees to have input into job goal setting, whereas in other countries such as the USA, job goals tend to be assigned.[6]

Performance criteria

Goals tend to be translated into performance appraisal criteria so specificity and measurability issues are important aspects and we need to recognize that hard, soft and contextual goals are often used as the basis for performance criteria. **Hard goals** are objective, quantifiable and can be directly measured – such as return-on-investment (ROI) and market share. **Soft goals** tend to be relationship or trait-based, such as leadership style or interpersonal skills. **Contextual goals** attempt to take into consideration factors that result from the situation in which performance occurs. For example, multinationals commonly use arbitrary transfer pricing and other financial tools for transactions between subsidiaries to minimize foreign-exchange risk exposure and tax expenditures. Another consideration is that all financial figures are generally subject to the problem of currency conversion, including sales and cash positions. Further complications arise because host governments can place restrictions on repatriation of profits and currency conversion. The nature of the international monetary system and local accounting differences may preclude an accurate measurement of results. The dilemma that this poses is that the use of transfer pricing and other financial tools is necessary because of the complexity of the international environment. Multinationals cannot allow subsidiaries to become autonomous in financial management terms and place controls on subsidiary managers. Hence the financial results recorded for any particular subsidiary do not always reflect accurately its contribution to the achievements of the corporation as a whole. Therefore, such results should not be used as a primary input in performance appraisal.[2] For this reason, a performance management approach is now advocated, rather than traditional performance appraisal, as it allows clarification of goals and expectations of performance against those goals.

Janssens[11] suggests that performance appraisal of subsidiary managers against hard criteria is often supplemented by frequent visits by headquarter staff and meetings with executives from the parent company. Soft criteria can be used to complement hard goals and take into account areas that are difficult to quantify, such as leadership skills, but their appraisal is somewhat subjective and, in the context of both expatriate and non-expatriate assignments, more complicated owing to cultural exchanges and clashes. However, relying on hard criteria such as financial data to evaluate how well a manager operates a foreign subsidiary does not consider the way in which results are obtained and the behaviors used to obtain these results.[27] Concern with questionable ethical practices led to the enactment of the US Foreign Corrupt Practices Act (FCPA), which may prompt an increased use of both behavioral and results data to appraise the performance of managers in foreign subsidiaries.[28] We discuss the FCPA in more detail in Chapter 11. However, an appraisal system that uses hard, soft and contextual criteria builds upon the strengths of each while minimizing their disadvantages.[6] Using multiple criteria wherever possible is therefore recommended in the relevant literature.

In addition, job analysis must, as Harvey[26] suggests, generate criteria that adequately capture the nature of international work as opposed to the domestic context, in order to provide valid appraisal information.

Who conducts the performance appraisal?

Another issue is who conducts the performance appraisal. Typically, employees are appraised by their immediate superiors and this can pose problems for subsidiary chief executive officers (or managers). They work in countries geographically distant, yet are evaluated by superiors back at headquarters who are not in the position to see on a day-to-day basis how the expatriate performs in the particular situation. Consequently, subsidiary managers tend to be assessed according to subsidiary performance, with a reliance on hard criteria similar to those applied to heads of domestic units or divisions. Of course, there is a danger that a subsidiary manager will take decisions and implement local strategies that favor short-term performance to the detriment of longer term organizational goals. His or her susidiary performance will not be affected if the manager leaves the position before the consequences of those decisions and strategies begin to take effect.

Appraisal of other employees is likely to be conducted by the subsidiary's chief executive officer, or the immediate host-country supervisor, depending on the nature and level of the position concerned.[6] With regard to expatriate performance appraisal, host-country managers may have a clearer picture of expatriate performance and can take into consideration contextual criteria. However, they may have culturally bound biases (e.g. about role behavior) and lack an appreciation of the impact of the expatriate's performance in the broader organizational context. As the IHRM in Action Case 10-1 illustrates, some expatriates may prefer to have parent company evaluators given that their future career progression may depend on how the appraisal data is utilized back at headquarters.

IHRM in Action Case 10-1

Expatriate performance appraisal

An Australian was expatriated to the multinational's Regional Office in Tokyo. Although his position was designated as Marketing Manager, he also performed a critical strategic role for global business development. One of his main roles was 'intelligence gathering and the identification of business opportunities' for his former supervisor back at the Australian headquarters.

The former supervisor, although located in Australia, was in the best position to evaluate the market and environment research and related material that the expatriate was collecting for input into the multinational's global and regional strategies. The Australian expatriate's appraisal was therefore conducted by his former supervisor at headquarters, rather than by a senior manager in the Tokyo Office. The headquarter-based supervisor was also most influential in subsequent decisions about this expatriate's post-repatriation career progression.

Source: Based on an interview with the expatriate concerned.

This may be especially so in cases where foreign operations are relatively less important than domestic US operations.[29] Others may prefer host-country appraisal if they perceive it as a more accurate reflection of their performance.

Multiple raters are sometimes used in the domestic context – such as the technique referred to as 360-degree feedback.[30] It has been argued that, given the cross-cultural complexity of the foreign assignment, a team of evaluators should be used for performance appraisal. For example, Gregersen *et al.*[18] found that most firms (81 per cent) in their survey of HR directors in 58 US multinationals used more than one rater when assessing expatriate performance. The immediate superior (in either the home or host country), the expatriate as self-rater and the HR manager (either home-or host-country based) were commonly used as multiple evaluators of US expatriate performance. Likewise, a survey of 99 Finnish internationally operating companies reported that 79 per cent of respondents indicated that expatriate performance appraisal was conducted by the superior located in Finland.[6] Often, however, this was simply because there was no suitable person in the host country to conduct such appraisals. The 2002 global trends survey conducted by GMAC Global Relocation Services, mentioned in previous chapters, found that host-country performance reviews were used by 65 per cent of responding firms, whereas 43 per cent used home country-based reviews (the numbers do not total as respondents were allowed multiple answers).

Certainly, for the virtual assignment situation, the use of multiple appraisers would most likely be the most accurate way to determine performance. However, the availability of knowledgeable, trained raters may constrain the approach taken in the international context.

Standardized or customized performance appraisal form

Domestic companies commonly design performance appraisal forms for each job category, particularly those using a traditional performance appraisal approach rather than performance management. Such standardization assists in the collection of accurate performance data on which personnel decisions can be made and allow for cross-employee comparisons. The question often posed is whether these standardized forms should be adapted when used for appraising international managers. As Gregersen *et al.*[31] argue:

> In principle, performance appraisal systems are designed carefully and often presumed to be static. Valid reasons exist for maintaining standard, traditionally used appraisals (e.g. when the system has been tested, has identified baselines and reduces future development costs). These reasons are valid as long as the context of the performance does not change. In the expatriate setting, however, the performance context does change and sometimes it changes dramatically. Given a global context, previous testing and established baselines grounded in domestic situations can become meaningless.

Despite this, they found in their sample of US firms that 76 per cent in fact used the same standardized appraisal forms for expatriate appraisal.[32] Employees who relocate within the multinational and non-expatriate assignees who also cross cultural boundaries in their performance context do not always feel headquarters-based appraisal forms allow for consideration of the critical success factors of their performance such as cross-cultural competence.[33]

Frequency of appraisal

In practice, appraisal is commonly on a yearly basis and this appears to extend to international performance systems, even though the domestic-oriented literature on this topic recommends ongoing performance appraisal and feedback. For example, the majority of the US companies in Gregersen *et al.*'s study[18] referred to above reported annual appraisal practices. It is interesting to note that the US companies using annual appraisal systems were more likely to use standard appraisal forms and hard criteria. In their discussion of this finding, Gregersen, *et al.* comment that replicating domestic practices requires less effort in collecting and interpreting the data and that the preference for following the domestic system might reflect lack of international experience within the companies in the sample. As only 28 per cent of the HR respondents in their study reported having been on international assignments themselves, they might not be aware of the need to take contextual criteria into consideration, or see a need for the customization of their expatriate performance systems.

Performance feedback.   An important aspect of an effective performance management system is the provision of timely feedback of the appraisal process. One of the problems with annual appraisal is that employees do not receive the consistent frequent feedback considered critical in order to maintain or improve their performance. It is also suggested in the performance literature that regular feedback is an important aspect in terms of meeting targets and revising goals, in addition to assisting in motivation of work effort. The difficulty for the expatriate who is being evaluated by a geographically distant manager is that timely, appropriate feedback is only viable against hard criteria.

For virtual assignees, this is further complicated when geographic dispersion dictates reliance on e-mail communication. Interpersonal relations and an effective choice of communication medium are two factors influencing virtual work-group relations. Milliman *et al.*[34] reported two critical incidents involving miscommunication between managers working on a virtual assignment in the USA and Malaysia. E-mail feedback about his Malaysian counterpart's good performance provided to the Malaysian by the American head of the project generated a cycle of cross-cultural conflict. This threatened the virtual team's performance when the Malaysian sought to transfer out of the team. Adopting an organizational learning approach, Milliman *et al.*[35] analysed the miscommunication and its consequences. They concluded that the two managers concerned had different views about what constituted 'the primary source of job performance, how performance feedback is provided, what role the subordinate will have in communicating with a superior, how conflict is handled and what communication styles are expected'. The approach used to analyse these incidents provides a useful IHRM starting point for developing effective cross-cultural performance feedback communication skills.

Appraisal of HCN employees

The discussion so far has omitted the issue of appraising the performance of HCN employees. To a certain extent, this reflects the limited research on the topic in the context of IHRM, although there is a growing body of literature on comparative

HRM practices. What is important to mention here is that the practice of performance appraisal itself confronts the issue of cultural applicability.[36] Performance appraisal in different nations can be interpreted as a signal of distrust or even an insult. In Japan, for instance, it is important to avoid direct confrontation to 'save face' and this custom affects the way in which performance appraisal is conducted. A Japanese manager cannot directly point out a work-related problem or error committed by a subordinate:[37]

> Instead, he is likely to start discussing with the subordinate about the strong points of that person's work, continuing with a discussion about the work on a relatively general level. Then he might continue to explain the consequences of the type of mistake committed by the subordinate, still without directly pointing out the actual mistake or the individual employee. From all this, the subordinate is supposed to understand his mistake and propose how to improve his work.

One way to overcome the dilemma of cultural adaptation is to use host-country nationals to assist in devising a suitable system for appraising subsidiary employees and to advise on the conduct of the appraisal. The need for local responsiveness may affect the multinational's ability to implement effectively a standardized approach to performance management at all levels within the global operation.

As we discussed in relation to PCNs and TCNs, the level of position involved is an important consideration. Should a multinational appoint an HCN as its subsidiary manager, then much of what we covered in terms of goals (particularly hard goals)

Figure 10-7   HCN role conception

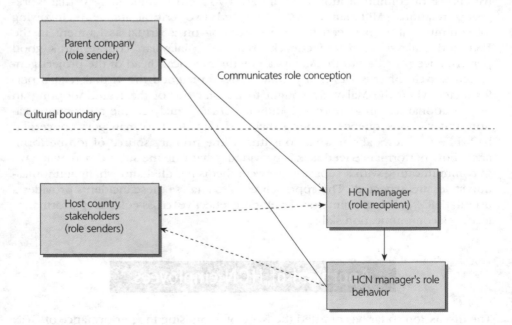

Source: Adapted from I. Torbiörn, The Structure of Managerial Roles in Cross-cultural Settings, *International Studies of Management and Organization*, Vol. 15, No. 1 (1985) p. 61.

and performance measures could be expected to apply to the HCN. In terms of task performance and potential role conflict, as can be seen from Figure 10-7, Torbiörn[10] recognizes that HCN managers face particular role concerns that are different from those of the PCN and TCN manager. The HCN manager is expected to perform a role that is conceptualized by a psychologically and physically distant parent company, but enacted in an environment with other role senders who are both psychologically and physically close.

Parent company role conception is communicated to the HCN, but it crosses the cultural boundary, as does feedback expressed as the HCN's role behavior (the solid arrows in Figure 10-7). Input from 'host-country' role senders, though, does not cross a cultural boundary. The HCN receives role expectations and enacts role behaviors in his or her own cultural environment. For subsidiary staff below the top management level, one would expect that the performance management system is localized to take into consideration local behavioral norms of work behavior. Torbiörn's model depicts only HCN managerial role conception and communication.

Conflict may arise in cases where HCNs report to a PCN expatriate manager who also conducts their performance appraisal. In a way, this is the reverse of discussion surrounding local managers appraising the performance of expatriates in terms of cultural bias. The difference, of course, is the impact that parent company standards have on the performance management system and the degree to which localization is permitted in a standardized approach. It may not be culturally sensitive to use appraisal techniques such as 360-degree feedback, for instance. In practice, US multinationals have often used the same appraisal form for HCNs as for their domestic employees. Sometimes the forms are translated from English and sometimes they are not. Both approaches have drawbacks. Although some companies are developing information systems to assist in performance appraisal, the widespread use of computer-generated data is hampered by the legal constraints imposed by some host governments or by concerns about personal privacy. This is, however, a dynamic issue. Despite these problems, it is possible to devise a standardized appraisal system that caters for local concerns, as can be seen from the approach taken by Pepsi-Cola International detailed in IHRM in Action Case 10-2.

An aspect that is overlooked in the limited literature is the potential for role conflict for those HCNs transferred into the parent's operations.[39] For that period, the HCN may be evaluated according to role behavior expectations communicated by role senders that are physically close but psychologically distant, in an environment that is also psychologically distant. The HCN is then transferred, usually back into his or her home country and may experience difficulties in readjusting role behavior.

In relation to performance appraisal generally, it seems that the process remains problematic, irrespective of cultural impacts. For example, recent research reported a common finding across 10 countries or regions, which was the failure of performance appraisal to fulfill its development purpose. The study formed part of the Best Practices in International HRM project, described as a multi-year, multi-researcher, multinational project.[40] The 10 countries/regions were Australia, Canada, China, Indonesia, Japan, Korea, Latin America, Mexico, Taiwan and the USA. The researchers noted: 'It appears that the potential of appraisal is not fully realized in current practice, not only (as widely believed) in the US, but also in most other countries.'[41]

Performance appraisal at Pepsi-Cola International[38]

Pepsi-Cola International (PCI) devised a common performance appraisal system that focuses on motivating managers to achieve and maintain high standards of performance. Administrative consistency was achieved through the use of a performance appraisal system of five feedback mechanisms: instant feedback, coaching, accountability-based performance appraisals, development feedback and a human resource plan.

The common system provided guidelines for performance appraisal yet allowed for modification to suit cultural differences. For example, the first step – instant feedback – is based on the principle that any idea about any aspect of the business or about an individual's performance is raised appropriately and discussed in a sensitive manner. The instant feedback message could be delivered in any culture; the important thing was not *how* it was done but *that* it was conducted. In practice at PCI, the successful delivery of instant feedback required some adjustment to local cultures. Americans used it because it fitted a fast-paced way of doing business. In most Asian cultures, feedback may be tough and direct but is never given in public; nor, in some Asian cultures, does head-nodding during instant feedback signify agreement, only that the message has been heard. Some Latins argue very strongly if they do not agree with the feedback and some employees, Indian nationals, for example, insist on a great deal of specificity.

The purpose of instant feedback was to improve business performance, not to criticize cultural styles. In using this system, PCI was trying to balance the cultural and administrative imperatives of successfully managing the performance of a diverse workforce.

Summary

Technical competence is a necessary but not sufficient condition for successful international performance. Cross-cultural interpersonal skills, sensitivity to foreign norms and values and ease of adaptation to unfamiliar environments are just a few of the managerial characteristics most multinational firms seek when selecting international managers. The added challenge is the effective management and appraisal of performance across all of the multinational's operations. Therefore, we have explored in this chapter:

- The basic components of performance management system that is conscious of and responds to, the organizational, national and international elements.

- Multinational performance aspects: whole (global) versus part (subsidiary); non-comparable data; the volatility of the global environment; the effect of distance and the level of maturity. Performance management as a control mechanism was briefly discussed.

- Factors associated with expatriate performance: the compensation package; task and role; headquarters' support; host environment factors and cultural adjustment.

- The performance management of non-expatriates and those on non-standard assignments. We used the virtual assignment as an illustration of some of the aspects that need to be considered in these non-traditional assignment types.
- The issues relating to the performance appraisal of international employees.
- Appraisal of HCN employees in subsidiary operations.

Broadening out the discussion to the multinational level and addressing performance management and appraisal concerns related to non-expatriates and those on non-standard assignments has been useful to remind us that there are many dimensions to international business operations that need to be considered when designing an effective performance management system in the multinational context.

Discussion questions and exercises

1 In the section on the volatility of the global environment, several world events were listed that have had profound implications for multinationals' global and local strategies. What were the implications for multinationals of the SARS epidemic? Can you identify specific HR implications of this world event?

2 Discuss the major factors associated with appraisal of expatriate managerial performance.

3 'One of the dangers of performance appraisal is that, because the focus is so much on a particular individual, the teamwork aspect gets lost. In an international location, it is perhaps desirable to focus more on how the PCN has settled in and is operating as part of a team rather than as an individual at the possible detriment of the team.' Do you agree with this statement?

4 Why is it important to include hard, soft and contextual goals when assessing managerial performance?

5 In what ways would the role of a manager working in a non-standard international assignment arrangement differ from that of a typical expatriate manager?

Further reading

J. Milliman, S. Taylor and A. Czaplewski, 2002. Cross-cultural Performance Feedback in Multinational Enterprises: Opportunity for Organizational Learning. *Human Resource Planning*, Vol. 25, No. 3, pp. 29–43.

V. Suutari and M. Tahvanainen, 2002. The Antecedents of Performance Management Among Finnish Expatriates, *International Journal of Human Resource Management*, Vol. 13, No. 1, pp. 55–75.

J. Milliman, S. Nason, C. Zhu and H. De Cieri, 2002. An Exploratory Assessment of the Purposes of Performance Appraisals in North and Central America and the Pacific Rim, *Asia Pacific Journal of Human Resources*, Vol. 40, No. 1, pp. 105–122.

M. Fenwick, H. De Cieri and D. Welch, 1999. Cultural and Bureaucratic Control in MNEs: the Role of Expatriate Performance Management, *Management International Review*, Vol. 39, Special Issue No. 3, pp. 107–124.

M. Harvey, 1997. Focusing the International Personnel Performance Appraisal Process, *Human Resource Development Quarterly*, Vol. 8, No. 1, pp. 41–62.

Notes and references

1   C.A. Bartlett and S. Ghoshal, Managing Across Borders: New Strategic Requirements, *Sloan Management Review*, Summer (1987) pp. 7–17.

2   V. Pucik, Strategic Human Resource Management in a Multinational Firm, in *Strategic Management of Multinational Corporations: the Essentials*, ed. H.V. Wortzel and L.H. Wortzel, New York: Wiley, 1985, pp. 429–430.

3   J. Garland, R.N. Farmer and M. Taylor, *International Dimensions of Business Policy and Strategy*, 2nd edn. Boston, MD: PWS-KENT, 1990, p. 193.

4   Pucik, Ref. 2, p. 430.

5   M. Fenwick, H. De Cieri and D. Welch, Cultural and Bureaucratic Control in MNEs: the Role of Expatriate Performance Management, *Management International Review*, Vol. 39, Special Issue No. 3 (1999) pp. 107–124.

6   M. Tahvanainen, *Expatriate Performance Management*, Helsinki: Helsinki School of Economics Press, 1998.

7   R. Hays, Expatriate Selection: Insuring Success and Avoiding Failure, *Journal of International Business Studies*, Vol. 5, No. 1 (1974) pp. 25–37. Tung appears to have based her initial studies on these categories [see R. Tung, Selection and Training of Personnel for Overseas Assignments, *Columbia Journal of World Business*, Vol. 16, No. 1 (1981) pp. 68–78].

8   H. Mintzberg, *The Nature of Managerial Work*, Englewood Cliffs, NJ: Prentice-Hall, 1973, p.54.

9   J.S. Black and L.W. Porter, Managerial Behaviours and Job Performance: a Successful Manager in Los Angeles May Not Succeed in Hong Kong, *Journal of International Business Studies*, Vol. 22, No. 1 (1991) pp. 99–113.

10 I. Torbiörn, The Structure of Managerial Roles in Cross-cultural Settings, *International Studies of Management and Organization*, Vol. 15, No. 1 (1985) pp. 52–74.

11 M. Janssens, Evaluating International Managers' Performance: Parent Company Standards as Control Mechanism, *International Journal of Human Resource Management*, Vol. 5, No. 4 (1994) pp. 853–573.

12 H.B. Gregersen and J.S. Black, A Multifaceted Approach to Expatriate Retention in International Assignments, *Group and Organization Studies*, Vol. 15, No. 4 (1990) p. 478.

13 M.G. Birdseye and J.S. Hill, Individual, Organization/Work and Environmental Influences on Expatriate Turnover Tendencies: an Empirical Study, *Journal of International Business Studies*, Vol. 26, No. 4 (1995) p. 800.

14 D.C. Feldman and H.B. Tompson, Expatriation, Repatriation and Domestic Geographical Relocation: an Empirical Investigation of Adjustment to New Job Assignments, *Journal of International Business Studies*, Vol. 24, No. 3 (1993) pp. 507–529.

15 A study of Finnish expatriates working in European contexts reveals interesting examples of culturally close postings and role behavior. One Finnish expatriate posted to nearby Sweden found it difficult to adjust because Swedes were used to more subordinate participation in decision-making than is commonly practiced in Finnish companies. One can assume that Finns posted to Sweden as TCNs would relate similar reactions. See V. Suutari and C. Brewster, The Adaptation of Expatriates in Europe: Evidence from Finnish Companies, paper presented at the 12th Workshop of Strategic Human Resource Management, Turku, March 1997.

16 For example, in one of the few articles on this topic, Chadwick looks at the TCN assignment in general and does not specifically address performance. Rather, the focus is on fair treatment and equity regarding compensation. See W.F. Chadwick, TCN Expatriate Manager Policies, in *Expatriate Management: New Ideas for International Business*, ed. J. Selmer, Westport, CT: Quorum Books, 1995.

17 M. Conway, Reducing Expatriate Failure Rates, *Personnel Administrator*, July (1984) pp. 31–37.

18 H.B. Gregersen, J.M. Hite and J.S. Black, Expatriate Performance Appraisal in U.S. Multinational Firms, *Journal of International Business Studies*, Vol. 27, No. 4 (1996) pp. 711–738.

19 Ref. 6, p. 226.

20 D. Welch and L. Welch, Linking Operation Mode Diversity and IHRM, *International Journal of Human Resource Management*, Vol. 5, No. 4 (1994) pp. 911–926.

21 F. Kahn, Living in Fear of Frequent Flying, *Financial Times*, 3 November (1997) p. 14.

22 The term 'intermittent spouse syndrome' (ISS) has been coined to explain the effect that the rapid and unrelenting cycle of partings and reunions can have on family members.

23 M. Fenwick, On International Assignment: is Expatriation the Only Way to Go?, *Asia Pacific Journal of Human Resources*, in press.

24 D.E. Welch, V. Worm and M. Fenwick, Are Virtual Assignments Feasible?, *Management International Review*, Vol. 43, Special Issue No. 1 (2003) pp. 95–114; D.E. Welch and M. Fenwick, Virtual

Assignments: a New Possibility for IHRM? in *Human Resource Management: Challenges and Future Directions*, ed. R. Wiesner and B. Millett, Brisbane: Wiley Australia, 2003, pp. 279–304.

25 See, for example, M. Armstrong, *Performance Management*, London: Kogan Page, 1994; P. Stiles, L. Gratton, C. Truss, V. Hope-Hailey and P. McGovern, Performance Management and the Psychological Contract, *Human Resource Management Journal*, Vol. 7, No. 1 (1997) pp. 57–66.

26 M. Harvey, Focusing the International Personnel Performance Appraisal Process, *Human Resource Development Quarterly*, Vol. 8, No. 1 (1997) pp. 41–62.

27 R.W. Beatty, Competitive Human Resource Advantages Through the Strategic Management of Performance, *Human Resource Planning*, Vol. 12, No. 3 (1989) pp. 179–194.

28 K.F. Brickley, *Corporate Criminal Liability: a Treatise on the Criminal Liability of Corporations, Their Officers and Agents*, Cumulative Supplement, Deerfield, IL: Clark Boardman Callaghan, 1992. Enacted in 1977, the FCPA addresses the problem of questionable foreign payments by US multinationals and their managers. The act was amended by Congress in 1988 to include substantial increases in the authorized criminal fines for organizations and new civil sanctions for individuals violating the FCPA.

29 E. Naumann, Organizational Predictors of Expatriate Job Satisfaction, *Journal of International Business Studies*, Vol. 24, No. 1 (1993) pp. 61–80.

30 For further details about this technique, see the Special Issue on 360-Degree Feedback, *Human Resource Management*, Vol. 32, Nos 2–3 (1993).

31 Ref. 18, p. 716.

32 It should be remembered that these authors take a traditional performance appraisal approach, rather than utilize the newer performance management literature that we discuss in this chapter. It may be that the goal setting stressed in the performance management literature will assist standardization.

33 M. Fenwick, *Control and Expatriate Performance Management in Australian Multinational Enterprises*, unpublished Doctoral Thesis, University of Melbourne, 2000.

34 J. Milliman, S. Taylor and A. Czaplewski, Cross-cultural Performance Feedback in Multinational Enterprises: Opportunity for Organizational Learning. *Human Resource Planning*, Vol. 25, No. 3 (2002) pp. 29–43.

35 Ref. 34, p. 37.

36 See, for example, N.J. Adler, *International Dimensions of Organizational Behaviour*, 3rd edn, Cincinnati, OH: South Western, 1997; S. Schneider, National vs. Corporate Culture: Implications for Human Resource Management, *Human Resource Management*, Vol. 27 (1988) pp. 231–246; G.P. Latham and N.K. Napier, Chinese Human Resource Management Practices in Hong Kong and Singapore: an Exploratory Study, in *Research in Personnel and Human Resource Management*, Vol. 6, ed. G. Ferris, K. Rowland and A. Nedd, Greenwich, CT: JAI Press, 1989.

37 J.V. Koivisto, Duality and Japanese Management: a Cosmological View of Japanese Business Management, paper presented at the European Institute of Advanced Studies in Management Workshop on Managing in Different Cultures, Group E, ssec, Cergy, France, 23–24 November, 1992.

38 For a complete description of PCI's system, see R.S. Schuler, J.R. Fulkerson and P.J. Dowling, Strategic Performance Measurement and Management in Multinational Corporations, *Human Resource Management*, Vol. 30, No. 3 (1991) pp. 365–392.

39 The performance appraisal of 'inpatriates' is briefly covered in M.G. Harvey and M.R. Buckley, Managing Inpatriates: Building a Global Core Competency, *Journal of World Business*, Vol. 32, No. 1 (1997) pp. 35–52.

40 J. Gerringer, C. Frayne and J. Milliman, In Search of 'Best Practices' in International Human Resource Management: Research Design and Methodology, *Asia Pacific Journal of Human Resources*, Vol. 40, No. 1 (2002) pp. 9–37.

41 J. Milliman, S. Nason, C. Zhu and H. De Cieri, An Exploratory Assessment of the Purposes of Performance Appraisals in North and Central America and the Pacific Rim, *Asia Pacific Journal of Human Resources*, Vol. 40, No. 1 (2002) p. 117.

CHAPTER

IHRM trends and future challenges

11

Chapter objectives

In this final chapter, we identify and comment on observed trends and future directions regarding:

- International business ethics and HRM.
- Mode of operation and IHRM.
- Ownership issues relating to IHRM requirements of organizations other than the large multinational, such as:
  - small- and medium-sized firms (SMEs)
  - family-owned firms
  - non-government organizations (NGOs).
- Theoretical developments and research issues in IHRM.

Introduction

In this book, we have explored the international HRM issues relating to managing people in a multinational context. To that end, we have focused on the implications that the process of internationalization has for the activities and policies of HRM. A major activity has been that of placement: who to place in charge of foreign operations and units to cater for the managerial and technical demands of international business growth. The chapters in Part II examined the various aspects relating to staff placement: managing and supporting international assignments. We also considered in the preceding chapters of Part III host-country issues, such as standardization of work practices, processes and procedures and the implications for human resource management. In this way, we tried to counter the imbalance towards expatriate issues, while recognizing the continued need to manage effectively international assignments owing to the important strategic roles of expatriates and non-expatriates in sustaining international operations. Throughout the preceding chapters, we also identified the HR implications of some of the managerial responses to the changing global work environment, particularly developing the required global mindset to accompany global operations, the use of informal control mechanisms, horizontal communication, cross-border teams and international assignments. We now turn our attention to developments that have not previously been emphasized in the general IHRM literature and the challenges that they present to IHRM: international business ethics, mode of operation, SMEs and family-owned firms and NGOs. The chapter concludes with a short discussion of theoretical developments and research issues in the field of IHRM.

International business ethics and HRM*

When business is conducted across national and cultural borders, the operationalization of an enterprise's ethics program takes on added layers of complexity. In particular, questions about the existence of universal ethical standards and global values are raised. This is especially problematic when multinationals operate in host countries that have different standards of business practice, are economically impoverished, whose legal infrastructure is inadequate, whose governments are corrupt and where human rights are habitually violated.[1] The question of ethical relativity arises not only in the context of different home- and host-country employment practices but also in the central operations and policies of multinationals. In this section we overview developments in four important areas of international business ethics and the challenges they raise for HR professionals: global values, international corporate codes of conduct, the criminalization of bribery and the emerging role of HR in operationalizing corporate ethics programs.

Ethical relativism or global values?

Global organizations face a challenge: should they apply their own values everywhere they do business, irrespective of the cultural context and standard of local practices? To appreciate the dilemma, take the situation of a multinational that has assigned a PCN to manage its operations in a host country where bribery is commonly practiced, child labor is used and workplace safety is wanting. Whose standards should prevail? – those of the multinational's parent country or the host country? There are three main responses to this question. The first involves ethical relativism, the second ethical absolutism and the third ethical universalism.

For the *ethical relativist*, there are no universal or international rights and wrongs, it all depends on a particular culture's values and beliefs. Thus if the people of Indonesia tolerate the bribery of their public officials, this is morally no better or worse than the people of Singapore or Denmark who refuse to accept bribery. For the ethical relativist, when in Rome, one should do as the Romans do. While ethical relativism may be appealing to those who fear cultural imperialism, it is a logically and ethically incoherent theory.[2]

Unlike the relativist, the *ethical absolutist* (or imperialist) believes that when in Rome, one should do what one would do at home, regardless of what the Romans do. This view of ethics gives primacy to one's own cultural values. Opponents of this view argue that ethical absolutists are intolerant individuals who confuse

---

* The contribution of Lorraine Carey (University of Canberra) to this section is gratefully acknowledged.

respect for local traditions with ethical relativism. It must be noted that while some behaviors are wrong wherever they are practiced (e.g. bribery of government officials), other behaviors may be tolerated in their cultural context (e.g. the practice of routine gift giving between Japanese business people). When PCNs discover too late that the political–legal environment in which their home-country policies were formulated is significantly different from that of the host countries in which they operate, the results can be extreme. Kelly[3] cites an example of a US expatriate bank manager in Italy who was appalled by the local branch's recommendation to under-report grossly the bank's profits for income tax purposes and insisted the bank's earnings be reported in the same way as they would in the USA – accurately. Later at the bank's tax hearing, he was told by the Italian Taxation Department that the bank owed three times as much tax as it had paid. This reflected the Italian Taxation Department's standard assumption that all firms under-report their earnings by two-thirds. The new assessment stood despite the expatriate's protests.

In contrast to the ethical relativist, the *ethical universalist* believes there are fundamental principles of right and wrong which transcend cultural boundaries and that multinationals must adhere to these fundamental principles or global values. However, unlike the absolutist, the universalist is careful to distinguish between practices that are simply culturally different and those that are morally wrong. But what are these shared global ethical values and principles?

Studies have identified honesty, compassion, responsibility, freedom, respect for life and nature, fairness, tolerance and unity (family or community) as core global values to which people subscribe irrespective of race, culture, gender or religion.[4,5] The challenge for business lies in how to incorporate them as core business values and, having done so, how to align staff to these values. For example, the value of respect might include valuing differences (gender, sexual orientation, race, religion, etc.), sexual harassment prevention and understanding stereotypes as well as workplace safety, product safety and environmental protection. The challenge for managers operating in diverse cultural environments is that different cultures will prioritize core ethical values differently and will translate values into specific behaviors differently. This is the main reason why cultures clash and is the essence of a true ethical dilemma. For example, in the USA, freedom is regarded as the most important global value whereas in Asia, family or community unity is selected as the most important value. Europe, representing a range of cultures, includes fairness, honesty and responsibility along with freedom and unity as top ethical values.

The existence of universal ethical principles can also be seen in the agreements that exist among nations who are signatories to the United Nations Declaration of Human Rights and a number of international accords such as the *Guidelines for Multinational Enterprises* adopted by the Organization of Economic Cooperation and Development (OECD) and the *Caux Roundtable Principles of Business*. Frederick discusses the moral authority of transnational codes and suggests that they indicate the emergence of a transcultural corporate ethic and provide guidelines that have direct applicability to a number of the central operations and policies of multinationals including the HRM activities of staffing, compensation, employee training and occupational health and safety.[6] However, the claim that there are global values and universal principles that should be followed in international business is not inconsistent with the view that there are a wide range of situations where variations in business practice are permissible. Donaldson and Dunfee refer to *moral free space* in a world of universal moral norms.[5]

Self-regulation initiatives: international corporate codes of conduct

The need for international accords and corporate codes of conduct has grown commensurately with the spread of international business. We touched on some of this in Chapter 8 in the section on managing subcontractors, multinational attempts to tackle hiring practices, health and safety issues and appropriate behavior through adherence to codes of conduct. However, translating ethical principles and values into practice in the international business domain, even allowing for some consensus within the international community, is an enormous task in the absence of a supranational legislative authority. As noted above, a number of mechanisms to facilitate the incorporation of ethical values into international business behavior have been suggested. Predictably, these have centered on regulation, both self-imposed and government decreed, the development of international accords and the use of education and training programmes.

One of the most interesting initiatives in international business self-regulation is the *Caux Roundtable Principles for Business Conduct* developed in 1994 by Japanese, European and North American business leaders meeting in Caux, Switzerland.[7] This was the first international ethics code for business and aimed to set a global benchmark against which individual firms could write their own codes and measure the behavior of their executives. The Caux Principles are grounded in two basic ethical ideals: *kyosei* and human dignity. The preamble to the Caux Principles states that:

> The Japanese concept of *kyosei* means living and working together for the
> common good – enabling cooperation and mutual prosperity to co-exist
> with healthy and fair competition. Human dignity relates to the sacredness
> or value of each person as an end, not simply as the means to the
> fulfillment of others' purposes or even majority prescription.

The Caux Principles aim to operationalize the twin values of living and working together and human dignity by promoting free trade, environmental and cultural integrity and the prevention of bribery and corruption. The general principles clarifying the spirit of *kyosei* and human dignity are presented in Section 2 of the document while the specific stakeholder principles in Section 3 are concerned with their practical application. The Principles have their origin in the Minnesota principles developed by the Minnesota Center for Corporate Responsibility in the USA. Following their adoption in 1994, worldwide endorsements have been sought and given.

The need for comprehensive and cohesive codes of conduct for multinationals and smaller firms involved in international business is widely recognized as an important issue.[8] Studies in the USA, UK, Canada and Australia consistently report that 80–95 per cent of companies have codes of conduct.[9–13] A good example of a multinational's corporate code of conduct which is cohesive and comprehensive in recognizing relationships between the company and its many stakeholders is Johnson and Johnson's Credo, which in part states:[14]

> We are responsible to our employees, the men and women who work with
> us throughout the world. Everyone must be considered as an individual.
> We must respect their dignity and recognize their merit. They must have
> a sense of security in their jobs. Compensation must be fair and adequate,
> and working conditions clean, orderly and safe. We must be mindful of
> ways to help our employees fulfill their family responsibilities. Employees

must feel free to make suggestions and complaints. There must be equal opportunity for employment, development and advancement for those qualified. We must provide competent management, and their actions must be just and ethical. We are responsible to the communities in which we will live and work and to the world community as well. We must be good citizens – support good works and charities and bear our fair share of taxes. We must encourage civic improvements and better health and education. We must maintain in good order the property we are privileged to use, protecting the environment and natural resources.

In addressing the core human values of good citizenship, respect for human dignity, respect for basic rights and justice and using them to define ethical behavior, Johnson and Johnson's Credo meets the standards of the Caux Principles, the UN's declaration of fundamental human rights and the OECD *Guidelines for Multinational Enterprises*.

A common difficulty with codes of ethics is enforcement. The attitudes of senior management play a crucial role in developing, implementing and sustaining high ethical standards. HR professionals can help multinationals to institutionalize adherence to ethics codes through a range of HR activities including training and the performance–reward system. The research on corporate ethics programs shows that while most large enterprises have corporate codes of conduct, training in and enforcement of the codes are problematic. For example, a 2000 study of the operationalization of ethics in Australian enterprises reports that while 92 per cent of enterprises had corporate codes of conduct, 66 per cent provided training in those codes, 53 per cent included ethics compliance in their formal performance management programs and 16 per cent included ethics compliance in their formal reward systems.[13] The US, UK and Canadian studies report similar findings. If self-regulatory mechanisms fail to shape the level of socially responsible behavior required of multinationals by society, then firms can expect legislative measures will be called for to resolve conflicts between themselves and host and home countries. Such is the case with bribery.

Government regulation: new global developments on the criminalization of bribery

Bribery and corruption top the list of the most frequent ethical problems encountered by international managers.[15] The World Bank estimates that about US $80 billion annually goes to corrupt government officials.[16] Macken[17] uses the following comment by a manager from the Australian multinational, BHP-Billiton, to illustrate the business reality for firms that have a policy of not accepting bribery:

Other companies were moving ahead in leaps and bounds. It took about 18 months for everyone to realise we were not going to buckle, then things started moving ahead. But very few companies can afford to tough it out for that long.

Bribery involves the payment of agents to do things that are inconsistent with the purpose of their position or office in order to gain an unfair advantage. Bribery can be distinguished from so-called gifts and 'facilitating' or 'grease' payments. The latter are payments to motivate agents to complete a task they would routinely do in the normal course of their duties. While most people do not openly condone bribery, many argue for a lenient approach based on the view that bribery is necessary to do business (the ethical relativist's argument). However, it is now generally agreed that bribery undermines equity, efficiency and integrity in the public service, undercuts public confidence in markets and aid programs, adds to the cost of products and may affect the safety and economic well-being of the general public.

For these reasons, there has been an internationally wide movement to criminalize the practice of bribery. In 1977, the USA enacted the *Foreign Corrupt Practices Act* (FCPA) to prohibit US-based firms and US nationals from making bribery payments to foreign government officials. In addition, payments to agents violate the Act if it is known that the agent will use those payments to bribe a government official. The Act was amended in 1988 to permit 'facilitating' payments but mandates record-keeping provisions to help ensure that illegal payments are not disguised as entertainment or business expenses. The FCPA was criticized for placing US firms at a competitive disadvantage since European and Asian firms did not face criminal prosecution for paying bribes to foreign officials.[18] However, the evidence on the competitive disadvantage of the FCPA is mixed. The FCPA was also criticized by some for being ethnocentric while others saw it as moral leadership on the part of the USA.[19]

In the absence of adequate international self-regulation to control bribery and corruption, the USA lobbied other nation states for almost two decades to enact uniform domestic government regulation to provide a level playing field. Finally, in December 1996, the UN adopted the United Nations *Declaration Against Corruption and Bribery in International Commercial Transactions*, which committed UN members to criminalize bribery and deny tax deductibility for bribes. A year later the Declaration was endorsed by 30 member nations and four non-member nations of the OECD adopting the *Convention on Combating Bribery of Foreign Public Officials in International Business Transactions (OECD Convention)*. Under the *OECD Convention*, members agreed to establish domestic legislation by the end of 1998 criminalizing the bribing of foreign public officials on an extraterritorial basis. The *OECD Convention* came into force in February 1999 and by mid-2002 it had been ratified by 34 of the 35 signatory countries. Each member state is required to undergo a peer review and to provide a report reviewing its implementation of the Convention. Country reports are available on the OECD website.[20] Some non-OECD countries have also moved to curtail bribery and corruption. For example, in Malaysia and Singapore, several foreign firms caught bribing public officials have been declared ineligible to bid on future government contracts. The *OECD Convention* requires sanctions to be commensurate with domestic penalties applicable to bribery of public officials. Under the FCPA corporate fines can be up to US$2 million and individual penalties up to US$100 000 and 5 years' imprisonment.

Given the seriousness of offences against the *OECD Convention*, it is imperative that enterprises involved in global business take active steps to manage their potential exposure. Also, although the OECD Convention currently addresses the supply side of corruption in the public sector, it is likely that the ambit of the Convention will be expanded to include bribery in the private sector in addition to the demand side of bribery. HR professionals have an important role to play in instituting a strategic plan for legal compliance and developing corporate codes for voluntary compliance. They can provide training in understanding the difference between corrupt bribery payments, gifts and allowable facilitation payments and developing negotiation skills to handle problem situations that may arise in sensitive geographical regions and industries. As noted above, they can also implement performance management programs to support efforts to reduce corruption.

	World corruption index		**Table 11-1**

Top 10 most corrupt countries	Corruption Perceptions Index score[a]	Top 10 least corrupt countries	Corruption Perceptions Index score[a]
Bangladesh	1.2	Finland	9.7
Nigeria	1.6	Denmark	9.5
Paraguay	1.7	New Zealand	9.5
Madagascar	1.7	Iceland	9.4
Angola	1.7	Singapore	9.3
Kenya	1.9	Sweden	9.3
Indonesia	1.9	Canada	9.0
Azerbaijan	2.0	The Netherlands	9.0
Uganda	2.1	Luxembourg	9.0
Moldova	2.1	UK	8.7

[a]The **CPI 2002** score relates to perceptions of the degree of corruption as seen by business people and risk analysts, and ranges between 10 (highly clean) and 0 (highly corrupt).
Source: Adapted from the Transparency International Corruption Perceptions Index 2002[22] (www.transparency.org).

The debate over payment to foreign officials is likely to continue for many years to come. The Berlin-based non-government lobby group Transparency International (TI) publishes an annual Corruption Perceptions Index. The index measures perceptions, not actual levels of corruption, for over 50 countries and is based on international surveys of business people and financial journalists. The ranking is scored from 0 (most corrupt) to 10 (least corrupt). Table 11-1 shows the 10 most corrupt and 10 least corrupt countries in descending order from the 2002 index. Finland and Denmark are the top two least corrupt countries and Nigeria and Bangladesh are ranked 101 and 102 on the list. Although not included in the Table, data for the USA show that it is listed in 16th position in 2002 on the list of least corrupt countries.[21]

The emerging role of HR in operationalizing corporate ethics programs

Recently there has been discussion in the ethics literature about the HR function taking on the role of ethical stewardship, with some writers suggesting that HR has a special role to play in the formulation, communication, monitoring and enforcement of an enterprise's ethics program. The US-based business ethics literature generally presents the view that the HR function along with finance and law is the appropriate locus of responsibility for an enterprise's ethics program.[23]

Empirical studies have begun to investigate whether ethics initiatives and strategies for ethics management should be HR driven. The 2003 SHRM/ERC[24] survey found that 71 per cent of HR professionals are involved in formulating ethics policies for their enterprises and 69 per cent are a primary resource for their enterprise's ethics initiative. However, the SHRM respondents did not regard ethics as the sole responsibility of HR. When asked to indicate the degree to which they thought other units or positions should be responsible for ethical leadership, 96 per cent of HR professionals said the Chief Executive Officer (CEO), 93 per cent functional Vice-Presidents, 90 per cent immediate supervisors, 77 per cent the Board of Directors and 65 per cent legal counsel. An Australian study on the operationalization of ethics in enterprises reports similar findings with almost 70 per cent of respondents reporting that the degree to which HR is currently responsible for the formulation of corporate ethics programmes is either 'a large amount' (38.4 per cent) or 'quite a lot' (31.3 per cent).[13]

A Canadian survey of CEOs provides some support for the US and Australian findings.[25] When asked which functional areas should have responsibility for the administration of corporate codes of conduct, 37 per cent of CEOs answered HR, 19 per cent law and 9 per cent senior management. In assigning responsibility for revising corporate codes of conduct, 40 per cent cited HR, 31 per cent law and 10 per cent the company Director or President. However, Robertson and Schlegelmilch[10] report that enterprises in the UK are more likely to communicate ethics policies through senior executives than HR departments. Their results show that the CEO and Managing Director have 'primary responsibility' for communicating ethics policies and codes in 69 per cent of the UK enterprises and 42 per cent of the US enterprises. This compares with the HR function which had 'primary responsibility' for communicating ethics policies in 15.7 per cent of the UK enterprises and 33.2 per cent of the US enterprises.

Taken together, these empirical findings recognize that HR is well positioned to make an important contribution to creating, implementing and sustaining ethical organizational behavior within a strategic HR paradigm. HR professionals have specialized expertise in the areas of organizational culture, communication, training, performance management, leadership, motivation, group dynamics, organizational structure and change management – all of which are key factors for integrating responsibility for ethics into all aspects of organizational life. At the same time, the findings suggest that responsibility for ethical leadership should cut across all functions and managerial levels, including line and senior managers.

Challenges for the HR function of the multinational firm

Although people involved in international business activities face many of the same ethical issues as those in domestic business, the issues are made more complex because of the different social, economic, political, cultural and legal environments in which multinationals operate. Consequently, multinationals will need to develop self-regulatory practices via codes of ethics and behavioral guidelines for expatriate, TCN and local HCN staff. Firms which opt consciously or by default to leave ethical considerations up to the individual not only contribute to the pressures of operating in a foreign environment (and perhaps contribute to poor performance or early recall of the expatriate), but also allow internal inconsistencies that affect total global performance.

When recruiting and selecting expatriates, their ability to manage with integrity could be a job-relevant criterion. The pre-departure training of expatriates and their orientation program should include an ethics component. This might include formal studies in ethical theory and decision making as well as interactive discussion and role playing around dilemmas which expatriates are likely to encounter. In an effort to sensitize managers to cultural diversity and to accept the point that home practices are not necessarily the best or only practices, there has been an emphasis in international business training on adapting to the way in which other cultures do business. Insufficient attention is generally given to when doing so results in unacceptable ethical compromises. In designing training programs to meet the challenges of multinational business, HR professionals must raise not only the issue of cultural relativities but also the extent to which moral imperatives transcend national and cultural boundaries.

It is also important for the HR department to monitor the social (ethical) performance of its expatriate managers to ensure that as managers become familiar with the customs and practices of competition in the host country, they do not backslide into the rationalization that 'everybody else does it'. To avoid the temptation to cut 'ethical corners', expatriates must not be placed under unreasonable pressure to deliver good financial results and they must be given feedback and reinforcement. Performance appraisals, compensation programs and regular trips home are important instruments in developing and maintaining ethical cultures. The HR department must also offer ongoing support to expatriates throughout their assignment. This is made relatively easier via technologies such as e-mail and video conferencing. One can envisage that an expatriate faced with a moral dilemma might have ready access to mentors at home or expatriates in other countries via these technologies.

The development of a truly international community is still in its infancy and there is not yet agreement about what should constitute a global ethic to resolve the conflicts which arise in such a community. However, there is an emerging consensus about core human values which underlie cultural and national differences and the content of guidelines and codes which help to operationalize the ethical responsibilities of multinationals. Those involved in the management of HR would do well to consider these issues when developing organizational strategies and selecting, training and developing expatriates. The complex world of multinational business demands no less.

Mode of operation and IHRM

We have stressed the need to broaden the scope of IHRM beyond that of subsidiary operations. Although not downplaying their importance, for many multinationals managing and staffing subsidiary units are only one aspect of international business operations, although the weighting given to subsidiary management will vary according to the nature of international activities and the size of the internationalizing firm. As mentioned in Chapter 2, some multinationals will combine different operation methods, including subsidiary operations, to exploit specific foreign market opportunities, while others may operate through a single contractual mode such as licensing and management contracting. Different HRM issues may come to the fore with different operation modes – compared with subsidiary operations. The fact that external parties are involved in contractual modes, joint ventures and strategic alliances imposes management and HR constraints that are not usually present in wholly owned operations.

Relatively speaking, the IHRM implications of international joint ventures have received considerable attention, but there remains a need for studies that consider the HR implications of contractual modes where the firm is operating at arm's length. Training, for instance, is often an important part of contractual modes, playing a key role in the transfer of technology and systems, inculcation of company

culture and acting as a screening process (for example, in selecting suitable franchisees). As a result, staff may be primarily involved in short-term assignments to
deliver training in foreign locations, rather than as traditional expatriates.

Firms engaged in international projects will not only utilize a variety of forms of
international assignments but will also need employees who can deal with multi-
lateral partners. For example, projects funded by the World Bank in conjunction
with a host-government agency raise HR issues that are not necessarily faced in
subsidiary operations, such as working with a multinational team whose members
come from various organizations with different skill levels and methods of working.
These types of projects are often in physically remote and challenging locations,
thus placing demands on risk management. For example, between 1998 and 2002,
74 per cent of reported kidnapping cases occurred in Latin America, compared
with 14 per cent in Asia-Pacific, 7 per cent in Europe and the former Soviet Union
and 3.5 per cent in Africa and the Middle East. The largest at-risk group are business
people (project workers, engineers and operatives and highly paid business executives) and their dependants.[26]

We mentioned in Chapter 8 some of the issues facing multinationals using
subcontractors in developing markets to manufacture their goods. We also
highlighted some of the HR implications of using management contracts. In fact, it
could be suggested that multinationals will be required to increase the range of
modes used to maintain and develop foreign markets in the future. The demands
thus created are likely to require a greater diversity of HR responses. To play a more
strategic role, corporate HR staff will need to have knowledge of the modes and
their HR implications in order to provide pertinent input to top management
decisions regarding different mode options. HR staff will need to become more
adept at dealing with 'foreign partners' who are not employees of the multinational.
For example, it may require training staff at varying levels and in various functions
and locations to deal with foreign licensees and franchisees.

Ownership issues

As mentioned previously, international firms vary in size, ownership structure, level
of international experience and geographical spread. However, the activities of large,
publicly owned multinationals and transnationals dominate the international business management and IHRM literature, reflected in the concentration on subsidiary
issues. Despite the paucity of empirical studies upon which to draw, however, it is
possible to outline briefly some features of SMEs and family firms that differentiate
these from larger multinationals, and to make some reference to the growing importance in terms of international business of non-government organizations.

Small and medium-sized firms (SMEs)

For manufacturing firms, exporting is often the important first step in internationalization, and this is recognized by governments through a range of measures, such
as export grouping schemes,[27] to encourage and assist SMEs to become internationally oriented. According to a *Far Eastern Economic Review* article,[28] SMEs are
expected to become the 'mainstay of South Korea's economy, replacing the long-
dominant, family-run conglomerates known as *chaebols* whose reckless borrowing
and poor management are largely blamed for the country's 1997 financial crisis'.

In the mid-1980s, South Korean SMEs were responsible for less than 30 per cent of the country's total exports. By 2002, they accounted for 42 per cent.

In Western countries such as the USA and Australia, a growing proportion of SMEs are owned and managed by females. This trend has been attributed to frustration with lack of career progression within larger firms (the glass ceiling) and the freedom that comes with managing one's own business. Many of these SMEs are involved in international business.

What emerges from entrepreneurship and small business management literature is the stress that international activity places on SME management. Resources become stretched, particularly staff. To sustain effective exporting, international travel to foreign markets to monitor agents and distributors, for example, can place particular demands on the Managing Director in addition to those directly responsible for international marketing. In very small firms, the Managing Director often is also the export manager. These key individuals develop the necessary knowledge and skills, thus representing the SME's stock of international competence. Little is known about the way in which IHRM expertise is developed at this stage, as we discussed in Chapter 2.[29] This is a challenge for academics and managers as the issues relating to international business travelers and forms of non-standard assignments appear particularly relevant to SMEs.

Family-owned firms

Often, family-owned firms are treated as a sub-set of SMEs. However, large multinationals can be family owned, although the definition of what constitutes family ownership varies across countries. Firms that later become publicly owned have retained members of the founding family as major stockholders. For example, families are said to wield influence at between 35 and 45 per cent of US Fortune 500 listed firms (depending on how influence is defined).[30] The Ford family in the management of the US automobile company Ford Motor Company and members of the Packard family during the merger of the US firms Hewlett-Packard and Compaq are recent illustrations where family concerns have received wide media coverage in the context of international business decision-making.

The bulk of the world's firms are family owned. For instance, the *Mittelstand*, or small, owner-run firms constitute the mass of German businesses.[31] According to an international survey of family firms,[32] 40 per cent cease to exist within the first 5 years. About 66 per cent of those who survive that critical period will either 'die' or have control pass out of the hands of the founding family within the first generation. Only 17 per cent of those still left will survive up to the third generation of the founding family.

A factor that may contribute to the demise, or take-over, of a family firm is the way in which management succession is handled. Replacing top management is often seen as a challenge, but handing over the 'reins of the business' can be fraught with conflict and turmoil when family businesses are involved. HR planning takes on a different dimension in the context of family-owned firms and gives rise to much speculation in high profile multinationals such as Michelin (French tyre company), Ikea (Swedish furniture manufacturer), Hyundai (Korean automobile firm), Aldi (German supermarket chain) and News Limited (Murdock's media group, including the London *Times*, New York *Times*, Sky Channel and Fox).

Another aspect is the way in which the internationalization process is handled within family-owned firms. There has been a suggestion that Asian family firms try to keep as much control as possible within the immediate or at least the extended family. As mentioned in Chapter 2, at some stage, international growth means that the firm will not be able to staff key positions with family members and the challenge then is to find and develop suitable employees, thus confronting the staffing concerns we addressed in Chapter 3. A study by Yeung[33] of three Chinese family-owned Hong Kong firms' internationalization found that these firms were able to meet the challenges of growth while still preserving their family management and structure, although control through socialization was used when non-family managers were placed in key positions. As Yeung points out, the globalization of family firms has been a remote topic in international business studies.

Non-government organizations (NGOs)

The desirability of globalization of trade and business has provoked a vigorous debate within national states, and often is expressed in anti-globalization rallies and protests. The activities of environmental groups such as Greenpeace highlight how these have also become internationalized. They tend to have national 'managers' in various countries, and variations of structural forms for coordination and accountability. Aid agencies such as the Red Cross, the Red Crescent, World Vision and Médecins Sans Frontières (Doctors without Borders) are international organizations that could be classified as non-profit multinationals. They may utilize different organizational structures and have members who may internalize to a greater degree the shared values and beliefs, owing to the nature of the organization's mission and activities, than may be found in a for-profit multinational. Nonetheless, in terms of global control and operations, there would be similar managerial concerns to those of, for instance, oil companies. Physical risk – such as the danger of staff being taken hostage and of having property damaged – is common to firms operating in hostile contexts.

However, as Fenwick[34] identifies, non-profit organizations have been ignored in strategic IHRM (SIHRM) research, arguing:

> It seems that SIHRM has not addressed the non-profit context because, despite its ideals of valuing human resources and commitment, it [SIHRM] reflects the traditional management ethos of effectiveness and efficiency rather than the non-profit ethos of values-driven, charitable and philanthropic ideals.

It would seem that the broadening of focus of the human resource implications from the current focus on foreign direct investment and large for-profit multinationals is imperative as the trends identified above are more than likely to continue well into the 21st century. Contractual modes of international business operation, SMEs and family-owned firms and NGOs are just three areas where IHRM issues remain to be fully explored.

Research issues and theoretical developments

The field of IHRM has been slow to develop a rigorous body of theory. There are three major reasons for this:

- Many management and HRM researchers have regarded the IHRM field as a marginal academic area. This attitude was reflected in the relatively small number of stand-alone courses in IHRM on the teaching side. Likewise, IHRM has a marginal position in the wider international business community.

The dominance of economics in the international business field to date, with its focus on foreign direct investment, has been a contributing factor. Recent developments, such as dedicated journals (e.g. *International Journal of Human Resource Management*) have raised the profile of the field. Overall, there is an emphasis on comparative HR and industrial relations, rather than IHRM in the multinational context.

- International studies are invariably more expensive than domestic studies. International research takes more time, involves more travel and frequently requires the cooperation of host-country organizations, government officials and researchers. Developing a stream of research is consequently much more difficult. An example, though, of how academics can overcome some of these difficulties is the 'best practice' country/regional study and analysis of 10 countries approaches to HRM, involving a diverse team of academics from various countries.[35]

- There are major methodological problems involved in the area of international management and IHRM. These problems greatly increase the complexity of doing international research and, as Adler[36] noted, frequently are impossible to solve with the rigor usually required of within-culture studies by journal editors and reviewers. The major methodological problems in this area are:

  - *Defining culture and the emic–etic distinction.* The problems of defining culture and the emic–etic distinction were discussed in Chapter 1.

  - *Static group comparisons.* An enduring issue in international research is that virtually all cross-cultural comparisons are based on 'static group designs'.[37–39] The difficulty with static group comparisons in international research is that subjects are not randomly assigned from a superordinate population to different levels of a treatment variable. In practice, it is impossible for cross-cultural researchers to avoid this methodological problem. This difficulty is further compounded by ill-defined notions of culture as an independent variable. As Malpass[39] has observed:

    > No matter what attribute of culture the investigator prefers to focus upon or to interpret as the causative variable, any other variable correlated with the alleged causative variable could potentially serve in an alternative explanation of a mean difference between two or more local populations.

    As a practical solution to this problem, Malpass recommends that investigators should attempt to obtain data on as many rival explanations as possible and then demonstrate that they are less plausible (by conducting *post hoc* statistical analyses, for example) than the investigator's favoured interpretation.[40]

  - *Translation and stimulus equivalence.* Researchers need to be aware that problems may arise when translating concepts central to one culture into the language of another culture. Triandis and Brislin[41] consider that translation problems should be a starting point for research, rather than a data collection frustration. The decentering technique – translating from the original to the target language and back again through several iterations – is advocated. This technique allows the researcher to test if there is any emic colouring of the concepts under investigation. A related point is that non-native speakers need to translate research findings into English for publication in English-language journals. Techniques such as decentering are important, particularly when dealing with qualitative data.

Theoretical developments

Over the past two decades, various researchers in the IRHM field have been developing a theoretical body of knowledge to provide the necessary robust frameworks and models pertaining to a more mature scientific field of inquiry. Many of these developments have been incorporated into the relevant chapters of this book where appropriate. Reviewing these theoretical contributions, it is possible to identify two streams of inquiry:

● The micro-level – concentrating on expatriation management issues. Early work in the IHRM field was dominated by large-scale quantitative studies by US researchers on expatriate management issues in US multinationals. These had a common approach in using HR managers as the respondents. The various studies by Tung, Black, Oddou, Mendenhall and Gregersen (reviewed in various chapters in Part II) are good examples of such contributions. These studies have been important in that the empirical findings identified key issues and challenges in the use of expatriates in staffing subsidiary operations. More significantly, these researchers raised the profile of IHRM as an area of scientific inquiry.

● The macro level. Surveying HR managers is a logical and useful contribution to research and theory building, but it has been inevitable that IHRM, as a scientific field, would need to consider other IHRM phenomena than expatriation management activities. As Bonachi et al.[42] point out, most studies in the expatriate literature have failed to analyse the relationship between expatriation policies and multinational strategies. Some researchers are endeavoring to address this shortcoming through a line of research termed strategic international human resource management (SIHRM). It considers the HRM issues and activities that result from, and impact upon, the strategic activities and international concerns of multinationals.[43,44] This line of inquiry parallels that of strategic HRM, which focuses the link between organizational strategy and performance and HRM.

Both streams of research are appropriate and critical to theory development. Further, it has been desirable for research to move beyond description and to broaden methodological approaches to include both inductive and deductive research. Researchers are endeavoring to overcome some of the methodological issues through collaborative work. For example, different cultures have different attitudes towards mail questionnaires that may influence a poor response rate. Harzing[45] found that the higher the cultural distance between the country of the researcher (the sender) and the target country (the receiver), the lower is the response rate. She admits that using English as the language of the questionnaire was probably a contributing factor and speculates that the international orientation of the respondent may have a positive influence on the response rate. A team of researchers from various countries – as with the Best Practice study referred to above – can assist in overcoming some of the problems inherent in mail questionnaire-based methods of data collection.

Contributions from qualitative research are valuable in analysing the process of internationalization, particularly longitudinal studies that explore connections between the internationalization process and determinants of IHRM policies and practices. Utilizing research methods that allow HR managers' perspectives to be supported by others such as expatriates and partners, in addition to archival material and documentation, has yielded additional insights into IHRM activities and issues and a consideration of broader organizational factors.

An example of a theoretical framework that has been derived from a strategic approach using a multiple methodological approach is that of De Cieri and Dowling. These authors argue that, while SIHRM as a distinct area of research has been a useful step, it may be more appropriate to speak of strategic HRM in multinationals. The framework is depicted in Figure 11-1.

Multinationals operate in the context of worldwide conditions, including the external contexts of industry, nation, region and inter-organizational networks and alliances, as shown in Figure 11-1. For example, the removal of internal trade barriers and integration of national markets in the European Union brought a new range of inter-organizational relationships. As we have previously mentioned in the context of performance management, external factors exert direct influence on internal organizational factors, SHRM strategy and practices and multinational concerns and goals.

The internal organizational factors are shown in order of most 'tangible' to most 'intangible'. MNE structure refers to both the structure of international operations, intra-organizational networks and mechanisms of coordination, such as those outlined in Chapter 2. The life cycle stage of the firm and the industry in which it operates are important influences for SHRM in multinationals, as are the various international modes of operation discussed earlier and levels of firm strategy. The most intangible organizational factors are experience in international business and headquarters international orientation. Following developments in the literature, such as that of Taylor *et al.*,[46] who take an integration of resource

---

A model of strategic HRM in multinational enterprises | **Figure 11-1**

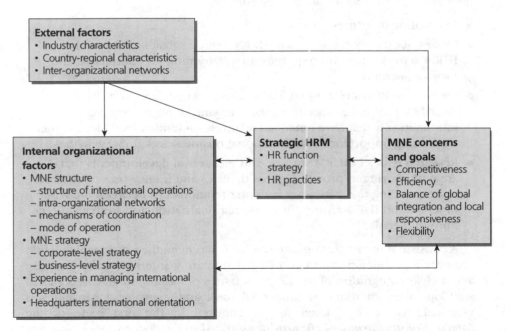

Source: Adapted from H. De Cieri and P.J. Dowling, Strategic Human Resource Management in Multinational Enterprises: Theoretical and Empirical Developments, in P.M. Wright *et al.* (eds), *Research in Personnel and Human Resource Management: Strategic Human Resources in the 21st Century*, Supplement 4, ed. P.M. Wright *et al.*, Stamford, CT: JAI Press, 1999.

dependence and resource-based perspective, the model suggests that there are reciprocal relationships between organizational factors, SHRM and multinational concerns and goals.

With regard to HR strategy and practices, reciprocal relationships between strategic issues and SHRM strategy and practices have been highlighted by research taking a resource-based perspective.[46,47] In addition, several studies have shown that HR activities such as expatriate management are influenced by both external and internal factors.[44,48] Effective SHRM is expected to assist the firm in achieving its goals and objectives. This view is influenced by the emerging body of SHRM literature that examines the relationships between endogenous characteristics, SHRM strategy and practices and firm performance or competitive advantage.[49] While some research has suggested that multinationals will gain by utilizing and integrating appropriate SHRM strategy and practices, to enhance firm performance,[50] the evidence is inconclusive and important questions remain about the nature of this relationship.[51] The model offered by De Cieri and Dowling aims to assist in the cross-fertilization of ideas to further develop theory and empirical research in strategic HRM in multinational firms.

Summary and concluding remarks

Throughout this book, we have endeavored to highlight the challenges faced by firms as they confront human resource management concerns related to international business operations. This chapter has been concerned with identified trends and future challenges – both managerial and academic – that are likely to have an impact on IHRM, as a function and as a scientific field of study. We specifically addressed:

- International business ethics and HRM.

- Modes of operation other than wholly owned subsidiaries, and the IHRM activities that are required, such as training for contractual and project operations.

- Ownership issues relating to SMEs, family-owned firms and NGOs and the IHRM challenges specific to these organizations as they grow internationally that have remained relatively underidentified, despite their continuing importance in international business and global activities.

- Research issues in IHRM studies, and theoretical developments that are endeavoring to provide rigoros theories and frameworks to assist in understanding the intricacies and inter-relationships between the IHRM function and IHR activities, firm internationalization and strategic directions and goals.

A consistent theme throughout this book has been the way in which IHRM requires a broader perspective of what operating internationally involves, and a clear recognition of the range of issues pertaining to all categories of staff operating in different functional, task and managerial capacities is essential. As Poole[52] stated in his editorial in the first issue of the *International Journal of Human Resource Management* in 1990, 'international human resource management archetypically involves the world-wide management of people in the multinational enterprise'.

Discussion questions and exercises

1 What is your view of the recent international initiatives to criminalize foreign bribery?

2 Identify a number of HRM problems that typically arise with expatriate assignments. In what ways might the core ethical values and guidelines identified in this chapter apply to them?

3 You are the Project Manager in charge of the construction of a new pipeline to bring oil from its source in the Andes down to the refinery on the coast of Colombia. What steps would you take to protect all your employees?

4 Why is management succession an issue for family-owned firms?

5 Key individuals in SMEs develop critical knowledge and competence about foreign market activities. How can an SME protect itself from losing this stock of knowledge should such a key individual leave the firm?

6 What IHRM activities are pertinent to the sending, by Médecins Sans Frontières, of a medical team into Iraq?

Further reading

D. Wiechmann, A.M. Ryan and M. Hemingway, 2003. Designing and Implementing Global Staffing Systems: Part I – Leaders in Global Staffing, *Human Resource Management*, Vol. 42, No. 1, pp. 71–83.

M.A. Lopez-Navarro and C. Camison-Zornoza, 2003. The effect of Group Composition and Autonomy on the Performance of Joint Ventures (JVs). An Analysis based on Spanish Export JVs. *International Business Review*, Vol. 12, No. 1, pp. 17–39.

Y. Baruch and Y. Altman, 2002. Expatriation and Repatriation in MNCs: a Taxonomy, *Human Resource Management*, Vol. 41, No. 2, pp. 239–259.

J. Donaldson, 2002. Multinational Enterprises, Employment Relations and Ethics, *Employee Relations*, Vol. 23, No. 6, pp. 627–643.

H. Harris and L. Holden, 2001. Between Autonomy and Control: Expatriate Managers and Strategic IHRM in SMEs, *Thunderbird International Business Review*, Vol. 43, No. 1, pp. 77–100.

Notes and references

1 For a more complete discussion of the factors impacting upon complexity in international business ethics, see R.T. DeGeorge, *Business Ethics*, 5th edn, Englewood Cliffs, NJ, Prentice Hall, 1999, pp. 514–521.

2 For a discussion of ethical relativism see Ref. 1, Chapter 2; L.P. Pojman, *Ethical Theory: Classical and Contemporary Readings*, Belmont, CA: Wadsworth, 1995, pp. 15–47.

3 G. Kelly, cited in R.T. De George, *Competing with Integrity in International Business*, New York: Oxford University Press, 1993.

4 R. Kidder, 1994. *Shared Values for a Troubled World*, Jossey-Bass, 1994.

5 T. Donaldson, 1996. Values in Tension: Ethics away from home, *Harvard Business Review*, Sept–Oct, pp. 48–62.

6 W.C. Frederick, The Moral Authority of Transnational Corporate Codes, (1991) in Beauchamp and Bowie, 1997, *op. cit.*, pp. 576–588.

7 Preamble to the Caux Round Table Principles, reprinted in Hartman, *Perspective in Business Ethics*, 2nd edn, 2002, pp. 737–740; see also http://www.cauxroundtable.org.

8 D. Payne, C. Raiborn, and J. Askvik, A Global Code of Business Ethics, *Journal of Business Ethics*, Vol. 16, No. 16 (1997) pp. 1727–1735.

9 *Business Ethics Survey Report*, Alexandria: Society for Human Resource Management/Ethics Resource Centre (SHRM/ERC), 2003.

10 D. Robertson and B. Schlegelmilch, Corporate Institutionalisation of Ethics in the United States and Great Britain, *Journal of Business Ethics*, Vol. 12 (1993) pp. 301–312.

11 R.M. Lindsay, L.M. Lindsay and V.B. Irvine, 1996. Instilling Ethical Behaviour in Organizations: a Survey of Canadian Companies, *Journal of Business Ethics*, Vol. 15, No. 4 (1996) pp. 393–407.

12 G.R. Weaver, L.K. Trevino and P.L. Cochran, Corporate Ethics Practices in the Mid-1990s: an Empirical Study of the Fortune 1000, *Journal of Business Ethics*, Vol. 18, No. 3(1999) pp. 283–294.

13 C. Brewster, L. Carey, P. Dowling, P. Grobler, *et al.*, *Contemporary Issues in Human Resource Management*, 2nd edn, Capetown: Oxford University Press, 2003. Ethics Policies and Procedures in Australian Enterprises: Survey Summary Results, unpublished manuscript, University of Tasmania.

14 J.R. Boatright, *Ethics and the Conduct of Business*, 3rd edn, Upper Saddle River, NJ: Prentice Hall, 2000, p. 11.

15 See R.M. Green, *The Ethical Manager*, New York: Macmillan, 1994, p. 290 for a list of practices that pose the most frequent problems for international managers.

16 C. Pacini, J. Swingen and H. Rogers, 2002. The Role of the OECD and EU Conventions in Combating Bribery of Foreign Public Officials, *Journal of Business Ethics*, Vol. 37, No. 4 (2002) pp. 385–406.

17 J. Macken, Dirty Money, *The Australian Financial Review*, 31 March (1998) p. 13.

18 T.L. Carson, Bribery, Extortion, and the Foreign Corrupt Practices Act. *Philosophy and Public Affairs*, (1984) pp. 66–90.

19 W. Bottiglieri, M. Marder and E. Paderon, The Foreign Corrupt Practices Act: Disclosure Requirements and Management Integrity, *SAM Advanced Journal*, Winter (1991) pp. 21–27.

20 http://www.oecd.org.

21 For an up-to-date TI Corruption Index, consult http://www.transparency.org.

22 Transparency International Corruption Perceptions Index, http://www.transparency.org/pressreleases_archive/2002/dnld/cpi2002.pressrelease.en.pdf, 2002.

23 G. Edwards and K. Bennett, Ethics and HR: Standards in Practice, *Personnel Administrator*, Vol. 32, No. 12 (1987) pp. 62–66; also see D. Driscoll and W.M. Hoffman, HR Plays a Central Role in Ethics Programs, *Workforce*, Vol. 77, No. 4 (1998) pp. 121–123; C. Wiley, Re-examining Perceived Ethics Issues and Ethics Roles Among Employment Managers, *Journal of Business Ethics*, Vol. 17, No.2 (1998) pp. 147–161.

24 See Ref. 9.

25 L.J. Brooks, *Professional Ethics for Accountants*, St. Paul, MN: West Publishing, 1995.

26 P. Ham, Enter the Kidnap Gurus, *The Australian*, 29 August (2003) p.12, Business Travel section. The article profiles an international kidnap and ransom firm, Control Risks Group. See www.crg.com.

27 D.E. Welch, L.S. Welch, L.C. Young and I.F. Wilkinson, The Importance of Networks in Export Promotion: Policy Issues, *Journal of International Marketing*, Vol. 6, No. 4 (1998) pp. 66–82.

28 Small Companies are Headed for the Big Time, *Far Eastern Economic Review*, May 22 (2003) p. 32.

29 D.E. Welch and L.S. Welch, Pre-expatriation: the Role of HR Factors in the Early Stages of Internationalisation, *International Journal of Human Resource Management*, Vol. 8, No. 4 (1997) pp. 402–413.

30 *The Economist*, Under the Influence, 17 November (2001) pp. 59–60.

31 *The Economist*, Slipped Disc: Germany's Mittelstand, 15 December (2001) pp. 56–57.

32 *IMD International Survey*, report and results obtained from www.rediff.com, accessed 1 April 2000.

33 H.W.C. Yeung, Limits to the Growth of Family-owned Business? The Case of Chinese Transnational Corporations from Hong Kong, *Family Business Review*, Vol. 13, No. 1 (2000) pp. 55–70.

34 M. Fenwick, Extending Strategic International Human Resource Management Research and Pedagogy to the Non-profit Multinational, *International Journal of Human Resource Management*, Special Edition on International Human Resource Management in the Asia Pacific, 2004, to be published.

35 For a review and related articles, see M.A. Von Glinow, Guest Editor, Best Practices in IHRM: Lessons Learned from a Ten Country/Regional Analysis, *Asia Pacific Journal of Human Resources*, Vol. 40, No.1 (2002) Special Issue.

36 N. Adler, Cross-cultural Management Research: The Ostrich and the Trend, *Academy of Management Review*, Vol.8 (1983) pp. 226–232.

37 R.S. Bhagat and S.J. McQuaid, Role of Subjective Culture in Organizations: a Review and Directions for Future Research, *Journal of Applied Psychology*, Vol. 67 (1982) pp. 653–685.

38 D.T. Campbell and J. Stanley, *Experimental and Quasi-experimental Design for Research*, Chicago: Rand-McNally, 1966.

39 R.S. Malpass, Theory and Method in Cross-cultural Psychology, *American Psychologist*, Vol. 32 (1977) pp. 1069–1079.

40 See L. Kelly and R. Worthley, The Role of Culture in Comparative Management: a Cross-cultural Perspective, *Academy of Management Journal*, Vol. 24 (1981) pp. 164–173, and P. J. Dowling and T.W. Nagel, Nationality and Work Attitudes: a Study of Australian and American Business Majors, *Journal of Management*, Vol. 12 (1986) pp. 121–128, for further discussion on this point.

41 H.C. Triandis and R.W. Brislin, Cross-cultural Psychology, *American Psychologist*, Vol. 39 (1984) pp. 1006–1016.

42 J. Bonache, C. Brewster and V. Suutari, Expatriation: Developing a Research Agenda, *Thunderbird International Business Review*, Vol. 42, No. 1 (2001) pp. 3–20.

43 R.S. Schuler, P.J. Dowling and H. De Cieri, An Integrative Framework of Strategic International Human Resource Management, *Journal of Management*, Vol. 19 (1993) pp. 419–459.

44 D. Welch, Determinants of International Human Resource Management Approaches and Activities: a Suggested Framework, *Journal of Management Studies*, Vol. 31, No. 2 (1994) pp. 139–164.

45 A.V. Harzing, Response Rates in International Mail Surveys: Results of a 22 Country Study, *International Business Review*, Vol. 6, No. 6 (1997) pp. 641-665.

46 S. Taylor, S. Beechler and N. Napier, Towards an Integrative Model of Strategic International Human Resource Management, *Academy of Management Review*, Vol. 21 (1996) pp. 959–985.

47 K. Kamoche, Knowledge Creation and Learning in International HRM, *International Journal of Human Resource Management*, Vol. 8 (1997) pp. 213–222.

48 M. Harvey, M.M. Novicevis and C. Speier, An Innovative Global Management Staffing System: a Competency-based Perspective, *Human Resource Management*, Vol. 39, No. 4 (2000) pp. 381–394.

49 B. Becker and B. Gerhart, The Impact of Human Resource Management on Organizational Performance: Progress and Prospects, *Academy of Management Journal*, Vol. 39, No. 4 (1996) pp. 779–801; L. Dyer and T. Reeves, Human Resource Strategies and Firm Performance: What do We Know and Where do We Need to Go? *International Journal of Human Resource Management*, Vol. 6, No. 3 (1995), pp. 656–670.

50 M. Festing, International Human Resource Management Strategies in Multinational Corporations: Theoretical Assumptions and Empirical Evidence from German Firms, *Management International Review*, Vol. 37, Special Issue No.1 (1997) pp. 43–63; S.J. Kobrin, Is There a Relationship between a Geocentric Mind-set and Multinational Strategy? *Journal of International Business Studies*, Vol. 25 (1994) pp. 493–511.

51 P.M. Caligiuri and L.K. Stroh, Multinational Corporate Management Strategies and International Human Resource Practices: Bringing IHRM to the Bottom Line, *International Journal of Human Resource Management*, Vol. 6 (1995) pp. 494–507; R.B. Peterson, J. Sargent, N.K. Napier and W.S. Shim, Corporate Expatriate HRM Policies, Internationalisation, and Performance in the World's Largest MNCs, *Management International Review*, Vol. 36 (1996) pp. 215–230; P. Sparrow, R.S. Schuler and S.E. Jackson, Convergence or Divergence: Human Resource Practices and Policies for Competitive Advantage Worldwide. *International Journal of Human Resource Management*, Vol. 5 (1994) pp. 267–299.

52 M. Poole, Editorial: Human Resource Management in an International Perspective, *International Journal of Human Resource Management*, Vol. 1, No.1 (1990) pp. 1–15.

Cases and exercises

IV

Staffing a new international venture

© Denice Welch, 1999

Your group comprises the top executive team of an Australian wine company that trades under the name of Yarra River Wines. The company is based in the Yarra Valley wine district in the hills outside Melbourne. It has its own vineyards, but also purchases grapes from selected Victorian vineyards to use in its blended varieties of cabernet, shiraz, merlot and grenache. The wine is sold under the labels of Yarra River for its blends and Yarra Estate for its shiraz and chardonnay. Like other companies in the Yarra Valley, it has a high-class restaurant attached to its winery that, along with winery tours and cellar door sales, attracts a constant flow of tourists. This is now forming an integral part of building domestic and international brand recognition.

Since the late 1970s, the company has built up reasonable levels of export sales of premium red and white table wines to three international markets: the UK, Scandinavia and, recently, the USA. Buoyed by rising global sales and industry predictions for future growth, the Board has given approval to acquire an existing winery in southern France. The French acquisition is an important step for the company as it is the first foreign direct investment. Exporting through agents and distributors has been the company's mode of operation until this point. The French operation is a middle-level player in its home market, with limited sales to neighbouring EU countries. Pre-acquisition evaluation revealed an efficiently run operation, in the French context, with modest profit margins.

To a certain extent, Yarra River Wines is a late starter, as its larger Australian competitors such as Orlando (Jacobs Creek) and BRL Hardy have been operating their own French wineries for several years. The renowned French champagne house Domaine Chandon has a successful operation in the Yarra Valley that produces sparkling and table wines, some of which are exported to France. However, Australian wine has gained a global recognition for quality wine, assisted by technological improvements and aggressive marketing, and your company expects this to assist Yarra River Wines to 'ride the Australian wave' and gain market share in Continental Europe.

The agenda for today's meeting is to decide on the staffing of the French acquisition. Control is paramount as the Board is especially cautious given the perceived and real risks the new venture presents. The top executive team is convinced there is room for improvement, particularly in terms of wine production techniques and marketing. However, the group recognizes that care must be taken with staffing decisions, given the potential for conflict between French and Australian management approaches and the need for sensitivity to local issues.

The HR Director will present the meeting with an assessment of the current management in the French acquisition, and provide a briefing document on

French and EC employment laws, including retrenchment. Key positions to be considered are: Managing Director, Marketing Manager, Wine Technologist (a new position), Production Manager, Finance Manager and Human Resource Manager.

In the time allocated, your group must decide on whether to use Australians (either from inside or outside the company), to retain the current French management team or to use a mixture of French and Australians. While you are free to make suppositions/assumptions regarding the HR assessment of the current French management team, you must be prepared to justify these, and provide the rationale behind the decisions your group makes.

Peter Hanson

Building a world-class product development center for Hi Tech Systems in China

© **Ingmar Björkman**, Professor, Swedish School of Economics, Helsinki, Finland
Visiting Professor, INSEAD, Singapore

Introduction

Peter Hanson, the Head of the Product Development Center (PDC) of Hi Tech Systems in Shanghai, had been in China for 5 months. He was the first person in the PDC when he arrived in Shanghai in April 2000. Thinking back at the period he had spent in China so far, he felt that things had gone fairly well. The PDC was now up and running and today, on 12 September 2000, Peter welcomed its 16th employee.

Nonetheless, Peter still had a number of concerns. The PDC was still rather small and it was possible for him to interact with and influence all employees. As the PDC would grow significantly over the next year, he wanted to make sure to create a healthy and positive atmosphere and orientation towards work. His vision was to create a world-class PDC in Shanghai, but how to do that in a country that mainly was a recipient of technological know-how from abroad, and what measures should be taken to convince other parts of Hi Tech Systems to engage in joint development projects with his PDC? And even if he managed to develop the competencies needed to build a world-class PDC through careful recruitment and selection as well as good investments in training and development, how were they to retain the employees in a market where job hopping was common, money apparently an important reason why people switched jobs and well-educated people had ample opportunities in other companies? Basically his question was: would lessons on how to manage human resources obtained in North America and Europe apply also in the People's Republic of China?

Product development in Hi Tech Systems

Hi Tech Systems was established in Stockholm, Sweden, in 1976. Already by the late-1980s, Hi Tech Systems had become known as one of Europe's most innovative firms in its industry. The growth continued in the 1990s, with firm profitability remaining healthy. The company is currently one of the three largest firms in its industry. Hi Tech Systems' global manufacturing comprises six production facilitates in five countries on three continents. Approximately 45 per cent of sales come from Europe but in particular the USA, and Japan and China have also become important markets.

Product development is seen as key to the success of Hi Tech Systems. Almost 20 per cent of Hi Tech Systems' employees are working in research and development. Hi Tech Systems has PDCs in Sweden, the UK, the USA, Japan, Hong Kong

(China) and, most recently, Mainland China. There is a global PDC management group headed by Johan Lind that consists of all the PDC heads and which convenes once per month. Johan Lind reports to the head of global product development in Hi Tech Systems, Anders Jonsson.

The responsibility for product development programs resides with the global business lines and the so-called 'platforms' (such as Japanese user interface). Research programs within the business lines that lead to actual products also draw on the work being done within the platforms. In each PDC, people work on projects related to both Hi Tech Systems' business lines and platforms.

A full-grown PDC has some 4–500 employees and a variety of competencies and is expected to have the capability needed to develop an entire new product. There are several reasons why the company has established a whole portfolio of PDCs. First, different areas differ in terms of technologies and standards relevant for the business. Therefore, it makes sense to locate Research & Development activities in locations where the technologies reside. Second, by dispersing PDCs to different parts of the world, the company can move product creation activities in response to environmental and market changes. Third, it enables Hi Tech Systems to draw on human resources not available in one location. Hi Tech Systems has traditionally done most of its product creation in Sweden, but as a result of the growth of Hi Tech Systems there are not enough engineering students in the whole country to satisfy its needs. Fourth, products need to be local adapted and this is easier to carry out locally than in a distant PDC.

In a typical research program, most of the work on the key components of a new product is done within one single 'core' PDC. Within each project there is a fairly clear distribution of responsibilities across the PDCs involved. Other, 'peripheral' PDCs are typically involved in developing locally adapted variances of the product. Most of the work has typically already been done in the core PDC before the other PDCs become involved (although in order to ensure that the necessary local adaptations of the final product can be made at a later stage, people from each of the geographical regions are involved in steering groups already during the conceptualization stage). The knowledge transfer mostly takes place through people from the PDCs who visit the core PDC for 1–3 months to work with the product development people before they return to their own units. At the point when the project has been established in the peripheral PDCs, the focal project leader reports to the global head of the focal product development project and to the head of the own PDC. Heavy emphasis is put on establishing and following up project milestones.

Hi Tech Systems in China

The People's Republic of China started to open up to the outside world in 1979. In 1992, the Hi Tech Systems group established a representative office in Shanghai and in 1995 a first joint venture was established. By the beginning of 2000, Hi Tech Systems already had four joint ventures and wholly owned subsidiaries in China. Hi Tech Systems had become a significant player in the rapidly growing Chinese market where it was competing with other Western, Japanese but also increasingly strong local competitors. China had become one of Hi Tech Systems' most important markets. Most of the products sold in China were produced in the firm's local factories.

However, Hi Tech Systems so far had no PDC in China. Towards the end of the 1990s, there was a growing consensus that this neglect had to be rectified. A decision to establish a PDC in Shanghai was made by Hi Tech Systems' management board in January 2000. Peter Hanson was chosen to head the PDC.

Peter Hanson

Peter Hanson was born in California in 1962. After graduating from college with a major in management, his first job was with a major US industrial firm. As a part of his job, in 1989–90 he spent 6 months in Hong Kong. During his assignment in Hong Kong, he 'fell in love with Asia and China. Since that moment he knew that he was going to return to Asia'. Peter also met his future wife, who moved with him to the USA. In 1991–93, Peter did an MBA and then started to work in a small start-up company. In late 1997, Peter was persuaded by one of his previous colleagues to join Hi Tech Systems. When joining Hi Tech Systems, Peter was appointed operations manager. After some months, he was asked to head the Engineering Unit of the new PDC that was built up in Philadelphia. Peter accepted the job, which meant that he would be responsible for the largest unit of the PDC. Peter and his new boss Curtis O'Neill soon became very close, with Peter acting as the second in charge of the PDC. Peter recalls:

> I learnt a lot from Curtis. He was very people-oriented. He would make sure that you get an opportunity to get into an environment where you either learn or you don't. He gave people lots of challenges, lots of learning opportunities, where they could prove themselves. He would also quite directly point to areas of improvement. He also underlined the importance of networking, how to build networks of people that you can draw on.

One of the things that Peter learnt soon after joining Hi Tech Systems was the importance of having good personal contacts within the company. The Hi Tech Systems global product development worked to a significant extent through informal contacts across units and it was crucial to be well connected. His choice of the five product line managers in his department reflected this view. While people in the Philadelphia unit expected and pressured him to choose local people for the positions, he selected three expatriates and only two local employees.

> People thought I was taking promotions away from Philadelphia. I had my own views in mind – we needed to be connected to the other centers. If you're well connected people trust you to do a good job within a research program, and it is also easier to get technical help if needed. I then used lots of interviews with the candidates to convince people about their capabilities and to get some buy-in from the other managers. I also made sure to tell people that the objective was to fill the positions with local people in 2–3 years. In fact, the line managers had as an explicit objective to develop a local replacement of themselves.

During the next 18 months, Peter visited Sweden several times. He often took part in the global PDC group meetings as O'Neill's stand-in. The global PDC management also knew that he was interested in returning to Asia, something Peter had mentioned from the outset in his performance management discussions.

Establishing the Product Development Center

During the summer of 1999, the global PDC management group decided that a feasibility study on the possible creation of a PDC in the People's Republic of China should be carried out. In October 1999, Peter was asked to become involved in the project. His task was to examine the data and write a report on whether or not a PDC should be established and, if so, where in China it should be located. By that time Peter also knew that he would be the preferred candidate as head of the PDC (if approved). In January 2000, the Hi Tech Systems global management board approved the establishment of a PDC in Shanghai. One of the advantages of Shanghai was that the PDC would be able to use the existing Hi Tech Systems organization in the city. It would be easier to learn from the experiences of Hi Tech Systems' largest Chinese production and its China headquarters, both of which were located in Shanghai. In February, Peter went to China on a pre-visit, mainly to meet with people in the Hi Tech Systems organization.

When it became clear that the PDC would be established, Peter started to look for people. There was no established policy for people management within the global product creation organization, but Peter was told to draw on the Human Resources (HR) department at the Hi Tech Systems group in China for support. He thought he would initially need approximately 10 positions for expatriates, and it would be of crucial importance to find suitable people for the key positions.

> It was networking all the way – the social networks were very important! There were many people who knew that I would do it and some of them contacted me. I contacted and spoke to lots of people in all parts of the Hi Tech Systems organization. I wanted the candidates to have experience in launching Hi Tech Systems products in China. They should know the Chinese environment and culture. This meant that there were only a very small number of people who fulfilled my criteria. And they had to commit to staying at least two or even three years, which is not usual in Hi Tech Systems. Towards the end of the period they start hunting for another job anyhow.

Peter finally identified four persons that he wanted: one Swede and three persons from the People's Republic of China who had studied and worked for several years abroad (two in the USA and one in Sweden). One of them he already knew in advance, the others he had identified through his networking activities. All the Chinese had a strong education background, with degrees from top Chinese universities before leaving the country for overseas graduate studies. Everybody had at least some experience in leading own teams.

> I talked a lot to them. Have they thought about living in China? Were they (the Chinese) conscious about the challenges involved in going back to China? For instance, people may be jealous of them making much more money, travelling abroad and having much higher positions than they themselves had? Have they realized that it's going to be a start-up operation, and that it may be difficult to get things started and people on board?

To persuade the persons he wanted to accept relocating to China, Peter tried to create a positive and challenging vision for the PDC. To date, Hi Tech Systems had probably not done enough to meet the needs of the Chinese-speaking countries. Did they want to become a part of the process of creating a world-class PDC in China? The PDC would become responsible for the Chinese user interface platform – did they want to participate in the challenge of its development? Being restricted by the company's expatriate compensation policy, which was built on a standardized job grading system, he was able to offer competitive but not exceptional salaries. He finally managed to persuade all four candidates to accept a job in his PDC. They all knew each other from their previous jobs. During the late Spring of 2000, he found some additional people in the global Hi Tech Systems organization who also agreed to taking up jobs in Shanghai.

> A part of my strategy was to get people from different PDCs. By having these people in my organization we are easily able to reach into the other PDCs, which is particularly important in the beginning as we are dependent on doing parts of larger projects in collaboration with other centres. If we have good people who have credibility from each of the other PDCs, we will be recognized and seen as trustworthy.

But Peter did not see technical competence as the only important criterion. In his view:

> 80 per cent is attitude. It doesn't matter what you can do if you lack drive. With drive you can always fill in the gaps .... Perhaps it has something to do with my own background. I have had to manage without an engineering education in an organization and industry that are extremely technology-intensive.

The PDC was to report to the Global PDC management and to the Hi Tech Systems China country management. As agreed upon with the Global PDC management group, PDC Shanghai would be responsible for product creation in the Chinese language area, including Mainland China, Hong Kong, Singapore and Taiwan. In the beginning it would mostly do limited parts of larger products in collaboration with other global PDCs, working on, e.g., software and Chinese-specific applications. The long-term vision was eventually to have the competencies even to be able to build new products in China.

The start of the Product Development Center

Peter and his family finally arrived in Shanghai on 12 April 2000. The next employee arrived from overseas in May, and already by September the unit had 16 employees, half of whom had been recruited from abroad. Peter's estimate was that long-term, 15–20 per cent of the employees would be from overseas but that it would take 3–4 years to decrease the proportion of expatriates to that level.

> When you build a home, first you build the foundations. You need to make sure that the foundations are in place – the recruitment process, human resources management, finance. Then you need key managers to build the organization around.

In the recruitment of local employees, the PDC was collaborating closely with Hi Tech Systems' HR department. After job descriptions and job grade levels had been determined by the PDC, the HR department would announce the position using both advertisements and the Hi Tech System home page, receive curriculum vitaes (CVs), do a first screening of the candidates and arrange for interviews and assessment of the applicants. The interviews were done by a minimum of two PDC managers, who also acted as observers in the assessment centers organized by the HR department. For the assessment of applicants in China, Hi Tech Systems used 'The Space Shuttle'. The Space Shuttle was a game where the applicants worked together in a group with the objective of reaching an agreement on how to build a space shuttle. By observing the applicants involved in a problem-solving situation where they also interacted with each other, the observers could draw their own conclusions about the applicants. Recruitment and selection of local employees largely resembled practices used elsewhere in the global Hi Tech Systems organization.

Some other Western firms had apparently made larger adjustments in their selection practices in China. For instance, Peter had heard that Shell had changed its selection practices based on an in depth study of its existing Chinese managers and entry-level management trainees. Traditionally Shell focused on analytical and problem-solving abilities. However, when, for example, applicants were asked to identify the strengths and weaknesses of the Chinese educational system and then say what they would do to remedy deficiencies if they were the Minister of Education, if there were any responses at all they tended to be uniformly bland. It was also found that the kind of 'Who would you throw out of the airplane?' question commonly used in the West also tended to engender a 'learned helplessness effect' on the part of Chinese university graduates, who have excelled at clearly defined tasks in a familiar environment and who had 'learnt' to respond to the unfamiliar by simply freezing. Shell's system identified the Chinese education system as the chief culprit. The educational system is hierarchical, extremely competitive and almost exclusively based on examination of rote learning. Problem-oriented interaction among strangers is unnatural and problematic for most Chinese. Therefore, to evaluate the decision-making skills, communication skills, analytical problem-solving abilities and leadership capabilities of the applicants based on hypothetical cases solved in assessment situations may be very difficult. As a result, Shell's study recommended the use of real case studies rather than hypothetical questions.[1]

Competence development would probably be key to the success of the PDC both in terms of localizing its operations and in producing good results. By mid-September, the new employees had mostly worked on small projects, such as setting up the IT system. A couple of people had also been sent to Hong Kong to work in the field with experienced engineers for 3 weeks. Formal training would be important, and the PDC would need to collaborate with Hi Tech Systems' HR unit on the course programme offered to the PDC employees. To what extent should the Chinese employees receive the same content and delivery as Hi Tech Systems' employees elsewhere? In China, the Confucianist and Communist-influenced Chinese educational system, in which the learner is a mostly passive receiver who is obedient to the instructor, tends to create linear rather than lateral thinking and precedent-based problem solving where the focus is on getting the 'right' answer.

Nonetheless, hands-on on-the-job coaching would be even more important for the development of the new employees. Most of the responsibility for coaching would obviously be on the experienced Hi Tech Systems' employees, but it would also be important to bring in people from other PDCs for visits in Shanghai. Coaching on the part of the expatriates would be extremely important, Peter thought. He had already been discussing it at length with the managers that he had hired, but he was not sure whether or not that was enough, especially not when the unit would grow over the next couple of years. He certainly would not be able to coach all expatriates by himself.

In Hi Tech Systems' globally standardized performance management system, all employees should carry out performance management discussions with their superiors. Within this system, individual objectives are established and followed up. According to company policy, the individual's objectives must be specific and, if possible, measurable, key activities for how to reach the objectives shall be specified, criteria for how to evaluate the performance agreed upon and, finally, development plans decided upon. Peter's aim was that every new employee would do their first performance management discussion within 1 month after they joined the organization. All Hi Tech Systems' superiors in China were trained in how to use the system but there was still a question of how the 'Western' system would be implemented in the Chinese culture characterized by respect for hierarchy, face and harmonious personal relationships.

Peter had also given the question of the relationship between employee competence development and career progress a lot of thought. In Hi Tech Systems worldwide, people achieved high status by having excellent technological knowledge and skills rather than having made a successful career as managers. However:

> In China especially the young people expect to get a new title every year; otherwise they had better start looking for another company. The speed of expected career progression clearly differs from the West. To develop the level of competence required for the next career step will be a challenge. Can they achieve it once a year? I think very few will.

The compensation of employees would follow the Hi Tech Systems policies. Managers and team leaders were compensated based on both business and individual performance. High-level executives and senior managers had a large business performance component in their bonus system, while the compensation of lower level employees was mostly based on their individual performance. In the Shanghai PDC, individual performance would be evaluated based on 4–5 objectives. Peter required that the objectives had to be measurable on a 10-point scale. For instance, a manager's performance could be evaluated based on the manager's ability to fill positions in his/her group, employee satisfaction (as measured in company-wide surveys), employee turnover, the team's ability to stay within the budget and some measure of quality (to be determined in discussions between the person and Peter). Each person's performance was evaluated every 6 months, and bonuses paid accordingly. The target bonus was 10 per cent of the person's base salary, with 20 per cent as maximum. People working on a specific development project were not evaluated every 6 months but the evaluation rather followed the milestones of the project. The bonus element was also somewhat larger for people working on projects than for other PDC members.

Peter believed that the compensation system would work well in China. Having clear objectives and rewards linked with their fulfillment would help send a clear message to the employees: your performance equals what you deliver – not the personal connections, or '*guanxi*', that you have! Nonetheless, at least in the start-up phase of the PDC it might be somewhat difficult to establish feasible objectives for the employees. Additionally, there had been reports from other foreign firms that there was a tendency among local employees to set objectives so that they would be reached by the subordinates.

Looking towards the future

Analysing the start-up phase of PDC, Peter found that many things had gone fairly smoothly. For instance, the two Chinese 'returnees' who had joined PDC so far (the third was still in Sweden but would relocate next month) seemed to do well. Although China had changed a lot since they left the country some 10 years ago, their interaction with the local employees seemed to go well.

Managing the growth would certainly be a challenge in the next couple of years, Peter thought. For instance, local employees would have to be taught to manage themselves and to take responsibility – behaviors not automatically understood and accepted in the Chinese environment. While the Hi Tech Systems culture was non-hierarchical and meritocratic, the Chinese culture is hierarchical, and the 'face' of superiors could be at stake if subordinates made own initiatives rather than waiting for orders from their superiors. Furthermore, during the Communist regime since 1949, the Chinese had been discouraged from engaging in competitive and entrepreneurial behavior. The Chinese proverb 'the early bird gets shot' aptly illustrates the reluctance on the part of Chinese employees to engage in the kind of innovative behaviour that Peter wanted to see in the PDC. On the other hand, Peter had seen several Chinese changing their behavior significantly abroad. What should they do to promote this behavior also in the Shanghai PDC?

Peter was also looking for somebody to work closely with Hi Tech Systems' HR function. This person would work closely with him and the line managers to define future competence needs and how they could be met. 'So far I guess I have fulfilled this role, but I'm afraid that neither me nor line managers will have time enough to pay sufficient attention to this issue in the future.'

Finally, Peter was concerned about retention. 'I have also been told by [a human resources expert] that a one Renminbi salary difference may make a person switch jobs.' Peter believed that money would not be key to retaining the employees, though. To create a positive, family-like atmosphere might help. Peter had started a tradition of everyone in his unit to meet for a snack on Monday mornings. He also made a conscious effort to spend time talking to people in the department. Furthermore, he had invited people out for lunch and dinner. To maintain a positive relationship between the foreign and local employees, he tried to coach the expatriates not to mention how much money they made, how they lived and how cheap they found most things to be in Shanghai (say 'reasonable' instead, was his advice). All this had apparently contributed to there starting to circulate rumours that 'things are done a bit differently in PDC'. He was now thinking of whether to involve the employees' families in some way. Formal team-building exercises should probably also be done.

There were so many things to do.... Peter looked out of his window in one of the many new multistory buildings in the Pudong-area of Shanghai – where should he start?

Reference

1. *China on the Couch*, The Economist Intelligence Unit, 28 September (1998) pp. 3–4.

IHR planning exercise

© Denice Welch, updated 2003

Golden Skis is a medium-sized Norwegian manufacturing company that currently has production facilities in Austria, the USA and Spain. It also has a local production facility in the town of Moss, situated south of the capital, and a sales subsidiary for the local Norwegian market located in Oslo. The company was founded in 1938, making sleds and toboggans, then moved into cross-country ski production in 1947. As skiing increased in popularity as a winter sport, Golden Skis expanded its product lines to include downhill ski equipment and snowboards, and recently introduced a special line of ski clothing. It began exporting to neighbouring Nordic markets in the 1950s and established its first foreign factory in 1969 in Austria.

Factories in the USA and Spain were established in 1986 and 1990, respectively. A regional office/sales subsidiary in Hong Kong is responsible for Golden Skis' subcontracting operations in China and the marketing of products in the Asia-Pacific region – to countries such as Japan, Korea and Australia.

Golden Skis has survived increased global competition through improved quality, R&D and aggressive marketing through the use of skiing champions, capitalizing on world attention during the Winter Olympics hosted by Norway in 1994.

You are the Manager of the International Staffing Division, reporting to the Group Human Resources Manager, at the global headquarters located in Sandvika, a suburb of Oslo. As part of your job, you have to manage the increasing number of international staff transfers. At present, the company has the following staff abroad:

Parent-country Nationals (PCNs). 30 Norwegians in total, of whom 20 will be due for either repatriation or reassignment in July. They are in the following locations:

Hong Kong. 6 PCNs in total:

Hans Bjørnsen, Managing Director, 55 years old, with wife Ruth. Both want to return to Oslo.

Carl Solbær, Marketing Director, 47 years old, wife Martine, three children aged 5, 7 and 15 years.

Erik Erikssen, Finance Manager, 66 years old, married, accompanied by wife Helle. Due for retirement.

Jan Holmen, Accountant, 33 years old, accompanied by partner Ellen and 2-year-old daughter.

Bente Sørensen, Sales Manager, 27 years old, single female.

Ole Magnussen, IT specialist, 26 years old, male, single.

Austria. 4 PCNs:

Magnus Petersen, Technical Director, 38 years old, divorced.

Runar Brønn, research technician, 33 years old, with partner Anna and 3-year-old son.

Thomas Gummersen, Marketing Manager, 41 years old, with wife Inger and two sons aged 12 and 9 years. Family want to return to Norway.

Reidunn Oddsen, HRM trainee, single female, aged 26 years.

Spain. 3 PCNs:

Gunnar Amundsen, Finance Director, 45 years old, wife Kari and two children, 12-year-old twins.

Peter Halden, Accountant, single male, 30 years old.

Marit Bensen, Factory Manager, 32 years old, accompanied by 5-year-old son, but partner, Thomas Alsberg, has remained in Norway.

USA. 7 PCNs:

Petter Solgaard, Finance Director, 48 years old, with wife Hanne and 16-year-old son. They want to return to Oslo.

Odd Husby, Accountant, 35 years old, wife Lise and three children aged 2, 4 and 8 years.

Tor Gunnessen, IT specialist, 28 years old, single male.

Maria Jensen, Marketing Manager, 31 years old, divorced.

Lars Overeid, IT specialist, 30 years old, partner Rigmor, 28 years old, without work visa (green card).

Knut Knutsen, software engineer, 42 years old, wife Heidi and 10-year-old daughter. Moved from Austria but want to return to Norway.

Katrine Ullesen, graduate trainee, 25 years old, single female.

Third-country Nationals (TCNs). 10 in total.

Henry Tung, IT specialist from Hong Kong, in USA, 65 years old, with wife Lucy, want to retire in Hong Kong.

Karl Meissner, Finance Manager, an Austrian in Spain, 52 years old, with wife Alessandra. Due for transfer in July.

Franz Kammen, ski technician, an Austrian in Spain, 43 years old, with wife Lotte and two sons aged 8 and 10 years.

Allen Powers, ski technician, American in Austria, 26 years old, single male.

Julia Claymore, Marketing Manager, American in Spain, 36 years old, single female.

Carlos Santino, Production Manager, Spaniard in Austria, 38 years old, with wife and four children aged 1, 3, 6 and 10 years.

Conchita Gonzales, marketing research specialist, Spaniard in the USA, 32 years old, single female.

Mary Robertson, Finance Director, American in Austria, 36 years old, husband Tom remains in the USA.

Hank Bonichi, R&D engineer, American in Spain, 35 years old, with wife Susan and one son aged 5 years.

Günter Strahl, Sales Director, Austrian in Hong Kong, 45 years old, with wife Maria and two daughters aged 6 and 8 years.

Host-country Nationals (HCNs). 5, all at Golden Skis's global headquarters (HQ) in Sandvika.

Elizabeth Moore, trainee, 26 years old, due to return to USA subsidiary in July.

Juan Bonnaro, trainee, 25 years old, due to return to Spanish subsidiary in July.

Klaus Kramer, trainee, 28 years old, due to return to Austrian subsidiary in July.

Julius Chong, Sales Manager at HQ, will return to Hong Kong in July.

Bill Johnson, trainee, 28 years old, just arrived from the US subsidiary for 1 year.

To assist in your planning, you have gathered the following information:

- The subsidiary in Hong Kong has notified that they need a marketing manager and a computer systems analyst: both positions cannot be filled locally.

- The Austrian subsidiary has three vacancies expected in July, all at the managerial level in the production area. Although they may be able to fill these locally, they are prepared to accept PCNs and TCNs as part of the company's geocentric policy. Although Norway is not a member of the European Union, moving Norwegians into European countries is possible under the European Economic Area arrangement.

- You have been advised that the CEO is proposing the closure of the Austrian factory and moving production to a new facility in Slovenia. Plant rationalization is being considered as a way of reducing costs and closure of the Spanish factory, and even the Moss factory, would follow if this strategy is implemented.

- Owing to expansion, the US subsidiary will require four additional ski technicians in July.

- The Spanish subsidiary has indicated a need for a Finance Director in July.

- Headquarters need six people to fill vacancies, but as yet you have not received further details about occupation or level. You also have been advised that the local factory in Moss may require a Finance Director to replace the current incumbent who has been on sick-leave for 3 months. The sales/marketing office in Oslo is under-staffed.

Task

Your group has 1 hour for the following exercise:

1 Draw up the required plan to handle the transfers outlined above.

2 What additional information will you need in order to assist in the proper repatriation and reassignment of these staff? How will you access this?

3 What will you do if you find you have more vacancies than you have staff (or vice versa)?

Spanning the globe

© **Allen Engle Sr.,** Professor of International Management, Eastern Kentucky
University, Richmond, KY, USA

Eric Christopher, Associate Director for Global HR Development at Tex-Mark,
was sitting in his car in an early-morning traffic jam. He had thought that by
leaving his home at 7.00 a.m. he would have been ahead of the heavy commuter
traffic into San Antonio's city centre. The explanation for the long queue was
announced by the radio traffic service. A large, portable crane, used to set up
concrete barriers around road works, had overturned, and inbound and outbound
traffic would be at a dead stop for at least an hour.

Eric had ended up at Tex-Mark, a computer input–output manufacturer and
supplier, through an indirect career route. Brought up in the Hill Country Village
district of San Antonio, Eric had graduated from Churchill High School and Baylor
University in Waco, Texas, with a major in History and a minor in Spanish. His
maternal grandmother lived in Tennessee, but was born and grew up in Edinburgh,
Scotland, and Eric had spent several summers while in high school and at university
backpacking around Europe.

His facility for languages was impressive and he had an excellent working use
of Spanish, French, Italian and German. He could converse in Cantonese, as the
result of working in a noodle restaurant during university, and had started a
tutorial course in Mandarin last fall.

Upon graduation, Eric backpacked around Europe and South America until his
money ran out. Returning to Dallas he took a ticketing job with SouthWest Airlines
and was quickly moved to the training unit. After four successful years at South-
West, he was contacted by a headhunter about a position as Global Development –
Assistant with Tex-Mark. The promised combination of global travel, more money
and a return to San Antonio proved irresistible, and Eric had been with Tex-Mark
for 5 years now. His career progress to date was outstanding, despite the extra
workload self-imposed by undertaking MBA studies at the University of Texas,
San Antonio, as a part-time student.

Tex-Mark had started out as a 'spin off' firm from Dell Computers in the late
1970s. Patents combined with an excellence in engineering, an outstanding
institutional sales staff, cost-sensitive production and pricing, all combined to make
Tex-Mark a major force in the printer and optical scanner industry. Tex-Mark
inherited a production facility in San Antonio from Dell, but the company also had
international production facilities operating in three countries: Monterrey, Mexico;
Leith, Scotland; and, more recently, Jaipur, India. A major new facility was planned
to start production in Wuhu, China, late next year.

Research and new product development activities were split between the home
offices in San Antonio, a printer center in Durham, North Carolina, and an optical

research 'center of excellence' in Edinburgh, Scotland. Major sales, distribution and customer service centers had recently expanded into Asia and are now located in Rheims, France; Memphis, Tennessee; Sydney, Australia; Rio de Janeiro, Brazil; Hong Kong; and Tel Aviv, Israel.

Faced with the long delay, Eric turned the radio volume down, turned up the air conditioning and telephoned his office on his hands-free car phone to advise of his situation. Fortunately, his personal assistant was already at work so Eric was able to rearrange his schedule. He asked that the 10.30 a.m. meeting with Fred Banks, a Plant Engineer recently repatriated from Jaipur, be pushed back an hour. His major concern was a teleconference meeting at 2.00 p.m. with his Director, who was currently visiting the sales center in Memphis, and the other four members of executive career development team in San Antonio. The general topic was a review and evaluation of training and development strategies for expatriate professionals and managers resulting from Tex-Mark's growth and the new production shift to Asia. Eric had indirectly heard that Juanita Roberto, the Vice-President for HR, wanted costs cut and her delegates on the team would be pushing for streamlined (Eric had mentally translated that as cheaper) training programs, shorter expatriate assignments and a faster appointment of HCNs whenever possible. While Eric had prepared for this crucial meeting, he needed to incorporate some information from his office files.

The radio announcer broke into Eric's thoughts, commenting that overextension or carrying too much weight probably caused the crane to overturn. 'I can identify with that,' Eric thought to himself.

Eric's meeting with Fred Banks had not gone well. Fred was one of the last of the 'Dell legacies', a Dell engineer who had stayed on with Tex-Mark after the spin-off in 1978. Fred had been a bright and promising young engineer back then, and was one of the first people chosen to go to Scotland in 1983. He was so successful in bringing that facility on-line in an 11-month assignment that he was made lead engineer of the team that went into Mexico in 1989. The 3-year Mexican project did not go as smoothly. Certainly there were many unavoidable economic uncertainties during that period.

Reviewing the files, Eric felt that a large part of the problem was that Fred's team did not relate well to their Mexican counterparts. Furthermore, the Tex-Mark team did not treat the local and national government agencies with enough respect and sensitivity. Eric noted that permits and authorizations that should have taken weeks instead took 6 months or more.

After the Mexican project, Fred stayed in San Antonio with occasional trips to Durham, North Carolina. His assignment to India in 1999 was by sheer chance, as a last minute replacement for another engineer whose father was diagnosed with a serious cancer some 2 weeks before the family was to set off on assignment. Eric had helped design the pre-departure training program for the original candidate and had even included a 1-week visit for the candidate and his wife.

Today Fred was angry and disappointed that an 18-month assignment in India had turned into a 3-year assignment, and that a research position in Durham 'promised' to him by a previous V.P. (two V.P.s ago) was filled by a younger Durham resident employee. Eric bluntly countered that the 18-month assignment had become a 3-year assignment largely due to Fred's unwillingness to train and hand over responsibilities to local engineers and his inability to work constructively with district and federal regulators in India.

The conversation took a hostile turn and, although Eric did not lose his temper, he was troubled by Fred's final comment: 'If this is how you treat the people willing to go abroad, you'll never get your best engineers to leave San Antonio.'

Preparing for the 2.00 p.m. meeting, Eric reviewed the unofficial, yet 'standard' expatriate training program that he had been instrumental in developing over the last 3 years (see Exhibit A, below). Although Eric recommended that all pre-departure activities should be undertaken, it was not compulsory.

With the Chinese operation adding to the number of expatriate destinations, Eric realized that Tex-Mark should have a more formal policy regarding international assignments. Feedback regarding the interviews and conversations with Tex-Mark employees with country experiences was mixed. Some had developed into longer term mentoring arrangements but other expatriates had found it not useful. Still, it was a low-cost way of providing information. Language courses were problematic. On too many occasions, there was not the time – employees left the country midway through their language courses. He recalled the idea of more 'extensive' assignments requiring more 'complete' and 'rigorous' preparation from an MBA course he took last year. Obviously, China is more a more challenging and difficult assignment than France, but can we differentiate treatment on the grounds of cultural difficulty?

Exhibit A

Tex-Mark Corporation: Policy for Expatriate Preparation and On-assignment Support

Pre-departure activities

1 *'Country briefings,'* outsourced to a consulting firm in San Antonio that had experience in dealing with the countries in which Tex-Mark operated. Tex-Mark was prepared to pay for four sessions each lasting 1 hour.

2 *Reading assignments.* Three to four books (depending on region of assignment) on national or regional culture and/or doing business in the focal region. Accompanying spouses/partners had access to a similar library.

3 *Interviews and conversations* with Tex-Mark employees with country experiences.

4 *Language courses.* Attendance at elective 'survival-level' language classes. These courses last from 8 to 12 weeks, with three course meetings per week. Tex-Mark will also pay for spouses/partners.

In country training and development
Upon arrival, Tex-Mark staff in the local operation will assist the accompanying spouse/partner with job-search activities. They will assist with finding children acceptable schooling situations. Where possible, Tex-Mark staff will endeavor to provide a social support network.

Repatriation
Upon return all expatriates are required to go through a debriefing and career counselling session with HR staff. This should be held within 2 months of the person's re-entry to the home location.

More importantly, Eric asked himself, how can I suggest we make our training more rigorous given the Juanita Roberto's focus on cost? Even if I win on this point, what will I answer when asked what methods or activities make up more 'rigorous' training? Finally, what is the role of language training? Eric knew that not everyone took to languages in the way in which he did and that Mandarin is not Spanish.

Finally, is now the time to raise the issue of repatriation? The meeting with Fred had been disturbing. Eric knew that the current debriefing and counselling sessions had a reputation for being more 'tell and sell' than a meaningful exchange of ideas and insights. Top management had recently signalled this as a growing 'problem'. Eric had planned to gather data on repatriate turnover. Perhaps this should be given a higher priority. After all, how could Tex-Mark decide to plan for international assignments, involving more TCN movements, and the transfer of HCNs into its US operations for training and development, without considering repatriation?

In the role of Eric

1 Summarize your thoughts on the problems at hand, alternative solutions and your strategy on how to proceed at the forthcoming meeting.

2 How will your proposal solve the problems you have defined?

3 How can you defend your solution from budgetary concerns? In what way is your approach both a solution to the problems of expatriates at Tex-Mark and a good economic investment?

Step back out of role and answer the following

1 Does Eric's personal background assist in his assessment of the problems he faces?

2 Would you have approached this situation differently? If so, what benefits would your different approach provide for Tex-Mark?

Quality compliance at the Hawthorn Arms

© **Allen Engle Sr.**, Professor of International Management, Eastern Kentucky University, Richmond, KY, USA

Sitting in his room at the Hawthorn Arms Hotel in Shannon, Ireland, waiting for a morning flight to London and then on to Marseilles, Alistair Mackay reflects on how uninspiring hotel rooms are. He had just completed a series of meetings with Irish officials in Limerick, concluding with a debriefing session over a Guinness with his Irish colleagues to plan their next move. Negotiations over a potential contract were proceeding well but there would labor implications that would require a formal response. Consequently, Alistair had missed the last evening flight out to London. 'Another night away from the family. Thank goodness I am not missing our wedding anniversary tomorrow. I must remember to find something really special in the duty-free shop.'

Six months ago, Alistair was appointed Director of Personnel Development, European Division, for Trianon, an Anglo-French avionics firm. Trianon had begun as a subcontractor for the Concorde, and gradually had gained a reputation in the 1970s and 1980s as a high-quality, if sometimes undependable, subcontractor for major French and British aerospace defense contractors. Attempts to expand into civilian markets by gaining contracts for the original European Airbus were unsuccessful, although today nearly 30 per cent of Trianon's sales are through civilian contracts. Now, under new executive management, Trianon is focused on major navigational display contracts for the next generation of Airbus production. Prior to joining Trianon, Alistair had worked in the legal department of a Scottish bank. European Union employment requirements had become his speciality, and provided a springboard into his current position.

His cell phone rings, and he receives an unexpected call from his colleague Henri Genadry, General Director of Joint Ventures, Mergers and Acquisitions, Display Division. Henri informs him that the expected outright purchase of a scanner–cathode ray tube production facility in Veceses, outside Budapest, Hungary, was not going ahead. Instead, the decision had been made at corporate headquarters in Marseilles for a 10-year joint venture with a Hungarian government-backed firm.

Henri goes on to explain that the Hungarian control and equity interests in this project are expected to make ministry officials in Budapest happy. Henri was hopeful that the decision will make executives and administrators at Malev, the State-supported airline, friendly to Trianon in the long term. 'We will now need a "Quality Compliance Manager" for a 3-year assignment in Hungary. It is an important position as we will need to keep tight control on this joint venture operation. There will be some travel to France and Germany – at least in the first year – until we see how things are working out with these new partners.'

Alistair asks, 'When do you expect this "Quality Compliance" manager to be available?' There is a pause on the other end of the line, after which Henri blandly responds, 'Five or six weeks if we are to meet corporate timetables. We expect the person to be in on the ground, so to speak. We will need a realistic assessment of current processes for a start. The person will need to be familiar with the joint venture's objectives and targets. We have some details through the due diligence process but skills audits were somewhat rushed.' Alistair then asks that details, including a job description, be e-mailed to his intranet address.

'Well,' Henry admits, 'this is the first joint venture the firm has been involved in outside the UK, Germany or France. The job description will be very precise on the technical – "quality" – side, but vague on the administrative – "compliance" – side. You may need to fill in the missing pieces as you see fit.'

After a few more minutes of general chatting, Henri finishes the phone call. Alistair plugs his laptop into the telephone port on his room's desk, and after a few false starts, logs on to the secure corporate web site and accesses three personnel files from a folder he had prepared some weeks ago in expectation that he would be asked for a decision. Of course, he had expected the position to be that of Project Engineer in an operation of which the firm would have 100 per cent ownership. Now he was looking for a Quality Compliance Manager in a joint venture.

Alistair doesn't like making these kinds of decisions when feeling so remote and 'disconnected' from the firm. He considers calling his friend and mentor, Manfred

---

Exhibit A

Alistair Mackay's shortlist of possible candidates

First candidate:

Marie Erten-Loiseau. Born in Prague, her family moved to Toulon when she was 12 years old. Brought up in France, she was educated as an aeronautical engineer in France and Germany. Marie has worked for Trianon for 13 years, in two divisions within France and Germany with increasing levels of project responsibility. Her leadership of two projects over the last 3 years in Lodz, Poland, and two sites in Czechoslovakia has been marked by remarkable success. Married, her husband is semi-retired. They have one child in university.

Second candidate:

Janos Gabor. Born in Gyor, Hungary, Janos was educated at the University of Pecs, Hungary. He has a good background in the production of cathode-ray tube and display systems technologies, albeit from the central European perspective. He has worked at Trianon for nearly 4 years, and has just been transferred into the cathode-ray tube division as a Senior Engineer. His family is reportedly very well connected with national government officials, particularly the old, ex-party members of multiple ministerial bureaucracies. Janos is single.

Third candidate:

Sinead Marrinan-McGuire, a production engineer on loan to Trianon's London office for joint venture analyses and 'due diligence' reviews on technical and legal grounds. She has spent 3 years in the R&D development team in Dublin and London, working on the very technologies to be applied in this Hungarian joint venture project. Alistair met and talked with her today in Limerick and was very impressed with her understanding of corporate level concerns and strategic issues. Most of her career has been in Ireland and around London, with only short, tactical trips to France. Married, her husband is a solicitor in Dublin. They have three children, aged 7, 9 and 13 years.

Heinrich, in Frankfurt, Germany, and asking him about the Hungarian project, as the German based-divisions had more experience dealing with Hungarian issues. He looks at his watch. It is 22.30. 'Not a civilized time to call any one, let alone Manfred.' Alistair knew that Manfred's wife Britt had presented them with a son 3 weeks ago, and they were having trouble getting the child to sleep through the night. 'I will call him from the airport and set up a meeting. I will have the job description by then.'

He is also feeling uncomfortable with the process he is going through. Surely we can do better than react like this after the event. Why were we not part of the decision-making process on the Hungarian venture?

Questions

1 Consider the three candidates in Exhibit A. If forced to make a decision tomorrow, which candidate should Alistair choose for the job? What major factors should determine his choice?

2 We are told nothing of the process that Trianon uses to recruit candidates for this level of final selection. Given what you know about the firm from the case, outline a general recruitment and selection process for Trianon. Describe how your proposed process fits with 'best' selection practices as well as the strategic needs of this company.

3 Should HR staff be involved in strategic decisions relating to international business operations such as finalizing a joint venture agreement?

Conflicting expectations
Where pay and performance collide[1]

UpTech Support is a medium-sized US company, based in Silicon Valley, California, operating in the intensely competitive computer industry. Its main area is the development of software support systems. It had survived the so-called 'Internet bubble burst', its management believed, because the company had resisted the temptation to move from its area of core competence. Instead, UpTech Support concentrated on building up relationships with its key clients. Consequently, it was now a successful company in its market niche, with sales offices in the major cities across the USA. Its international operations, however, were small, with a sales subsidiary in Canada, one in France and, recently, a sales subsidiary in Australia. The Canadian office had been established early in the 1990s and was treated by staff within the US headquarters as merely an extension of the US operation.

The choice of the other international markets was somewhat fortuitous. UpTech Support's major US client had formed a strategic alliance with a French counterpart, and UpTech Support had been successful in extending its service to the French-based entity. The Australian initiative was likewise due to following US clients. In both of these markets, international activities were confined to sales and client service with the US headquarters responsible for product development.

This morning, two top executives of UpTech Support are trying to understand how what had seemed a simple salary decision developed into a major issue. Jessica Kellaway, the Vice-President of International Operations, was particularly perplexed. She read carefully the report Steve Hegworth, the Human Resource Director, had compiled. Pierre Lecruet had seemed the logical choice to send to Australia to head the local operation. Why was he now focused on his salary package rather than concentrating on improving UpTech Support's market position?

Jessica voiced this concern aloud. 'I am at a loss here, Steve. We hired Pierre 5 years ago when we established the French operation. He did an excellent job in terms of the French market, but now he seems to be only interested in how much money he can extract in terms of pay and benefits.'

Steve agreed, 'It is strange. Pierre had discussed his career aspirations with us during a routine performance appraisal session before the Australian position arose. The company was performing well in France, and Pierre had considered that the job was losing its challenge. As Managing Director, there was nowhere else for him to go within the French operation.'

Indeed, it was with some relief to all concerned that Pierre accepted the challenge of repeating his French success in the new Australian initiative. At the time, Jessica and Steve were in agreement that using a trusted manager with a proven track record seemed to be less risky than employing an unknown local Australian.

Steve continued, 'Pierre knew that if he performed as expected in Australia, there were plans to move him into a position within the top management team here at headquarters in Silicon Valley. What that position may be is, at this stage, somewhat vague, Jessica. As I said, it is strange we are now having problems.

Pierre is so ambitious. He must know that his current behavior will have a negative impression here and affect his future with us.'

'Yes,' agreed his colleague, 'and perhaps with hindsight we should have employed an Australian. After all, that is what we did in Canada, and France, for that matter, when we hired Pierre. Or perhaps we should have sent someone from here.'

His American colleagues were right. Pierre was ambitious and had taken on the Australian position with great eagerness. Here was an opportunity to prove that he was deserving of a top management position within the US operations. The decision to relocate to Sydney had not been so straightforward on the personal side, though. The expatriate contract stipulated a minimum period of 2 years, with the possibilities of an extension should the situation warrant it. Pierre's wife, Sabine, had her own career and it was difficult to ask if she would be prepared to resign her current position – to put his needs before hers. Sabine had just recommenced her teaching position after spending several years at home. Their youngest child was now of school age, and Sabine was happy to be back in a part-time position at a local high school. In the end, they agreed that Pierre would spend the first 6 months in Sydney alone. That would give him time to settle into the new work environment, find suitable accommodation for the family and explore suitable schools for their two children. It would give Sabine an extra 6 months working as a teacher, and minimize the disruption to their children's education.

Work consumed Pierre's time – apart from two quick visits home to Paris. It had been agreed that Pierre would be paid according to his home base salary, with the usual variable bonus linked to performance. When Pierre received his first payment in Sydney, he was surprised to find that Australian base salaries were higher on average. However, he has too busy establishing the new operation to spend much time worrying about it. Besides, he was being paid in Euros, which were enjoying a favourable exchange rate with the Australian dollar.

It was when the family joined him in Sydney that the problems started. First, he moved from a small flat into a family-sized house. Sydney is the most expensive city in Australia, and rental charges reflected this. As they owned their own spacious apartment in Paris, paying rent in Sydney was a noticeable outlay. Although they were renting out the Paris apartment, they had financial responsibilities at home that needed to be covered by that relatively small income. Second, the children were shocked to find that they were expected to operate in English at school. Sabine had investigated the possibility of the children receiving additional French lessons provided by the organization Alliance Françoise. During discussions with the staff at the Sydney office of Alliance Françoise, Sabine was informed that a private school in Sydney offered students the option of 'immersion French' – a study stream where all subjects were conducted in French. Both Pierre and his wife were impressed by their visit to this private school but not at the cost involved. Sabine was firm in her opinion that UpTech Support should pay for school fees and expenses. Pierre e-mailed this request to Jessica, as head of the international division. Jessica promptly forwarded his e-mail to Steve, as she saw this as an HR concern. After much consideration, Steve offered to meet half of the cost of the children's educational expenses.

Sabine had also found that there was an informal social club, formed by expatriate spouses, which met once per month. Attending her first meeting, she found that other companies were paying more benefits than those UpTech Support were providing for them. 'For instance, Pierre,' Sabine told her husband over dinner that night, 'some of the women had a company car for their own use. You have a company-provided car, but I must use public transport or take taxis. Other women were talking about something called COLA, which I discovered was shorthand for cost of living allowance.'

'I had not thought of that,' Pierre commented, 'I start from a lower base salary compared with my Australian counterparts. A cost of living allowance would help to bring that up to a level that would compensate for some of the loss of purchasing power.'

Pierre was fully aware that the Australian assignment had to be a success on the home front as well. Sabine's attitude to international assignments would be critical to any future moves other than back to France. Maintaining their accustomed standard of living was proving to be a key factor in assuring that his family was content with their expatriate situation. He admitted to himself that his work performance was being affected by family concerns and the salary issue needed to be quickly resolved. Another e-mail was sent to headquarters.

Steve had groaned when he read the e-mail from Pierre. A second company car? Cost of living adjustment? It could not cost him more to live in Sydney than it did in Paris, surely. Steve realized that he would have to discuss these latest requests with Jessica. He quickly got an assistant to surf the Internet to find comparative data on salary levels between France, Australia and the USA. The results were included in the report he had taken to this morning's meeting.

Questions

1 What information, other than comparative salary levels, should the HR Director, Steve Hegworth, have specifically asked his assistant to collect prior to his meeting with Jessica Kellaway? How would you access these extra data?

2 How would you recommend that the company proceed in this case?

3 Should UpTech Support develop expatriate compensation policies or continue to treat each expatriate case on an *ad hoc* basis?

Note

1 This hypothetical case was prepared by Denice Welch and Peter Dowling. The idea was prompted by one written in the early 1980s, although its author is unknown. We have extensively rewritten and updated the case for teaching purposes. We have made extensive efforts, to no avail, to trace the author of the original idea so that due acknowledgement can be made in future editions. Anyone who could assist us trace its origins is encouraged to contact us via the publisher.

'Keep safe ducky': or, when Sally met a not-so-nice Harry[1]

© Denice Welch and Lisa Hewerdine, 2003

The Business Class Lounge in Singapore Airport was relatively deserted when Sally entered. It was 22.00 hours local time. There seemed to be only one staff member visible – the woman who checked her boarding pass at the front desk of the Lounge. After two hectic days with distributors in Hong Kong, coupled with a departure delay due to thick fog that caused her to miss her connecting flight to Delhi, India, a quiet environment was just what Sally wanted. She sank gratefully into a sofa in the middle of the Lounge complex, placed her handbag on the coffee table, and pulled her travel case beside her. She sat for a few minutes idly watching the goldfish in a large tank in front of her seat. 'Four hours to wait,' she thought, 'Oh well, I can get my weekly sales report written up, so I will only have to add the updated sales figures when I connect to e-mail when I check-in at the Ribero Hotel in Delhi. It will be in the boss's inbox in Sydney on time, not that I will get any praise for that.'

Sally Palmer was the modern version of the travelling salesman. At 26 years old, she had been just 2 years in her present position as Marketing Manager, responsible for selling medical equipment for a US firm, although Sally was hired by, and reported to, the Australian subsidiary. The sales department was small. Sally was one of four sales representatives – but the only female – who sold products into the various countries that comprised what the US parent defined as the Far East Asian Region, taking in South-East Asia, the Middle East and Africa. The position involved frequent travel to each country, with the primary tasks of maintaining good relationships with current distributors or signing up new ones, and making presentations or arranging for demonstrations of medical products to potential and current clients in the large hospitals.

Sally's immediate boss, the head of the Australian subsidiary, Bill Burton, was one of the four who travelled. Apart from his overall responsibilities for the Asian Region, Bill took the Middle East markets as his territory. Sally was responsible for Hong Kong, Indonesia and Indian markets. Bill was unconcerned about the stresses and strains that the lifestyle of an international sales representative imposed on the individual. After all, he travelled as much as they did. Consequently, there was definitely a hands-on, learn-by-doing approach to conducting business internationally. None of them had been offered the possibility of cultural awareness or international negotiations training. The only concession that Bill seemed to make where Sally was concerned was his parting comment if he happened to be in the Australian office when Sally was preparing for yet another international sales trip: 'Keep safe, Ducky'. This comment amused Sally. Occasionally, Bill's expressions would reveal his Welsh–English upbringing. 'Ducky' was one such expression. Sally did not expect to receive any special treatment from her colleagues because of her gender, neither did she need telling how important it was for her to observe local customs. She was very careful about how she dressed and behaved, particularly when travelling into Muslim countries. This aspect had been stressed when, as an undergraduate student, specializing in International Business, she undertook a Country Studies course that included visits to South-East Asian countries.

The important performance objective was the sale. Bill's mantra was: 'Don't come home until the deal is closed,' which Sally sometimes thought contradicted his unwritten, but often articulated, policy that they should only stay in one country for 2 weeks at a time. This was Bill's way of recognizing that country visits could be gruelling work and that a tired sales force was counter-productive. However, there was no formal policy regarding travel. Sally's last contact with any staff in the subsidiary's HR department had been 2 years ago upon her appointment to her current position.

The job was Sally's dream come true. Ever since completing her undergraduate degree, she had worked hard to obtain a job in which she could travel. Selling came naturally to her and, being single and unattached at the moment, she did not mind the long stretches of visits to the various international markets. It was exciting, even exotic, and she knew she was the envy of some of her friends. Travelling in business class, using lounges like the one she was sitting in now, staying in quality hotels, enjoying new sights and sounds, novel locations, duty-free shopping, who would not like it? Sally could count on one hand the number of weeks she had spent in her own home in the last 2 years.

It was hard work, though. The past 2 days were typical. Sally had arranged with the firm's local distributor in Hong Kong to demonstrate a piece of medical equipment to theatre staff in two major hospitals. She had arrived on a late-evening flight from Sydney and it seemed that she had only just got to sleep when the telephone rang. The bedside clock indicated 3.50 a.m. She picked up the handset to find it was the distributor ringing from the hotel lobby, asking if she was ready to go and that he had a takeaway hamburger and coffee in a bag for her breakfast. It was 10 p.m. before Sally returned to her hotel. Both days had been long as there had been small dramas with the demonstration equipment and lengthy sessions over endless cups of coffee negotiating the deal. 'We did it though,' Sally smiled to herself, remembering the celebratory meal with the local distributor last night. 'I must look a mess, not enough sleep, no make-up on,' she thought.

Sally booted her computer and started her weekly report. One hour passed quickly. Her mobile phone beeped, and she read the text message. It was from a friend and Sally was returning the message when a voice interrupted her: 'Can I sit here?' Sally glanced up as a man who looked to be at least 50 years old sat down on the sofa adjacent to her, and placed a plate of food and a glass of what looked like whisky on the table beside her laptop.

Sally looked around. The adjacent sofas and armchairs all around her were empty. In fact, the lounge looked deserted still. The man had already sat down, so what answer was he expecting? Sally finished sending her text message, and then recommenced her report. The man interrupted her again, asking if he could fetch her a drink or some food from the buffet across the room. Sally absently answered, 'No thank you. I am fine.' He pressured her, seemingly refusing to take no for an answer. In the end, Sally suggested a cup of tea. She thanked him, but then found herself being handed a plate of ice cream and a glass of white wine. Sally declined both and made a point of returning to her work on the laptop.

Seemingly undeterred by Sally's attitude, the man got up out of his seat and returned immediately back with a bowl of chips, and then a plate of sandwiches.

The coffee table was soon cluttered with untouched plates of food and glasses of untouched drinks. Sally suddenly realized that every time the man returned from the buffet, he took a different seat. This time, he was sitting on the same sofa. He then offered Sally his business card and for a moment, the situation appeared normal. The man asks where Sally is going, and remarks that India is also his destination, and wants to know if she is going there on business. Sally politely returns the small talk for a minute and then returns to her computer. Undaunted, the man leans forward and picks up Sally's boarding pass, which was poking out of a side pocket in her handbag. 'Well, this is fate. We have adjoining seats on the same flight.'

The man moves closer and puts his hand on her knee. Sally is now alarmed. 'This is not normal. This is not happening.'

Questions

1 How would you have handled the situation in which Sally finds herself?

2 Would such a situation have occurred if Sally had been a male?

3 Should Sally report this incident to her line manager, Bill Burton?

4 Should the Australian subsidiary's HR department be made aware of this incident?

Note

1 This case is based on a true incident. Names and locations have been altered to preserve the anonymity of the person concerned.

Jaguar or bluebird?
(A) Mark Chan's decision to stay overseas or return home after his expatriate assignment[1]

Günter K. Stahl (INSEAD Singapore), **Chei Hwee Chua** (University of South Carolina) and **Rebekah France** (INSEAD MBA 03J),

Sitting in a field filled with yellow buttercups, Mark Chan took in a deliberate deep breath of the fresh English country air and felt a sense of contentment as he basked in the warm summer sunshine. He and his family were having a Sunday picnic with their neighbours, the Howards, in their neighbourhood park. Some distance away, his wife Linda was happily chatting with the Howards while his two children and the little Howards played with their dog.

Looking at them brought back fond memories of their time in England so far. Almost 5 years ago, Mark accepted an expatriate assignment and moved to England from Singapore with his family. Mark was glad that his family had settled down happily. They made new friends and assimilated well into the English culture and lifestyle.

Mark gave out a sigh. The thought of having to decide on his next career move hit him again. His international assignment in England was coming to an end in 3 months' time and he could either continue pursuing an international career or return back to Singapore. Mark felt that deciding on his next career move had never been so difficult. This time, he had a lot more to consider. He not only had to take into account his own career development needs, but also the needs of his wife and children. Mark knew that his company was expecting his answer within the next few days, but the numerous discussions he had with Linda in weighing the pros and cons of each career option could just never come to a decisive conclusion. The more Mark thought about it, the more confused and frustrated he got.

Mark's thoughts triggered his memory back to the critical career decisions that he had made in the past and the series of events that led to his current predicament.

A bachelor on the road: an initial string of international assignments

Mark started his career at the Singapore subsidiary of a Japanese consulting company and embarked on a string of international assignments that lasted about 1 year each. These international assignments brought him to Japan, Thailand, Indonesia, Vietnam and Malaysia. His job was to help foreign companies to scout and evaluate merger or acquisition opportunities in Asia, as well as the negotiations and closing of the deals. Deciding on taking up these international assignments was easy. He had always liked the idea of living and working overseas and learning about new cultures. He was a bachelor and his parents were not too old then and could take care of themselves. There was nothing to tie him down.

Homeward bound: starting a new job and family

After working overseas for 6 years, Mark got married and decided that it was time for him to settle down back in Singapore and start a family. He joined the Singapore subsidiary of Energem,[2] a diversified, global company with market-leading positions in a number of industries, including speciality chemicals, polymers, health care and gases and related products. Headquartered in the UK, Energem employs over 60 000 people worldwide and has extensive operations in Europe, North and South America and Asia Pacific. Joining Energem at mid-career, Mark was offered a position as a marketing manager at its Speciality Chemicals division, with responsibilities for corporate accounts of multinational companies in South-East Asia. Based on Energem's global management ranking structure,[3] it was a level 4 middle-management position. Mark was attracted to Energem because it offered international career prospects and had a well-known leadership development program for 'high potentials,' including those who had been recruited locally.

A year later, Mark had a job change and a promotion to level 3. He accepted the offer by Energem's corporate unit, Group Mergers & Acquisitions (M&A), to join its team as M&A manager and analyst for Asia-Pacific. Energem was starting to embark on M&A activities in this region and Mark's past experience fitted well with the requirements of the job. Mark reported directly to the global M&A Vice-President who was based in the UK and Mark's responsibilities included scouting for M&A opportunities, conducting due diligence and negotiations and liaison with Energem's various country heads and global business line heads.

An international assignment opportunity

At the end of his third year at Energem, Mark was offered a 3-year international assignment opportunity at the corporate headquarters in London by Energem's Group Information Technology (IT) unit. Mark was very excited about the offer. The job was to conduct M&A activities for the strategic IT needs of Energem's joint ventures globally. Accepting the offer would mean another promotion for Mark and he would enter Energem's senior management category. He would report directly to the Chief Information Officer and would be close to the 'Gods' at corporate headquarters. Mark also relished the challenge of living and working overseas, and the salary and expatriate benefits package were very attractive. Mark remembered that although making the decision to accept the assignment was not as easy as it had been during his bachelor days, he did not find himself in a huge dilemma. Although Linda would have to give up her job as a private banker to follow him on the assignment and they had two children, they both agreed that it was a small window of opportunity for them to go overseas since their children were still very young and Linda could take a break from her career and spend more time with the children.

An expatriate again

Mark recalled his first day at work in the London office. He felt comfortable and settled into his new office easily. Since he had been to the London office rather often in the past, he knew the place well and also knew a number of colleagues based there through past projects. By early evening, he was already having a beer with a few colleagues in the pub near the office.

Despite the initial friendliness, Mark soon realized that there were some colleagues who felt that he got the job because Energem needed a 'token Asian' in the team to show that it valued diversity. Since Energem's M&A activities in Asia were of a smaller scale compared with those in Europe and the USA, they did not think that someone from a subsidiary in Asia would have the knowledge and ability required for the job. Mark knew that there was nothing much that he could do about this perception, except to prove them wrong. Leveraging on his expertise in conducting due diligence and consummating M&As gained within Energem and through his 6 years as an M&A consultant prior to joining Energem, Mark learned quickly and performed well on the job. As time went by, he earned the respect of those colleagues who had their doubts initially. Mark also used the expatriate assignment opportunity to hone his cross-cultural skills and expand his network of contacts within and outside Energem. When his 3-year contract came to an end, he was offered an extension of 2 years. He had a promotion to level 1 and was now responsible for special M&A projects within Group IT that were confidential and of a larger scale.

On the home front, Mark and his family had settled down in England happily and found the English lifestyle appealing. Energem provided them with a large house with a big garden in the countryside, less than an hour by train to Mark's office in London. They also bought an old English sheepdog – something which they had always wanted but were unable to do as their apartment in Singapore could not accommodate such a big dog. As Mark and his family were Christians, they got to know the people in their neighbourhood quickly through attending church services and activities. Some colleagues also lived in the same neighbourhood. Mark and his family found it relatively easy to integrate into the local community. They became close friends with several neighbours and often had dinner parties or Sunday picnics together.

After having been a working mum, Linda was thrilled at her new 'occupation' as a full-time home-maker. Linda found herself busier than when she was working. She had always felt guilty for not spending enough time with the children and was glad to make it up to them during their time in London. She felt that it was important to spend as much time as she could with them during their formative years. Linda made friends with the other home-makers in the neighbourhood quickly and often met up with them for afternoon teas to exchange gardening tips and cooking recipes. Linda was fascinated by the gardens of their neighbours and became interested in gardening. Soon, their garden was as lovely as those of their neighbours and Linda was especially proud of her plot of red roses which bloomed beautifully in spring and summer.

As Mark continued to reminisce about how they had spent their time in England so far, he realized that the time they spent together as a family had been much more than when they were back home in Singapore and they had became more close-knit. Being away from relatives and friends in Singapore and having to travel a lot during the week, Mark made it a point not to work during the weekends and often brought the family out on weekend excursions and holidays. Back in Singapore, Mark's family led a typical Singaporean lifestyle. When they went out, they would shop, eat and watch movies at the various large shopping malls found in the city. Hence they found the typical English countryside lifestyle a refreshing change and eagerly adopted it. They especially enjoyed the long walks in the parks nearby, the drives around the English countryside, visits to the castles and the horse rides on the hilly greens. The family also often went on weekend holidays to the neighbouring countries. Moreover, compared with the year-round hot and humid climate in Singapore, they preferred the English temperate climate and were fascinated by the changes in seasons.

Being a car enthusiast, Mark was thrilled by the affordability of cars in England. Owing to the Singapore government's efforts at preventing traffic congestion in the small city state, even ordinary cars are luxury items. In Singapore, he could only afford a Nissan Bluebird. But in England, Mark had two cars and they were a Jaguar and a Triumph convertible. With an expatriate salary and benefit package, a temperate climate, a large house with a big garden in the countryside and two fancy cars, Mark's family found themselves living a life that they could only dream of in Singapore.

A bugle call for return

At the end of their fourth year in England, Linda's father passed away unexpectedly after a heart attack. After the funeral, Linda stayed back in Singapore with the children for a month to take care of her mother. The months after her return to England proved to be very difficult. Although she had a younger brother who could take care of their mother and she had always been happy and satisfied with life in England, she was often worried about her mother and felt the need to return to Singapore permanently to take care of her.

An international career or return home to Singapore?

Seeing that Linda was yearning to return home, Mark started to look for a position back at the Singapore subsidiary of Energem. After 8 months of searching, Mark was beginning to lose hope when he learned that the Regional General Manager (Asia-Pacific) for the Specialty Chemicals division had unexpectedly left for a job at one of their competitors, and Energem had to fill his position quickly with a manager who was familiar with the Asia-Pacific markets. Given his familiarity with the markets in this region and his extensive international experience, Mark thought that he was the natural candidate for this position. He was prepared to accept it on the spot.

Mark remembered clearly the Monday morning when he received the phone call from the Global Vice-President of the Specialty Chemicals division telling him that although nobody doubted his qualification, they had offered the job to one of his former colleagues who was based at Energem's Singapore subsidiary.

The memory of that phone conversation and the resulting emotions of anger, disbelief and betrayal all came back to him. 'It's ridiculous,' he told Linda when he informed her about the bad news, 'they selected someone with zero international experience! What happened to all that talk about being a global player and the importance of international experience? It's all crap!'

Having the door closed on this option, Mark was left with the offer of a middle management position in the Polymers Division to consider. The Global Vice-President of the Polymers Division told Mark that he was impressed with his track record and that he valued his international experience. However, there were simply no senior management positions available at the moment and he could only offer Mark the position of regional marketing manager for its rubber and coatings business in Asia Pacific. He added that this would be a temporary position and that Mark would be given first priority consideration as soon as a senior management position becomes available at the Singapore organization.

The other option that Mark had was to continue pursuing his international career. Having proved his abilities in handling global M&A activities, Mark was offered a 3-year international assignment at Energem's subsidiary in The Netherlands to where they were about to relocate the headquarters of the corporate unit, Group Mergers

& Acquisitions, reflecting Energem's attempts to decentralize critical functions and units. Mark was offered the position of Global Strategy Manager for Energem's special M&A projects. This would mean a promotion to level D. Naturally, the promotion would also mean a higher salary and he would continue to enjoy the perks as an expatriate. On the other hand, taking up the regional marketing manager position in Singapore would essentially mean a demotion. He would have to accept a salary cut and would lose all the expatriate benefits.

The question that Mark continually wrestled with was: 'Does it make sense to give up an attractive international career and a good life in Europe for a return to Singapore at a lower rank position?' Career-wise, the answer was clearly 'No'. On the other hand, Linda had been pressuring him to return to Singapore. Moreover, looking at things on a long-term basis, Mark knew that moving back to Singapore now would be the best option for Linda and possibly also the children. If they stayed abroad too long, Linda would find it even more difficult to continue her banking career. As for the children, they had started to go to school. Unlike England's educational system, on which the Singapore's system is based, The Netherlands is Dutch-speaking and has a very different educational system. Mark thought, 'If we don't move back now, it will be even harder for everybody in the future. But I have worked so hard to be where I am now! I don't want to throw my career away.'

Having been absorbed in his thoughts for some time, Mark suddenly heard giggling and felt a tiny hug from behind. It was his younger son, John. 'Daddy! It's time to eat now! The shepherd's pie that Mrs Howard brought looks really delicious!' As Mark walked towards the rest of his family and the Howards, he felt torn between his career aspirations and the long-term needs of his family. Mark knew that whichever decision he made, either his career or family would suffer.

Notes

1   This case is intended for classroom discussion rather than to illustrate either effective or ineffective handling of an administrative situation.
2   This is a fictitious name.
3   Energem's global management ranking structure is as follows: levels 9, 8, 7, 6 and 5 are junior management positions, levels 4 and 3 are middle management positions and levels 2, 1, D, C, B and A are senior management positions.

Jaguar or bluebird?
(B) Mark Chan returns home after his expatriate assignment[1]

Günter K. Stahl (INSEAD Singapore), Chei Hwee Chua (University of South Carolina) and Rebekah France (INSEAD MBA 03J)

Home sweet home

After several more rounds of long discussions with Linda, they finally decided to move back to Singapore. The needs of his wife, children and mother-in-law were the over-riding factors in his decision.

The following months were spent packing and shipping their things and bidding farewells. Other than that, they did not have much time to think about their return to Singapore until the day of the departure. In fact, it did not cross their mind that it was something that they had to be mentally prepared for. 'After all, Singapore is home,' they thought.

Reality bites

It had been half a year since Mark and his family moved back to Singapore. To their surprise, adapting back to life in Singapore turned out to be not as easy as they had imagined. After getting used to living in a large house with a big garden in the countryside for 5 years, their apartment in Singapore seemed much smaller than before. Although they lived in a luxurious condominium complex with facilities such as swimming pools, jacuzzis, saunas, gym and tennis courts, they simply missed the vastness of the English countryside and the lifestyle that they led in England. Mark no longer had his fancy cars and drove a Nissan Bluebird, as he used to do 5 years ago, before he left Singapore. Linda had to give up her gardening. The children missed their teachers and friends at school. And they all missed their dog terribly. It was impossible to bring it back since it would have been too large for their apartment.

While the whole family was having dinner one evening, Mark's elder son, Jeremy, suddenly blurted out, 'I really *don't* want to go to school *any more*!' '*Me too*!' John, the younger one, followed.

Total silence fell upon the dining room. Tears started to trickle down Linda's face and she began sobbing uncontrollably. She, too, was unhappy. All the tensions and unhappiness that had built up over the past 6 months suddenly came out in the open. She could no longer pretend that it was great to move home. She knew that all of them were, in one way or another, unhappy with their new life back in Singapore.

Five months ago, Jeremy and John went to school on the first day with a bright and cheery face, but came back quiet and gloomy. Especially Jeremy; he hadn't been quite his usual chirpy self since then. Except for the weekends, the boys were either tired or felt ill every morning, and wanted to skip school. Mark and Linda found out that they did not like going to school because they felt out of place and were unable to make new friends. They said that very often, their teachers and classmates could not understand what they were saying and neither could they fully understand what their teachers and classmates were saying. Having lived in England since they were 2 and 3 years old, respectively, both boys grew up speaking English with a clear British accent. So, being in an environment where their new teachers and classmates spoke 'Singlish' – English with a Singaporean accent and Singaporean slang words – communication became a problem. Sometimes, their classmates made fun of their accent by imitating them. They also found Mandarin classes tough since they did not have Mandarin classes in England and they spoke English at home. Therefore, Linda engaged a private tutor to give the boys additional Mandarin classes. Linda and Mark consoled them and told them that they should give school a try and that things would get better. The sudden outburst at the dinner table showed that things obviously did not get better.

Linda and Mark could empathize with their children. Although Linda was happy to be back in Singapore so that she could take care of her mother, she found her life back in Singapore less satisfying than she had imagined while she was in England. In the beginning, her friends were glad to have her back and listened to her about her life in England with interest. However, this interest waned and they started switching topics whenever she mentioned England. Soon, Linda found it difficult to identify with her friends. Sometimes, she couldn't help feeling that some of them who had always lived in Singapore were rather myopic and uninteresting, whereas at other times, she felt left out when they talked about their jobs and office politics. Another problem was job search. Linda was keen to start working again, but with the economic downturn in Singapore, there were few suitable job openings. The application letters that Linda sent either had no replies or were rejected.

For Mark, he began to regret his decision to accept the job in Singapore. When he accepted the position, he knew that it would be a demotion in rank and the scope of his responsibilities would be less. However, he did not expect that he would be feeling bored with the job after just a few months.

Mark started asking the Global Vice-President of the division about more senior positions, but was told that such positions were not available at the moment and that he should be patient. With the downturn of the global economy, there was no growth in the Division's business, particularly in Asia-Pacific. And nobody at the senior management level was leaving or retiring soon. Mark also got the same answer from the other Divisions. After 6 months, Mark realized that his 'temporary' position might not be 'temporary' after all, since senior management positions in Singapore would not be available for quite a while. He felt trapped.

The outbursts by his two children and his wife reminded Mark of his own frustration with his current job situation and his anger of being not offered the Regional General Manager position in the Specialty Chemicals Division. 'This is simply unfair! What's the point of getting international experience when it doesn't get you a decent job back home?,' he thought, bitterly. 'How long am I supposed to wait? I've had enough! There must be companies out there that value international experience.'

After consoling his wife and children, Mark went to his home office and dialled the mobile phone number of his friend Nigel, who was head of the local office of an international executive search firm.

Note

1   This case is intended for classroom discussion rather than to illustrate either effective or ineffective handling of an administrative situation.

Andrew Robinson goes to Taiwan
The challenges of a short-term assignment[1]

© Catherine Welch, University of New South Wales, Australia

Andrew Robinson had been working as a software developer in the computer industry for 10 years and had recently joined the subsidiary of a major multinational telecommunications equipment supplier in Sydney, Telequip Australia. Andrew was born in Australia, had studied at an Australian university, did not speak a foreign language and had never worked abroad, although his family had lived abroad when he was of pre-school age and while still a student he had visited parts of Asia and Europe. Andrew knew he had outstanding technical skills as a software programmer and troubleshooter, and he had accumulated extensive experience in developing software for the telecommunications industry.

When Andrew joined Telequip Australia, he was assigned to the company's network management division, which was in the process of developing a management platform for its main domestic customer. A network management platform is the nervous system of a telecommunications network. When something goes wrong in the network, the management platform sends messages to the 'brain' of the network, the control center. The platform was always designed to be generic and to be sold to other telecommunications operators in the world market. It would be Telequip Australia's first 'world product'.

Andrew worked on the network management system for the domestic customer for about 6 months. The first releases of the product had been installed when a Taiwanese telecommunications carrier, Taicom, became the first foreign company to sign a contract with Telequip Australia for the network management system. Because of the many different requirements of telecom operators, the network system would require extensive adaptation and new features to be developed, so initial estimates were that the contract would require 6 months of development before Taicom would have the new system up and running. It was anticipated that a large degree of re-use from the project for the domestic customer would be possible, particularly for the first few releases.

In addition to the software to be provided by Telequip Australia, Telequip North America was providing hardware and finance. The total value of the hardware was about 10 times the value of the Australian software.

Andrew was asked if he wanted to join the Taiwanese project and, happy at the prospect of a change, agreed. All the development work for the project would be done in Australia, with just a single manager, Jonathan Samuels, being sent to Taipei from Sydney on a full-time basis. The most senior manager on the project, Malcolm Donaghue, was based in Australia, but the understanding was that he would spend about half his time in Taipei. Because of shortages of staff and demands from other projects, most of the staff on the project were newly hired subcontractors from India with no experience of the industry.

Andrew knew that it was likely he would have to make a few short trips to Taipei to install and test software during the life of the project, but he didn't mind the idea of visiting a city he hadn't been to before. He liked Chinese food and had a lot of friends of Chinese descent, so he didn't feel that Taiwan would be too alien.

Andrew joined the project in November and in January was on the plane to Taipei for a 4-week visit. His initial few weeks on the project had been very positive and he felt that the technical aspects of the project were on track. The small development team in Australia had been making progress and hitting deadlines. The view from Taipei was very different. Taicom was not happy with progress: the system was frequently down, and even when it was running it was incapable of handling the promised load.

Andrew also had the feeling that Jonathan, although a hard worker, was not comfortable in Taipei. Although Jonathan rarely complained, he never seemed happy either. He never went out, worked 7 days a week, had not made any friends among the locals and had not made any attempts to learn Chinese. He never had a good word for his Chinese colleagues and it had not occurred to him to get business cards in Chinese. Andrew began to have his doubts about whether Jonathan was the most suitable person to act as Telequip's liaison with Taicom.

It seemed that Malcolm was also not entirely at ease in Taipei. This surprised Andrew, because Malcolm had worked in Hong Kong for some years and was the only one on the project with Asian experience. However, Malcolm's problem seemed to be that he was having trouble managing a project that now spanned two countries. He was not able to prevent further delays to the project and his only solution to a problem seemed to be to ask his staff in Taipei to work harder. He worked himself harder still. Andrew became frustrated that Malcolm did not send more work back to the development team in Australia, and that communication between staff in the two locations was so poor.

One day, Andrew's wife rang him during office hours to report that they had exceeded their limit on their credit card and she had not been able to use it. 'That doesn't sound right,' he responded, 'I haven't paid the hotel bill yet, so I don't see how we could have run up such a large amount on the card. I have been keeping track of how much I am spending.'

It transpired that the hotel had placed a hold on his card when he had checked in, pushing the amount on the card to its limit.

'Couldn't Telequip have given you a company credit card to use while you are over there?' his wife said.

'I'm afraid that's not how they work. They will reimburse me when I get back home and hand over my receipts.'

'But in the meantime I am going to have to use cash,' his wife grumbled. 'Why couldn't they have at least warned you about this? We could have increased our limit in advance.'

'It could be worse,' said Andrew. 'One of my colleagues has shown up here without a credit card at all. A couple of others had space on their cards so his hotel bill and expenses have been shared between them.'

Andrew returned to Australia after his 4-week stay in Taipei, slept 40 hours in 3 days, then went back to work as normal. He and his wife had been house-hunting and on his return from Taipei found a house they liked, so signed a contract on it. Under the terms of the contract, settlement on the house would take place in May and he and his wife would move straight in.

In April, a few weeks after he had signed the contract on the house, Andrew was approached by Malcolm and asked if he would be prepared to go to Taipei for a more extended period of time. Taicom was complaining that they didn't have any visibility over the project since the work was being done in Australia, so Malcolm was convinced that Telequip needed more people on the ground in Taipei. Andrew pointed out that he had just bought a house and needed to be in Australia for settlement, but Malcolm felt confident that that could be accommodated in the schedule and assured Andrew that he could put together an attractive though unspecified financial incentive for the short-term assignment. Andrew went home to consult his wife and both agreed that since it would not be a good career move to turn Malcolm down, and since the extra money would be welcome in view of the fact they were about to start making repayments on a mortgage, Andrew should take up the assignment. 'I'll come back to Australia to help you move, anyway,' Andrew assured his wife. 'Malcolm knows about the house and knows that's something he has to work around.'

Accordingly, Andrew let Malcolm know that he would accept the assignment, but requested 2 weeks' grace so he could get himself ready. He also asked that he receive in writing the terms and conditions of his assignment. At this stage it wasn't clear how long the assignment would last, but under the terms of his visa he would not be able to stay in Taiwan for more than 60 days at a time.

Two days later, Malcolm came to him and said, 'Look, it's bad news. Taicom have told us that if we don't meet the next deadline they'll cancel the project and we'll be kicked out. I am flying out tomorrow and need some technical staff to come with me for backup. I know you said 2 weeks, but this is urgent.' Andrew didn't like the idea of having to break this latest development to his wife, but he agreed and his flight was booked. He spent the afternoon trying to finish the most urgent tasks on which he was working, leave instructions for the team he was supervising and copy his most important files on to the laptop he would be taking with him to Taipei. At 5 o'clock his personnel officer e-mailed a short memo setting out his financial entitlements for the short-term assignment. It was 8 o'clock in the evening before he arrived home, by which time his wife had packed his suitcase.

On the plane he took out the document outlining his entitlements. Now that he was classed as being on a short-term assignment, rather than a business trip, the financial arrangements for his stay in Taipei had changed. He would still be paid his usual salary and would remain on the Telequip Australia payroll, but he was entitled to an additional daily per diem. Jonathan had already told him to claim the per diem at the end of each month, and the money would be paid straight into his bank account in Australia. The per diem was generous, but Andrew knew his wife wouldn't be pleased that he would still be using his personal credit card. He had at least arranged with the bank to raise his credit limit while he was back in Australia.

When he and Malcolm arrived in Taipei, a full-blown crisis had indeed developed. Taicom was very concerned about missed deadlines and, even worse, complained that the product that had been delivered so far did not meet their requirements. There was a strong sense that if Telequip did not devise a way to meet some of Taicom's grievances then the project would be cancelled. Failure of the project would have serious ramifications for the global marketing of the product. Malcolm was working 12-hour days, 7 days a week, and expected Andrew to do the same. Andrew didn't mind hard work but he wondered how long he could keep up such a demanding schedule.

Andrew was staying in a hotel but there was an expectation that he would find alternative accommodation. Telequip did not provide him with any assistance in finding an apartment, however. The whole issue of accommodation started to trouble Andrew. He didn't want to remain at a hotel, but as a foreigner with no Chinese and no knowledge of the city, how was he going to find something else? And how was he going to find the time to hunt for an apartment when he was spending such long hours at the office?

April turned into May and Andrew began to realize that he was not going to make it back to Australia in time for the move into his new house. His wife said she understood and she would manage on her own, but he knew she was upset and was finding it hard to cope. But he didn't see how he would be able to leave Taipei for a week or two. The crisis was nearing its peak, and in desperation Malcolm was transferring more and more staff from Sydney to Taipei. At one point there were 30 Telequip staff in Taipei, including many of the subcontractors who had been hired from India. Many had left behind children as well as their spouses, something which Andrew was glad he did not have to do.

Andrew was beginning to feel tired of the long hours and the sterile environment of the hotel. One night he accompanied some colleagues to a nightclub – not something he would normally do at home, but he felt that he was entitled to some entertainment. The night was not a success, however. He danced with a Taiwanese woman who propositioned him, despite his protestations that he already had a wife back in Australia. He eventually managed to shake her off, but when he went back to his room early in the morning, he realized that he had lost his mobile phone on the dance floor. When his wife heard a carefully edited account of the night she was not impressed, and because he did not obtain a police report he was not able to claim the loss of his mobile phone on insurance.

Andrew had been looking for an apartment with the assistance of a Taiwanese colleague. He had looked at two flats which were spartan but adequate. However, in Taiwan, a 12-month lease is standard. He was unwilling to sign such a long-term lease and unable to negotiate a shorter one. Andrew found that Jonathan had also tried and failed to find an apartment, opting instead to stay in a serviced apartment. Their Taiwanese colleagues were amazed at how much the Telequip Australia employees were spending on five-star accommodation.

On his way to lunch one day, Andrew noticed a board in English advertising a flat for let. He phoned the number and found out that the real estate agent spoke English and that he had a different apartment on offer which was not far from where he was working. Later in the week the real estate agent took him to view the apartment. It was very basic and lacked a kitchen, but it was reasonably cheap, its owner spoke English and was prepared to agree to a 3-month lease. Andrew decided to take it. He had to provide 3 months' rent in cash, so he took out a cash advance on his credit card, and moved in as soon as the apartment had been cleaned.

Andrew's mood improved when he checked out of the hotel. At least he had overcome one hurdle and he was secretly proud of having managed such a complex transaction in a foreign city. He began eating at local restaurants rather at the hotel, even though he often didn't understand what he was ordering. The first time he visited an eatery he would choose a meal at random. If he decided to return, he always ordered the same meal again.

The hurdles he faced in the office remained. Malcolm had returned to Sydney but had started to behave erratically and was perceived to be suffering from burnout. Control of the project had been placed in the hands of a more senior manager who was based at Telequip headquarters rather than in Australia. The long hours and the uncertainty over the project's future continued.

Approaching the end of the first release, the project looked like being cancelled. Much of the promised functionality was missing. As Andrew explained to his wife, 'There's a piece of functionality we promised in the contract. It doesn't fit nicely into anyone's responsibility and no one's done anything about it. The customer really needs it right now and, the problem is, it's going to take months to develop it.' He explained their planned approach.

'That sounds awfully complicated. Isn't there an easier way to do it?'

'I don't know. No one's looked for one. Maybe there is.'

There was. Three weeks later, Andrew explained, '90 per cent of the work was going to be in writing a program to display the data. But frankly, there wasn't anything in the data that couldn't be displayed in any web browser. I wrote a small program that turned each record into a file and posted it to a web page. Taicom still aren't satisfied with the release as a whole, but they've agreed to overlook the other deficiencies for the moment and we can start work on the second delivery.'

After this, life in Taipei started to settle down a little for Andrew. He took the odd day off on the weekend and explored some of the hills near his apartment. One day on the way home from work he stopped off at a coffee shop that looked fairly lively, and was invited to sit down with some students eager to practise their English and prepared to give him some tips on Chinese in return. He had bought some books on Chinese characters and could distinguish about 200 characters by this stage, although he still had great trouble working out what he was being served in restaurants and could only speak a handful of words. He had noticed that his colleagues preferred to stick to restaurants that had menus in English, and were not interested in learning any Chinese. As May turned into June they also had the humid summer to complain about.

Andrew's 60-day term was approaching its end and his wife was busily making plans for his return. Again, she was to be disappointed. He was asked to go back for another 2 months. He contemplated saying no, but the telecom industry was suffering a severe downturn at the time and Telequip Australia had recently laid off nearly 20 per cent of its staff. Perhaps because it was under pressure, the Taicom project went unscathed. Now, he thought, was not the time to make trouble and he knew he should be feeling relieved to have a job at all. There were a lot of people worse off than he was.

He told work he needed 10 days in Sydney and no one objected loudly, so he packed his bags eagerly. He really needed a break and was looking forward to a chance to rest and unwind. When he arrived home, however, he realized his wife had other plans. She wanted him to help her move some furniture upstairs, unpack boxes, start filling out their tax returns, go shopping for a new dining table, prune the roses in the garden and catch up with relatives he hadn't seen for months – there seemed to be no end to the chores awaiting him. At one point he burst out, 'Look, you have no idea how much stress I have been under. I just want a bit of time to do nothing'. His wife snapped back at him, 'And do you think life has been a holiday for me? I still had to keep working, yet somehow manage the settlement of the house all by myself, and move, and unpack, and organize all the urgent repairs to this place that needed doing. And now you're about to disappear again. You can't leave me to do everything. You just don't understand what it's been like back here. There are some things I just can't do on my own, I need your help, and now's the only time I can get it.'

The personnel officer also wanted to catch up with him. She informed him that the per diem that Malcolm had arranged for Andrew's first 2-month stay in Taipei was considerably above company guidelines and would be scaled back by an unspecified amount. She promised to send him a letter outlining his new entitlements, but the letter did not arrive in time for his departure. She also told him to ring a number at an accountancy firm to check if he had any tax liability in Taipei. The accountant sent him a three-page e-mail on the matter. In part, the e-mail read:

> Based on our discussions with our Taiwanese office we understand that where an individual is seconded to work in Taiwan and receives any income from a Taiwan entity, that individual will be subject to Taiwan individual income tax regardless of the days spent in Taiwan.
>
> However, where an individual is paid by a foreign entity with no recharge to a Taiwanese entity of the compensation costs associated with the assignment, it is the number of days spent in Taiwan which will determine whether there is a Taiwanese tax liability. Where an individual has been in Taiwan for a period of less than 90 days cumulatively during a Taiwanese tax year (being the calendar year), the employment income will be exempt and no Taipei income tax return is required.
>
> Prima facie, owing to the International Tax Agreement (ITA) between Australia and Taiwan, where an individual:
>
> 1 is physically in Taiwan for less than 183 days (in a calendar year);
>
> 2 is paid by an employer not resident in Taiwan; and
>
> 3 their compensation costs are not being recharged to a Taiwanese entity their salary will also be exempt from tax in Taiwan.
>
> However, even though the salary income is exempt according to the ITA, an individual must still lodge a Taiwanese tax return if their stay exceeds 90 days. Taiwanese tax is also payable at this stage but a full refund is available at a later date if all the following can be substantiated with the Taiwanese tax authorities:
>
> 1 the individual remained a tax resident of their home country (e.g. statement of residency from the Australian Tax Office);
>
> 2 Australian notices of assessment cover the relevant period; and
>
> 3 there is proof that the individual was paid and employed by a foreign company.
>
> We understand from our Taiwan office that the process of claiming a refund is difficult even with the above substantiation. This is especially in the case of an Australian taxpayer due to the difference in tax years. Practically, the costs of claiming the refund can often outweigh taxes paid.

'So does that mean you are liable for tax in Taiwan or not?,' asked his wife when she read the letter, 'and if you do have to pay tax in Taiwan but can't get a refund, or have to wait years for one, is Telequip going to reimburse you? I'm beginning to think that we're not going to do as well out of this assignment as we initially thought. Take the way you are being paid the per diem, for instance. They never pay it to you in advance. You wait a month, then put in a claim form, and then we wait around for them to give you a cheque for the amount you have claimed. But in the meantime you have racked up all those bills on your personal credit card. So in the end they owe us thousands of dollars.'

His 10-day interlude in Sydney was soon over. Back in Taipei, the routine was disturbingly familiar. Another crisis involving Taicom was brewing. This time, however, Andrew had a real sense of impending disaster. He had a sobering talk with a

Taicom manager who told him that even if the system were made to work, Taicom would not use it. It simply did not provide the functionality that Taicom required.

Despite these pressures, Andrew was determined to keep some balance in his life and make sure that he take at least one day off each week. He certainly didn't want to end up like Malcolm, who probably should have been on extended sick leave but was still working. He also decided he should take the initiative to study Chinese in a more formalized fashion. He started ringing around some language schools that other expatriates had mentioned and found one with weekend classes. He had to pay for 10 weeks of classes in advance. He was unsure he would still be in Taipei for that long, so enrolled in the cheapest course he could find.

Meanwhile, his Australian colleagues were complaining about the food, the hot and humid summer, the unreasonableness of the Taicom staff and the pollution. One day was spent in suspense waiting to see if a typhoon threatening the city would hit. All the local staff stayed at home, so it was only the expatriates who gathered in the darkened, empty Taicom building. At about noon they received a call from a manager at Telequip headquarters ordering them to leave the building. In the end, the typhoon missed Taipei, but struck a village that some of the Telequip staff had visited the previous day. By this stage most of the Australians working on the Taicom project were openly expressing the hope that the project would indeed be cancelled. If the project were to fail, Andrew and his colleagues nevertheless anticipated that they would remain in Taipei for a number of weeks to wind up the project.

In mid-August, 6 weeks into Andrew's second 2-month assignment, senior Telequip Australia management announced that the company would be pulling out of the Taicom project. Telequip informed Taicom of a revised schedule that included delays of more than 6 months beyond previous estimates, which had already slipped by almost 6 months. Telequip management did not expect that the offer would be acceptable, and indeed Taicom responded by cancelling the project. Andrew and his colleagues in Taipei were informed of the cancellation the following day. Telequip instructed its staff in Taipei to shut the system down, pack up and return home as soon as possible. Andrew and his colleagues disabled the system, collected all their belongings and left the building by the end of the day. All of them wondered if they would have jobs to return to. All felt defeated and dispirited after now having nothing to show for their months of effort. That evening Andrew ended up at a nightclub and drank until 4 a.m. with colleagues from a different but related project.

The following day, and rather hung over, Andrew was told by a Telequip secretary that she had managed to book him on a flight back to Sydney that evening. He was advised to collect the ticket from the airline's sales office in the city, after which he raced back to his apartment to pack. He caught his flight, but did not have time to retrieve his deposit from the real estate agent. A colleague who was remaining behind for a few days handled the matter on his behalf.

Back in Sydney, the Taicom team was briefed on what had happened. The Indian subcontractors were gone within an hour of the meeting. The rest of the company quickly found out through word of mouth. Morale, already low since the first round of retrenchments, plummeted even further.

'I hope this time you're back for good,' his wife said when they met at Sydney airport. 'It's truly amazing, you know. Telequip is such a large company that operates all over the world and has so much international experience. So why is it they couldn't manage to run this project in Taiwan?'

'The worst thing is,' Andrew said, 'if we had been better prepared I think we could have made this project work. I don't think it had to be a failure. The technical problems were real, but the major problem was that we weren't "buddies". We never understood them and they never understood us.'

Malcolm was retrenched the following week. Two weeks later, so were almost all of the managers and a majority of the employees who had been involved in the project, although Andrew survived. The remaining staff were reallocated and a number of other retrenchments were made elsewhere, including the whole product sales team. The 'world product' vision was dropped and Telequip Australia's focus shifted squarely to its domestic customer.

Note

1   This case would not have been possible without the generous and extensive input provided by 'Andrew Robinson'.

Appendix

http://www.shrm.org/
This is the (US) Society for Human Resource Management (SHRM) home page list of international HR websites.

http://www.shrmglobal.org/
Homepage of the Institute for International HR, a division of the Society for Human Resource Management (SHRM). This home page is valuable in details of the *International Human Resource Management Reference Guide*, mentioned later in this Appendix.

http://www.aibworld.net/
The Academy of International Business home page.

http://fernando.emeraldinsight.com/vl52000297/cl519/nw51/rpsv/index.htm
Emerald publishes a wide range of management and library and information services journals. The electronic databases allow instant access to the latest research and global thinking.

http://www.ihrim.org/
The International Association for Human Resource Information Management (IHRIM).

http://www.ipma-hr.org/
Home page of the International Personnel Management Association (IPMA), a professional association for public personnel professionals, primarily those who work in federal, state or local government. The page includes a list of useful HRM sites around the world.

http://www.ipd.co.uk/
Home page of the Chartered Institute of Personnel and Development, UK.

http://www.workindex.com/
A search engine (based at Cornell University) targeting work and HR-related websites.

http://www.fedee.com/index.shtml
The Federation of European Employers.

http://www.eurunion.org/
The US site of the European Union.

http://www.ibrc.bschool.ukans.edu/
The Kansas University International Business Resource Connection home page. Aimed at small- and medium-sized companies, this website includes a good list of other websites.

http://ciber.msu.edu/
The World Wide Web server of the Center for International Business Education and Research (CIBER) at Michigan State University.

http://ciber.centers.purdue.edu/
CIBERWeb, the Internet Hub of the USA's Centers for International Business Education and Research.

http://www.ita.doc.gov
This site is produced and maintained by the International Trade Administration, US Department of Commerce.

http://www.windhamint.com/
GMAC Global Relocation Service provides information about international relocation and expatriate management.

http://www.meridianglobal.com
Meridian Resources website is designed to help pre-departure training for expatriates.

http://www.expat-repat.com/
ExpatRepat provides coaching for expatriate performance in international assignments.

http://www.ilo.org/
International Labour Organization.

http://www.ey.com/global/content.nsf/uk/institute_for_global_mobility
The Ernst & Young Institute for Global Mobility.

http://www.erc.org/
Employee Relocation Council's website provides information about international relocation and expatriate management.

http://www.fedworld.gov/
Fedworld information network hosted by the US Department of Commerce.

http://www.livingabroad.com/
Magazine for expatriates.

http://www.expatforum.com/
Site aimed at expatriates, with a chat line.

http://www.unctad.org/
United Nations Conference on Trade and Development.

http://www.transparency.org/
Transparency International's Corruption Index – ranks 102 countries on perceived level of corruption.

http://www.towers.com
Towers Perrin is a global human resource consulting and administration firm. It claims to help organizations manage their investment in people to achieve measurable financial performance improvements.

http://www.eiro.eurofound.ie/
The European Industrial Relations Observatory Online.

http://www.eiu.com/
The Economist Intelligence Unit.

http://ethics.acusd.edu
The site provides both simple and concept definitions and complex analysis of ethics, original treaties and sophisticated search engine capability; covers ethical theory and application.

http://commerce.depaul.edu/ethics/
Has many valuable ethics and professional resources.

http://www.eben.org
The European Business Ethics Network, EBEN, is an International network dedicated to the promotion of business ethics in European private industry, public sector, voluntary organizations and academia. It provides links to many other relevant websites.

Other resources

The Institute for International Human Resources, a division of the Society for Human Resource Management, produces a *Reference Guide* that is updated regularly. It lists resource organizations, expatriate policies, embassy listings and websites. It contains a glossary of terms used in IHRM, classified and alphabetically grouped into six major HRM functional areas: Management Practices, Employment, Training and Development, Employee and External Relations, Compensation and Benefits, and other HRM (such as travel).

Index

Note: page numbers in bold refer to Figures, Tables and boxed material